Japan: A For...
The Biogr...
Anthony Reynolds

Nicola Tyson

For Cathy in Glynneath

Published by Burning Shed
Third printing August 2019
978-0-9933036-1-6
Copyright © Burning Shed 2015

Photographs are reproduced with kind permission of the respective photographers. All efforts have been made to correctly identify said photographers. If you believe an error has been made we will be happy to correct it in any future editions.

The right of Anthony Reynolds to be identified as the author of this work has been asserted by him in accordance with the Copyright, Designs and Patents Act 1988.

All rights reserved. No part of this publication may be reproduced, stored in or introduced into a retrieval system, or transmitted, in any form or by any means (electronic, mechanical, photocopying, recording or otherwise) without the prior written permission of the publisher.

This book is sold subject to the condition that it shall not, by way of trade or otherwise, be lent, resold, hired out, or otherwise circulated without the publisher's prior consent in any form of binding or cover other than that in which it is published and without a similar condition including this condition being imposed on the subsequent publisher.

'...And seeing your age and ashen hair
I'll curse the thing that once you were,
Because it is changed and pale and old
(Lips that were scarlet, hair that was gold!),
And I loved you before you were old and wise,
When the flame of youth was strong in your eyes,
—And my heart is sick with memories.'

Rupert Brooke 'The Beginning'.

Designed by Carl Glover at Aleph Studio
Typeset in Times New Roman

Printed in EU
www.aforeignplace.com
www.burningshed.com

Contents

4   Chapter 1
        Back in the Beginning

18   Chapter 2
        Whatever Gets You Through The Night

30   Chapter 3
        Mastering Obscure Alternatives

50   Chapter 4
        Alphaville

72   Chapter 5
        1980

92   Chapter 6
        1980 2

110   Chapter 7
        Art and Parties

130   Chapter 8
        The Tin Drum

150   Chapter 9
        Burning Bridges

170   Chapter 10
        Voices Raised in Welcome

200   Afterword
        'Who would have dreamed of love never ending?'

Chapter 1
Back in the Beginning

The time and place into which David Alan Batt entered the world was very ordinary. He was born on 23 February 1958 (the Year of the Dog) in Stone Park, Beckenham, Kent in England. That day Michael Holliday's 'The Story of My Life' was the UK number one single. Its sweetly melancholy, whistled refrain would have provided the perfect soundtrack for any parents elated at the arrival of their first son. A sister Linda had been born three years earlier. The Batt parents, Bernard and Sheila, were, like their surname, from solid working-class Anglo-Saxon stock. 'The first thing I remember was my parents standing on a balcony outside the house, telling me I couldn't go out there because it might collapse,' David would recall in 1984. 'It didn't occur to me to wonder why *they* could go out there.'

Over a year later another son, Stephen, was born on the first day of December in Sydenham, south east London. For the earliest years of the brothers' childhoods, the family home was a sturdy Victorian terrace on Venner Road in the borough of Lewisham before the Batts moved to Hither Green in December 1962, again in Lewisham. Lewisham was then a model of suburbia, predominantly (but not exclusively) working class, and still re-establishing itself in the wake of the war. The borough was also in flux – bottoming out in terms of prosperity while at the same time acclimatising to the influx of an immigrant population: Jamaican, Pakistani, Italian and Greek. Still, it was far from some of the bombed-out slums of inner London and in the early 1960s, Lewisham was as good a backdrop for the dream of childhood as any other. There were parks and recreation grounds, civic retreats, leisure facilities and shops. You could catch the number 47 bus from Catford to go canoeing on Peter Pan's Pool. There was Mountsfield Park, which had a tea room where every Sunday afternoon you could listen to live music playing on the bandstand. There was the Sunday market in the Broadway which sold day-old fluffy yellow chicks; a linen shop called Pecry's where the money flew around tubes in the ceiling from the counter to a central cashier; along the main road there was proof of the new Italian population in an ice cream parlour called Marcantonio's. The town centre had a new Sainsbury's, the requisite Burton and the ubiquitous Woolworths, which sold almost everything that was wanted and needed: plugs, linen, batteries, washing powder, string, clothes pegs, bulbs. And pop music.

The Batt household was not musical and nobody in the family played an instrument. Their record collection consisted of the same three basic albums that probably existed in every other English home at that time - *The Flight of the Bumblebee*, *South Pacific* and *The King and I* - yet music itself seemed to be inherent in the Batt brothers. 'My brother and I had these little toy guitars when we were around five or six and I would play them until I had blisters on my fingers,' remembered David. 'I just loved music, even though I really had no introduction to it.' Stephen: 'There was eventually a record player and I'm not sure what year that arrived, but it played host to *South Pacific* and *The King and I* as well as my dad's two albums by Johnny Cash and Hank Williams.' This then was the first musical soundtrack of David's life – classical, dramatic, expansive. And in Cash, a baritone intoxicated by the pain and power of spiritual awareness and longing.

In 1962, with 'Love Me Do', The Beatles would change everything forever, everywhere. Although David and Stephen were still too young to partake actively in this pop phenomenon that was star-bursting around them, they couldn't help but be aware of it. 'We didn't listen to much music in the house,' David would recall several lifetimes later. 'My dad used to repair this one wireless we had – once a year it used to work for 24 hours then break down again – but I remember music coming out of that old radio: 'Ticket To Ride', 'A Hard Day's Night' – the first things that hit me as being just an amazing sound.' David would have been seven in 1965 when 'Ticket To Ride' flooded the airwaves. But in fact his brother remembers the impact of The Beatles being less dramatic: 'We were a bit young when they first took off,' recalls Steve. 'However, our sister bought the early singles so they were very familiar since they were played on repeat.' It would be another few years before the next step in David's formative musical education took place and once again he would owe this to his older sister and her love of Motown. David: 'I loved certain sounds. Motown had it and The Beatles had it. I guess that was the first attraction, then realising that I had an innate love of music and that it was second nature to me.'

Throughout the 60s the Batt brothers' childhoods developed in the most ordinary way. Their father, working variously as a builder, labourer and plasterer struggled, the same as everyone else the family knew, to provide a decent standard of living for his family. He succeeded (everyone was clothed, fed and raised to respect themselves, their surroundings and their elders), but there were no exotic holidays, flashy cars or cultural indulgences. David: 'As a family we never ventured far on our infrequent travels. My family never had money to burn.' Nevertheless, there were trips to the English seaside and the occasional visit to the cinema. There was a dog called Tim who had a passion for sniffing visitors' armpits and who murdered the neighbour's tortoise. Stephen would write about their childhood years later: 'When I think of memories with my brother David, I remember best our summer holidays. We got on well and played together. I hardly remember playing with my sister because she is much older than I am. But I played with David; we were mischievous, had adventures and did stuff that every child does. I was often with David, playing in the street, riding bikes, playing musical instruments and so on. Compared to him, I think I was a sociable child whereas David was quiet and shy. I liked to make others laugh but then again I was very timid as a young kid. When I was four I started going to school. My mother used to take me there every morning. When I first realised she was going home and leaving me, I cried and followed her. I stopped crying as soon as she said, "I'll tell Dad!" David had no problem going to school and I think he gets along with my mother better than I do, and I get along with my father better than he does. We sometimes skipped school pretending to be ill; we rubbed our eyes and pretended to have hay fever. We didn't like school at all. We enjoyed watching TV and we collected models of spaceships … we treasured these toys. I was not good at sports but I wanted to be a member of a football team at our school and when I was seven or eight at last I was able to be a member of the team. My father was pleased and came to see me playing one Saturday morning. But our team lost with a score of 11-0. I stopped playing football then.'

Over 2000 miles away, Andonis Michaelides had been born in Cyprus on 24 July 1958. In his autobiography he writes of a cold, loveless upbringing by distant, neurotic parents. These factors were exasperated when the family moved to London in late 1961. 'The stereotypical view of a warm Mediterranean family, openly showing their emotions, had nothing to do with the family I belonged to,' he would recall. Andonis was a sensitive and naturally affectionate child with no outlet for such feelings. Moving to Catford's Forest Hill and starting school in England brought no respite. 'Skinheads were in, while Indians and Pakistanis, to which my appearance had me fit snugly between, were most definitely out,' he'd recall. Andonis would struggle to sustain himself emotionally until he was old enough to find the music in himself. Music and art would increasingly become both a need and a release for him, something on which he was emotionally dependent.

Eventually he would be lucky enough to recognise the same need in his new friends, particularly in a 'long haired whitey' called David who felt the same stigma of alienation and was drawn to its antidote – the solace and transcendence of music. 'It [music] is the first thing that's completely removed from family concerns,' David would reason. 'It's an important identification. It grabs and excites you and creates some kind of passion, and that's important.'

By the mid 1960s, the Batts had moved to the house on Hither Green, which backed onto a railway line. David and Stephen now began seriously to pursue music together at home. By then they had acquired 'proper' acoustic guitars and practised as a duo in their bedroom. It was a distorted, sonically overloaded 'fab four' summer of 1968 release that upped the ante. Stephen: 'It was the release of The Beatles' 'Revolution' that inspired David and me to start composing on guitars. We had a cassette tape recorder with a very low-grade microphone. It stood on a tilting stand and a "stomp" board [a piece of leftover white linoleum which ended up as a piece of graffiti art]. We overloaded the record level of the machine by both strumming, stomping and singing to create the sound of distortion à la 'Revolution'.' 'I remember a lot of stuff I wrote around 12 or 13 when I first got a guitar,' David would recall. 'We had no musical background, no one in the family knew how to play instruments. Stephen and I just taught ourselves and made things up as we went along.'

Around the same time in nearby Beckenham, David Jones, a tightly-permed waif with another (albeit 12-string) acoustic guitar had launched the Beckenham Arts Lab at The Three Tuns pub. 'There's a lot of talent in the green belt and there is a load of tripe in Drury Lane,' the 20-something David Jones told *Melody Maker*. 'I think the arts lab movement is extremely important and should take over from the youth club concept as a social service.' David Jones, soon to be David Bowie, was Beckenham's very own Buddha of suburbia and, during this time, he and his wife Angie walked the same streets as the Batt brothers. The future Bowie would have an enormous effect on David, Steve, and Andonis in particular, but even though 'Space Oddity' had been a top five hit in 1969 it was seen as something of a novelty song and its effect was negligible on these future members of Japan. 'We weren't aware of him at all at that point,' confirms Stephen. Bowie is also probably the only person ever to name-check Penge in a pop song, which he did in 'Did You Ever Have a Dream,' a song about astral projection from 1967.

In September 1969, David, Richard and 'Mick', as Andonis was now known (this abbreviation of his surname was obviously more user-friendly in England), began secondary school at Catford Boys'. Many children do not enjoy going to school and neither David, Mick, nor Steve in particular, would recall the place with any affection. 'From the very first day,' Mick would say, 'I knew I'd entered a battleground, a traumatic exercise in survival.' Such a place and time at least opened up the possibility of new friendships. In addition, Mick, a natural musician, was also able to follow his skill formally. 'I always thought when I was a little kid that there must be something in music that makes you feel really good when you're playing it,' he would recall, 'and the first chance to try it out was in junior school, where there used to be a little orchestra to play and sing the hymns to, and I used to play mouth organ in that. But I wasn't really enjoying it, so I began playing the violin, which I did for about three years. But still something wasn't quite clicking, and I gave it a break. Then when I went to senior school and started playing bassoon in the school's symphony orchestra.' Shortly before this, Mick had sought refuge in the school's music room, number 206, to escape the horrors of sport. There he struggled with the violin, but eventually found he disliked using the bow. Anything that got between his fingers and the instrument had a dislocating effect upon his muse. The same would eventually apply to using a plectrum with a bass guitar. Such barriers would be abandoned allowing his own particularly idiosyncratic style to personalise his playing of all instruments.

In the third year of senior school, destiny introduced Mick to one of the most important figures of his life: David Alan Batt. 'He was quiet,' remembers Mick, 'and often blushed when spoken to, and had long hair.' Mick made David laugh and, more importantly, David was perceptive and sensitive enough to see the hurt behind his new friend's joker persona. Mick and David sat at the back of the class when able (Mick, a disruptive presence, was sometimes forced to shift his desk to the front in order to be better supervised), but there was another boy they noticed, 'a goody-goody' according to Mick, called Richard Barbieri. Barbieri had been born in the much more salubrious surroundings of Kensington, and lived in Paddington until he was five at which point a south London council flat became available to his parents in Sangley Road. 'I was fortunate to have kind and loving parents who were very tolerant and supportive,' Richard would recall. 'My father, who was born in London but grew up in Italy, worked as a waiter at most of the top hotels in the West End and my mum was a secretary. My sister was four years younger than me. I took her to quite a few concerts in the 70s, including her favourite band Queen. I have aspects of my parents' personalities, but I think my aunt was quite an influence as well. She was very different from my parents in that she was totally into the arts. She was definitely a character, very glamorous à la Joan Crawford and a free spirit. She attended an acting school, loved film and music and was an animal lover. She signed me up with the RSPCA. I spent a lot of time with her when I was a kid and there were no rules, so I could stay up until four in the morning listening to music. On Saturday mornings she'd take me to Shepherd's Bush market where she did her rounds of inspecting the pet shops to check that the animals were being suitably looked after.'

Back in school, Richard found himself on the front row of Catford Boys' year three where, unlike his future friends, he worked studiously and had an appreciation of sport. He was more socially adept and, while not traditionally musical himself, also had a growing interest in music, though compared to David, Mick et al., he was a late developer. During one lunch break over a shared loaf of bread stuffed with chips, David introduced his brother Stephen to Mick. At this point Mick had never even seen a bass guitar in the flesh and Stephen was still limited to bashing out trills on bongos, his knees and a school desk. The meeting between the two future rhythm brothers was casual and as unremarkable as the street and day on which they met.

Nick Huckle was another local lad in the same year as David, Richard and Mick and a friend of Barbieri's from the earliest days of Catford Boys'. Huckle would go on to become a friend and colleague to what would become Japan for the next decade. 'I was aware of David from about the age of eleven years old,' he recalls, 'but we didn't become friends until a bit later.' Richard remembers Nick as, 'Very funny in an "Eric Morecambe" kind of way. It's hard to describe, but he could make you laugh with just certain gestures and expressions.' Steve: 'Nick was brought into the group via Richard as they were good friends at school, so once Richard joined the group he was a subsequent addition to our socialising. I always felt he was someone with a good sense of humour and had an independence, which meant he wasn't looking for approval from any of his peers. He seemed very uncomplicated as a person, but at the same time he never opened up emotionally so it was impossible to determine what was actually going on with him.' Huckle: 'In September 1972 there was some disruption in class and the teacher, Mr Spencer, moved everyone around. I ended up sitting next to them in three seats at the back of class and that's how we met. We discovered we had a love of pop music in common. We were about 14 at this point. We weren't that popular with the rest of the school. Pretty soon it was a gang of me, Dave, Mick, Steve and Richard. That was about it. This was before the band. I knew that Dave used to muck about on acoustic guitar with Steve. I was fascinated by Dave's endless doodling of the T. Rex record label logo all over his exercise books [the one showing a silhouette of Bolan with his then long corkscrew hair]. It turned out Dave was a big fan and had all his albums from early Tyrannosaurus Rex through to *Electric Warrior*. 'Metal Guru' was just out as a single and *The Slider* album was being eagerly anticipated.' Bolan was a huge presence on the UK pop scene in the early 1970s, a brand new supernova who was arguably the architect of the glam rock revolution. In addition, Bolan was peculiarly English, androgynous, beautiful, sexy, witty, decadent, groovy, and boogied in full make-up. David Batt would borrow at least three of these components to great effect. So, for that matter, would the artist previously known as David Jones. Huckle: 'One day at lunchtime we were all doing a crossword in a pop magazine called *Popswap* and there was a clue we couldn't get. The next morning Mick came over and said he'd found out the answer was "David Bowie". I don't think any of us had heard of him at that point. Within days of that, Bowie did *Top Of The Pops* with 'Starman'. He joined Bolan as one of our heroes. Dave and Mick both bought the *Ziggy Stardust* album and it was endlessly being played and talked about. Dave quickly started to get hold of his back catalogue too, but I've no idea as to where he got the cash from as we were 14 at that point. Then *Aladdin Sane* came out in 1973 and Mick got it first from the local record shop in Catford [Diamond Records] and we all went round to his place to listen to it in his bedroom. We were in awe.' The 'Starman' appearance was seismic, having a profound effect on countless other British boys that night, many of whom would go on to form bands that, like Japan, would peak commercially a decade later.

Back at Catford Boys' School, the daily grind continued. David gravitated towards art and English and his brother likewise, although the younger sibling, true to his natural perfect timing also had a penchant for maths. Sport, despite the sanctuary of room 206 (dominated by a teacher called Mr Cave), was mostly unavoidable. 'Everyone had to do games,' recalls Huckle. 'While Richard and I did football or tennis, Dave for the first three or four years or so did fencing, and only a very elite few got to do fencing.' (Taught by the unfortunately named Professor Fairhorn). 'It was a good gig to get as it meant you didn't have to run around in the rain in shorts. I can't remember if Dave represented the school or not, but Catford Boys' [unusually for an inner city secondary modern] taught it then and was supposed to have had a rather strong team.' Sporting activities seemed only attractive to the boys as a means of getting out of other even less desirable activities. 'When I was 13 or 14 I took tennis lessons only because the students involved were allowed to play in the park without a teacher supervising,' says Stephen. 'I didn't play tennis at all, I would just chat with some friends. And I can say the same thing about swimming. I tended to skip lessons pretending to be ill.' Only Barbieri had any true inclination towards sport; a lifelong soccer fan, he also had a natural aptitude for tennis, which he would play well into his adult life. Barbieri: 'Much of my childhood revolved around sports. I was a very shy kid but became captain of the school football team and was soon selected to represent Lewisham Borough. I was actually better at tennis though and won the Kent doubles title aged 13. I didn't get to know Steve until much later, when I joined the band, as he was two years below me at school. Mick was the joker, always in trouble. This was born of survival instincts I guess, as he may have been picked on. School was not unlike a prison hierarchy. Being the football team captain meant I had some friends who were "hard", so maybe that's why I didn't get picked on much.'

Although none of Japan remembers their school days with affection (Richard: 'There was always a fear and dread associated with school'), David especially would go on to be candid about what he considered to be an unhappy childhood. 'I was overly sensitive,' he'd remember. 'I found the environment rather brutal. I wanted to protect myself from it. I was and am very shy – cripplingly shy as a child – so I'd spend a lot of time alone. Drawing and painting were my outlet at the time.' This is a refrain that would echo through the press interviews of his adult life but it's truer to say that such childhood trauma had more to do with his sensibility than it did with any circumstances of his upbringing and environment. Most parents at that time dealt with their children's discipline physically. Corporal punishment in schools was a given. David did not come from a broken home or extreme poverty and the school, while undoubtedly occasionally brutal and unforgiving, was merely a run-of-the-mill Church of England state school. Had it been Catholic, the beatings and abuse could have been much more pronounced. Millions of other boys of his generation, including his friends, just accepted their lot and dealt with it but, for some reason, for most of his adult life David would refer to the unhappiness he felt as a child and pinpoint the cause of that misery as being fundamentally environmental.

Not that he was a problem child. 'I remember Richard and David particularly,' says ex-Catford Boys' School's English/History/Economics teacher, William Newman-Norton. (Huckle: 'Norton was rather dapper as I remember. Used to walk around with a large rainbow umbrella and a silk handkerchief sticking out of his jacket pocket. He read us H Ryder Haggard stories and stuff and was quite cool.') Norton: 'Of course I don't know what their lives were like outside school but in class they were quiet, sensible, well mannered, hard-working. Richard seemed the most refined. They were extremely polite. David Batt was a very nice boy. His brother Stephen was more of a smart aleck. He always had a smirk. I remember saying to David, "Why can't your brother Stephen be as well behaved as you?" He sort of laughed it off and said, "Oh, you know, we're just different." But then Richard and David were so pleasant and co-operative that, by comparison, a lot of the other boys were badly behaved. I don't remember having the slightest problem with David or Richard – they just got on with their work. They were charming. Catford Boys' had a social mix – there was the rougher end and the slightly less rough end. But these two obviously came from decent homes – that was clear. They were always smartly turned out.' Although David in particular would go on to pursue a spiritual path, his schooling was not particularly God-fearing. 'It wasn't particularly a religious school,' affirms Norton. 'There were some active Christians on the staff and one had in fact been a missionary, but they weren't preachy. The headmaster was quite a dull man… he taught me how to cane the boys – "Make them wait first" etc., all these kind of techniques. There was, however, a good art department.' This at least would allow David to gain one academic qualification. 'Dave went off and did art,' says Huckle. 'He walked through it; it was the only exam he passed. But at this time he was totally focused on his music.' Barbieri also recalls Catford Boys' staff caustically. 'What a bunch of dodgy teachers there were at that school. There was one who stood watching the boys while they showered. Another used to invite boys back to his house!' 'I think the only way I can view it is that it was so unbearably dull,' David would say. 'It was a place of such convention. There was no colour, and it was an incredibly insensitive world. You couldn't be different. You weren't allowed to show certain sides of yourself, you know. It was tough.'

There was another influential figure at Catford Boys'. Jack Stafford was a slightly older pupil than David and Mick et al. but he was outspoken, apparently openly bisexual, and had the confidence to dye his hair. He also played guitar. Although he was never a bona fide member of the 'inner circle', he was nevertheless a notable influence on the future members of Japan and on Mick in particular. 'He opened our ears to Lou Reed, The Velvet Underground, and Iggy Pop,' Mick would recall. 'Jack liked to experience everything to extremes and experimented as much as he could with alcohol, drugs, and sex.' Occasional lunchtimes were spent at Jack's house but most time was spent at the Batt household, particularly on weekends when David and Stephen's parents would enjoy a night out. It was now that Mick discovered that 'Dave had an acoustic guitar and Steve a set of bongos, which they would sometimes play while I was there. I would have liked to have joined in, but didn't feel the bassoon was appropriate.' Thus the friendship between David, Mick, Rich, Steve and Nick deepened. Barbieri was still a satellite figure and, despite being raised as part-Italian, felt no particular affinity with Mick's Mediterranean roots. 'I'm not sure I did feel any particular kinship in that respect,' he says, 'it was very much a multicultural school and the majority of my friends were black. Mick was obviously more "foreign" than I was. And more foreign-looking. Unlike Mick, I was born in London and though I have Italian heritage I've never thought of myself as an Italian. By contrast Mick was born in Cyprus and had to learn English as a child.' Years later, David in particular would perpetuate the idea that the fledgling Japan were the school's rebel outsiders, but it seems this alienation was exaggerated. 'Neither Richard, David nor Michaelides [Karn] seemed like outsiders,' muses Norton. 'They didn't strike me as odd or different. Maybe Michaelides. He was a real character and he mixed more with Jack Stafford who was very unconventional. I remember that the head of the sixth form was an ex-military man called Radcliffe. An awful man who was obsessed with the length of the boys' hair; it couldn't go below the collar. He was always attacking them with a ruler and measuring their hair… a dreary, petty, obsessive man. But I only remember Jack Stafford actually dyeing his hair, none of the others, although Michaelides had quite an exotic haircut.' Huckle elaborates: 'There was always this myth that they'd been thrown out of school for wearing make-up but I don't remember that as being true. There may have been one occasion where Dave was sent home for wearing his hair too long. In our school it was a rule that your hair couldn't go over your collar, and he broke that rule! We used to find ways of putting it up at the back.' Unlike Mick, David was not known in his school as having any particular musical ability.

In school, drawing and painting were his means of artistic self-expression. And rather than being labelled as a 'rebel', if anything, David was considered a doodling daydreamer by the adults around him. But as David saw it he was 'dreaming to a purpose'. 'I never had any myths or models,' he would say years later, seemingly dismissing the role models of Bolan and Bowie. 'I've always wanted everything to be real. I've always wanted that all my dreams become reality. You know, I come from a working class family and I fled from school as soon as I could. My school was terrible: more than a school, it seemed a reformatory. I was always a quiet boy, very introverted and endlessly lost in his own world. When I began to write songs (I was 12 or 13 years old), I stopped drawing altogether.'

As Mick, Richard, David and his brother grew into teenagerdom, in Stephen's words, 'Everything changed.' Pop music had now become an obsession – a window into a world far preferable to the one in which they lived. The first single David had ever bought with his own money was either The Jackson Five's 'ABC' or T. Rex's 'Telegram Sam'. (He has stated both). These were purchased at either Diamond Records, a small independent on Rushey Green, or Harlequin Records on Catford Broadway. 'This is where we did most of our vinyl browsing after school and at weekends,' confirms Huckle. 'They had a sister too, an older sister, Linda. I only met her a few times. She was nice and loved pop music too. Whenever I was there the big thing was always who was gonna make the coffee! On Thursday evenings and weekends the parents were out and we'd be able to crank up the music. I remember also at this time David had a girlfriend who was two years older than him from the girls' school down the road and that was considered quite a thing at the time.' By now, music had also replaced sport as Richard's main interest. 'The best thing about my teenage years though, and my obsession, wasn't sport or even girls, it was buying albums and going to concerts,' he says. 'I was just so obsessed and absorbed by those great artists and albums in the early 70s. Against the grey backdrop of 1970s suburbia, this music took you to other places and pointed the way to a possible future.'

In May of 1973, David, Nick and Mick attended a Bowie concert at Earl's Court. 'It was part of that massive tour he did over 1972/73,' says Huckle. 'For all of us, I think, it was our first proper rock concert; we were 15 now. Apparently it wasn't one of Bowie's best, but we didn't know any different. And having rushed to the front of the stage when the show started we were ushered back to our seats in the interval only to find them occupied by Angie Bowie and several of Bowie's entourage. Angie autographed our badges and then the show recommenced and we were off to the front of the stage again.' 'She looked stunning and was so kind and gentle to us,' Mick would recall, 'we certainly weren't going to complain.' David recalled the show itself as a joy and 'wonderfully theatrical'. Huckle: 'After that show, for Dave, Bolan began to rapidly slide down the pecking order, and all things Bowie related took over, including Lou Reed, Iggy, Warhol. Dave had Bowie pics all over his bedroom wall. As for the others, Rich wasn't quite as much into Bowie, favouring Alice Cooper and Queen. Mick seemed to have a broader palate back then including 10cc, Todd Rundgren, Hawkwind and Stanley Clark.' There was a later attempt to witness a more local Bowie gig on 24 May but only Richard got in. Barbieri: 'That was the Lewisham Odeon show. David and Mick came along to stand outside but didn't have tickets. It's also weird to think that when I was about 14 David Bowie was making *Hunky Dory* and was living up the road from my house, in the same drab suburbia.'

If the peerless glam pop of this era – made by working class London boys just like themselves – provided a view on to a whole new vista, then maybe playing music seriously would provide an entry into that world. 'It was the only open door on the horizon,' says David, 'I knew that I had to get out of that environment and that creating music was my only means of escape. Which is no good reason for making music. There aren't that many noble ideas in a young boy's mind, but at that time it didn't matter.' Looking the part would also help. 'I remember when we were like 13 or 14,' says David, 'and Mick and I were getting our ears pierced at that time, and oh! the grief we got for it, you know, from everyone! The traditional, usual places, building sites and what have you.' Changing their appearance was an important step towards self-sufficiency for David, and Mick in particular. 'I would say there was a survivalist element to a lot of it,' says David of the gradual manipulation of his appearance. 'It was like putting on a spacesuit to walk on the moon. If you didn't have it, you wouldn't survive. That's the only way it made sense to me.'

Around this time Stephen gave up the guitar: 'Being left-handed I couldn't keep up with the learning curve of chord shapes – everything upside down, with certain chord changes tough to implement because of having to use the wrong fingers – so unless I restrung the guitar it was too tricky. I then started to play an electronic organ for a while but it was too drab and limited the energy we were feeling and expressing. So I then got a set of bongos which were much more akin to the Bolan/Finn set-up, and things progressed from there.' 'Steve was a pretty atypical younger brother,' says Huckle. 'He was in the same class as my brother who was two years younger than me. And my brother then was an embarrassment to me, but Dave and Steve hung out together.' There was a moment when Huckle himself could have joined the trio, but he had already realised that while he loved music he wasn't particularly musical. 'Mick, of course, was learning the bassoon then,' he remembers, 'and I did try and join in musically. I took guitar lessons from an old granny down the road but I wasn't very good – I didn't have any talent! Unlike the other Catford boys, we weren't into playing football at lunchtime … we used to go down to Dave's house and listen to records. Either that, or hang out in a corner just talking music. It was literally just music, music, music.' Mick, the most musically talented of all, struggled to find a place within Stephen and David's musical activities. 'I tried numerous ways to join David and Steve,' he'd recall, 'like taking up the Rosedale organ Dad had bought me a few years back, but it meant getting to know what chords are and all those black and white keys are terribly testing. I gave up on that and tried vocals next. David didn't want to sing, so it would be easy once I'd learnt the words.'

With little money between them, finding their musical feet was an effort, mostly enabled by the kind of good luck that blesses the young. In a school corridor Mick had bought a battered bass guitar seemingly on a whim from Jack Stafford. In a seemingly random moment, Mick had found his calling. 'It didn't feel right until I got a bass,' he'd say. At this point Mick was still concentrating on being a singer. Still, he reasoned that it wasn't unheard of that a bass player could also be a vocalist. Although still nameless, Japan had begun. 'In 1973, we formed the band and began to practise,' confirms Steve. A few years later David would sum up their almost nonchalant formation: 'We got together right, and I could only play a little bit of rhythm guitar right, and Steve could play a few percussion instruments. We said, "Mick, why don't you try bass?" and that's how it came about. None of us has been taught, none of us knows a technique. We only know exactly what we do now. That's why we'll be progressing for a long time.' Now that Mick had an actual electric instrument, things were looking up. But this also posed a stumbling block. 'I had no amplifier,' says Mick, 'so at the Batt household on Saturday evenings we used their hi-fi system, which enabled me to be just about heard against the acoustic guitar.'

Right on cue, Steve got his first drum kit. At 13 he acquired it for £30 (the equivalent of over £200 in 2015). 'I was very pleased when I got them; they were delivered at night and I sat in front of them smiling until morning,' Steve says. The gift was from his parents, the wisdom of which they would question. 'My parents were kind enough to buy it for me; it didn't seem like such a lot at the time,' remembers the drummer. 'My mum saw it advertised on the noticeboard where she worked. She could have easily kept quiet about it, bless her. I can only wonder how many days they spent regretting that decision when we turned electric in the upstairs bedroom. I remember constantly being asked to go light on the floor tom.' Thus another problem hovered into view. 'At first we had a difficult time finding places to rehearse,' continues Steve, 'so for the first six months we played in our house and for the next six months in Mick's house. We played for two hours every day. It was very noisy and my sister got angry, especially with the sound of the drums. After that, we practised on the third floor of Mick's father's butcher's shop'. Huckle: 'The Batt parents were good people. They didn't have any money but they didn't put up any barriers between Dave and his musical ambition. One of my favourite memories is when I went round their house to listen to music in the evenings and you'd always get beans on toast.' Thus the legendary rhythm section of Jansen and Karn was born. It was pivotal that they began playing seriously at the same time. Mick: 'A lot of it [the rhythm section's unique chemistry] has to do with the fact that Steve Jansen got his drum kit at exactly the same time as I got my first bass guitar, which was a very cheap and nasty instrument. It only cost me £5 at school and the action [distance between strings and fretboard] was very high, which meant I had to use a lot of strength to press down the notes. Because we were learning our instruments at the same time, we were both constantly pushing each other forward, constantly showing off to each other going, "I can do this, what can you do?" and trying to keep up with each other. We'd also insist the other person progressed all the time.'

In the spring of 1974, having given up on academia, David and Mick took to walking the streets of Lewisham when they played truant, dreaming out loud to one another. They would have looked an incongruous pair: the exotic looking Mick, still slightly overweight, brown eyes and skin gleaming beside the rail-thin, paper-white David. They often attracted aggressive unwanted attention and, even without make-up, were already labelled 'weirdos' and 'poofs'. On one such wander, abetted by a recent photo of Bowie, they found a hairdresser who would give them a lookalike haircut. The crude mullets they now sported would have further alienated them from both skinheads and bus drivers alike.

In late May 1974, Mick's older brother offered them a spot at his wedding with only weeks to prepare. The trio were still rehearsing half an hour before the gig when the hired PA arrived. Barbieri was not involved at this point. Mick: '1 June was Japan's first ever concert. It must have sounded dreadful, but up to that point we had been writing music based around songs that David had written. We were only 14 [Mick was actually 15, David 16, and Steve 14] and I was the vocalist but it was only moments before the curtain went up that I froze and said, "David, I can't do this – you should do it as they're your songs and you know the vocals off by heart." I was so nervous, I couldn't even remember half of the lyrics. He reluctantly became the vocalist there and then.'

Such was the panic in preparing for their debut 'concert' that the trio had forgotten to call themselves anything. When asked who they wanted to be introduced as, a hurried discussion followed. David's suggestion, apparently plucked from the ether, was agreed upon. Thus the trio were instantly christened 'Japan'. Mick recalls that they performed covers of songs by Bowie ('The Jean Genie' was the opener), The Velvet Underground, and Lou Reed, as well as original material with some pieces as long as 20 minutes. Other songs included 'The Man Who Sold The World,' 'Queen Bitch,' 'I'm So Free,' 'Sweet Jane', and a Batt original 'Tongues of China'. The trio played heads down until the wedding guests wandered off to the buffet. And then they played some more. 'How I wish somebody had recorded the event,' Mick would say. 'It must have been awful.' (In fact an ad for a reel-to-reel recording of the gig did surface in the mid 1990s). The name Japan would be dropped and taken up again over the coming months. It held no particular meaning for any of its members. David: 'The name? No reason whatsoever. We just needed a name because we were about to do our first show and I came up with the name. I didn't know anything about the East – it was a temporary name because no one particularly liked it and it stayed; you just get attached to things and think, "Why bother changing it?" So it stayed.' Mick: 'It came from a fascination with the country itself. We planned to use the name only once.' Steve: 'The name was chosen out of innocence, we had no knowledge of Japan at all. It may have come from a lyric or something. I often think that the influence might have all come from one of Bowie's lyrics, maybe even 'Ziggy Stardust' ['Like some cat from Japan']. This was about 1974, and so we named ourselves Japan. In those days we listened to Bowie and Roxy Music and things like that, and I think that might have triggered some imagery – I think Bowie had some costumes and things like that and it all just filtered through, but our actual knowledge of it [the country] was very little.'

Richard, David, Mick and Nick finally escaped Catford Boys' in 1974. David left with the least – a solitary O level in art. 'When we left school,' explains Huckle, 'the idea was that Richard and I would go on to sixth form. But I couldn't stand the idea of going to school for another two years, so I got a job. And Richard turned up at my house on the first day of sixth form to find I wasn't there. And my mum said, "Oh, that nice boy Richard came to get you this morning, but I told him you'd got a job." So then, because I wasn't going, Richard decided not to bother as well and he got a job in a bank. Meanwhile, Mick was working for some charity at a place on Tottenham Court Road. And occasionally we'd meet on the train going into town, but generally we lost touch for a couple of years.'

These years were consumed by live music, both as spectator and participant. The trio attended gigs, such as their friend Jake Airport playing in a pub band, and as many others as they could afford. Huckle: 'We attended a Roxy Music show. We also saw Todd Rundgren at the Victoria Apollo [the *Ra* tour]. We all went to see Lou Reed there as well. Alice Cooper at Wembley and Be Bop Deluxe at Drury Lane also spring to mind as group outings. Eno/Manzanera's 801 at the Festival Hall and Steve Harley and Cockney Rebel at Wembley.'

By 1975, Huckle had been invited back into the gang. He was surprised at the progress his friends had made. 'I remember they asked me to come and listen to them play for the first time. It was in Steve's bedroom and I was all prepared for it to be not too good. But actually I was really impressed! And I said so. I told them that it was the kind of stuff I'd buy. And it was all Dave originals. I was amazed. He was doing really long guitar solos then too.' Barbieri was still an outsider at this point but his interest in pop music was also growing: 'I used to go to a lot of concerts and possibly being a bit shy and introverted, I was more drawn towards the boffins behind the big rig of keyboards and controllers than to the front men/performers.' The trio were not content to follow the usual three chord path that so many of their peers pursued. 'I think practically everyone influenced me bass-wise; every time I listened to a song, I'd be listening to the bass,' Mick would explain. 'I always had two guitars, one of them to play at home, without amps, the other to play in rehearsals. The one I had at home, I took all the frets off, so basslines I was making up at home I'd find increasingly difficult to play in rehearsal. So I (eventually) bought myself a fretless bass. I can't say who influenced me more than anyone else. The one bass player I really admired was Percy Jones, who played with Eno a lot. Anyway, I think it's a bad thing on certain instruments to learn sequences, scales and what have you. We're all self-taught and I think if you learn scales you can become too dependent on them as part of your style. It's art like any other art and it has to be felt.'

Steve: 'The rhythm part I set about learning to play on my first kit was 'Hot Love' by T. Rex. The bass drum is very clear to pick out in the mix and it was a pretty regular, medium tempo with some interesting accented parts during the coda of the song (I do recall noticing how it speeds up during the line 'she's faster than most' and wondered if that was on purpose or subconscious – I decided on the latter). Another big influence then was Billy Ficca from Television. I felt he was a very imaginative drummer and I probably picked up some of that quirkiness from him (Marquee Moon is a great example – you can also hear how this track builds towards the end in a similar way to the track 'Television' on our first album: it was a bit of a nod to that band). Another important drummer for me was Aynsley Dunbar for his work on Bowie's *Diamond Dogs*, and with Nils Lofgren and on Lou Reed's *Berlin*. We didn't get much encouragement from our parents, because we were putting aside our "prospects" for something of which nobody except us believed in the outcome. We must've had real naivety, but without it we'd never have started.' Another early and seminal influence on Steve's drumming was witnessing the Sadistic Mika Band supporting Roxy Music that year. As Steve focused on their drummer, Yukhurio Takahashi, he could never have imagined that the two would eventually become lifelong friends.

Even on Japan's earliest recordings the rhythm section stands out as ambitious, pushing the capabilties of the young men playing. Mick: 'There were very few bass players I could look up and aspire to sound like, but that was because I was basically only listening to rock bass players or Tamla Motown. I didn't want to be just in the background, I wanted to be in the front. I've been thinking about this a lot recently, trying to remember which track first really inspired me and I think it was Lou Reed's 'Walk On The Wild Side', which suddenly made me think, "That's the way I want to play." I couldn't understand why I was unable to play like that; though, of course, I later learned it was played on a double bass and there were two of them. But that was a turning point where I decided I was going to do something to make the bass dominate the track. That was right when I started playing the bass.'

As Japan progressed musically, their confidence grew and this was reflected in their appearance. More attention in particular was given to their hair, with dyes and hairspray being experimented with, and the group finally stopped wearing the clothes their parents had bought for them. 'We started dressing that way since we were 13, 14,' David would recall, explaining their eventual trashy, androgynous look. 'So it was about 73, 72. The glam rock thing was happening, but it was a theatrical thing. It wasn't something you carried off into the streets, especially where we came from in the tough suburbs of London. We had lots of threats of violence, because the way we looked conjured up certain things. People thought that if you looked that way you had to be homosexual and that was a thing in that time and place that just wasn't accepted.' Mick: 'It was hell, to put it in a word. It was really difficult. There were occasions we had trouble, though not so much fights, more like beatings up and lots of running away from people. At that point there was only the three of us in the band, me, David and Steve and the only way we could find any strength at all was in numbers. We stayed together, did everything together and tried to protect each other, if that was at all possible. I guess that was the foundations of our anti-social feelings that we all grew up with.'

Out of school, and all living at home, there was the ever-nagging issue of money. David would spend some time signing on at the Labour Exchange, later describing this period as one of 'intense boredom'. Thus began the occasional foray into 'brainless work', as Mick would describe the various odd jobs he and David endured. 'The first was at the United Friendly Assurance Company where they called us Antony and Cleopatra,' Mick remembers. Needless to say, no job lasted long and the two sustained the band by working as messengers for a while, travelling between offices in London by bus and tube. While waiting for a train at Catford station one morning, Mick ran into his old school friend, Richard Barbieri, 'dressed in a suit and tie and carrying a briefcase, also on his way to work (at a respectable bank).' Mick enthused about his band and Richard came to a rehearsal straight from work. It was the first time he'd seen his old friends in nearly a year. 'David was very quiet and kept out of any groups or gangs, but he had a self-assurance of sorts. The first time I saw him out of school after a while (I worked at a bank for just over a year) he was walking along the road in a white suit with bright orange hair. I thought he looked great.' Richard obviously thought the band sounded good too, because he joined that night despite never having played any instrument of any description. Barbieri also had the advantage of a steady, well-paid job and was able to contribute funds to the band's kitty every month, the treasurer of which was the more mathematically inclined Steve. Richard also brought a more expansive musical taste to the melting pot with his love of prog rock being incorporated into the staple diet of Roxy, Lou Reed and Bowie.

The base of musical operations was now at Mick's dad's butcher's shop in Archway, North London. This entailed an epic journey from South London, exacerbated by Steve's unwillingness to travel by tube (he would suffer from claustrophobia for years). Richard would come straight to

First rehearsals with Dean, Catford youth club 1976
Lorraine Braid

rehearsal from work, and photos from the time show him still sporting his office clothes while sat behind a Jem Jumbo organ purchased from Woolworths (this 'clerk on stage' look was one he would refine to great effect in the coming years). 'All I had was a cheap Jem Jumbo organ with four sounds and no talent for playing either of them,' says Richard. 'Offering nothing beyond chordal backing with a fizzy organ tone wasn't really enhancing the music (any musical feature or solo would rightly be assigned to Rob Dean when he eventually joined the band). The fact that I had a job and could contribute to the band "moneybox" probably kept me in the band.'

There was only one gig in 1975, at the Bunch Of Grapes, Duke Street in April. Richard stayed in the audience, still lacking confidence in his ability. 'I was actually kicked out of the band once in the early days, then soon after welcomed back into the fold,' he remembers. 'To this day I don't know who instigated the sacking or whose two votes

of confidence got me back in.' As a result of occasional performances in front of indifferent audiences, the band was disappointed with the progress it was making. As a result, Japan decided to enlarge their line-up by recruiting a lead guitarist via the obligatory advert in *Melody Maker*. Advertising themselves as a 'funk/rock band', they waited by their respective family phones for the calls to come in. After chatting to one candidate, a meeting was duly arranged.

Enter Rob Dean: 'Japan were my first group, pretty much. I'd played with friends and at school and stuff, but I'd realised I wasn't band leader material, so I thought it better to join a band and follow someone else's direction. I was working in offices and stuff purely so I could buy gear. I mean musical gear, not other kinds of gear. I was 21, even though the ad in *Melody Maker* said "18 year old wanted" or something. I think the ad mentioned Roxy Music as an influence and I was a big Roxy fan. That was our common ground because I really wasn't into Bowie

and Lou Reed that much. Not to the extent that the others were.' Steve: '[The ad said] "Japan seek lead guitarist aged between 17 and 18" and Rob comes along – 21 and married with two kids! Not really.' Dean: 'The weird thing was, I didn't reply to many ads. In fact that was the first. And I was the first guy that turned up too. I don't think they saw anybody else. And we clicked. And that was it. Do I believe in fate? Very much so.' 'Well, it's the only time we've ever done it [placed an ad],' explained David, 'because we've always believed in only forming a band on friendship. But we just sort of had this feeling at the time and we felt the time was right.' Dean: 'The audition was at Dave and Steve's mum's house. I'm from Hackney so I'd never been to Catford before. It was a long way to go! It's a strange area … not that exciting. I remember when they opened the door they were pretty distinctive looking. Dave had long hair but it was spiky on top and it was dyed red. Definitely a Bowie influence. But other than that he just had on a T-shirt and jeans. Mick's hair was fairly similar but black. Steve was still at school at this point so he wasn't looking so distinctive. I wouldn't say it was glam because there was no make-up. My own look? Oh, I don't know. My hair was probably some kind of blow-dried bouffant thing! Later, Bolan was an influence on my look but not at that point. Rich wasn't there and when I arrived we went straight up to Steve's bedroom and plugged in two electric guitars and Dave started playing me one of his songs. He told me what key it was in first.'

'Rob was an East Ender,' Mick would recall, 'who listened to Eric Clapton, Frank Zappa and Steely Dan, and made funny shapes with his mouth when he played, just like professionals do. It seemed he could play anything and was leagues ahead of us technically. Pushing us all to try harder.' Dean would return the compliment: 'Mick, Steve and David were obviously very tight, and that was very impressive. They were very focused about what they wanted to achieve. I mean the fact that they had their own PA! Very impressive. I don't know where they would have got it from but it showed real drive.' At the audition David sat on Steve's bed playing his songs on a second-hand 12-string guitar, while Dean played along on electric through a tiny practice amp. 'Dave would have played me an original song of his, not a cover,' Dean explains, 'and I was at the house about three hours. Once we'd decided I was "in", we didn't play that much. We were talking mostly. Just chatting. Soon after we started rehearsing in this small place, somewhere in Catford. Some crap place. Dave was very, very prolific in those days. He seemed to come up with new songs all the time. They weren't fully formed focus-wise but he had tons of ideas. And the influences of the day were pretty obvious as they are with young bands – Bowie, Roxy etc., and the songs sounded pretty free-form, yet were in fact very intricate as well. There was this song called 'The Apple', which was a 10 minute extravaganza that went through all these changes; different riffs and time changes, key changes, underpinned by Mick and Steve who were from day one really tight together. It was a real epic. Part of that was the influence of Todd Rundgren in those days. We were all into Todd and we went to see a solo tour he did, a gig at the Hammersmith Odeon. And we were all bowled over by it. It was very impressive. Of course he also produced the Hall & Oates album *War Babies* and that was the one David liked best. It's their most extreme album. David was also listening to Michael Jackson a lot.'

Mick and Steve were also becoming interested in jazz-funk and in the Stanley Clarke album *School Days*, which exemplified Clarke's fretless bass and Gerry Brown's intricate groovy drumming to great effect. This was music to aspire to. 'Now there was a bass player to look up to,' Mick would state, 'and who wasn't lost in the background.' Although all of Japan listened to and loved music on a daily basis, there was little intellectualising about it at this point. 'We didn't talk much about the music, we just got on with it,' says Dean. 'The songs were fairly open to our input and the arrangements just happened. It was quite organic. The guitar interplay between Dave and me, it just happened. And it wasn't merely him playing rhythm and me on top, it was more intricate than that, but we didn't discuss it much. There was no musical director as such but obviously Dave came in with the songs already written.' In 1976, the five piece practically toured London, playing enthusiastic but sparsely attended gigs at social clubs, universities and colleges. 'We worked hard at getting our music out there,' remembers Dean. 'We'd play any place at all then. And we had our own white van. A little white van with "Japan" painted on the side that Richard used to drive because he was the only one, apart from Mick, who could. That van ended up in the knackers' yard well before we "made it". I don't think it'll turn up on eBay.' Huckle also had his part to play. Steve: 'He seemed to fall into the role of working for the band as comfortably as, perhaps, someone who would prefer to be handed tasks as opposed to initiating things for himself. He had no apparent musical talent or big ambitions so it seemed like a natural path for him to step up to the job of assisting the four of us to make a success of what we wanted to achieve.' Finally, Japan were a fully formed group, ready to take on and be loved by the world at large. All they needed was a manager.

Chapter 2
Whatever Gets You Through The Night

Sylvian at
The Lyceum
November 1978
Jan Kalinski

While Japan made a noise in Archway, Simon Napier-Bell was bored in the Mediterranean. After already living what seemed like several lifetimes in the first 30 years of his life, he had announced his retirement in 1970. 'I had a house built in Spain, a beautiful place with a pool and guest suites, and I sold up and moved there,' he recalls. 'I was bored stiff. Got very drunk, danced alone to Rolling Stones records, fell asleep on the sofa. After three days, I called up an estate agent and told him to put the place on the market. I missed it all – the travel, the argy-bargy, the interesting people.'

Napier-Bell was a born wanderer, a hustler, an aristocrat without the inheritance. He was also, through imaginative wheeler-dealing and luck, occasionally wealthy. Raised in England in the 1940s and 1950s, educated both privately and by the state, his original ambition was to be a wandering jazz trumpeter. By the mid-1960s, he had put his own musical ambitions behind him and had fallen into management. His first notable client had been The Yardbirds. With the group's bassist, Paul Samwell-Smith, Napier-Bell had co-produced their first studio album. He also oversaw the entry of Jimmy Page into the group alongside Jeff Beck. Although the groups with which he was associated were high profile, historically Napier-Bell himself was a marginal figure throughout the 1960s when compared to the likes of Brian Epstein, Andrew Loog Oldham and Peter Grant. Yet he was also much more grounded, pragmatic and level-headed than many of his neurotic contemporaries. While he enjoyed a drink, he was no alcoholic and drugs were not his tipple and, unlike Epstein, he wasn't tortured by his sexuality. Along with his flamboyance and love of a lush life, Napier-Bell possessed a sturdy common sense.

There were other associations throughout the 1960s, most notably with Sylvian's one time deity Marc Bolan, whom Napier-Bell had auditioned while Bolan was still totally unknown. 'Marc rang me up and said, "I'm a singer and I need a manager. Would you like to hear some of my songs?" and minutes later he was knocking on my door – tiny character, like a Dickensian urchin, guitar slung over his shoulder. He chose the biggest of my armchairs, disappearing into it, and sat cross-legged and played every song he'd ever written. I was utterly fucking entranced. I booked Kingsway Studios and we drove over and recorded them all.' Napier-Bell looked after Bolan as a member of the Dada-esque rock happening that was John's Children, but by the time Bolan had become T. Rex, Napier-Bell was no longer in the picture.

Possessed of restless feet and a curious mind, Napier-Bell spent the next few years working in South Africa, America and Spain, often hustling huge advances from gullible record labels with his friend, ex-comedian turned record producer Ray Singer. By the mid-1970s, after SNB had found himself back in London again, Japan were pinballing around the capital's circuit, taking any gig that was offered. A series of seemingly random appearances ensued at pubs, universities and polytechnics. In February 1976, they found themselves at Goldsmiths College, London. 'The Goldsmiths gig supporting the Fab Poodles was the first time I saw them live,' says Huckle. 'The Poodles wouldn't move anything on the small stage so the guys had to fit their gear on it as best they could. Steve ended up behind the PA rig. I remember his floor tom fell off the stage halfway through their set.' Such gigs would become the stuff of comedy in retrospect, but at the time they took enormous effort and preparation on behalf of the band. The rewards were negligible. Often the only remaining audience at the end of such a show would be Nick Huckle and Jack Stafford, but at one rehearsal, kismet offered up another witness: Danny Morgan.

Morgan had originally approached Napier-Bell with celebrity aspirations of his own, as the manager would recall: 'One day in the mid-70s, a guy called Danny Morgan turned up at my flat in South Audley Street hoping I'd turn him into a rock star. He wore horn-rimmed glasses and had a nose like a toucan. He was short and stocky and limped. "But I've got a wonderful voice," he explained. "Forget it," I said, but he stayed on the doorstep smiling broadly. "I'm a haemophiliac," he told me. "I have permanently bruised knees, so the government give me a car. It's only a mini, but I could drive you around if you like."' Napier-Bell dismissed the intriguing character but, like a moth obsessed with a naked light bulb, Danny kept coming back. In between Danny's stalking of Napier-Bell, the diminutive music fan had been intrigued by an advert in *Melody Maker* for a totally unknown group seeking a manager. After phoning the group, he drove to the butcher's shop in Archway where they rehearsed and was instantly enamoured by what he saw and heard. A few days later, when Danny finally got Napier-Bell in his car (only due to a taxi strike), he enthused about what he had seen. 'I've met a fantastic group,' he told his captive audience as he drove the irritable manager to Olympic Sound Studios one day, 'they're called Japan and they advertised in *Melody Maker* for a manager, but I'm afraid they didn't think much of me. They'd sign with you though and you could give me all the work to do.' Napier-Bell recalls sitting impassively throughout the drive, determined not to be seduced by Danny's enthusiasm. Luckily, Danny seemed indifferent to indifference. 'The lead singer is stunning,' Danny went on, while Napier-Bell huffed, gazed out of the window and checked his watch. 'He has yellow hair down to his waist, and his brother, the drummer, is a dead ringer for Elvis at 17. The bass player's hair is the same as the lead singer's but red, so they look like twins. The singer's as beautiful as a girl, but he has a voice like gravel, like Rod Stewart. And they write amazing songs.' By the time they had reached their destination in Barnes, Napier-Bell had barely said a word. As he stepped out of the car, determined never to see Danny again, he was informed that an audition had been set up on his behalf. 'I'm not interested,' snapped the manager. 'I'll pick you up at 11,' replied Danny. 'You'll love them.' The next day Danny did and, in no time at all, Napier-Bell would.

The initial audition was apparently with Sylvian only. He turned up at Napier-Bell's office in Wigmore Street and played his original songs to the manager on a battered acoustic guitar just as Bolan had done a few years previously. 'I knew I was under scrutiny, as if it were me being auditioned not him,' Napier-Bell would recall. 'His voice was as much self-created as his look – Bowie out of Bolan, a flirtation with Jagger and sometimes a rasping Rod Stewart.' The manager listened carefully to the 'rambling' songs and was impressed by their 'haunting' quality even then. Sylvian sang 'arrogantly' with 'a defiantly cold stare into my inquisitive eyes,' Napier-Bell remembers. 'He was a natural – irresistibly stamped with instant success.' Napier-Bell offered to sign him on the spot, but soon came round to taking on the whole band (some of whom were waiting downstairs as Sylvian sang). Morgan, who had by now formed a company with Napier-Bell called Nomis-Morgan, was elated. 'Danny wasn't at all managerial,' Karn would recall. 'Simon, on the other hand, was the epitome of a music manager right down to the Rolls-Royce, fur coat and fat cigar.' Huckle: 'Actually, both SNB and Danny did the fur coat and cigar thing. I think maybe Danny felt he should imitate SNB. And yes, Danny was irrepressible.' 'Danny was a good man,' recalls Jansen, 'a real music lover.'

In the beginning, Sylvian was as impressed by Napier-Bell as much as anyone, later describing him as 'a wit and raconteur, he enjoyed nothing more than attempting to extract large sums of money from record companies. He could charm his way out of the most difficult situations.' The overriding attraction, however, was that Napier-Bell offered a lifeline, a rope ladder to the next level. Japan had no back-up plan, no other options they could seriously consider and, left to their own devices, they were perhaps damned to move in ever decreasing circles. Their lack of alternatives also suited the manager, who preferred to take on groups for whom failure was not an option. Japan were not Napier-Bell's sole clients at this point as he also managed a group called Urchin (two members of whom would later join Iron Maiden) and an 'authentic' punk group called London, comprising nice middle-class English boys (among them, future Culture Club drummer Jon Moss). Napier-Bell was not as flush as he would seem, either. Huckle: 'When he first started managing them, he was making a few quid here and there writing and producing jingles for radio and TV commercials.' When Japan signed to Napier-Bell in the spring of 1976, for a time at least the love between them was mutual.

In the flush of this fresh infatuation, some mistakes were invariably made. 'Contracts were handed out within weeks, not just for management but also for publishing,' says Karn. Japan even used Napier-Bell's own lawyer to go over these contracts. The song publishing agreement was for Sylvian only. There was some discussion about splitting the publishing between the group, but this idea was soon discarded, with the manager apparently telling Japan that it 'looked much better' to have only one name in the brackets under each song listed on any album. The group were assured that this could change in the future if need be. Except for a few co-writes years down the line, it never would. 'They really had no idea about how the business side of it all worked,' says Huckle. 'I remember at a dinner with SNB one day where he explained to us the difference between publishing and recording and between mechanical and performance royalties etc. After that, back in someone's bedroom, I remember a discussion on how they might split the publishing, and they talked about 50% going to Dave and the rest being split equally between the other four. I suspect that somewhere down the line SNB talked them or Dave out of that arrangement, as it was never formalised. But they were kids on a high from being signed by a big-time manager and couldn't conceive of money or any kind of contractual difficulties getting in the way of friendships and the common cause. It was "All for one, and one for all," back then! There were no band politics in them days.' 'I think David had quite a big ego about his creative importance within the band,' says Napier-Bell, 'And about that he was both right and wrong. But it's a constantly recurring problem with the lead singer-songwriter of all bands. Perhaps he could have been a bit more generous. Or perhaps it was me who persuaded him to take that much – I can't remember.'

At the time, the group were simply elated to have a reputable manager on their side and money was rarely discussed. All Japan wanted to do was make music, leave home, travel, find the world, have the world discover them, become stars. Napier-Bell, on the other hand, lived and breathed money and put a large amount of it where his mouth was. 'Initially, I thought Danny might be able to help me manage them,' he remembers. 'I gave him £15,000 to buy a van and equipment. After three days the van broke down. When he went back to the car lot where he'd bought it, the place had closed down. And he'd forgotten to take out insurance.' This was the first in a series of bad luck episodes that would dog Japan throughout their career, but it was a minor stumbling block and soon forgotten. Nomis-Morgan came with other characters – Richard Chadwick, an ex-post office worker/civil servant who would work as Napier-Bell's accountant; Ray Singer, a music producer with whom the manager gleefully extracted cash advances from record companies; and Connie Filippello, a beautiful half-Australian, half-Italian office girl, – 'Attractive and definitely over-glamorous for a mere office worker,' according to Karn. With Japan came Nick Huckle, who instantly fitted into the new picture.

The next step was to get Japan down on tape. Barbieri duly took some rudimentary piano lessons from his new manager, and Danny booked the band into TPA studios in Denmark Street. Overseen by Napier-Bell and an in-house engineer, the band played their live set straight to tape. Although the recording quality and Sylvian's strained vocals lend the songs a superficially rough quality, the playing is in fact incredibly assured and intricate. Jansen and Karn's mutual syncopation is already in place: 'You two are so tight,' the engineer told the confused rhythm section who were still not au fait with such musical jargon. On this foundation Sylvian and Dean played *off* each other rather than with one another, with the latter pouring out expansive, brittle solos. Barbieri is the quietest presence, occasionally coming out of nowhere with long, doodling Moog solos or less often providing a basic chordal backing. 'I was just hanging on musically in those early days,' admits Barbieri. The group's mood, apparent in both the adrenaline-fuelled playing and the exuberant banter, is cocky, excited, enthusiastic, raw and happy, just like the music. 'I could hardly sleep at all during those three days,' Karn would recall.

A photo shoot was arranged in Denmark Street itself, capturing the band as some exotic potpourri of badly blended styles with clothes mainly lifted from the women's sections of charity shops. Huckle: 'The white flared sleeve thing Rich wore then was made for him by his aunt. Soon after, SNB hired a stylist who met the guys once in a pub. She came back with some clothes for them to wear and put Steve in a boiler suit, for example. Her concept though was soon dropped and from then on they did their own styling.' Make-up was not yet a daily ritual but it soon would be. Sylvian: 'I think the whole glam rock thing was a big influence. I mean it was Marc Bolan who first opened the door and it was just a release. I think there was a whole generation there just waiting to stick the pancake make-up on.' 'One day David turned up in full make-up,' Napier-Bell would recall. 'I presumed he'd done it because he simply couldn't wait any longer to be a star.' The manager's theory was that by 'looking like a star' Sylvian would '*feel* like a star'. This suited everyone's plans just fine – to an extent. Sylvian apparently encouraged the others to follow suit with Dean being the least enthusiastic, but he too would eventually acquiesce, finally losing the moustache he had recently sported. 'What was I thinking?' he'd reason decades later, 'even Bryan Ferry didn't look good with a 'tache!'

Now that their manager had a tape and a suitably arresting photo to go with it, he was confident that the band would be signed within weeks. After all, he had pulled off major deals in the past for acts that were mere fabrications of his and Singer's imaginations. The climate had changed, however. This was no longer the voluptuous 'swinging 60s'. Punk was at its peak in London and while Japan were certainly something, they were certainly not punk. 'I thought they might buck the prevailing trend and take off in a flash,' their manager remembered ruefully. Sylvian: 'When it came to the punk thing we were outcast again, not just because of the style of music, but because of the appearance, which was flamboyant in a way that punk was fighting against. You know, they were more about getting back to basics and they associated [our look] with glam rock again, which was wrong.' The group Japan resembled most was, of course, the New York Dolls. While Jansen and Sylvian had been temporarily enamoured by the New York trashters, the obsession was fleeting. 'We were aware of the New York Dolls, or at least some of us were,' Sylvian would explain, '[but] we never consciously copied anybody intentionally. We were naive and just doing things, and people made reference to them.'

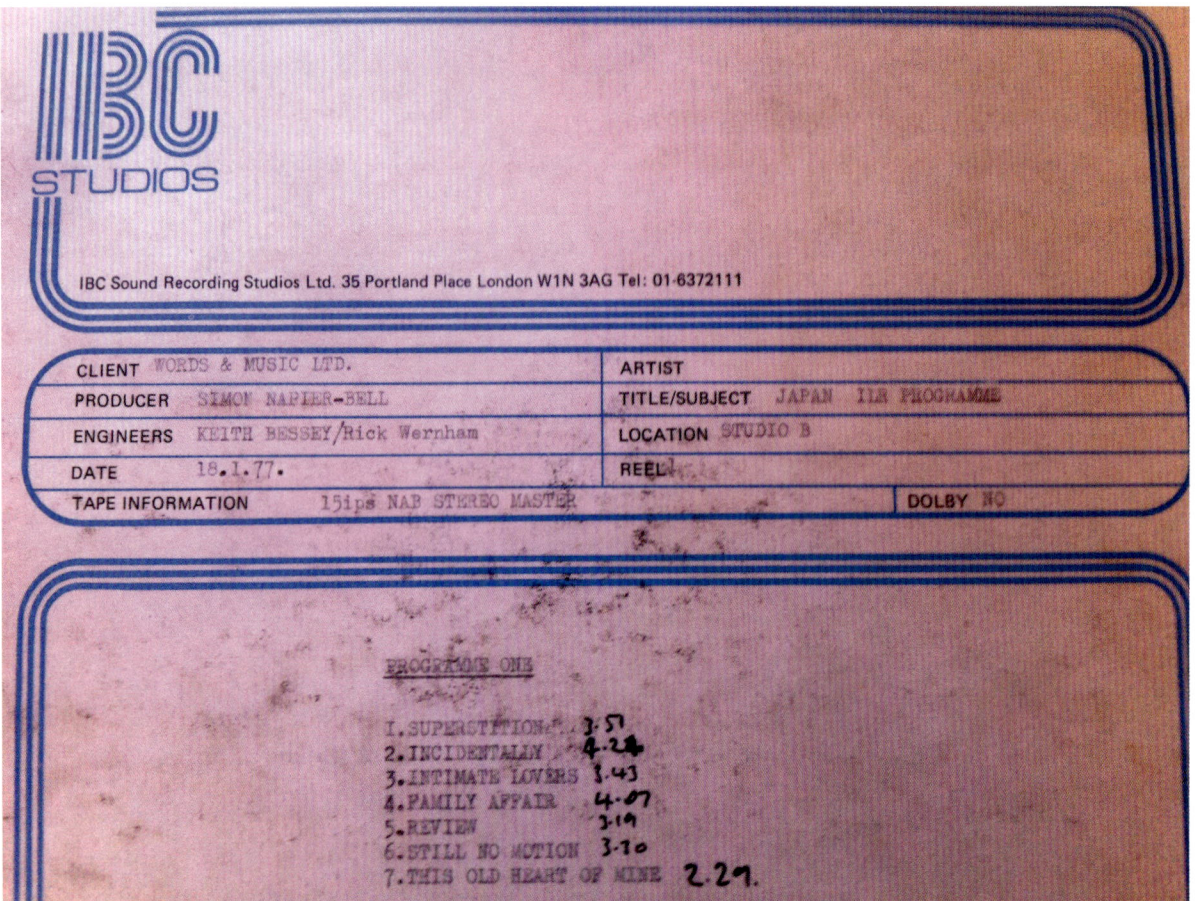

First proper recording session
Courtesy of Richard Barbieri

Napier-Bell was at least enough of a name within the music industry to get a quick reaction to the Japan package he had sent out. That the reaction was instantly negative, sometimes with particular reference to Karn's oblique bass playing, was one that initially threw the manager. In response he asked the band to record again, this time interspersing their original songs with well-known covers. In the first week of January 1977, while Johnny Mathis, Abba and Queen topped the UK singles chart, another recording session, this time at ICB Studios in Portland Place, was booked. Twenty songs were recorded in four days, with Japan laying down versions of songs by Clapton, Sly and the Family Stone, Stevie Wonder and Rod Stewart. A few Japan originals peppered the covers, including 'Lovers on Main Street' and the soon to be forgotten, 'Assassination'. Rick Wernham was assistant engineer at the sessions. Rick: 'They really were nice guys. I did a sort of "goat bleat" as an impression of David's singing voice to amuse the drummer. David overheard and Steve grassed me up by telling David that I thought he sounded like that. David got all upset and asked if he sounded stupid and said that he had a different singing voice and should he change? At least I had enough sense to jump up and down and tell him not to as I thought his voice was great – and I really did. You have to remember that David's singing voice was pretty unusual for the time. They were a really good-sounding band. Tight and – um – rocking. I'm surprised that 'Knock On Wood' didn't get a wider hearing. To my memory (and I haven't heard it since we recorded it) it was a really committed performance from David. To my shame, I hadn't heard that song before then, and when I later heard

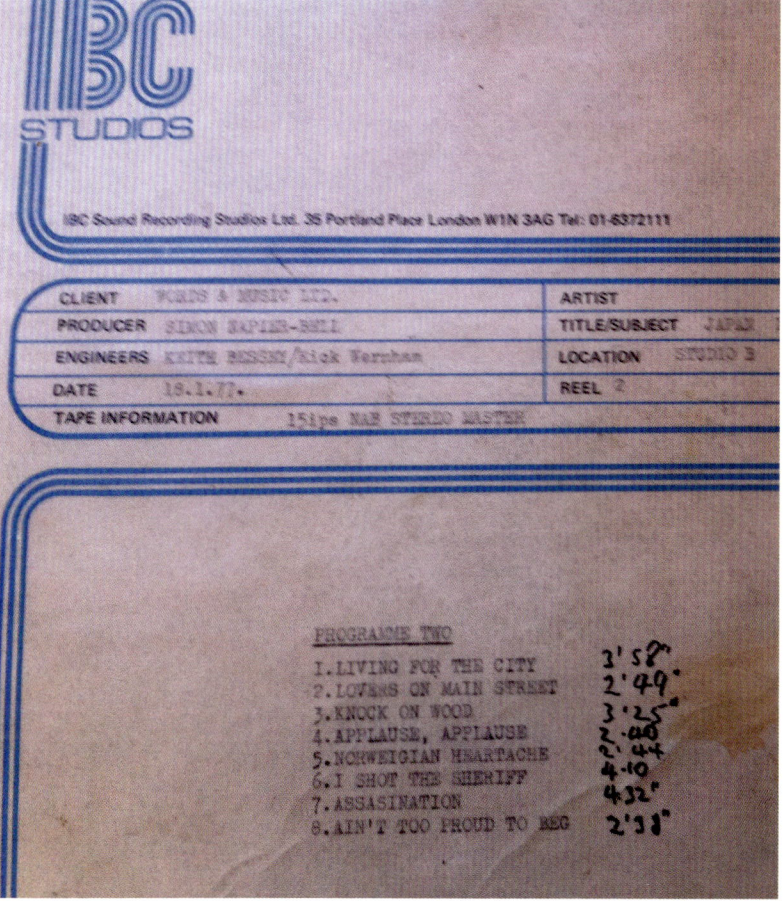

it was like they were expecting us.' Without a record deal to their name, Japan were merely 'potential' and, as one label had told their manager, 'We are not in the business of potential.' The gigs were also a financial drain. Napier-Bell calculated that each appearance the band made cost at least £50 while bringing in only £10 at most. It wasn't even as if the gigs prompted any progress. 'There was one gig at a club in Rupert Street, Soho,' remembers Huckle, 'a very poor booking by Neil Warnock as it was essentially an out-and-out disco. The club manager insisted they leave the stage after about five numbers. The dance floor was empty and his Friday night disco crowd were all leaving. Simon had me handing out flyers all over Soho for this gig as he wanted a full house because he was expecting A&R guys to show. They didn't. They also played a gig at the School of Architecture students' bar in Bedford Square. Again, Simon was expecting some A&R guys to turn up. They finished their set but no A&R had yet appeared. So Simon kept getting them to play a song called 'Diamonds' repeatedly as an encore to the now rather small but inebriated student audience, some of whom were dancing to that particular song. He thought it would look good if the A&R guys walked in to an enthusiastic audience. They must have played it at least four or five times as an unrequested encore. But, as usual, no A&R showed.' Japan were occasionally well received by their random audience, but the payback for even a good gig was paltry. The instant fame that was expected to come with signing to a big-name manager was as far off as it had ever been. 'Yes, those early years were often chronically painful,' says Huckle, 'but then the many lows did make the fewer highs seem so much higher. I think a combination of enthusiasm, self-belief, dedication, not knowing any different, and strong friendships (along with not having a plan B) got them through. It's a credit to everyone, band and management, that everyone stuck with it.'

Such gigs were a honeymoon compared to the one overseas trip Japan made that year. Neil Warnock had secured a residency at The PN club in Munich. No doubt inspired by the folklore of The Beatles' adventures at the Star Club in Hamburg, the group set off to pay overseas dues in a Rover Estate borrowed from Mick's dad. 'It broke down in Belgium and is probably still under the motorway bridge where it was abandoned,' remembers Huckle. Somehow a diesel van was borrowed and the torturous journey continued. 'I remember we arrived in Munich after this terrible journey and the leaking diesel van had somehow turned our faces nearly black with the dirt and fumes,' recalls Barbieri. 'Maybe that's

the original version, I thought it didn't have the passion that Japan had put into it.' With recording completed, more photos were added to the package and the reel-to-reel tape hurriedly couriered out to record labels. The reaction was again negative. Napier-Bell was, for once, stumped.

Meanwhile the band played on, appearing at such diverse venues as military bases and regional social clubs up and down the country. Napier-Bell had at least now secured Japan a powerful live agent in Neil Warnock but even he was sometimes at a loss as how to book them, as the seemingly random one-off gigs illustrated. Warnock: 'We had a meeting at the Bron agency and I liked 'em straight away, although even then they were very private as people. But they were already acting like stars. Even though we were a big agency, where 'Wish You Were Black' came from. We then arrived at our accommodation, which was one cockroach-infested room in a high-rise block. I wonder how many groups would have given up at that point.' Huckle: 'We only just made it there, what with vehicle breakdowns and running out of money, only to find that the club weren't expecting them and a local band was already in residence. Following fevered negotiations between Neil Warnock and the club owner Peter Neumann, they were allowed to play for five or six nights, not the two weeks originally scheduled.' The truncated residency was probably a blessing, and little is remembered of the gigs themselves. 'I just remember the cockroaches where we were staying,' shudders Dean. The group boarded the leaking diesel van and made their way home, black-faced.

When they weren't struggling to make music, the band found solace in each other, hanging out in each other's bedrooms, playing records, talking and scheming long into the night. 'We'd usually just chill out playing records,' remembers Dean, 'and occasionally have some wine or a spliff. It was fun. Danny Morgan had a huge record collection and he brought a lot to the table. We used to go to the movies a lot. I was a movie freak. In the mid to late 70s I used to go to the cinema all the time. Dave was really into the movies too, and we all had our favourite actors and stuff. Dave loved Dirk Bogarde, but I was more into De Niro. We both really liked Scorsese's *New York New York* a lot. Yeah, we were very impressed by De Niro in that.' There were also the inevitable romantic liaisons. In February of 1977 Japan, for some long forgotten reason, supported jazz-pop veteran Georgie Fame at Covent Garden's Rock Garden. Huckle recalls the three consecutive Monday night gigs as 'tough, with barely anyone bothering to watch them play. The stage at the Rock Garden was in the basement and I seem to remember most of the audience used to stay upstairs in the wine bar bit while Japan were on. I think at one of the gigs they played to Danny Morgan, myself, Rob's girlfriend and a drunk.'

There was some relief when, after the show, David was introduced to a friend of SNB assistant Connie Filippello; a girl called Charlie who was a Swiss model. The attraction was instant and the blonde model insisted on taking David, Steve and Mick back to her Kensington apartment to meet her flatmates. Once back at the flat the foursome settled into a late wine and spliff-soaked evening until eventually Charlie's flatmates turned up. In this case, they turned out to be a dark-skinned young woman with peroxide hair, and Angie Bowie. The chemistry between Angie and Mick was almost as instant as that between David and Charlie, and for the next seven months the Kensington apartment became a home from home for Mick and David. These glamorous, jet-set girls, no doubt beguiled by their almost unfeasibly cute young toy boys, even taught their willing 'boyfriends' how to apply make-up. 'It reminded them of doing the same for David Bowie and his band,' reckoned Mick. Huckle: 'Back in her homeland of Switzerland, Charlie had some kind of regal title by birth, a baroness or something. She was very attractive, as were all her friends, and to us young South London lads they appeared to be very exotic. She was a character too; I remember her travelling to a gig with us in Brighton at a place called Shelly's or Chaplin's and not being at all afraid to use the men's loos so as to avoid the queues of disco girls outside the ladies'. The local Brighton disco boys were open-mouthed when this Swiss glamour babe sashayed past them all standing at the urinals blatantly checking out their manhoods. The thing between her and Dave lasted only a few weeks. She was a fair bit older than him but, again, that was par for the course with Dave.'

Back in the rehearsal room, Barbieri was by now concentrating more on the noises he could summon from his synthesiser rather than the chords he wrought from his stage piano. Anxious to keep up with the band's musical progression, he was finally carving out a sonic space for himself within the band. He had worked in isolation on the recording of one song, 'Applause Applause', adding a simple five-note phrase that countered Sylvian's melody. This basic overdub transformed the song for all who heard it. 'Rich was beaming, knowing he'd become our hero,' Karn would say. 'Rich had found out what was missing from his own playing and also from the band's music. Electronic programming was to be his forte and all the piano lessons in the world couldn't help him with that.' 'At that stage, Richard wasn't a great keyboardist,' confirms the manager. 'He really came into his own when synthesisers and computer music came to the fore.' Karn was also making innovations. Now the owner of two bass guitars, an Ibanez and a Jedson, he decided to remove the frets from the cheaper Jedson. 'It felt good to me,' he said, 'it allowed so much more freedom to move around, uninterrupted by frets.' He continued to use his superior fretted bass with the band, but was frustrated at not being able to play the fretless parts that he had practised at home in actual rehearsals. A new ambition, when money allowed, was to own a real, decent fretless bass guitar. Karn: 'I'm sure Frank Zappa said once, "If you learn on the worst, you can do anything on the best."'

While Japan practised DIY carpentry on their instruments, partied with David Bowie's wife and continued to play poorly received and pitifully attended gigs, Napier-Bell sat in his office and wondered what he had let Danny Morgan talk him into. The group's debt to him was mounting and not one label seemed interested in helping him recoup his investment. Then suddenly, out of the blue, the mountain came to Muhammad, manifested in a series of tacky posters that suddenly appeared around London. The poster featured an impressive looking woman astride a motorcycle, stating 'Wanna be a recording star? Get your ass up! Take your chance!' 'The poster was so amazingly non-credible that I was embarrassed even to notice it,' the manager remembered. The source of the tacky ad was the German record label Ariola-Hansa who were, in effect, staging a talent competition. With nothing to lose, Napier-Bell had Connie send off a tape and photograph and then he forgot about it. Three uneventful weeks later, Japan had an audition.

The audition for Hansa took place at London's Morgan Studios on Friday 13 May 1977. The engineer in charge of the auditions was Chris Tsangarides. 'Hansa had the auditions at Morgan Studios number one in Willesden,' he remembers. 'I was engineering the lot. It was 15 minutes for each act and they were recorded onto a two-track tape and were filmed by a stand-alone video camera. I thought Japan were great! I thought, "If Hansa don't sign this lot, they're mad." They were punky and funky and had outrageous haircuts and full make-up and I was just like, "This is great!"' Although it was another London-based band, The Cure, who won the competition, Japan were also offered a contract. Within five weeks of their manager accidentally noticing that tasteless poster, Japan had a record deal. Hansa was a successful German-founded record company best known for its Disco hits with Donna Summer and Boney M, and was a wealthy if not exactly cool label. Whatever Hansa's image, the band was elated and their manager was relieved. The first phase, after investing in new equipment (Karn finally got his first fretless, a Travis Bean with the serial number 002, but it was soon stolen), was to get Japan in the studio. In the next few weeks, demos were recorded in an effort to find the 'correct' approach for Japan's debut album.

These first professional recording sessions were produced by 1960s pop producer Steve Rowlands, who was brash, loud and American, and totally unsuited as a producer for the embryonic Japan. 'I remember him as a complete non-entity, creatively,' says Jansen. The result was a mishmash of overproduced styles and genres which, while often impressive, was unsatisfying to all concerned and to Sylvian in particular: 'We'd been signed but hadn't yet been given the freedom to make a record. We'd been demoing away, trying to please everybody else with what kind of music we should be making and it would change on a weekly basis – whatever was happening. Nobody was happy with anything – we weren't, the record label wasn't. It was atrocious. When we were finally allowed to make a record, we just had this pile of material that had been kicking around for years and a lot of the good stuff had been dropped along the way because it supposedly wasn't commercial enough. The first album ended up a mishmash, a caricature of whatever and whoever.'

It was an ignominious start to Japan's recording career and the demo sessions were mercifully halted while they went on their first proper tour with ex-Traffic drummer Jim Capaldi. 'Capaldi was a gentleman,' Dean would recall. 'He took an interest in us and treated us like proper musicians. It was refreshing.' Huckle: 'The tour with Jim Capaldi was a useful experience. It was Japan's first "proper tour", albeit of the university circuit variety. The audiences were only mildly enthusiastic though as they were, of course, Traffic fans!' By the time Japan finally entered Audio International Studios to record their first album in late 1977, punk and disco were still raging and Marc Bolan had recently been killed in a car accident. Japan owed something to these phenomena; they were in debt to the recent glam past but full of spunk and righteous youthful energy. With their dyed, elaborate hairstyles and women's clothes they were also authentically glitzy. As such, they didn't really fit in anywhere and it would be a challenge for Napier-Bell's friend and appointed producer Ray Singer to assemble their sound into one cohesive whole. 'They were either behind the times or ahead of them,' says Neil Warnock. 'It was hard to tell. They just didn't fit in. But it was obvious that they had something going for them. Just hearing Mick's bass playing told you that.'

Japan's listening tastes in the late 1970s were as eclectic as it gets. Barbieri reveals their music of choice as the following: 'Circa 1975/1976, it was jazz/fusion rock (for example, Stanley Clarke, Jeff Beck, Return to Forever, Weather Report, Mahavishnu Orchestra, Al Di Meola), pop/rock (Todd Rundgren, Utopia, Automatic Man, 10cc, Hall & Oates, Sensational Alex Harvey Band, Brian Eno), reggae (Big Youth, Bob Marley, Steel Pulse), and Stevie Wonder. Prior to the first two albums in 1977/1978, we liked Patti Smith, Television, Tom Verlaine, Talking Heads, and Bowie's *Low*.' In the recording studio, Peter Silver was Singer's number two at the sessions and his impressions echo Warnock's observation. 'I recall thinking that the band were perhaps either ahead of their time, or maybe a little confused about their overall direction. They certainly had a few interesting ideas here and there and the album had an eclectic tracklist.'

The parade of depressing gigs so far had at least worked to their advantage. Japan had played so much and under such diverse circumstances in the preceding years to have become unequivocally tight and confident. It was also obvious which songs in their repertoire worked and which ones didn't. Once ensconced in the studio, Japan were not intimidated at all. The actual recording and mixing of their first album would take only a few weeks. Barbieri: 'We'd rehearsed most of the material long before the recording, so it was more about getting the performances as good as possible. We'd already been in professional studios recording various demos and cover songs. In those instances, we'd often record 10 or more tracks in a day in just one or two run-throughs. I found that intimidating. The difference with making the first album was that we had time to perfect the sounds and performances. Being able to record multiple parts separately was exciting and our first real experience of a professional recording.' Singer and Silver were a good humoured and highly efficient team with a straightforward approach that, at least for now, suited Japan's firstborn. 'They had a really good feel,' says Singer. 'I tried to record what they were doing live in rehearsals – very much a Rock band, with that great bass sound of Mick's. I think because his background was Greek Cypriot or something, you'd get this weird "wnnn wnnn wnnn" in the bass-playing – a sound unlike anything I'd heard before. Those sessions were lots of fun – they had a great sense of humour.'

In stark contrast to Japan's later albums, *Adolescent Sex* was mainly about Singer setting up the band and simply capturing what he heard. Jansen: 'We were extremely prepared as we'd been playing most of the tracks for a while, so they'd been rehearsed and performed live to quite an extent. Working out drum patterns was done strictly in rehearsals over a period of time. I never had any feelings of intimidation in a recording studio. We were so used to playing music together by this time that it just felt like a natural progression.' Sylvian explained how they approached their work in the studio: 'What we try to do musically, is to record the bass and drums and do something totally different with them than the track needs or desires. So we get the bass and drums sorted out so that they play something

Sylvian, Jansen
1978
Keiko Kurata

totally unique on their own, then we put Rob and Richard on the top so we get an emotion out of the song. So when you listen to it you get into it, and you feel either aggression, happiness or sadness, but you've got to get something out of it. Every track has got to give you something, and motivate you to think something.' The album, as Sylvian had pointed out, was something of a mishmash of styles, although this wasn't particularly a conscious, stylistic decision. 'No one ever sort of comes in and says, "this is a Reggae song," so we all play Reggae, it's not like that, we never all play the same thing,' explained Karn. Dean: 'Sometimes we play against each other rather than with. We're influenced by just about every type of music there is and it comes out in our songs.' The songs, bar the one cover version ('Don't Rain On My Parade'), had mostly originated in Sylvian's childhood bedroom via the 12-string acoustic guitar and, true to the publishing agreement, were credited to Sylvian exclusively.

'But it's not like I'm dominating the band in any way. I don't,' Sylvian would argue. 'I think I play a smaller part than the rest of the band, you know. I think my part is small compared to what is actually produced in the end. I mean I write the songs and the lyrics, okay, but when I come into the room it's just sort of a skeleton of a song. It's just me and a rhythm guitar.' The songs would have sounded completely different if anyone but Japan had been playing them and Sylvian recognised this, acknowledging that (unlike himself) his bandmates had 'found their styles very early on.' In particular, the studio was much

Jansen, Sylvian, Barbieri 1978
Keiko Kurata

more of a natural habitat for Barbieri than the stage at this point. The keyboard player, who 'had a nice little set-up of gear' (Wurlitzer Electric Piano, Solina String Ensemble and a small Moog synth with a Roland Space Echo) was able to play to his strengths in this new environment. The producer too was consistently sympathetic, as Barbieri confirms: 'There was genuine enthusiasm from Ray Singer. He created a really relaxed atmosphere in the studio and he was a joy to work with. We got on very well with Ray. He was a real character and I think his positive energy in the studio made me feel very comfortable in that environment. I'd previously felt quite intimidated on those rushed demo sessions in various London studios. There was much fun and laughter during that album, and in fact during the next two as well.'

Indeed, contrary to the 'serious' and 'humourless' image that Japan would become known for, while at work on *Adolescent Sex* they were as fun-loving and mischievous as any young men. Silver: 'During breaks or overdubs the band had competitions to see who could set fire to their shoes with meths [normally used only for cleaning off chinagraph markings on the desk] and bear the heat for the longest. Farmyard sound effects were also played exclusively into Steve's headphones while laying down backing tracks. This resulted in great hilarity all round. Steve would say, "I can hear chickens – can't you?" Us: "Nope." "Nor in the control room." Of course, these could be added during playback as well to compound the confusion.' Jansen adds: 'Singer at the time was great fun to work with, a really relaxed and humorous guy. We were obviously completely inexperienced and found his recording knowledge a great help in putting our naive ideas into practice.' Jansen's inexperience was particularly evident on one occasion. Silver: 'One day during the extended mixing schedule, Steve turned up with his kit and set it all up. I had it mic'd up all over as per the original tracks and got a sound together, assuming a new track was going to be laid down. He then announced he wanted to re-record the drums on one of the tracks. My heart sank as this would have been a non-starter due to spill on the original recording. It turned out that all he wanted to do was double-up on the kick drum during the chorus of one of the numbers – I forget which one – and had assumed that it would be necessary to redo the entire drum track. I simply used a tape delay to double-up the original during the mix and that was that.' Such innocent mistakes aside, it was generally accepted that of all the group, Jansen (along with Rob) was the most accomplished and most natural musician in Japan. The first of December 1977 was Jansen's 18th birthday and Danny Morgan presented him with a birthday card at the studio, which said, "You're now too old to be a child prodigy!"

It was around now that the Batt brothers and Michaelides legally changed their names by deed poll. The most obvious sources for Sylvian would have been the line in Bowie's song 'Drive In Saturday' ('He's crashing out with Sylvian/ The bureau supply for ageing men'), or Sylvain Sylvain of The New York Dolls. David himself would never satisfactorily reveal where he got the name from. 'Um, I always thought it was a boy's name,' he'd say quixotically, although he was open about why he changed it, 'The name change wasn't for commercial purposes only. It was also a very private need that generated the change.' Sylvian denied any conscious reference to either the New York Dolls or Bowie saying, 'Unless there's something going down on the subconscious level for which I cannot account, wrong … on both counts.' The source for Jansen was more prosaic. 'Mine came from browsing a telephone directory. I was into the New York Dolls at the time and being a teenager ... falling victim to a fad, J(oh)ansen was certainly steering my way of thinking. I'm pleased it did though cause I feel very much a Jansen. I'm glad I didn't opt for anything daft as that's the age when you do things you regret later in life.'

'Andonis Michaelides' would also be consigned to history: 'I'd always been known as Mick,' explained the bassist.

'It came from my surname which most people found unpronounceable. A surname to go with Mick was difficult. I felt that Mick rolled into most, making one long name, as in MickRock or MickRonson, so decided to have the surname start with the same letter that Mick ended with. For a while it was going to be Kar, but after going through the appropriate phonebook and finding Kahn, I chose to put an 'N' to it and became Karn.'

With the album recorded and mixed, Singer was not quite satisfied. 'Ray came back saying that "something was missing" and that a total remix would be required,' remembers Silver. 'I don't think I really relished more long mixing sessions and as we had recently acquired a Scamp Rack FX with various units I almost jokingly suggested simply compressing the mix as an alternative. Ray said we should give it a go, so I fed the mix through the Scamp compressors without even setting up anything – I think they had been left on some rather fierce 20:1 compression from a previous session. Ray seemed to love the instant transformation in the overall sound and agreed that the compression had done the remix brilliantly and saved us all a lot of time.' Considering the years of struggle and hard work that led up to it, the recording of Japan's debut was put to bed relatively quickly. Huckle: 'There's not a lot to say about the recording of that first album. It was, as Steve and Rich point out, a straightforward recording of the numbers they'd been performing for the past year or so, aside from 'Communist China' which was a new track that they'd only started to rehearse a week or so before the session and which took its final form in the studio. Other than that, it was a relatively straightforward and, for them anyway, quick session of circa two to three weeks from start to final mix. This is probably fairly typical for a lot of bands with first albums, where the material has already been extensively rehearsed, played live, reworked and honed over a long period. I do recall a discussion on whether or not to include one song, 'Diamonds', but in the end it was dropped, I suspect to make room for 'Communist China'.' Sylvian summed up the experience a year later: 'We knew we were good and we just wanted to get down the stuff we'd been doing. We were just interested in getting it done.'

The results of Singer's and Japan's efforts were unusual. Unless you were privy to their unique history and specific listening tastes, *Adolescent Sex* was confusing on all fronts, especially when Japan basically looked like the New York Dolls, with even some of their surnames being similar. But the Dolls weren't much of a musical influence on Japan. 'All you have to do is listen to the LP to convince you. There is no comparison,' explained Sylvian. 'The only thing that's similar between the Dolls and ourselves is that we are both self-indulgent; we are totally into ourselves.' It was yet another curveball thrown out to critics and punters alike that Japan didn't look like their disparate musical influences, and as a band they actually seemed to gain sustenance from confusing both the press and audiences alike. The album's opening track, 'Transmission', started off sounding like a Jeff Wayne production, before collapsing into a queer, anaemic pop-rock funk. 'It's like not wanting to be involved with a style or a phase that's going around already. We want to stand outside of that,' Sylvian would explain, 'so like the punk phase or whatever comes next, we are not going to be part of it, we are determined to stand outside of it. If people into punk, or whatever is next, get into us, well that's okay.' This outsider attitude sometimes resulted in *Adolescent Sex* sounding like a compilation album. Which, in effect, it was. The prodding, spiky title track rubbed uncomfortably beside the Streisand cover and the last minute 'Communist China' sounded tacked on. 'Performance' (also the title of another film Sylvian admired) was closer to the abandoned Barry White sheen of the Steve Rowlands demos than it was to the strangled funk of 'The Unconventional'. The lack of unifying concept behind the album was blatant. *Adolescent Sex* was what it was – merely the best songs of the last few years from a band barely out of their own adolescence. Its gawkiness had a goofy appeal and the production was at least as lush as the group's hair. For a debut, it sounded big time.

As Christmas came in, everyone involved in Japan and their debut album were confident that anyone and everyone would get into Japan once the album was released. The group had paid their dues. They had struggled to come this far. Even their manager had taken setbacks in getting them signed – and Napier-Bell was not used to disappointment. Yet a deal had been made, the album had been delivered and it sounded great (strange, sexy, big, ambitious, perverse, and accomplished). The group themselves looked fantastic. Everything was in place for a universal commercial breakthrough and instant critical plaudits.

It would take another four years of ridicule, effort, luck and agonising growing pains for Japan to crack the UK Top 40.

Opposite page: Richard Barbieri personal archive

Chapter 3
Mastering Obscure Alternatives

Blue Öyster Cult tour *David Sowerby*

In January 1978 in San Francisco, the Sex Pistols imploded on stage at what was their last true show. This was surely the authentic end of punk, although now that the phenomenon was actually making money for the labels, selling a pasteurised version of the movement would endure indefinitely. Sharing the same planet but on a different world, the Bee Gees and *Saturday Night Fever* were speedily becoming a pop phenomenon, a falsetto-fuelled bushfire that raged across the airwaves and discotheques from Basildon to Berlin. Somewhere in between these two extremes, and utilising elements of both (although infinitely less popular than either), was Japan.

David, Steve, Rich, Mick and Rob still co-habited with their parents but in all other respects were living the dream. Their debut album was in the can, they had a devoted and powerful manager at the helm, and they looked the business. All they had to do now was find a paying audience. To this end, more painfully inappropriate support slots were fixed, with the band supporting The Damned on their February 1978 tour of the UK. They would not make it to the end date. 'The Damned fans were hardcore,' Karn would recall, 'for once, I envied Steve and Rich being further back and way from the front of the stage and out of spitting range.' Within the first few songs, the immaculately coiffured and made-up Japan were covered in green and grey phlegm. 'Where did it all come from?' wondered Karn, 'and would there be any left for the main act?' As the fuchsia-haired bassist observed, the irony was that The Damned fans spat to show both their affection and their disapproval. Japan couldn't win. Even if they had somehow managed to convert the audience, they would have ended up matted in mucus. 'I was working the live desk,' remembers Huckle, 'and I can still see the look of pain and disgust on David's face. He even had a go at some of the more ardent gobbers with his microphone stand.' Dean: 'It was all a pose, that punk thing. And The Damned were definitely into that and considerably more successful than us. They were also *NME* approved, which we weren't. I found them quite snooty.' Inverted elitism aside, the consequences of the audience's hostility were real. 'Someone threw a lit cigarette,'

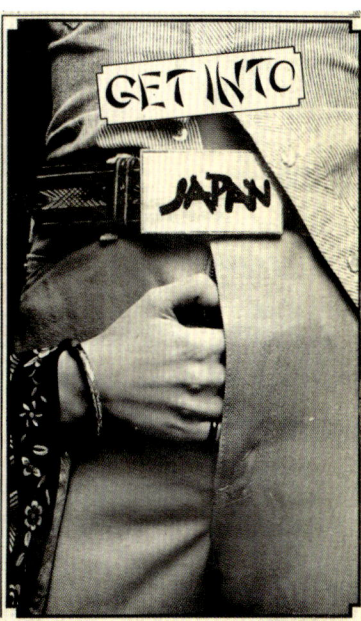

laughs Dean, 'and it landed in my hair and set fire to it.' While his lead guitarist's perm burned, and the catarrhal snot rained down, Karn's temper snapped and he kicked a monitor into the audience. Blood flowed and the crowd rioted. Japan were rushed backstage by security as the audience surged forward, resulting in a mob outside the barricaded dressing room. 'The door was hammered from the outside and bulging,' recalled Karn, 'all windows smashed, with hands reaching in and threatening to kill the "red-haired poofter".' Police, armed with German Shepherd dogs, eventually came to the rescue, and Japan were escorted back to their digs, still dodging, as Karn put it, 'long-range missiles'. The tour was abandoned. 'It was deemed too dangerous to continue,' says Huckle. With typical understatement, Sylvian summed up the farce: 'The Damned's audience didn't like us much. But it was a good experience.'

A few weeks later in March, a less saliva-sodden gig was arranged at the Camden Music Machine to coincide with the release of Japan's debut single, 'Don't Rain On My Parade' – the classic show tune popularised by Streisand in *Funny Girl*. Rob Dean was to blame: 'It was my idea. Me and Dave liked musicals ... the backing vocals are out of tune on purpose by the way.' Sylvian: 'Originally we played it live because we thought we'd do a song that no band had done before, and we thought we'd stick it on the B-side of the single. So we recorded it – it was very rough – but when Hansa heard it they went overboard about it and we didn't really give a damn about a single anyway because we are not interested in the singles market.' This was just as well as, with the exception of Australia, the single picked up next to zilch airplay although, due to Hansa's powerful presence in the industry, it was at least reviewed across the board. *Sounds* wrote it off as 'a nice joke'. *Record Mirror* optimistically stated, 'Goodbye Streisand, hello Japan.' The *NME*, then the most negatively predisposed towards the group called it 'a bit too clever ... smacks of some gimmick merchant's idea of the easiest route to a fast buck.' Still the *Shields Gazette* liked it: 'It's actually better than the original. Forget about your prejudices – Japan are best at making everything these days.'

Despite what could be kindly called 'mixed press' and a garish promo video that no one outside of Sydney saw, 'Don't Rain On My Parade' was met with a monsoon of indifference. It was after all an incongruous choice for Japan's debut single. It showcased neither their original material nor their true tastes. Hansa presumably thought that having an 'outrageous' looking group release a classic show tune was odd enough in itself to reap publicity and sales. But the rendering was too musical to be punk and too weird to be pop. The band's visual image just confused the effect further. The *NME* was right. Japan's debut single reeked of novelty.

However, it was a fact that the group's tastes were eclectic. This was proven when Sylvian chose his 'Star Tracks' for *Record Mirror* that month. His choices were basically the ingredients of Japan's first two albums, minus Bowie and Roxy Music. His picks featured Patti Smith, the reggae of Steel Pulse and Bob Marley and the out-and-out pop of David Cassidy. Only Eno's cover of 'The Lion Sleeps Tonight' hinted towards other more masked influences. Patti Smith was perhaps the least surprising choice, while punk was nowhere to be seen. The latter was too one-dimensional for Sylvian to relate to, whereas Smith embodied a literary sensibility that transcended her musical genre. 'You could recognise an intellect at work, particularly in Patti's early work like *Horses*, which was quite an important album at that time,' Sylvian would reflect years later. 'I was never attracted to the British punk movement at all. I celebrated the spirit of it. As unlikely as it seems, we were very much part of that spirit at that time. It was a matter of, "Well we can do that, pick up our instruments and go."' The difference was that Japan were too naturally adept at their instruments and too refined as people ever to emulate the amphetamine and lager-fuelled noise that The Damned and the Sex Pistols were brimming with so gloriously. 'They didn't own a punk album between them,' says Huckle, 'except Rob. He had *Never Mind The Bollocks*, but that was it.' Japan also differed from the New York punk school of Patti Smith in that they had a keen interest in how their songs were both arranged and produced, as opposed to merely being recorded. In 1978, it seemed Japan belonged nowhere apart from the alien ecosystem which they themselves had nurtured.

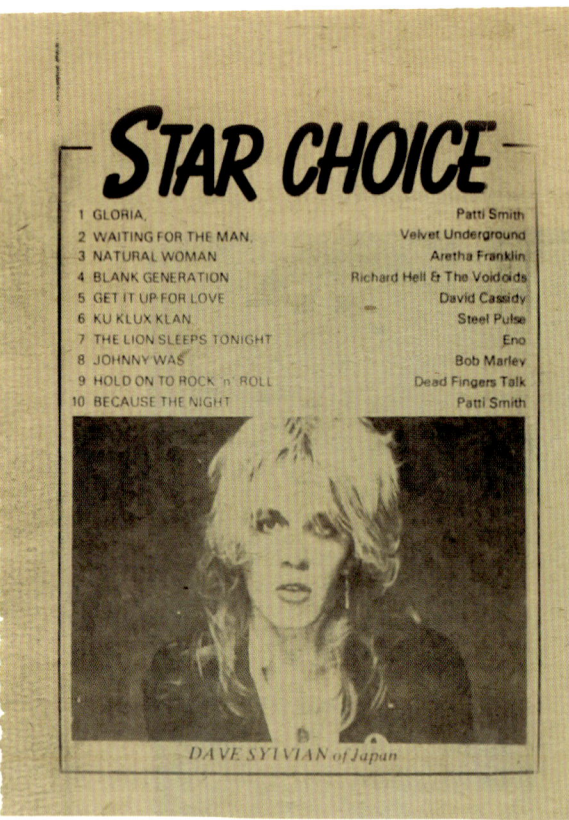

In April, the *Adolescent Sex* album was released on vinyl, cassette and eight track amid a tsunami of Hansa-generated hype. 'Get into Japan!' screamed the tacky ad, showing a manicured hand sliding into the straining fly of skin-tight jeans. (The jeans belonged to a mannequin and the hand to Hanne Jordan, a secretary from the agency behind the advertising). The album title itself was an honest and fitting description of the music within. The cover was a mess and a mistake, with the front image supposed to have been on the reverse and vice versa. By the time the band realised the error and protested, Hansa explained to them that to re-manufacture the cover would screw up the meticulous schedule planned for them. Although annoyed, the band let it go. Hansa weren't bluffing – there truly was a glut of press awaiting the group, even if the curiosity was not born of much musical appreciation. Japan's visual image was at this point so powerful that much of their publicity centred on what it meant for a young man to preen himself to the point where he was prettier than the average girl. Then there was the album's title. Once again, Sylvian was nothing if not contrary. 'I don't enjoy sex,' he declared flatly. 'It's just a part of life, no more important than breakfast. The album has got three songs that are specifically about sex.' A natural pop star, Sylvian played the game but was relieved to move onto other aspects of the band, trying to explain why it was that so many people already reacted so negatively. 'It's people that listen to it once and gauge it on first impressions who don't like it. It's one of those albums that you've got to listen to, get into and try to understand what we are doing, because we are not going to come along with what's been done already. We are trying to do something completely different.'

As ever, journalists were never happy to take the songs at face value. They wanted them decoded by the author. Sylvian was already sounding wearied at what was for him the beginning of a lifetime of being asked a recurring question. What were the songs actually about? 'I don't like doing this, but, well, I'd say 'Performance' is for minority groups in politics and 'Lovers On Main Street' is about prostitutes.' Next to explicating what he had already set out to express in song, answering questions about hair dye and panstick was a relief. Asked for the umpteenth time if his appearance meant that he was gay, Sylvian responded: 'No. I think a lot of boys are very good-looking – a lot better looking than girls. It's up to the individual – they shouldn't feel inhibited. Nothing to do with the sexual side of anything – if you like a boy – you think he's really good-looking – there's nothing wrong with saying it. I'm not asking everyone to go out and wear make-up – just wear it if you want and don't feel inhibited by the people around you.'

History has it that in the UK *Adolescent Sex* was met with across-the-board contempt. And while there were unfairly hostile reactions there were also gamely positive reviews that conciliated Hansa and Napier-Bell's confidence in their investment. However, when the reviews were bad they were cruel. Tony Stewart, writing for the *NME*, began his assassination thus: 'Hello? Is that Cadavers Cruising Coffins? Tricky one for you here. I want a circular coffin, 12 inches in diameter, quarter of an inch deep, and with a self-sealing lid.' The eager young band, no doubt initially jostling for a peek at the first review of their first album in the UK's biggest selling music weekly would have been advised to stop reading there. One can imagine each member of the band in turn, his face a mask of hurt and revulsion slowly twisting away from the review, leaving it in the hands of a more stoical Steve or perhaps Rob as they alone read it aloud to a slowly emptying room. Stewart continued: 'I've got the first offspring by a band called Japan here and it's stillborn. There's such a grotesque stench of musical decay that my stylus refuses to go near it again. Flowers? Well a bunch of pansies will do.' No doubt even the most pragmatic member of the band never made it to the end of the piece. One could imagine the paper abandoned and fanned out on the floor rearranged by the stomping of an elegantly Jelly-shod heel via a chain-smoking Mick or Dave.

They had a right to feel insulted and Sylvian's reaction revealed his still prevalent south London working-class genes. 'But the cunt can't have listened to the LP. What he said was that the LP went along at a funeral march pace, which means he must have listened to either 'Transmission' or 'Television' and missed all the other tracks.'

It's such vitriolic print assassinations that inform to this day the general critical consensus that Japan began as a joke. In fact, the critical reception was generally positive. *Record Mirror*, admittedly the least cool of the weeklies, even deemed *Adolescent Sex* a 'masterpiece'. They would also give Japan – or at least Sylvian – their first front cover that year.

Jane Suck in *Sounds* was under the false impression that 'David Sylvain' [sic] was actually somehow 'Sylvain Sylvain' of the New York Dolls (this occasional misspelling of Sylvian's name endures to the present day), but she still liked it. Sort of. Given the parlance of the Nick Kentisms of the time it was hard to tell: 'Japan make the bomb that got detonated AKA the Heartbreakers look all Ivy. Filthy rock and roll utilising everything we ever pimped for the '70s ... given a modicum of radio play, they stand a fair chance of breaking even.' In Geoff Barton of the same weekly, the band made a rare ally, albeit one who would lose affection as the band fulfilled the very potential he predicted. 'You know what they say about it being difficult to recognise true genius at the outset?' enthused Barton. 'Well maybe

Kate Bush launch party 1978
Keiko Kurata

Sylvian and Dean, Newcastle 1978
David Sowerby

this applies to Japan, the most interesting debut release from a British band so far this year.'

The monopoly of weeklies was not the only platform for music writing in the UK. The world of fanzines – home-made, Xeroxed magazines whose ardent content often outweighed the tatty format – was booming. Chris Carr, the editor of a Reigate-based fanzine called *Now*, was instantly smitten by this new group who 'kind of looked like the New York Dolls, but sounded nothing like them.' He contacted Hansa requesting an interview and hit it off with the band immediately. They soon became friends. 'I also got very friendly with Danny Morgan from the off,' remembers Carr. 'He was a total music fan and a very knowledgeable one. He was a very, very nice man who, if you liked music, you got on with. We shared very catholic tastes. He educated Japan in some musical respects.' At an after-show gathering, Carr put a proposal to the group: that he edit and write their very own fanzine. 'I told them that they were going to get nothing but damaged by the weekly press and they should have their very own printed platform as it were. The *NME* would never like them because they weren't wearing the right "uniform". The group were enthusiastic, but Carr thought little more of it and headed back home to Reigate. The following morning at 8.30, he was awoken by a call from a 'Mr Napier-Bell'. Carr: 'He said, "I love your idea," and I said, "which one?" It was a bit early for me, but it showed how driven Simon was, calling me at that hour.' Despite being broke, Carr somehow made it to Napier-Bell's Burton Street offices in London. A deal was soon made whereby Carr would write and publish Japan's very own fanzine, 'giving them a right to reply to all the negative press they were getting,' as Carr put it. The initial press run of a thousand was given out free at gigs. 'The costs were paid but *I* don't remember being paid. Maybe something nominal, but that didn't matter. I loved doing it.'

For the next year, Carr would hang out with the band as much as anyone. 'We'd sit around talking about films and books … they were funny and, behind the appearance, just regular guys. Pretty much. But, walking down the street,' says Carr, 'people would shout at them, spit at them, physically threaten them. Wherever we went we'd cause some reaction so I'd walk slightly ahead of them to be a kind of scout, as protection. It depended where we were. In the right club a certain kind of woman would be intrigued, but on the street it could be like running the gauntlet.' Huckle: 'Most of the time, feeling vulnerable on the streets was more to do with people staring, pointing or sniggering; this was one of the reasons they became such an insular group. It was worse in Catford than it was in the East End, but we could get hassle when we went to the cinema there. Although Bowie, Bolan and the whole glam thing had happened in the early 70s, the look hadn't truly translated into youth culture, so for your average south east Joe to see a gang of young men walking around wearing colourful clothes, with brightly dyed hair and make-up invariably sparked the "you wanker/poof/queer!" reaction.'

Chris Carr

Although aloof from such skirmishes – he rarely walked anywhere – Napier-Bell was becoming a hugely influential figure for the band. It was a given that from day one he had kept the boys afloat financially, but his management style was not cut and dried or geared to office hours only. He enjoyed his job and he enjoyed his clients. 'I was a fan of the group,' he'd say years later, 'I loved them – the best bunch of people I ever managed – sharp, funny, intelligent and good to be with'. He also relished showing them the nicer things in life such as upmarket restaurants, members only clubs, fine dining and wines. 'He taught us a lot about life and people along the way,' remembered Karn, 'teaching us to enjoy the finer things in life through his example. He was in many ways a much-needed mentor during our late teens and early twenties. We'd all get drunk over dinner where I spent half the time sobbing and spluttering thanks to Simon for having such confidence in our imminent stardom.' Although charmed by the group as a whole, Napier-Bell was already turning his focus toward Japan's singer. 'Simon was a little bit Pygmalion with David, and as a group he enjoyed educating them in matters outside of music,' says Carr. 'They were essentially working-class boys. I remember the first time he took us to a cocktail bar. He showed us the drinks menu and said, "What do you want?" We just laughed. We had no idea.

We also had a running joke about which knife and fork to use at the table. Simon moved in such rarefied circles that we were out of our depth to begin with. It was a steep learning curve, but they took to it like a fish to water. Especially Mick and David. David in particular thought, "Yes. Put me out there into that big ocean and out of this small pond." He was like a fish swimming towards the sea.'

Beyond the cocktail bars of Mayfair, Japan may have been mocked, reviled or simply treated as a camp freak show but they were not ignored. The volume of press was enough that Karn was able to begin a scrapbook, but at the end of the day *Adolescent Sex* spawned no hit and didn't chart. Eventually, Hansa's product would do the business in one territory. In the second biggest record buying market of the world, in the very country with which Japan shared a name, *Adolescent Sex* would go top 20. Earlier in the year Japan (minus Rob) had crashed a Kate Bush album launch party. A popular Japanese music magazine, Ongaku Senka, was in attendance and 'went crazy' photographing the photogenic foursome. The published photos would cause a frisson of arousal back in Japan. This would prove to be the first step towards Japan (the band) becoming hugely popular in Japan (the country). But all of this was some months off. Back in Britain there was the Blue Öyster Cult tour to survive.

Through April to June, the band endured 14 misjudged dates in support of an utterly inappropriate headline act. Blue Öyster Cult (whose keyboard player Allen Lanier, was currently dating Patti Smith) were a heavy, if thoughtful, denim on leather rock group whose audience barely applied deodorant, let alone eyeliner and foundation. 'We weren't fans of them,' says Dean. 'We weren't into that type of music. Not even Richard.' Japan's agent, Neil Warnock, would in retrospect consider the booking a mistake. 'I think we were also offered the Talking Heads tour which came a bit earlier in the year [January and February] but it was a small club circuit as opposed to playing large theatres with BÖC. So we went with that, but their audience was never going to appreciate Japan. The Talking Heads tour would have been cooler and had more kudos. I regretted booking them on the BÖC tour.' The tour started ignominiously for Japan. Owing to their late arrival for the opening night in Bristol, the group had to set up their gear on stage in front of 2,000 people. Even before Japan had played a note, these 2,000 people did not like what they saw. When Japan did finally plug in and play, the place went hate-crazy. The audience reaction in the whole was extremely hostile towards what they saw as a musically perplexing amalgam of plastic rock and faux funk played by a gang of transvestites.

Sylvian began the tour overwhelmed at the negative reaction and the night before Glasgow he apparently asked his manager to cancel the remaining dates. Simon considered this before giving Sylvian some advice: 'Play as much of the set as you can before the audience gets totally out of hand. Then, when you're on the edge of losing it, announce you're going to sing *a cappella* … Whatever reaction you get, it will be you who's caused it not them. That way it becomes you who is in charge.' Sylvian took the advice. The group took to baiting the hateful audience, incorporating musical passages into their set that would never make it to record. The new intro to 'Suburban Berlin' – in fact, the group had already been playing this musical prologue prior to the BÖC tour - consisting of Sylvian's solo vocal and Barbieri's stage piano, it was a haunting and seductive piece of music if you could make it out above the caterwaul.

At another show, an audience member recalls the group lurching into a waltzing circus show tune while Sylvian repeated 'welcome to the fairground' over and over in an exaggerated faggy croak, but Barbieri thinks this was in fact 'Suburban Berlin'. By the end of the Glasgow show, Sylvian had broken through the pain barrier. 'He was never again fazed by anything an audience did to him,' summed up Simon. There was a new respect among the headliner's entourage too. Huckle: 'The BÖC road crew, who were nearly all American, were initially as perplexed by Japan as the audiences. However, they grew to admire and respect the guys more and more as the tour progressed. It went from comments like, "Why the fuck are you guys even on this show?" to, "That was great – it gets better every night".' The audiences on this tour, however, remained unmoved.

An apprentice lighting technician, Par Can, helped set up the lighting at the Newcastle show. 'I was employed by BÖC to help set up their lighting rig,' he recalls, 'I remember Nick Kent was hanging around backstage, but he was there for the headline act. I had loved *Adolescent Sex* and was thrilled to see Japan arrive. They were even more striking in person, but incredibly shy. Newcastle then was a heavy metal town, but I don't think the band had any idea. It was like lambs going into the lions' den. They didn't seem overly confident, shall we say. I had a lot of mates in the audience and their heroes were Greg Lake and Lemmy. When they saw Mick Karn go on stage it was, "What the fuck is that?!"'

Karn and Sylvian,
Newcastle 1978
David Sowerby

Left: Karn, Music
Machine 1978
Keiko Kurata

Centre: Sylvian,
Music Machine
1978
Keiko Kurata

Right: Karn,
Sylvian, Music
Machine 1978
Keiko Kurata

Left: Karn, Fan,
Music Machine
1978
Keiko Kurata

Centre: Barbieri,
Lyceum 1978
Keiko Kurata

Yet dotted among the acne and dandruff-afflicted forest of denim, there was the occasional Japan fan. 'I was completely captivated by their image,' remembers Brian Cogan, then a schoolboy in Birmingham. 'I bought *Adolescent Sex* when it came out and loved it but was also into heavy metal, so when I saw they were supporting BÖC at the Birmingham Odeon I thought it the perfect opportunity to see two of my favourite bands for the price of one.' Brian was an alienated anomaly, as he soon discovered: 'I had no idea what a reaction they would get. It was bad, to say the least.' Brian and chums had good tickets, placing them near the front row. 'When they came on, my friend immediately said to me, "Bunch of fucking poofs". I tried to argue that they were actually really, really good but within seconds of Japan starting there was no way he could have heard me.' Brian states that, 'usually at such a gig the audience would ignore the support group but as soon as they saw Japan the place went crazy. There was this enormous wail that came out of the audience, a sort of scream of pure hatred and anger but you could just about make out, "Get off you fucking queers", "Go home you bent cunts", stuff like that. People were screaming and throwing stuff at them. I'd never experienced anything like it.' Amid the roar of adrenaline and testosterone-fuelled fury, Brian was besotted. 'I thought they were great, but I didn't want to make much of a show of it so I sort of clapped politely. I didn't want to get beaten up.'

On the raised stage, Sylvian perched like a peacock at a grouse shoot unable to retreat from his microphone, taking the full brunt of the crowd's animal rage. Jansen and Barbieri were relatively safe in their rear positions, but even so, the latter – a more confounding looking freak in his black lipstick and white lab coat – would have been unable to programme anything into his Moog to compete with the wall of angry white noise enveloping him. As the singer, Sylvian would bear the apex of the audience's insults, but from his guitarist's point of view the tour was not as testing as others remember it. 'It didn't feel that horrific,' says Dean. 'We were happy to be playing big theatres. When Dave did the *a cappella* intro to 'Suburban Berlin', the crowd went crazy booing, but they loved it – loved booing, I mean. To me, playing with The Damned was worse. We felt safer in a big theatre. Anything thrown would be harder to hit us, for a start.' By now, the torturously elongated intro to 'Suburban Berlin' had become an oasis for the group. 'As the tour progressed and Dave became more confident, he extended the silent pause bit in the middle longer and longer each night,' says Huckle. 'He would just stand there with the spot on him and that big Sylvian grin of his, while the denim-clad hoard went wild with fury. I think he must have peaked at nearly 30 seconds of silent grinning. After this, the BÖC stage manager asked me to ask Dave to ease off on the wind-up a bit as BÖC themselves were concerned that "their" audience were reacting more to the support act than to BÖC. I forgot to pass on his request.'

Their audience remained as perplexed as they were affronted. One BÖC disciple at the Manchester show recalls that, 'My abiding memory from watching Japan was this bloke from Sheffield looking at the lead singer and saying, "I'd give her one". When I pointed out that it was actually a man, he replied, "I don't care, any port in a storm."' Brian remembers confusion, sexual and otherwise, among the loathing. 'People were just aghast as to why a group like Japan were supporting BÖC. It made no sense, they were completely wrong for that gig and even that made people angry.'

The booing continued unabated throughout the whole tour. Occasionally, the music cut through the squall. 'I knew much of the material and it sounded great when you could hear it, but they weren't exactly preaching to the converted,' continues Brian. 'Mick was doing backing vocals occasionally, so he had to come to the microphone now and then and take the abuse with Dave. Dave didn't actually look hurt; it was like he was camping it up even more. The reaction was worse by the end of the show. You couldn't say Japan won them over. In a funny way I found it heart-warming though. Dave obviously had a lot of balls.' BÖC and Japan didn't mix socially either. 'I don't remember an occasion when the BÖC members and Japan members ever spoke,' says Huckle. 'It must have happened of course, but there was certainly no effort to make friends there. I think they were a bit embarrassed by Japan and didn't know how to approach those strange looking English guys.' 'They were both very shy groups and never the twain shall meet, I guess,' says Par Can. 'After the second Newcastle date we all ended up in a bar at the hotel and Nick Kent was still there, staggering around at three in the morning. Japan and Nick Huckle were there too, with the exception of David and Richard, and we had a chat. They seemed quite relaxed. There were birds about, but these were women into the glam scene rather than Japan particularly.'

Back on stage, the baiting exercise worked for a while, but by London Sylvian was bored and pissed off, at one point theatrically unfastening his guitar and letting it clang to the floor before sulking off, ending the set early. Yet, on the whole, the tour was a positive experience. Japan had been greeted with utter hatred and had not dissolved or resorted to the bottle or wrap. It had been a bonding experience. They had got through it, won a few fans and become tighter as a group. 'I know some people I knew were impressed by them as musicians on that tour, especially by Mick,' says Par Can. Huckle: 'I was always surprised that, despite the drubbing the audience gave them each night, there were invariably two or three brave souls who would be waiting outside the stage door each night amidst the denim-clad BÖC fans trying to grab a Japan autograph.' Dean adds that, 'We were treated well by the band and got on with their crew, even if they did set off a huge explosion on the last night of the tour during our quietest song. They let off every spare firework and explosive thing they had left and it was bloody loud. I don't think that tour did us any harm. Quite the opposite, in fact.'

Despite its poor sales, *Adolescent Sex* had not been ignored. In fact the title track was re-recorded that spring, released as a single and was a minor sleeper hit in Europe. Hansa recognised that they had signed something of potential and this was backed up by Japan's powerful management. This was also still an era when groups were nurtured and invested in and not dropped if they initially failed to chart. Japan's contract with Napier-Bell and Hansa was long term and as *Adolescent Sex* collapsed into bargain bins, the band was ushered into Morgan Studios in Willesden to record a follow-up in June. It was no secret that the band was disappointed with the production of their first album and initially they had sought more esoteric options than Ray Singer. Huckle: 'Dave had wanted Robert Fripp to produce *Obscure Alternatives* and had asked Simon to send him some demos etc. Simon reported back that Fripp was too busy and that it was now too late to find anyone else, saying, "So let's go with Ray Singer again". Personally, I always wondered about this. After all, Ray and Simon had been long-time friends and doubtless Fripp would have been quite expensive.'

Such was the growing interest from Japan (the country) that a journalist from Tokyo's *Music Life* magazine was in attendance for the sessions, although the resultant article focused more on the band's make-up and hair than the making of music. No demos were played to Singer in advance; the band simply turned up and went for it. The majority of the songs had already been broken in live. Morgan Studios was a well-equipped, mid-range studio with enough space for Black Sabbath to be recording in the main ante while Japan set up their equipment in studio two. Ray Singer had a new assistant – the very same man who had engineered Japan's audition a year ago, Chris Tsangarides. He recalls: 'I was 20 and just learning my trade. Ray was very open to any ideas I had and before the band came in I asked him, "What do we need?" and so I went out and got in a load of Marshall amps, a drum riser, the lot. So when Japan arrived they had three Marshall stacks each! And they came in and saw this lot and said, "Oh no, this isn't us, we want it trashy sounding, synthetic!" I was a bit crestfallen, but I said, "Oh all right then, never mind," and got rid of the lot. And it was fine then – once we knew what they wanted.' Dean: 'We were still with Ray Singer, which was probably a mistake; we wanted to make a different sounding album from the first one. We'd moved on, but I don't think Ray had. There was no way I was going to play through a wall of amps. It just wasn't my style. I used a small amp and the engineer wasn't best pleased.' In fact, with the exception of Karn, the whole group were perturbed by the engineer's presumptions, but at this point decided to bite the bullet and get on with the job in hand. 'Tsangarides went to great pains to find the right sounds,' offered Karn in the engineer's defence, 'and so did we. There was much joking around and time taken every day to create a relaxed and productive environment.' As usual the advance from Hansa went directly to Napier-Bell and he, in turn, would pass on cash to the band for any equipment that was needed.

In the studio, Sylvian favoured a Gibson Les Paul for his rhythm parts while on stage he used copies – 'Arbiter and El Mayo, because I tend to smash them up.' He also said that in the studio he was already assuming the role of director/auteur, reclining at the desk for much of the sessions and contributing physically only when he had to. 'I try to play the least amount I can, I don't like to play much; even if I come up with an idea I give it to Rob and he can do whatever he likes with it. I'd rather listen to what everybody else is doing. I like to leave the musical side to the band.' The one thing he could not abstain from was singing. In this regard, his approach and instrument had matured since the year before. 'I think the actual quality [of my voice] has changed; I've intentionally taken away the roughness of the first LP and the range has increased just through constant touring.' Dean and Barbieri in particular would both praise Sylvian's talents as a rhythm player, but the majority of the guitar work was left to Dean. 'I would up come up with the actual riffs on a lot of the stuff,' Dean confirmed. 'The lead part on 'Automatic Gun', for instance, was mine. I wasn't merely following Dave's directions, not at all.' In the studio, Dean used a Gibson Firebird through an HH amp, alternating with a Stratocaster via a Music Man combo.

Barbieri's confidence and ability had grown since the last album too. He was encouraged by the rest of the band to pursue electronic avenues rather than purely musical ones. His studio equipment included a Wurlitzer piano, a micro Moog and a string synthesiser. These were supplemented by either hiring new gear in or using the studio's resident equipment, in this case an ARP2 600, a Poly Moog and a Yamaha CS80. Jansen favoured a standard Tama kit with added Octobans and whatever percussion instruments were lying around the studio. This would be the last Japan album to feature such traditional percussive elements like bongos and shakers, as Jansen would explain: 'Certain percussion such as bongos or congas seemed a tad uncool since they were such a standard sound of the 70s. I was already edging towards things more electronic.'

The sessions flowed. The songs were well rehearsed and Japan were still fresh enough in the game to be overjoyed at simply being in a recording studio. To all intents and purposes, the sessions were happy ones and, although Sylvian would later state that there were tensions between the band, producer and engineer, no one else seemed to notice at the time. Tsangarides: 'It was fun! They were well into Bowie and the New York Dolls – that was obvious from the look of them. But one time I was talking to Mick and of course he had all this make-up on and red hair with pink bits, but I was really looking at him and suddenly something occurred to me and I said, "Mick – where you from?" and he said "South London," so I said, "No, before that," and it turned out we were from the same village in Cyprus! So we spent the rest of the time taking the piss out of the others in Greek. It was great! What wasn't so great was that they still had another producer that was with them, Steve Rowland.' A throwback to the initial Hansa signing, Rowland was fast becoming a dinosaur in the current climate. Tsangarides: 'He was more of a hindrance than anything. He was famous for being "tank driver number 22" in the battle of the Bulge or some such shit, and he never let us forget it. He was a dick, bless him.' Huckle: 'Yes, Steve Rowland was a bit of a prick, a kind of medallion man type. He was still working as Hansa/Ariola's in-house producer/A & R guy and was tasked with keeping an eye and ear on what Japan were doing in the studio. Hansa were uncomfortable with the guys doing their own thing. As a label they were used to controlling the recording process of the likes of Boney M, Donna Summer, and Child. Rowland soon gave up though, as everyone just ignored him, which I think it hurt his ego.' Tsangarides: 'He was kind of a big mouth who didn't really know what he was doing. At one point, we got hold of a Murphy Richards hairdryer and took the innards out and put a microphone in it. We then put it on Steve's bass drum. Rowland walked in and said in his laconic American accent, "Hey, what's that?" We told him it was a new type of mic, the "MR 1". "Awesome!" he said, "let's use it on everything!" To be fair, it was basically a real mic and so sounded fine, but it was hilarious to see people singing into a fuckin' hairdryer! Yet, in a way, a hairdryer-cum-microphone suited Japan perfectly.'

Chris Tsangarides

Sometimes the japes got out of hand. 'Japan set me on fire,' chuckles Tsangarides. 'They saw me messing around with this pure alcohol that you used to clean the tape heads; you could pour it on the desk and set fire to it and it made a pretty flame but went out quickly leaving no trace or damage. But they – Steve and Mick – put half a bottle down my trousers not realising what they were doing. There was no malice in it. So they set fire to it and I was kind of going along with the joke saying, "God, I'm on fire again. How many times has this happened?" You know, treating it like an everyday occurrence, but then it wouldn't go out. The flames were getting bigger and we started getting worried and someone had to go and get a fire extinguisher. They put it out and that's when the pain started.' Karn: 'It was not a pretty sight to see him seated in the reception area with his trousers around his ankles holding two halves of cucumber against his thighs as he waited for an ambulance.' 'I was rushed to hospital,' remembers the engineer, 'and they cut the blisters off my arse and dressed the wounds. It was a whole world of pain. For some time, I couldn't sit down normally and had to use a pile cushion while wearing dungarees. I still have scars. Ozzy Osbourne was working with Black Sabbath in the adjacent studio and when he got to hear about it he seriously offered to petrol bomb Japan for me. I had to convince him it was just a joke that got out of hand, but he kept insisting, "I'll do it, I'll petrol bomb them for you." I said, "I'm sure you would, and I appreciate it Ozzy, but really, there's no need."' Huckle remembers a saner side to the Black Sabbath singer. 'I do recall Ozzy Osbourne sitting in the studio during a mix. He was quite quiet and polite. He left saying it sounded really good.'

Near-fatal practical jokes aside, the group – Barbieri and the rhythm section in particular – were coming into their own. Tsangarides: 'I was watching Mick play his Travis Bean and I said, "Bloody hell, you make it sound like a fretless," and he goes, "Well, um, it is a fretless." He had simply drawn lines on the fretboard so it looked fretted.' Karn played through an Ampeg acoustic amp.

In terms of arrangement and delivery, many of the songs on *Obscure Alternatives* shared much with the previous album. They were, after all, written within the same period. Yet the group were keen to experiment with actual sound this time round and in the material itself there were major differences. Sylvian was writing more objectively, exploring themes outside of his own immediate reference. According to the lyricist, 'Automatic Gun' was about 'different [political] parties and revolutions taking over governments and about the people they leave behind, refugees.' 'Love Is Infectious' (a very early song of Sylvian's) was 'about a feminist.' 'Suburban Berlin' was 'about the National Front in England and comparing it to pre-war Germany ... we are against it. Everything it [the NF] stands for, we hate.' Such intent could be considered worthy for one so young yet the explanations attributed to the material summed up the then failures in Sylvian's writing. For all its glorious pomp, the listener would be hard pressed to ascertain from listening to 'Suburban Berlin' what the author's intent or feelings were or even what the song was about.

Against a rock template, musically the album hopped from funk to dub. 'Rhodesia' revealed an obvious short-lived reggae influence. 'Mick and Rich do listen to a lot of reggae, we all do to a certain extent,' explained Sylvian of this one-off. 'And the road crew are really into the music as well. I must admit, I don't know a lot about it, although there is one Big Youth album, I forget its title, which I really do enjoy. It's like another facet to the band, it makes us sound even more unusual I suppose.' Lyrically, Sylvian was less expansive in his explanation of the song. 'Rhodesia' was 'about Rhodesia and what's going on there.' Despite Sylvian's half-hearted intellectualising, once again the lyrics were so oblique that the listener would have been hard pressed to recognise much political intent. This was politics sexed up. The synonym for an 'Automatic Gun' could of course have had more carnal connotations. In fact, the one song so far released by Japan with an explicitly political title, 'Communist China', was actually 'about shagging Chinese girls,' according to its author. If the vocalist's lyrical attempts to appear worldly and clued in to current global events was unconvincing, then the music itself was beguiling; funked up, atypical, confident, brash and pulsating with youthful energy and spunk. On 'Sometimes I Feel So Low' ('a love song' written in the studio), Barbieri programmed a drum sound into his ARP and this was mixed in with Jansen's snare, resulting in a crudely effective, bargain basement Bowie harmonised snare sound. Karn's root bass notes on the title track were supplemented by Barbieri's Moog. These were subtle textures that hinted towards a more sophisticated future. It was the album's final track, however, that really signposted the way.

'The Tenant' sounded completely out of place on the album. With the exception of 'Sometimes...' it had never actually been performed prior to being recorded in the studio. Although written towards the end of the sessions for *Adolescent Sex*, 'The Tenant' was in fact a time capsule from the band's future, marking exactly where they were headed. The title came from the Polanski film and matched the movie's paranoid mood perfectly although its actual origins were more personal. Sylvian: 'I was sat in a hotel room somewhere. There were all these signals running through the air; I don't know where they came from, just these little noises running through the air.' In another interview from the time, he would cite that the idea for the odd glacial sounds that open the track came to him in the departure lounge of an airport. Barbieri confirms the latter. 'I was messing around with the Polymoog in the studio and found I was getting quite close to the unique Tannoy sound that they used at Charles de Gaulle airport. This was the little signal before a flight announcement was made. So I persevered and found that by scrolling the sliders or levers through the octave transpose setting in a quick up and down motion – I arrived at this really nice "signal" tone sound which had elements of white noise and hiss behind it.' The genesis of the piece had come to Sylvian alone. 'I was feeling very claustrophobic and quite depressed and I just wondered if it was possible to put all that down on record and to get that same feeling from a piece of music. Because I'd never got it from anybody else before. I'd already written the piano riff and I just thought that lazy flowing feel would describe the whole situation. It was an experiment and to me it's the most successful thing we've done to date. And the most emotional as well.' The 'found sounds' Sylvian heard in the air were perfectly reproduced by Barbieri's programming. 'I believe that industrial and mechanical sound can be far more original and easy to adapt than musical sound. I am constantly inspired by just listening to everyday noise,' stated Barbieri at the time. In saying so, he was shrewd enough to concentrate on his then strength, which was a unique ear for sound, rather than his weakness, which was the ability (or inclination) to play keyboards 'conventionally' in the style of a traditional 12-bar boogie. Nevertheless, Barbieri played the track's lilting mournful refrain on acoustic piano adeptly, with a Satie-esque panache. Sylvian himself did not perform on the track at all. Karn was still learning sax but contributed a mournful wail to the track, which was in turn treated to sound 'more like keyboards'.

Meanwhile, Dean attempted, and pulled off, his best Fripp impression, injecting the piece with a slow burning burr of a guitar line that seemingly had no beginning and no end. 'I don't think E Bows were around then,' he recalls, 'so I used a Big Muff pedal to get the kind of fat sustain I wanted. It took a while getting the right sound, but I think I got there in the end.' In the absence of a vocal, the group seemed more inclined to experiment with pure sound. Tsangarides: 'On that track I suggested we use a water gong. Steve was instantly curious. "What is it?" So I explained that you get a dustbin full of water and you immerse a tubular bell in it and it drops a whole octave. The secret is we record from the top and from below by putting a microphone under water. They looked at me aghast – "How do we do that?" So I explained that you wrap a mic in condoms and put it in and record it quickly before we electrocute ourselves. But none of them would go and buy the condoms. As usual they'd come into work fully made-up like tarts and were a bit embarrassed to go into a chemist to buy rubber johnnies, so they sent Nick Huckle out to get 'em.' 'It was my first time,' remembers Huckle, 'but not my last!' 'The Tenant' was obviously reminiscent of Eno's instrumentals from *Before And After Science,* but Sylvian attempted to argue the differences: 'Eno does things where you don't actually have to listen to the music, he creates an atmosphere – it's just background music. It's a backdrop for something. ['The Tenant'] isn't a backdrop for anything – this is just an instrumental song that creates a lot of emotion; it connects more to me more than anything else on the album.'

The title of the album itself was Japan's manifesto. 'It's about not accepting what's given to you … you shouldn't just follow a pattern that's been laid down for you, you should choose for yourself what you want to do and adapt a certain way of thinking,' said Sylvian, speaking for the group. Karn added 'We're reflecting our own feeling about the society we live in. You can't ignore the political mess that's going on in England.' Sylvian summed up their self-imposed predicament: 'We alienate ourselves wherever we are. I don't think we fit in anywhere. We really don't get on with many people. We think

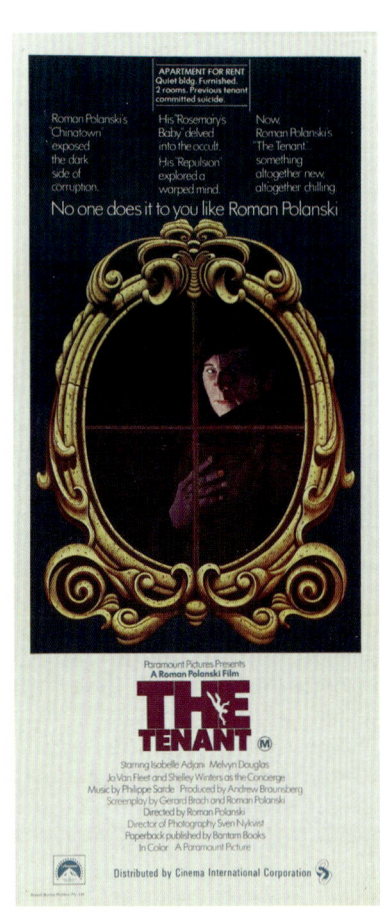

Poster for Polanski's *The Tenant*

totally differently from most people and the way we live is totally different and I just don't think wherever we settle we'll ever be a part of society. I don't think there is a place where we'll be happy or content to become one of the public.' The group's appearance would ensure that. Tsangarides: 'A bit later on Tony Iommi cornered me and asked me who that beautiful "bird" was that I was working with. I looked around and it was Dave standing there. So I said, "What her?" and Tony goes, "Yeah! Would you introduce me to her, she's gorgeous?" So I said, "Well, sure, okay, but the trouble is she's probably got a bigger dick than you."'

Their manager was rarely at the studio. 'I hardly saw him,' says Tsangarides, 'I don't think he had any creative input at all, musically.' Napier-Bell concurred: 'I kept out of the studio. It is the producer's job to be there, not the manager's.' However, there was another important presence in the studio that summer: the photographer, Fin Costello. 'I had set up a photo agency called Words And Faces with a few other people and one of the bands I photographed in 1978 was Japan. The pictures from that agency were distributed through the pop type magazines worldwide. Dave played me *Adolescent Sex*, which I liked and so we agreed to do another session when the time was right. Up to that time I had worked as a photojournalist and had very little studio experience. They subsequently became (with other bands) the models with which I learnt studio craft.'

Fin's photos of the sessions would eventually adorn the inner sleeve of the album. He would also take the cover shot. '*Obscure Alternatives* was a test shoot I did to practise using a new wide angle lens I had bought for the Hasselblad,' says Fin. As with 'The Tenant', the cover was another snapshot of Japan's future. Whereas the first album had portrayed Japan as the group they were, this time Sylvian was set apart, seemingly contemplating only his own future while the band stood regimentally in the background. Yet, all covers were approved by the band themselves. 'I would generally get Dave and quite often Mick and Steve up to the studio and we would go over the pictures together. It often gave rise to some interesting battles over picture choice but nothing ever went out without agreement.'

The album took 10 days to record and a few further weeks to mix. Soon after, the band attended Tsangarides's 21st birthday party. 'They bought me a wooden duck on a string,' he remembers, 'and my dog promptly ate it. We had great fun, I got on with them well. They were nowhere near as serious as they appeared.' In fact, Sylvian was already disappointed with the album and had vowed never to work with either Singer or his engineer again. 'We just couldn't get on with the engineer this time around,' Sylvian would say. 'He had his ideas, we had ours, and that was it, we couldn't seem to be able to find any middle ground. And the strange thing was that producer Ray Singer started taking sides with the engineer guy and we kind of felt left out in the cold, even though it was our album they were supposed to be recording. In the end we started doing things ourselves, just not involving the other two … it was the only way we could work. Partly as a result of all that we hope to be coming to America, probably New York, for the recording of the next LP. We're going to try to get Ken Scott [David Bowie, Lou Reed] to produce it.'

In July and August there was an ambitious seven-date residency at Camden Music Machine. The run was not as impressive as it appeared. Huckle gave out thousands of free flyers in the area, which admitted free entry on the quietest night in London. 'We broke the record for Monday nights,' Karn would state optimistically. Such tactics ensured a full, if mixed, audience: geeks, freaks, glam groupies, the odd alcoholic punk, and punters who simply enjoyed the visceral thrill of live music. 'The Music Machine gigs tend to merge into one as there were so many of them around that period,' says Huckle. 'There was one where Dave's brand new guitar was stolen. Another where the truck was broken into after the show and nearly all their instruments were nicked. Another where the PA's echo chamber stuck on a deep echo for five minutes or so. But they did begin to acquire a bit of a following as a result of all those MM shows. I remember one occasion I was asked to take a call in the ticket office. It was someone from Big In Japan's fan club in Liverpool [which at the time featured Budgie on drums and Holly Johnson on vocals] who wanted to confirm that we were going to be on again the following day, as she could arrange for a coach load of Liverpool fans to come down to London to see the gig. She of course was thinking we were Big In Japan. I didn't shatter her illusions and merely confirmed we would indeed be playing again the next day. Hopefully that may have helped swell Japan's audience at that gig while not disappointing the Liverpudlians too much.'

As Huckle points out, by the end of the booking, Japan had added genuine fans to the growing mailing list. These fans were hard won, the result of endless gigs, interviews, photo shoots, hype and advertising. It was ironic then that in a country where Japan had never played a note, things were starting to happen on a major scale without any effort whatsoever from the band. In April, while the group had endured the BOC tour, 5,936 miles away in Japan itself, magical things were happening for them. To be blonde, pale and thin in Japan was to be exotic, seductive and mystical. Richard Clayderman, the French, toothsome, blue-eyed MOR pianist was at this time considered a minor deity there. This particular androgynous and asexual image was designer-made for mass consumption by the mostly female pop audience. Previous figures in this mould had included The Walker Brothers and David Bowie. Yet unlike Clayderman, Bowie and Walker had offered the kind of music on the back of their light-haired and pallid personas that was much more mature and challenging than the usual MOR or teen-pop fodder. Furthermore, the London-centric Tokyo was not immune to the new wave and punk movements that were dominating the UK at the time, while being far from saturated by them. Sylvian and Co, with their strange uncompromising music (which was actually neither punk nor new wave, but with the patina of both) and their tailor-made look were perfectly poised for mass adoration in the country from which they had taken their name.

Based in Tokyo, Mr Akira Yokoto, was the A&R man for Victor Records' international division. In the spring of 1978, via Hansa's international division, he received a tape of the group. Significantly, it came with a promo shot of the five piece. Apart from their obvious 'prettiness' he was attracted to the sullen, unsmiling demeanour. Yokoto recognised 'an air of decadence' about the group tied in with the latest changes in pop music. It dawned on him that this particular look, coupled with the odd but serviceable music, would make the perfect replacement for the waning appeal of the Bay City Rollers. In tandem with Japanese publishing giants Taiyo, Victor licensed Japan from Hansa in May that year.

The hugely popular and powerful Japanese pop press had already gone into action in April, with *Ongaku Senka* magazine publishing seemingly endless photos of the band's gatecrashing appearance at Kate Bush's album launch party in London. The impact of the photos was such that a Japanese fan club was immediately established. This was prior to the release of any of Japan's music, although the debut album would begin selling there on import. Soon, and with minimal radio exposure and having not even visited the place let alone played a note there, Japan were tremendously popular in a country that they had only ever experienced via TV and books. Their manager had flown out to assess the situation soon after the signing. At a meeting with JVC officials (who owned Victor Records) Napier-Bell was told: 'We have now heard some rough mixes of the album (*Obscure Alternatives* presumably) and we think they are very unsuitable.' Napier-Bell assumed their English was at fault. 'You mean "suitable" don't you?' In fact he had heard them right the first time. 'No! We mean unsuitable, but we have great faith in the group and we think one day they will record music which will be suitable for the market; consequently we are going to get behind them.' Even Napier-Bell, as a well travelled, experienced gunslinger in the wild west of the rock and roll business was taken aback at such a strategy. 'I'd never heard of such a thing,' he would recall. The JVC boss continued, 'Normally, 13-year-old girls who buy records by these soft looking Western stars grow tired of them a couple of years later. With Japan, they will stay with the group because the music is more challenging. Through photographs and publicity we can build a fan club. Once they've bought [the music] they'll learn to like it. So you see – your group has much potential.' Napier-Bell was 'flabbergasted' but it strengthened his faith in the band. 'If the record company in Japan could be so far-sighted, maybe I should be too.' On returning to London, for the next six months he left home at 6am every day and drove to the local Anglo-Japanese foundation to study Japanese language and culture. Japan, it seemed, were going to be big in Japan.

Coincidentally, Japan's popularity was foreshadowed by a million selling comic book entitled *La Rose De Versailles* by Riyoko Ikeda. This graphic novel tells the story of Oscar, a beautiful aristocratic French girl posing as a man whilst endeavouring to save Marie Antoinette during the French

Oscar of *La Rose De Versailles* by Ryoko Ikeda

Above: Bilzen festival, Holland 1978
Anon

Right: Japanese pressing of *Sometimes I Feel So Low*

revolution. The winsome Oscar bears a spooky resemblance to the 1970s incarnation of David Sylvian. Finally released in Japan in September 1978, Japan's debut album – unwanted pretty much everywhere else – was an actual hit, staying in the international chart for 11 weeks. Such was the demand for all things Japan (the band) that a competition was launched to write 'Japan style' lyrics and even to design the next few covers for the band's singles. Back at home, the only proof of this for the band was the sudden influx of overseas fan mail. In their everyday lives, nothing had changed and they continued their exhausting circuit of gigging and press in the UK and Europe.

Europe was deemed a more fertile soil for the band than their home country and their next gig was at the Bilzen festival in Belgium, where Blondie were among the headliners. Besotted fans already awaited Japan's arrival. Margot: 'I received a letter from Mick, telling us that Japan were going to play the Bilzen festival that August. So of course we wanted to go. They were staying in a hotel in Maastricht, which is a city about 15 minutes from Bilzen. It was a good hotel and we were invited, but then it got weird. We understood that it had been arranged for us to stay there, but we had no details. The concert was on the Saturday afternoon and they asked to come over on the Friday. I was very ill with flu though so I wasn't sure I could go, but my mum fixed me up and so with two friends I made it there on Friday. We were waiting in the lobby and a strange woman came up to us. She introduced herself as Gaubi Hauser from Hansa. An attractive woman in her early 40s, Hauser was then enjoying a brief fling with Sylvian. Margot: 'And she said, "The boys will come out in a minute, they are having dinner." So we waited and she came out again and said, "Oh, I've heard all about you. Are your rooms okay?" We said, "No, we're waiting for you to show us to them." Then it dawned on us there had been some confusion. It seemed we had to pay for our own hotel rooms! We were invited and thought it was all arranged. We had no money. So she said, "Oh, I'll try and sort something out." It took hours with us just sat there until something was fixed, but by then we still hadn't seen the band. We were hungry too. Finally Mick came out and was very happy to see us, kissing us "Hello, how nice to see you etc." and lots of photos were taken. Then we gave them some space, as they were tense about the forthcoming concert. We went down for dinner that night and they were in the restaurant but involved in some sort of intense conversation with their manager so we left them to it. We were the only fans there and spent a long afternoon in the sun waiting.'

Eventually Margot and friends travelled to the festival in a van with Japan's crew. The gig itself was underwhelming. 'Japan were somewhere in the middle of the bill,' says Huckle. 'It was their first experience of playing in the open air, in the daylight at a festival. It was a fairly nondescript 20 minute set that received polite applause but no great enthusiasm from the crowd.' Margot: 'They seemed tense and I don't think they enjoyed it. The crowd reception wasn't special, they were just another foreign group to most.' Karn added, 'It was weird for us, because being an open air festival there wasn't much atmosphere'. Sylvian: 'Us and Blondie were the only good bands that didn't get encores.' Margot and friends were still there the next morning when after breakfast, 'There was a sudden commotion. Then I saw Mick and David looking very upset. They were carrying Steve into a car. They set him down first and people were bending over him. Steve looked so sick. Suddenly someone said to me, "Here, hold this," and handed me a carrier bag. I opened it and it was full of vomit. Meanwhile there was a photo session going on! Some photographers were taking photos of the band; "Can you sit like this, stand just so" etc. Steve was in agony.' Jansen: 'It was at that festival that I had one of my final appendix attacks and spent the night throwing up only to be asked to do a photo shoot around town (in which I do look palpably ill) before being rushed to the local doctor who said I was unable to fly home. SNB drove me back with Rob and every bump in the road was pure agony.' Margot recalls, 'Then suddenly everyone was leaving. The band kissed us goodbye and went off to the airport while Steve was driven off in a van somewhere, waving weakly at us through the window, looking even paler than usual.'

Somehow, despite Steve's condition, immediately after Bilzen the group played Frankfurt. 'I remember the Frankfurt gig itself being rather good reception-wise,' says Huckle, 'though Steve was in agony on stage, and had to be virtually carried off after the show.' Their manager recalls the post-show activities with more clarity. 'They'd just played a midnight gig at the Batschkapp Club in the centre of Frankfurt and at 2 am we still hadn't eaten. We set off to try and find some food. but Frankfurt 1978 proved not to be a midnight festival of gourmet cuisine. The only place we could find was an outside café opposite the railway station – beer, wine, sausages, and potato salad. Actually, it wasn't too bad. It was August, and warm, and we ordered wine and a huge communal dish of potato salad and sat outside at cheap metal tables in the early hours of the morning, not at all unhappy. Until, suddenly, a fridge appeared from nowhere and ran me over. It was a Westinghouse. The lady in charge of it was around 80 and was pushing it along the pavement on a single roller skate, moving rooms in the middle of the night. As she approached us she encountered a slight downward slope and lost control.

The result? One minute I was sitting gracefully holding a glass of red wine and scooping up a forkful of Kartoffelsalat; the next I lay crushed on the pavement under a 10-cubic-foot freezer-refrigerator in white with automatic ice dispenser. Worse still, she was a hit-and-run driver. No sooner had I been smashed to the ground than she gathered up her fridge, re-positioned it on its roller skate and scooted off, leaving me floored and bruised, and everyone potatoless, because the dish of Kartoffelsalat had fallen underneath me. And if that wasn't enough indignity, my companions thought it was the funniest thing they'd ever seen and sat roaring with laughter. The owner of the café, hearing the commotion, came running outside. He saw me lying next to an upturned table, the potato salad mashed beneath me, the broken glass on the pavement, the wine dribbling down to the gutter, the group in stitches. "You're all drunk," he shouted. "Rock and roll people, I hate you. Go home." He carried the tables and chairs inside, put up the closed sign, turned out the lights, and at 2 am left us hungry and without food with nowhere else to go.'

Back in London, Jansen was finally admitted to hospital for a burst appendix on the direction of the band's doctor, Barrington-Cooper. Jansen: 'I am indebted to the man because it was only he who insisted I have my appendix removed despite suffering attacks for a few years, and the NHS refusing to do the op even after admitting me into the Royal Free and running tests which they said proved inconclusive.'

With their drummer barely recovered, the last gig of the month was at the Edinburgh Rock Festival followed by yet another appearance at the Music Machine in Camden. The review of this show illustrated that, despite Japan's progress in the last year, much of the UK music press were still no closer to being charmed. 'They're just exquisitely awful,' said Mark Ellen in the *NME*. 'It's appallingly superficial … glutinous vocal drooling … a mass of chaotic noise … highlighting the worst of the most synthetic and misdirected aspects of rock.' Japan were no doubt glad to leave the country, when that November the band made their debut trip to the US. 'We just hope they have better ears than the jerks in London,' opined Sylvian. *Obscure Alternatives* had been released in September. 'Despite nice production values, it's basically a mix of early 70s glitter rock and late 70s new wave,' ran a typical US review. *Billboard* added, 'It has the art pose appeal of early Queen tempered with the post-apocalyptic chic of the Dead Boys. While this LP is rough, the band has the chops and ideas to grow considerably stronger than the sum of its parts.' These reviews summed up Japan in 1978. Neither album so far was cohesive enough to be regarded as an instant classic, but both reeked of potential.

There were five concerts planned in total, taking in LA, San Francisco, Boston, and two in New York. It was hardly a nationwide tour, but nothing could temper the fact that Japan were going to America. For a bunch of Londoners in love with much of American culture, its movies, music, and art – this trip was a momentous occasion. 'The long-haul flight on a jumbo jet was exhilarating enough,' Karn would recall, 'the Californian sunshine, the Hollywood sign in the distant hills … everything added to our star status, or so I liked to believe.' The band travelled with Nick Huckle and Napier-Bell along with a new soundman from the Camden shows, Pink Floyd's Nick Griffiths.

Although the commercial reception of their two albums in the US was negligible, Japan already had friends awaiting them. Marina Muhlfriedel: 'I was in a band called Viva Beat but also working for the Hansa office in LA, Beverly Hills in the publicity department. We were dealing with acts like Sarah Brightman, Boney M … kinda novelty disco rock. And one day we received a package that was so unlike any other band on the label. These guys in make-up, totally glammed up. [My friend and colleague] Pam and I were like, "Oh God, these guys are so totally us!" We were so excited, we couldn't wait to meet and work with them. So they came over with Simon, straight into the office and we kind of adopted each other. We fell in really well together. They didn't look that striking compared to the other bands in LA, but compared to other English bands of that time, they stood apart. They weren't really part of any scene. They were naive. They didn't say, "Hey, let's go hang out at the Rainbow," or whatever. They were excited but shy and kind of in their manager's shadow. Steve and Mick were the most confident. Mick was really grooving to be in LA. David was very guarded, almost uptight. He didn't want to reveal much of himself while the others, after a couple of days, were much more open. I never got to know David well.'

The first show, at the Starwood Club in LA, was hampered by the usual technical difficulties and a bemused audience. 'There were about 14 people there. It was just a couple of days after they arrived and Japan were exhausted,' remembers Marina. 'And the dry ice machine wouldn't shut up! It was like they were playing in a cloud. You couldn't see them at all. It was hilarious, pure Spinal Tap!' The audience were, according to Karn, 'politely receptive enough'. But such muted reactions along with the malfunctioning dry ice machine were wearing Sylvian's patience thin. It was no longer enough just to be living the life. Sylvian already felt as if he were going through the motions. 'They weren't "rock stars" at all,' says Marina. 'Even then, David wanted to lean toward being more of an art statement. But I loved what they were trying to do. It was quite original. The musicianship for such young guys … they were so locked in, it was amazing. The rhythm section mixed with David's voice was really unique.'

Sylvian was beginning to feel trapped in a caricature he had strived to create. It had gotten him out of Catford and all the way to Hollywood and as such had outlived its usefulness. He was already growing bored of endlessly playing 'The Unconventional' and 'Adolescent Sex' mere months after having recorded them. But the way forward was unsure, so what else was there to do besides keep the carnival going? 'After the show at the Starwood,' remembers Sylvie Simmons, then a freelance journalist, 'they all came up to the rooftop of the Hyatt House Hotel. There was a large swimming pool with loungers around it. I think the whole band was there, but David and Richard Barbieri went off to another corner of the roof. I do remember that David – still in his stage clothes and heavily made-up, including very pale foundation – was sitting on a sun lounger and staring out in space, looking as lost and out of place as anyone I'd met. Questions would be answered with just a few words or a sentence or two by David, and Richard seemed a little more accommodating. Mostly though, unlike a lot of UK bands that came through LA at that time, David's reluctance to talk didn't strike me as being deliberate, or some kind of stance; he just looked like he wished he wasn't there. Mostly when he did talk it was to emphasise that he and the band were serious about themselves and their music. One quote he said was, "Most people think it's hype in some way. Nobody could believe a band could be that serious about what they're doing, the way we look." And again, "They can't put the two things together, the way we look and what we're doing. They'd rather think there's hype in there or something to sell the product. That's the record companies." He did say something good about his view of punks though and it was the longest answer he gave me. "Punks, it's like they come out and tell you what you should be thinking, and what punks do, and so on. That's forming a new society, almost as bad as the old one they're trying to get out of already. They're making rules for themselves immediately, things to believe in. They're trying to get out of a system, but they're putting themselves in another one immediately. The way they dress as well. They say they dress as they do for reasons to go against society, but they all dress the same. We have no rules whatsoever."' As Sylvian was discovering, to be without rules was just as disadvantageous as to be beholden to them.

The group flew on to San Francisco. The Hansa staff were still smitten. 'I loved their music,' says Marina. 'I was a synth player and had spent time with Brian Eno and we knew Ultravox.' It's telling that neither of these names would make any commercial impression in the US (Roxy Music shared the same fate). Additionally, in America especially, Japan's communal shyness gave the impression that they were simply aloof. 'A lot of people in LA were sceptical of them,' continues Marina. 'Despite the way they looked, they didn't have the open, spiky, punky demeanour of the New York Dolls. There was a sense of "who do these guys think they are?"'

Japan's arrival in New York was a momentous occasion for the group personally. 'We loved so many movies filmed there,' said Dean. 'We loved *Taxi Driver*, so to actually be there was amazing.' The band booked into the Taft Hotel, before moving on to the Gramercy Park Hotel, Unfortunately, the group's bad luck continued to follow them. Richard Chadwick was arrested for inadvertently passing a fake $100 bill – he was soon released; and Karn fell down a flight of stairs the night before the debut gig, fracturing his ribs and having to be admitted to casualty in the early hours of the morning. The band slogged through bottom-tier magazine interviews as the day progressed with a medicated Karn joining them for the sound-check in the early evening.

Hurrah's was a famous and cool venue with a suitably low-key entrance at 36 West 62nd Street. At the base of a tower block, two medium-sized aluminium-framed glass doors opened out on to a long, dusty corridor. Inside, its dance floor was a huge pitch of varnished pine boards stretching for square yard upon square yard. At the far end was the stage, a small, hastily constructed affair, cluttered with equipment and shrouded by a black bin liner backdrop. Closer to the entrance was the mixing/disco desk, and closer still was the bar, adorned by an Art Deco sign lit by tasteful orange and red lights that said simply 'Hurrah'. It seemed a perfect setting for Japan, but while they seemed a little overwhelmed, the serious local media continued to be underwhelmed. Marina: 'We'd tried to get them on radio and TV and invited everyone to the gig, but we weren't too successful unfortunately. The boys were disappointed, but stoic.' The show too was a let down, best summed up by a random punter who sounded off to anyone who would listen: 'Aww, they wuz great! Rilly great! But look it this! Look it these people!' – referring to the NYCers and the cool reception they had given Japan: 'These people are terrible! They are shit!'

Following the show, the band headed out to some bars where they were introduced to the New York Dolls' Sylvain Sylvain and friend of their manager, soul singer Nona Hendryx, before heading on to Studio 54. Although excited to meet their heroes, by comparison Japan were well-mannered Englishmen. 'They weren't on the prowl,' confirms Marina. 'They weren't dudes looking to score, knocking back pints. That was not their style. They liked to go out for dinner, they didn't like to make a scene. They were quiet. They were less like pop stars and more like sociology students. David was the most self-consumed. He was so aware of what people thought of him. He was someone I couldn't crack. We didn't connect.' Neither had the first night's audience. The group were not happy with the tour thus far and their debut in New York had proven to be anti-climactic, with the majority of the under capacity crowd lingering near the bar throughout the show.

There was a better reception at the second gig with a marked increase in potential groupies swarming the front of the stage. But, as ever, the aloof and introverted Japan returned to the hotel alone. The usually sociable Karn was no doubt in too much pain to do much else. The next day the group took the ferry to Staten Island where their appearance continued to cause a stir. 'It gets to be a joke when there are dozens of people flocking around you just because you look a little different from most other people,' observed Jansen. 'In England people usually just stare, but here they come up and ask you for your autograph, then ask you who you are in the same breath.

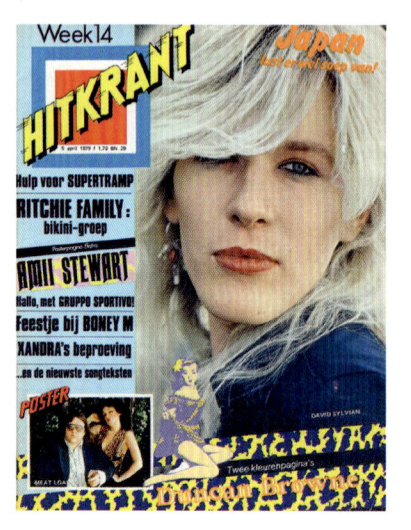

They don't care who or what you are,' he sighs, 'it just all seems totally ridiculous!' The final gig was in Boston and it was well received. 'The audiences seemed more clued in on the east coast,' says Huckle. The show was recorded direct to desk and the version of 'Heartbreaker' that survives shows the band on ebullient form, confident, swaggering and horny. While the rest of the group flew home, Karn and Sylvian stayed on to deal with more, mostly teen-orientated press. 'It would be nice if we could get to the point where we didn't have to do non-stop rounds of interviews,' moaned Karn who, despite the prescription painkillers he was high on, already sounded like a fagged-out showbiz veteran.

Back in Britain, an extensive 12 date tour to promote *Obscure Alternatives* awaited the group. In their absence, another single 'Sometimes I Feel So Low' had been and gone. This latest tour at least saw Japan headlining, playing only to their own audience. In the UK, their fan base had – against the odds – grown in the previous year. Brian Grogan: 'Nick Bates, or Nick Rhodes as he was later known, was then a huge Japan fan. We were friends and we'd hang out at [Birmingham's] The Rum Runner where I was a DJ. Him and his friend Nigel were in a band but I didn't think they were going anywhere. Nick had been DJing at the Runner but left to concentrate on his band and I took over as DJ. He even gave me a live bootleg tape of Japan. He was a huge fan and would go on to base his look on David totally. We'd sit and talk for hours about Japan, he was obsessed with them – whatever he says now. For some reason though, I didn't go to see them when they played Barbarella's on the *Alternatives* tour.'

Nick and Nigel did, however. 'They changed my direction when I saw them in 78,' remembers Nigel, soon to become John Taylor. 'They were in that post-punk interzone. It was clear that the aggressive stance led by The Clash et al. was getting a bit tired, quite quickly, so one was looking in other directions to see what was happening, for something kind of interesting, and Japan were one of the bands that I went to see in 78 at Barbarella's. Oh, I loved *Obscure Alternatives*. You know I'd been going to a lot of gigs and I'd seen a lot of bands in that room but they were something different. I hadn't seen anything with a rhythm section like that and I just loved it. I didn't know the first album but when they played 'Television' and 'Suburban Love' it was music to my ears, you know? And that was just about the time I was starting to play bass. So I was starting to think about a rhythm section. And punk wasn't about that – it wasn't rhythm section orientated. Japan had some other colours in there as well. Their keyboard player gave their sound something else; they had Kool & the Gang in there and I could hear a song like 'Why Did You Do It' by Stretch. And Heatwave. There were a few English soul bands of the early 70s and I can hear that in that era of Japan.' Within two years, Nigel and Nick's group would be sharing recording studios with Sylvian and Co, but as yet that was a hundred haircuts away. For now it was enough that, along with Chic's Bernard Edwards, Mick Karn would help shape the way John Taylor thought about bass and in turn go on to influence the sound of one of the most successful pop bands ever.

The press were less enthused. The reviews for *Obscure Alternatives* took up from where those for *Adolescent Sex* left off. 'The bass player is out of tune,' said the *NME* mistakenly. 'The songs adopt poses that were fashionable five or six years ago; no doubt in America people will think Japan are part of the new wave …none of this adds up to a reason for buying the album.' The album failed to chart and airplay (with the exception of Tommy Vance's Radio One *Rock Show*) was negligible.

It had been an exhausting, thrilling, depressing, exhilarating year and yet it was hard to judge what real progress had been made. The mediocre record sales didn't justify the money Hansa and Napier-Bell were spending and Sylvian had already outgrown the songs he had written. That Christmas he headed for the exclusive London Clinic to have his tonsils removed. As he recovered in a private room with 1978 dying outside, even he couldn't imagine the new audience and voice that awaited him.

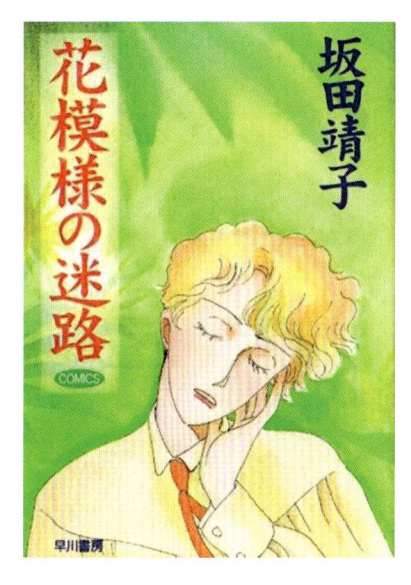

Chapter 4
Alphaville

Karn, Sylvian,
The Rainbow
April 1979
Jan Kalinski

David Sylvian, his brother Steve Jansen and Rob Dean had all been hospitalised during the last few months of 1978. While their career was somewhat healthier, Hansa were far from satisfied with the band's sales. Outside of the sudden freakish success in Japan itself, for all the travel, gigs and hype the group had endured (and enjoyed) they had still managed only one minor hit on the continent. They were in major debt to both their label and manager – sometimes there seemed to be confusion about which. Sylvian himself was already disillusioned with the music they had so far made. He would soon be saying that he 'didn't think the first album should have been released'. For the group to survive, the new year could only be one of betterment. It was with a new sense of hope and focus that the group determined not to make the same musical mistakes. To this end, the Hansa-endorsed trinity of Singer, Rowlands and Tsangarides was jettisoned like sandbags thrown from a rising balloon. Eager to develop but without the time or material to warrant a brand new producer, Japan instead went into DGM Studios that January with their manager as co-producer.

The bones of a new song 'European Son' and a cover version of The Velvet Underground's 'All Tomorrow's Parties' were recorded that month. 'European Son' was, of course, also the title of a Velvet Underground song, but this was the only similarity. The former, obviously inspired by the trip to the US, had been written by Sylvian on guitar that January and was specifically intended to be recorded at the same tempo (132 bpm) as the Earth, Wind & Fire hit 'Boogie Wonderland', presumably in an attempt for it to harvest similar airplay. This is Napier-Bell's version of events, although Barbieri doesn't recall it so. The tempos of both songs do not actually match. Of the Velvet's song, Sylvian would say, 'The album it came from [*The Velvet Underground & Nico*] has so many good songs that it was hard just to choose one. I took that one into the studio not telling the band it was a Lou Reed song and played the chords on the piano. They just thought it was one of my songs.' This was an inspired approach to covering a familiar song, ensuring that the band interpreted it without referencing the original and it was only when Sylvian began singing that the band recognised it because of the lyrics. Karn would also add some scratchy violin to the recording (heard most clearly in the coda) referencing John Cale's famous viola drones.

With the impending trip to Japan looming, there was no time to finish the tracks satisfactorily and they were put into hibernation while the group got on with rehearsing. Japan were still frequenting the same dank rehearsal room, a damp, mildew mottled space at the back of a bookmaker's situated in similarly grotty Kilburn. The actual location seemed to have little influence on the music Japan were now making. Or if it did, it was in fact pushing them to make music that transcended such grim realities. 'I don't know why,' remembers Dean, 'but rehearsing with Japan was never boring. There was always something to be getting on with. This is unique in my experience.'

Free of the rockist tendencies of Singer et al., Japan couldn't help but evolve. Jansen's playing was pin sharp but increasingly oblique in its construction, aided and abetted by the drummer's increased interest in electronics. His timing was as accurate as any drum machine and this meant that he could easily play along with Barbieri's sequencers, something with which the majority of drummers would struggle. Barbieri himself was intoxicated by the possibilities of sequencers and much more interested in pursuing the electronic/programming aspect of being a keyboard player than the Moogy virtuosity of Rick Wakeman, or in providing simple piano accompaniment. And then there was Karn, whose yearning, insidious bass playing was drifting further away from any notion of four to the floor root notes and was sounding increasingly exotic and beautiful in itself. Dean rooted the whole with his more grounded, but still often atypical approach. Sylvian now had more room to breathe, quite literally, and his vocals would soon leave the snarling, somewhat forced approach he had adopted until now, settling into a range that was much more natural even if, stylistically, it was even more affected. All that Japan needed now was a sympathetic producer to weave these disparate elements together. It was obvious that their first choice, Ken Scott, was not going to happen, and so Fripp was once again approached. While the band awaited both his response and the forthcoming Japanese tour, it was a good time to take stock of how far they had come and how much further they could go.

Since signing to Napier-Bell in 1976, Japan had secured a major recording contract with an international label, released two albums and various singles worldwide, and toured extensively in the UK and Europe. They had played five dates in the US and featured in countless magazines across the globe. They were on the precipice of touring Japan and were booked to play the country's biggest and most prestigious venue, the legendary Budokan. Even as they packed for the trip, the tour was already sold out. While they were still considered a tasteless joke by many in the UK, by most standards Japan were a raging success compared to the vast majority of groups. Even so, a warm-up show at London's Marquee venue just prior to leaving was poorly attended and as disheartening as any the band had played, despite the full-length white plastic mac that Sylvian rocked. Although they still lacked a bona fide hit, now that Japan the country had opened up to them, even their sales were becoming respectable. Individually, the band members were often enraptured by the luck of their day-to-day lives yet, like any budding pop star, they also took such success as their right. 'I didn't think of it as being phenomenal at the time, I took it all rather for granted,' Sylvian would say years later. 'I thought, "I'm owed this," for some ungodly reason. But looking back, I realise, yes, that I was obviously very blessed.' On the last day of February, a week after Sylvian's 21st birthday, Japan made ready to leave for Japan.

'I probably couldn't sleep, I was so excited,' says Dean. 'And I'm sure the others were the same.' In March the band flew from Heathrow via Sabena Airways to Japan for the first time. It was a long-haul, economy flight – the parsimony of which would puzzle certain members years later. Nevertheless, this was the consummation of a great mutual love affair between Japan and Japan and, in the case of Jansen and Sylvian in particular, one that would endure a lifetime. The bulk of their equipment would be awaiting the band at their destination. Japan's entourage included Nick Huckle, lighting technician Martin Disney, sound man Nick Griffiths, Napier-Bell's partner Richard Chadwick and their tour manager, Robbie Wilson. Sylvian's on-board reading was a slab of classic 1970s airport trash, *The Venice Plot* by Raymond Rudorff, and, between drinks, endless cigarettes and the in-flight films, the group dozed, shaved and touched up their foundation and eyeliner. Their manager travelled in first class at the front of the plane but would occasionally deign to visit his charges in economy. 'He was well travelled and good company on any journey,' says Dean. 'We'd talk about art, music and stuff.'

Such an economy flight involved many stops along the way including Frankfurt, Athens, Bahrain, Bombay, Singapore and Hong Kong. From this point on the band changed planes, flying on to Japan via Thai Air. 'We weren't allowed into Singapore,' says Dean, 'because we had long hair, so we had to stay in the lounge. Funnily enough there was actually a barber in the lounge, but we would have been like, "No way are we getting our hair cut just to be allowed into Singapore."' There was one final stop before Hong Kong. 'The pilot missed the first landing,' says Dean, 'and so we had to land somewhere else first to refuel and try again, only adding to the flight time.' Nevertheless this delay meant the group got to spend a day in the city, with Karn and Napier-Bell in particular enjoying the exotic food stuffs on offer there. Eventually, their destination glimmered into view.

Although the group had an inkling of how popular they were in Japan – the fan mail, press and sales affirmed that – nothing could prepare them for the reality awaiting them. Just before the 'fasten seatbelts' sign came on there was time to stub out a final Gitane and make one more trip to the toilet to fix their make-up. The next time they looked into a mirror, they would be rock stars.

'It was a long, cramped 22-hour journey,' remembers Huckle, 'and we were very tired and stiff. But it was like landing on a different planet. Suddenly, we were all being treated like proper megastars.' Although the flight touched down at Tokyo's Narita Airport at 6.25 am, there were hundreds of screaming fans already there, the majority of whom had camped out the night before. 'It was an incredible scene,' says Dean, 'I felt at the time that this is what it must have been like for The Beatles.' In the airport itself, photographers and TV camera crews jostled for position, buffeted by the waves of screaming female flesh around them. Some of the girls, giddy with shrieking and flooded with hormones and emotion, threw notes, flowers, gifts, phone numbers, cookies, gonks. The group immediately found themselves under the efficiently protective wing of UDO security guards (employed by the UDO live promotion agency) and the local police. 'UDO weren't afraid to give a shove when it was needed,' noted Dean, remembering how the bulky, sunglasses-wearing security would not hesitate to bat aside the more enthusiastic female fans if they got too close.

Sylvian's actual copy of *The Venice Plot* left behind in hotel

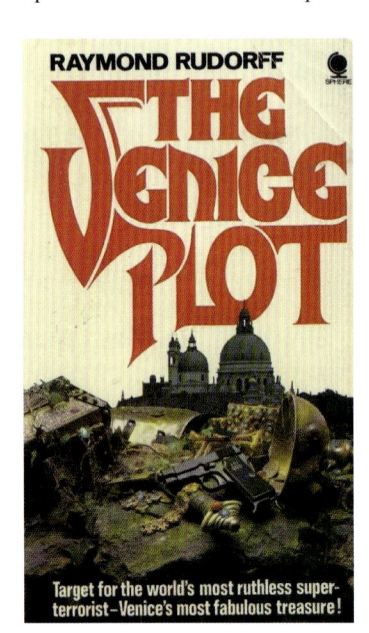

This sudden transition – from wannabes to contenders – was a shock. A few minutes earlier the group had been reading stale in-flight magazines, smoking cigarettes and exchanging small talk in the early morning light of a stuffy, sleepy aircraft cabin and suddenly they were in the eye of a storm of which they were both the cause and victim. As they were hurried through the chaos, Mick, David, Steve, Rich, and Rob could barely make out what the person next to them was saying, such was the ferocity of the screaming. There was no time to think, just to surrender as they allowed themselves to be guided by the over-enthusiastic security guards' shove and grip. All around, women were wailing. Dean: 'It was otherworldly, because in the UK we couldn't get arrested and now we had bodyguards. It was great.'

Their luggage having been claimed for them, the band were jostled through the throng of the terminal into a waiting fleet of limousines. As the windows wound up and clicked into place the screeching outside was compressed to a distant flat roar, a sound that was almost calming, like the ocean. The limos tentatively edged away from the terminal, feeling their way through the ranks of teeming, screaming fans. This was not the end, however. The fans immediately took off in pursuit. 'For the whole journey to the hotel there was an endless stream of taxis, over-filled with fans following us,' recalls Huckle, 'sometimes six or seven to a cab, all leaning out the windows waving, shouting and swooning at the band.' Somehow, around 10 am, the band made it to the Keio Plaza Hotel, where they were ushered into their rooms via the service lift and kitchens. 'I'd never stayed in a hotel in Japan before,' says Dean, 'but it was obviously a good hotel. All mod-cons and complimentary slippers and kimonos. It sure beat staying in digs in Dunstable.' The band went straight to sleep, awaking at 8 pm that night for dinner. They returned to bed around 11 pm. None of the group would ever see the lobby of the hotel in which they were staying. They were secretly smuggled in and out and always under guard.

There were a few days until the first concert, but no time for the band to decompress. Almost every minute was accounted for by a typically efficient itinerary of tea parties, interviews and endless photo shoots. There was the opportunity to visit temples and restaurants, but all beneath the elegant umbrella of a photo shoot. There was a seemingly insatiable demand for images of the band doing just about anything – lighting a cigarette, blow drying their hair, waiting for a train, watching each other waiting for a train, etc. In contrast to every other market, Japan were an instantly saleable commodity in Japan and as such were respected for the very things for which they were ridiculed back in Britain. Despite this, the band were still sharing hotel rooms. No one questioned this, as all expenses were covered by the promoter, but surely he would have allowed enough budget for each member to have their own room? In fact, years later the group would ascertain that this trip had been paid for in advance – and first class too – with the savings being pocketed by their manager, who would justify this by offsetting it against their debt to him. Whatever the economics were, Sylvian shared with Barbieri, and the rhythm section roomed together.

Karn would be amused at Jansen's propensity for sleepwalking, while Dean was shunned for his nocturnal habits. 'I had to share with Richard Chadwick,' says Dean. 'Because I snored, no one else would room with me.' The first full working day in Japan began on Friday 2 March with a press conference in the Silver Room of the Hilton Hotel from 1 pm. The group answered typically banal questions like, "What do you think of Japan?" and, "Do you like the food?" with good-natured, if fazed, aplomb. Jansen, always amongst the quietest of the band, was noted to have drunk two glasses of orange juice. Karn found the experience 'nerve wracking'. 'It was pretty boring,' reckoned Dean, 'we just got on with it.' The evening ended for most of the band at a French restaurant while Sylvian and Karn ventured out to a disco. By midnight everyone was wrapped up in complimentary kimonos in their rooms.

The fans – 99.9% female, with a higher proportion of slightly older ladies than was common – were everywhere, always. Many booked into rooms of the Plaza, with sometimes up to 10 girls splitting the cost of a double room, forming mini-harems on the floors below Japan's rooms. These oestrogen-fuelled masses had been waiting for this moment since the initial Onganku Senka photo shoot a year before. Victor Records had engineered the ultimate media foreplay on behalf of the band. The excitement was accelerated with each public appearance the band made, whether planned or not. 'On the Saturday, we went to see Linda Ronstadt at the Budokan,' says Dean. 'We weren't fans especially, but we were asked if we wanted to go so we said, "Yeah, sure". We got in there and she was already playing and we were led to the balcony area, which was empty. But then some girls in the audience looked up and saw us walking about and started screaming. Then the place erupted and we were asked to leave as we were disrupting the show. We couldn't believe it was happening.'

```
                    UDO
                    ARTISTS, INC.
        #2 Miya-chu Bldg., 3-8-37 Minami-Aoyama, Minato-ku, Tokyo 107 Japan
        Telephone: (03) 402-7281  402-7581  Cables: UDOARTISTSPRO  Telex: J26552
        ─────────────────────────────────────────────────────────────────────

                            I T I N E R A R Y

                        "JAPAN" TOUR OF JAPAN - 1979

                            GROUP (1) - BAND


Mar 1  Thu   6:20 AM   Arrive Tokyo (Narita Airport) by SQ #58
                       Check in Keio Plaza Hotel (Tel: 344-0111)

    2  Fri             See Promotion Schedule

    3  Sat                      "

    4  Sun                      "

    5  Mon   9:30 AM   Leave hotel, proceed to Budokan (15-20 minutes by car)
                                          (Tel: 216-0789)
            10:00 AM   Rehearsal
                /
             4:30 PM
             4:30 PM   Support band set up & check
             5:30 PM   Doors open
             6:30 PM   Support band ARB show
             7:00 PM   Intermission
             7:20 PM   JAPAN show

    6  Tue   3:00 PM   Leave hotel, proceed to Budokan
             3:30 PM   Sound check
             4:30 PM   ARB set & check
             5:30 PM   Doors open
             6:30 PM   ARB show
             7:00 PM   Intermission
             7:20 PM   JAPAN show
            11:00 PM   Baggage down
```

```
                                "JAPAN"  GROUP (1)  /  PAGE 2

Mar 7  Wed  10:15 AM   Check out of hotel, proceed to Tokyo Station
            11:12 AM   Leave Tokyo for Nagoya by Super Express "Hikari" #71
             2:22 PM   Arrive Nagoya
                       Check in Nagoya Kokusai Hotel (Tel: (052) 961-3411)
             3:30 PM   Leave hotel, proceed to Nagoya Shi Kokaido
                                                  (Tel: (052) 731-7191)
             4:00 PM   Sound check
             5:00 PM   ARB set & check
             6:00 PM   Doors open
             6:30 PM   ARB show
             7:00 PM   Intermission
             7:20 PM   JAPAN show

    8  Thu  11:00 AM   Baggage down
            11:45 AM   Check out of hotel, proceed to Nagoya Airport
             1:00 PM   Leave Nagoya for Fukuoka by All Nippon Airways #225
             2:10 PM   Arrive Fukuoka
                       Check in Nishi-Tetsu Grand Hotel (Tel: (092) 771-7171)

    9  Fri   3:00 PM   Leave hotel, proceed to Kyuden Taiiku-Kan
                                                (Tel: (092) 531-6961)
             3:30 PM   Sound check
             4:30 PM   ARB set up & check
             5:30 PM   Doors open
             6:30 PM   ARB show
             7:00 PM   Intermission
             7:20 PM   JAPAN show

   10  Sat  10:00 AM   Baggage down
            11:00 AM   Check out of hotel, proceed to Fukuoka Airport
            12:25 PM   Leave Fukuoka for Osaka by All Nippon Airways #206
             1:25 PM   Arrive Osaka
                       Check in Osaka Grand Hotel (Tel: (06) 202-1212)
             3:50 PM   Leave hotel, proceed to Osaka Festival Hall (same building)
                                                (Tel: (06) 231-2222)
             4:00 PM   Sound check
             5:00 PM   ARB set & check
             6:00 PM   Doors open
             6:30 PM   ARB show
             7:00 PM   Intermission
             7:20 PM   JAPAN show

   11  Sun   1:45 PM   Leave hotel, proceed to Osaka Expo Hall (Tel: 877-3370)
             2:30 PM   Sound check
             3:30 PM   ARB set & check
             4:30 PM   Doors open
             5:00 PM   ARB show
             5:30 PM   Intermission
             5:50 PM   JAPAN show
```

The group took refuge in the nearby Fairmount Hotel and then returned to the Budokan at 7.30 pm where they watched the concert from the wings. The group must have been euphoric. The venue was huge and they had caused a major incident there by simply turning up as audience members. What would their own concert provoke? The group went on to the now familiar French restaurant and were eventually ferried back to the sanctuary of the Keio Plaza where, despite the buzz, they all managed to sleep soundly. 'The excitement kind of staved off the jet lag, but a few sakes helped you to wind down,' explained Dean. Sylvian particularly enjoyed the view of Tokyo at night and was instantly inspired to write of the life he observed in the city below.

Sunday was not a day of rest, but filled with interviews and a TV appearance on *11 pm*. Monday 5 March was the day of the first show. The band were smuggled from their hotel at 9.30 am to begin the rehearsal at the Budokan at 10.00 am sharp before returning to their hotel in the early afternoon, when the support group, the Japanese Alexander's Ragtime Band, began setting up and soundchecking. The headliners would eventually take the stage at 7.20 pm. There were six shows booked in all, taking in Tokyo, Nagoya, Fukoka and Osaka and the set list utilised the first two albums with the addition of 'European Son' and 'Heartbreaker'. 'The way we dropped songs was dependent on how they fitted in with new material,' says Dean, 'and David

Itinerary for Japanese tour, March 1979

Japanese tour,
March 1979
Keiko Kurata

would put the set list together. I remember we weren't too fond of 'The Unconventional' by then, but we didn't have a lot of material so we made do with what we had.'

Keiko Kurata, a young Hyogo girl, was already a committed fan and would get closer to the group than most: 'My friend had met Japan in London and when she came back she started the fan club and asked me to help her. When they finally came to Japan we followed them everywhere, went to the same restaurants and clubs and stayed in the same hotels as them. It was difficult to connect because my English wasn't so good, but I connected most with Mick; he was very kind and helpful,

writing us letters and providing us with material for the fan club and newsletters. There was a big buzz about the concert because Japan were following in the footsteps of The Beatles, Dylan, The Walker Brothers, Cheap Trick, Eric Clapton and Queen – all of whom had popularised the venue in the West with a series of 'Live at the Budokan' albums. I slept on the street for one week to get a front row ticket. I got tickets for all my friends and in all those concerts we had the best seats.'

For many, the experience was closer to that of a religious ritual than a musical one. Japan could have merely got up on stage and simply bowed to the audience before trotting

Japanese tour,
March 1979
Keiko Kurata

off and the reaction would still have been hysterical. The group, however, treated it as just another gig, albeit their biggest by far. 'It was actually less intimidating playing a big venue than a small one,' says Dean. 'You didn't feel as scrutinised.' Most of the band's equipment was supplied for them, but they took their own guitars and FX. 'I had a pedal board which is modest by today's standards,' says Dean, 'but it was customised and built by Pete Cornish and had about ten effects – phase, distortion, graphics, just the basics.'

Backstage, the band huddled in a group hug before walking into a wall of human noise. 'It was just this deafening waterfall of screams,' says Dean, 'but UDO had provided a decent enough sound system, so it wasn't quite like The Beatles – we could actually hear ourselves.' 'Different kinds of missiles were aimed at us,' recalled Karn, referring to the recent BOC tour, 'soft toys, jewellery, chocolates, flowers.' The group apparently remember little of the gig itself, but bootlegged recordings (the second concert was broadcast on radio) show that they played as tightly as ever, neither rattled nor fazed by the sudden and drastic change of reception. 'I mean, only the week before, we were playing the Marquee,' says Dean 'and we couldn't even half fill it.' Japan played for an hour, including encores. It was a blur of noise and colour. 'It was all over so quickly,' says Keiko. 'We had waited so long to see them and it went so fast.' The group celebrated their success with dinner at what was now becoming their local – the French restaurant in Roppongi. They then checked into a new hotel, the Plaza having been deemed too dangerous to stay in due to being overrun with fans. Their crew stayed on at the Plaza as decoys.

Japanese tour,
March 1979
Keiko Kurata

Aside from the remaining gigs outside of Tokyo, the trip continued to be packed with interviews, meetings with the head of Victor Records, visits to temples and private invitations, all documented by the ever present Japanese photographers and journalists. There was also the occasional TV appearance. The group were captured in their almost innocent pomp at the NHK television theatre for the show, *Let's Go Young!* Huckle: 'It was a bit of a cross between *Top Of The Pops* and *The Old Grey Whistle Test* where the bands played live, but was a bit of a mix of pure pop acts and rockier bands. Each act set up on a mini mobile stage, which was then wheeled on and off the main NHK theatre stage for each live performance. [On the footage that survives] you can just see the preceding act's stage going off as Japan come on. I do remember that all the other acts were Japanese and that the audience sat reasonably quietly through their numbers, and then politely applauded at the end, as was the Japanese custom in those days. However, as you see when the guys go on the audience are pretty loud and excited throughout their performance. There was a rather clever revolving stage so that the acts could all set up and were then just revolved around to face the audience for their bit.'

The audience were by now beyond smitten. Kumiko was another typical fan, between childhood and adulthood, but with enough pocket money to indulge her newfound obsession: 'The NHK TV show was the very first time that I saw Japan live. My friend and I paid 5,000 yen each for an invitation ticket to see this programme. I was very lucky to see David Sylvian for the first time when he was backstage. I was the only one there. When I opened the backstage door, David was standing still, waiting for the elevator all by himself. He was so beautiful that I became speechless.' The group were under

Japanese tour,
March 1979
Keiko Kurata

no illusions that their initial success at least had little to do with their music. Their look was by chance primed to appeal to the female Japanese youth. 'We didn't like masculine looking men,' explained Keiko, 'we liked them thin and aesthetic looking, like the boy who was in the *Death In Venice* film [Bjorn Andersen]. That movie was so popular in Japan.' There was of course 'a massive groupie situation', according to Barbieri. 'Some of us took advantage of that,' says Dean. 'I know I did… The crew and Nick Huckle certainly did!'

The Xeroxed and glossy pages now devoted to Japan were enough to wallpaper Mount Fuji. In *Music Life* etc., the photos were mostly shot with soft filter and in high contrast; they resembled, for the most part, non-explicit porn.

In contrast to the UK, everywhere Japan turned they were wanted, adored, desired and congratulated. 'After the TV appearances we were each given very expensive (well, they seemed expensive) watches each as a gift by the TV producers,' remembers Huckle. 'They did another TV show for another channel on that tour [the aforementioned *11 pm* where the group mimed to their biggest single there, 'The Unconventional'] and were given cameras each.' 'We were constantly given gifts,' says Dean, 'I loved it. It was the first time I ever saw a Walkman.' In their few hours of downtime, Japan attempted shopping trips, which were curtailed by the intense reaction and harassment from their fans who seemed to be everywhere. 'I don't think they knew what they would do if they got hold of us,' says Dean of the fanaticism. 'It was like an unconscious, mob instinct that took over.' Dodging the hordes, there was still time for Dean and Barbieri to purchase some shoes at the international Ginza shopping arcade, while Karn treated himself to a lighter. Sylvian chose to spend his downtime in his room when possible, although he would admit to getting high at the experience of being a pop star for the first time. His initial reactions on Japan were mixed. 'My first impression of Tokyo was that it was too westernised,' Sylvian told *Music Life*, 'like a cross between America and West Berlin. It seemed to lack a character of its own.'

Years later he would reflect on the experience more soberly: 'Japan has many faces, some of which I could only glimpse, rather frustratingly, though overwhelmed and somewhat over-saturated, from the windows of hotel rooms, cars, trains, television, and the media at large. At the time of our first visit to Japan, the band was at the height of its popularity there. The local promotion and security were so fearful for our well-being that we were treated as virtual prisoners by our hosts. I'd read up on the culture to some degree, had seen a couple of exotic documentaries that tended to play up the otherness of Japanese culture rather than explore or explain it. The novelty value of visiting a culture so radically different from one's own, especially when young, can't be understated. That first visit was one sustained intake of breath, a real high. On another level there was a sense of homecoming. I believe I wasn't the only member of the band to feel this sense of belonging. This ease might also be attributed to the comedy of manners, another essential aspect of social interaction. Being shy and, as a consequence, occasionally fearful of social interaction, I enjoyed the formality, and therefore a certain comforting predictability, of the exchanges.' In short, Japan had found their spiritual base, a refuge where their sales would allow them to grow even as they were ignored in the rest of the world. On the way back to the UK, Karn cried all the way home. 'Why was I leaving a place where I was so wanted?'

Although it had offered a morale boost and financial relief, in other ways the success in Japan only accelerated the pressure. Now more than ever, Hansa were pushing for a hit. If Japan could be superstars in one country, they could be superstars in others. Disco was still enormously popular and one of the few genres Japan hadn't explored. One of the more intriguing hits of the pantheon was Donna Summer's 'I Feel Love'. Released in 1977 it bestrode the globe's pop, R&B, and disco charts like some unstoppable, throbbing robo-orgasm. Its innovation lay in the fact that, apart from Summer's super sensual vocal, the track was completely synthesised, relying on a driving, sequenced bass line that propagated Summer's exquisite voice across airwaves and into dance floors and living rooms the world over. Its futuristic, aggressive/progressive production impressed both the teeny-boppers and the so-called cognoscenti. Bowie himself would recall, 'One day in Berlin, Eno came running in and said, "I have heard the sound of the future". He put on 'I Feel Love' by Donna Summer and said, "This is it, look no further. This single is going to change the sound of club music for the next 15 years."'

The producer of the track was Giorgio Moroder, an Italian and natural born maverick with a populist touch who had been obsessed with music from the day he was born. He also had a working relationship with Hansa. In addition to his pop genius, Moroder also scored films and would win an award for his soundtrack to 1978's *Midnight Express*. Sylvian had been to see the film and was impressed by the harsh and seductive electronic score. The idea of the group collaborating with the producer had been touted before the trip to Japan and the plan was to have him produce 'European Son', the live arrangement of which, although still obviously in debt to the guitar it was written on, was becoming increasingly 'Morodered' as time went on, with Barbieri's sequencer driving the song atop Jansen's metronomic, machine gun fill drums. Moroder had been sent the Napier-Bell-produced demo of the song and had responded that he'd be happy to work with the band on condition that they co-write together. Japan acquiesced. Sylvian: 'I think we were ready to move into an area of music that was more electronically based, and at the time I'm not sure whether it was management or the record company that was pushing Moroder. He had just produced an album for Sparks, which we thought was interesting, so we thought we'd give it a go.' Moroder had in turn played a demo tape to Sylvian entitled *Foxes*, probably in reference to a film soundtrack Moroder was then working on for the movie *Foxes* starring Jodie Foster. Musically it was closer to the likes of Boney M than either his soundtrack or Donna Summer work and the lyrics were typically disco-trite. Sylvian abandoned the given melody completely and rewrote the lyrics, instead riffing on his recent experiences in Japan. 'You have to give credit to Dave,' said Barbieri. 'He really reinvented the song he was given.'

From Japan, Sylvian and manager had flown to LA to meet Moroder. By 15 March, the rest of the band had joined them and engineer Harold Faltermeyer at Rusk Studios, 1556 N La Brea Avenue, Los Angeles, CA 90028 to work on what would become 'Life In Tokyo'. The music itself was, by nature, a collaboration, a compromise with Japan struggling initially to find themselves within the song. 'It was almost like being a songwriter for hire,' affirmed Sylvian. 'It was one of those experiences – "We'll throw you into a studio in LA with Moroder," and he dishes out some old demo from his stack and says, "Try working with this," and it's like, "Okay." It was odd, but not unpleasant.' Perhaps in deference to Moroder's usual tendency for drum machines and sequencers, the rhythm section are at their most pedestrian and Barbieri's contribution is assimilated into Moroder's standard sequenced sound. 'Giorgio already had everything set up,' says Dean. 'The drums, the keyboard sounds.' Karn described it as an 'interesting and educational experience, but personally I was very unhappy with 'Life In Tokyo', after I came up with several basslines, all of which I was told were not right. I felt betrayed by the others, who kept taking Giorgio's side and moving me further and further away from my own style of playing and into what I can only describe as a simple country and western pattern that any bassist could have written.' The Hansa Hollywood staff popped into see how it was going. Pam: 'It was amazing being in the same room as them, but basically at that point it just sounded like every other Moroder track only with David's vocal on top. I don't think they particularly wanted to be there. I think it would have been much more interesting, say, if they had been working with George Clinton at that point.'

The atmosphere in the studio overall was jovial, as is evident from the photos of the session. As serious as he was about his work, Moroder was often a subtly comic

The Rainbow,
12 April, 1979
Jan Kalinski

presence. Sylvian: 'He used to remind us of Clouseau. He was this kind of funny, little, slightly bungling character.' Japan took to their newfound jet-set lifestyle with aplomb and felt at home in LA. 'It was also the first time we were offered coke,' says Dean. 'It was no big deal, but our first exposure to it. Overall, I got the sense it was just another working day for Giorgio. It was fast. I was surprised though that the keyboard parts weren't actually sequenced. Faltermeyer played them manually.' 'It was an odd little experience,' Sylvian would sum up, 'and I just think it set the ground for *Quiet Life*.'

Before heading home, the band had some time to indulge in a little light shopping. A show at the prestigious Rainbow venue was booked for later that year and Sylvian wanted to wear something special for the occasion. It was now that the original seed was sown for what would become the *Quiet Life* album cover in the form of a red leather box jacket. Napier-Bell would claim that Sylvian spent $3,000 of the band's money on the item but no one else remembers it that way. 'That's absolute balls,' says Dean, 'the jacket never cost that much. We all went shopping on Melrose Avenue and bought stuff – I got some shirts; Simon's version doesn't ring true at all.'

While the mixes of 'Life In Tokyo' were sent off to be mastered, Japan returned home briefly before embarking on another tour of Europe. Another single, 'Deviation', was released in the Netherlands that March and like most of those before it, flatlined. The New Sound Rising Tour, as it was called, took in 14 dates around Europe that March and April before heading home for the final stop at the legendary Rainbow where it seemed only yesterday Japan had been among the scuffle of Ziggy fans braying for

The Rainbow,
12 April, 1979
Jan Kalinski

Bowie. Before the show, the group headed to the famous hairdressers Mane Line for a a haircut, losing the poodle look once and for all. Even this occurrence was captured for posterity by a Japanese photo shoot.

Their set, as well as their look, was evolving, as evidenced by the inclusion of a new song 'Halloween' and the injection of sequencers and synth lines replacing the trashy guitar sound so prevalent only months before. Yet it was too early for Japan to be presenting their newfound half-formed selves and the show was more of a public workshop, presenting them as neither the old nor new Japan, musically or visually. The group were, in effect, a butterfly emerging from a chrysalis – ultimately a beautiful thing but a messy transition to witness. The effect was disorientating. Japan were known and derided in the UK for their glam look and for incorporating funk, rock, and reggae into their music. Now there was disco to

contend with. One incident during the gig added an unwanted farcical element to the show. Huckle: 'Embarrassingly, and I believe unknown to the band, Simon had hired a Japanese guy to run on stage during 'Life In Tokyo' in the guise of an over-excited fan. When he got behind Dave, he just started doing a strange sort of jig and was immediately bundled off by the crew. Only to be handed a wad of fivers by SNB.'

The Rainbow show was hyped as the final date of a triumphant world tour. Instead (with support by a band called Reggae Regular, only confusing things further), it only reflected the flux that the group were in; the venue was half full and, in the main, the critics remained unmoved. 'They have worked very hard, particularly on their haircuts, and will undoubtedly appeal to those who prefer style to substance,' summed up *Sounds*. Backstage, the band were unconcerned. 'We really were never that bothered about critics. We weren't especially upset by bad reviews,' says Dean. 'I always felt that there was nothing that anyone could tell me that I didn't already know about myself,' explained Sylvian.

Soon after the Rainbow performance, the great white disco-rock hope of 'Life In Tokyo' came and went. Despite being released in an array of formats and mixes around the globe, in the UK it picked up only late night regional airplay and failed to improve on the chart placings of the previous singles. 'If someone could figure out how to market Japan, they'd be enormous,' said *Sounds*. 'They have more relevance than all those snobbishly serious records pressed into one mucky little lump of plastic. Japan have feelings, yeah … I bet they get scared sometimes.' US *Billboard* flatly noted that, 'The trademark Moroder sound is apparent with its haunting use of synthesisers. Sylvian's vocals add to its throbbing appeal.' 'We weren't especially down about its failure,' says Dean, 'we just moved on. Personally I was jazzed just to have worked with Moroder.' The failure of this single in the US would lose Japan their record label there and it would be another three years before they warranted a domestic American release. The promo video by Mike Mansfield, shot at Elstree Studios was another mish-mash of stilted miming shot through a low-grade porno filter. The song had at least pointed the way forward for the band, whose mission now was to enter the studio and transmute their recent growing pains into a music that finally spoke of and for them. Frustratingly, no producer of choice was yet available.

As negotiations were ongoing, when the band weren't writing and rehearsing there were previous commitments and seemingly endless Japanese photo shoots to fulfil. In late May, the group made an irreverent appearance on Belgian TV miming to 'Automatic Gun', 'Adolescent Sex' and 'Life In Tokyo'. Sylvian, either stoned or tipsy or both, clearly had little feeling for the earlier material and didn't bother to hide it. 'We were always more into our newer material. It's only natural. Of that TV show, all I remember is how boring Brussels was,' says Dean. That June there was another gig at a festival in Amsterdam, booked months previously. Japan were billed above Golden Earring, which showed how big they were in the Netherlands. As Sylvian was impatient to get back into the studio, gigs at this point were becoming a bore and, as if in psychosomatic protest, his voice gave out. 'He suddenly started sounding like Donald Duck,' says Dean. 'We had to abort the gig, the crowd went crazy there was almost a riot.'

Following a week-long promo trip to Toronto by Karn and Sylvian, it was time for a break. 'It was suggested we take a holiday,' remembers Dean, 'in the States. Originally we were all going to go to different places, but as Mick and David were already in New York we ended up going there. We had an apartment near Times Square.' Decades on, Karn would reflect that, 'Dave and I spent a lot of time together, as best friends do. It didn't bother us that we had no friends there, we hadn't any in London and could rely on each other.' 'It was great fun,' says Dean. 'We hung out, went shopping, clubbing. We saw a lot of movies. Woody Allen's *Manhattan* had just come out. It was a great time to be in New York. We went to Max's Kansas City a lot. We met Sylvain Sylvain there.' The group were also courted by Bill Aucoin, then manager of Kiss who were at the height of their fame. 'He wanted to manage us in America and took us to see Kiss at Madison Square Gardens. God, they were awful,' laughs Dean. 'I think he saw us as a British equivalent of Kiss so for obvious reasons our negotiations with him went nowhere.'

Karn would write about this summer as a further period of painful transition for Sylvian. The two often met up with the singer Nona Hendryx, an associate of Napier-Bell's whom they had first met at the Hurrah show the year before. An apparently besotted Sylvian, unable to express his attraction to the singer, got routinely drunk instead, 'until no longer able to hold up his head,' according to Karn. 'She was a sexy lady,' adds Dean, 'she really had something about her and she was very kind to us. I'm not surprised that David fancied her.' Karn recalled how he would escort Sylvian back to the apartment after each drunken encounter. 'Those walks home were tearful and full of self-loathing for Dave, leading to the type of inner searching and questioning we all go through at some point in our lives, hating the person we have become and committing ourselves to promises of change for the better.' Sylvian himself summed up this difficult period: 'There was a period of about six months where we weren't really sure where we wanted to go, who we wanted to work with and what style of music we wanted to do. We were living in New York during that time, and we were trying to settle a new American record deal, because we'd lost the one we had. It was like re-evaluating what we'd done up to that point. We didn't want to go back to the old material and start playing that live again, so we decided to wait until we'd finished a new one [album]. Initially we'd planned to record in America because John Punter, who we wanted to produce us, was very tied up, although he wanted to do it. We didn't

Patti Nolder and Mick Karn, AIR Studios, September 1979
Patti Nolder

really want to wait, so we left for the States and talked to a few producers, but none of them seemed right – they didn't suit the album.' Japan's initial choices for producers – Robert Fripp, Roxy Music's Chris Thomas and Bowie's Ken Scott, had all proved to be unavailable at the right time, but this would prove to be fortuitous. 'We wrote most of the material and got it together over there,' continues Sylvian, 'but in the end we rang John Punter again, who by that time was free. So we came back because he wanted to work at AIR.'

Japan's next studio album would be the perfect opportunity to reinvent themselves. Sylvian would eventually refer to *Quiet Life* as Japan's 'debut album'. John Punter – as recommended by Thomas – would in effect become a sixth member of the group. Punter, born in 1949, had a fatherly, friendly and utterly unpretentious air about him. Lightly bearded, receding, bespectacled and with a cigarette always on the go, visually he was an unlikely addition to the group. Outside of the music industry at least, he was not a 'name' producer but well respected and in constant employment. His past credits included Procol Harum, Slade and, more significantly, Roxy Music and Bryan Ferry's recent solo albums. At heart, he was an enormously competent, astute and inventive engineer and not predisposed to push his ideas onto artists with whom he was working. He saw his job as being both to collaborate with and ultimately serve the artist. He did so with consummate professionalism and good humour. In short, despite the lack of hair dye and make-up – or because of this – he was the perfect component that Japan had up until now lacked.

The autumn of 1979 was now a good time for all concerned. Although encouraged by their success in Japan, it didn't overly affect the fivesome's insular path. 'I don't think the success in Japan affected how we approached composition as a band, but it did afford us the luxury of using a well-equipped studio and more accomplished producers, as Hansa were willing to invest that bit more,' says Jansen. 'Achieving recognition does perhaps escalate the process of moving on artistically. However, I don't think we were fooling ourselves that the recognition received in Japan in those early years was for our music. I seem to remember always being keen to get into the studio – it was an exciting opportunity to make a statement

Far left: Mick Karn in Patti Nolder's office, AIR Studios, September 1979, *Patti Nolder*

Left: Jansen, Paris hotel room *Patti Nolder*

as a musician and this was more important than live work.' It could be read that Japan – both country and group – were right all along and it was merely a matter of time before the rest of the world caught on.

With this new sense of vindication, a meeting had been set up between the band and Punter. The group were already considering a more expansive approach before they met him. Dean: 'I remember us sat in a car talking about the album just before we went to meet Punter. I recall David saying that he wanted strings on some tracks. We were like, "Wow, that's a concept! That's different."' 'Punter came for a meeting at our management office in Bruton Street,' recalls Barbieri. 'We obviously wanted him because of his Roxy Music production, so it was probably just a case of checking that he would be a nice personality to work with.' Punter: 'I remember meeting them there. Simon had got in touch with my then manager, John Burgess. It was love at first sight! They looked immaculate. Their glam appearance wasn't off-putting at all, probably because of my experience with Roxy. I had the same kind of feeling as when I met Roxy for the first time as I did with Japan. They were close. Any hierarchy there was wasn't as obvious as it would become. David was often stern and serious, but Mick was hilarious, a very funny guy. But despite their appearances they were very normal, all of them.' Jansen: 'I don't doubt the meeting went well because of the type of person John is and the fact that we had no reservations about working with him. Of course, this was a big step forward in terms of collaborating with a producer that had a vision similar to ours and was able to facilitate ideas with an endless enthusiasm.' In short, Japan and Punter clicked and the decision to work with one another was unanimous. Now that Japan had found the right producer, they were finally poised to become the group they were always meant to be.

The recording of Japan's third album would begin at London's Basing Street Studios on 3 September. In the world outside, things were as ever changing, only this time in Japan's favour. Punk was dying off and the pop charts were reflecting a more postmodern, optimistic and progressive sounding music with the likes of The Police, Blondie and, most notably, Gary Numan all riding high. Japan's new aesthetic – visually and sonically – was, perhaps by coincidence, much more in tune with the new wave of music and fashion than it had been just six months ago. The working title for Japan's third album was initially *Alien*. However, Sylvian was beaten to this title by Ridley Scott, who was about to release the film of the same name in the UK that September and for a while *European Son* was considered as a title instead. *Alien* was one of the few demos in existence at this point; recorded on a four-track portastudio at Richard Chadwick's flat in the Barbican by Sylvian and Barbieri, it was an eerie, industrial sounding downtempo track that could have been an outtake from

Barbieri, Karn,
AIR Studios,
September 1979
Patti Nolder

Moroder's *Midnight Express* soundtrack, with Sylvian's new croon oscillating throughout. Dean: 'I remember the *Alien* demo. It was played in a rehearsal and was very different to what we know as *Alien*; it was very obscure sounding.'

Eventually, both album titles and the original 'Alien' song and 'European Son' would be dropped from the album. Prior to entering Basing Street Studios, John had apparently heard nothing of the band's music they were due to record, either live on record or even in the rawest demo form. Punter: 'Dave or whomever would never come into the studio and say, "This is the demo". They would just play the song live in the studio and we would just throw ideas around and go with it. The first time I heard them play, I was struck by how unusual they were; the most traditional player was Rob. The rhythm section were totally unconventional and Rich was like a hybrid. I mean, he was more musical than Eno. Rich had a musical foundation of chords and melody but he also excelled at putting together the sequential stuff, which was so archaic at that time, practically steam-powered.'

Barbieri was a key element in Japan's new musical arsenal. His lack of traditional musical 'chops' encouraged the electronic aspect of the group and yet the acoustic piano playing on the album, while basic, is assured and confident. Despite this, Barbieri would never be considered an authentic keyboard player by many. He himself explains the reasons for this: 'I think it's the absence of any obvious stylistic approach in my playing,' he offers. 'There are variations on blues and jazz licks that we all recognise and hear in part in most musicians' work. Classical and folk as well. I never learnt any of these styles and even now for me to incorporate some standard riffs or licks wouldn't feel right. Electronic and minimal music were more of an influence. Although many would argue that a musician should practise to attain a higher degree of technique, which is admirable of course, I find that I can be more creative when I'm in my comfort zone, technically speaking. And while some will play 100 notes in 10 seconds, I prefer to play one note that lasts 10 seconds and that does something interesting in context with the track or in isolation. This isn't unique; it's just my instinct and not dissimilar in approach, at least, to artists like Eno, Harold Budd, etc., who play with space and let the sounds breathe. Because so much of what I do is about the sound, this inevitably slows everything down a degree so that the qualities of the sound can be heard. If you are playing something very fast and technical, then by default the sound has to be very linear and can't have that much textural interest.'

The awakening of Barbieri's musical philosophy was timely. Sylvian was now writing increasingly on keyboards although, as he didn't yet own a piano and wrote mostly at home, the majority of songs on the album were still born of his battered, second-hand 12-string acoustic guitar. This would provide a rich basis for an album that would combine uptempo, guitar-driven songs such as 'Fall in Love With Me' and sombre, brooding melancholic piano ballads like 'Despair'. Karn and Jansen were also blooming. 'We worked hard,' Karn would recall. 'I knew I'd discovered something new in my playing, breaking barriers with a distinctive, melodious style.' Karn's sumptuous, unfolding fretless bass playing was in part a response to the absence of traditional melody in Sylvian's vocal lines, and attempting to compensate for them.

Sylvian would state that he wrote many of his songs 'in one setting' and unlike traditional classic songwriters did not pore over top lines for any amount of time. 'I am suspicious of melody and tend to go with melodies that, hopefully, seep into the consciousness with repeated listening,' he said. He would write the basis of a song in isolation and then present the basic tune to the band in rehearsal, giving chords and tempo. The band then did what they liked with it. 'Writing together as Japan,' Karn stated, 'would invariably begin with Steve and I playing along to a sequence of chords and an often complete vocal line, keyboards and guitars would be experimented with, the preliminary chords would then often be discarded and the song built from the foundation we had laid.' At the time, no one questioned why the song-writing credits remained solely with Sylvian. 'It was not cool to talk about money back then,' Barbieri would reflect. 'It just never came up,' says Dean. Punter: 'I'm surprised that the credits went to just Dave. For some reason, I thought they'd done the diplomatic thing and shared the writing credits. Certainly they were all involved with the completion of the songs although the original idea may have been Big Bad Sylv's (as we used to call him affectionately). But it was a group effort. And it's a valid point – at what point does arrangement become co-composition? My recollection is that they were all working around a nucleus of a song and making it different and better. In that regard they should all have got some publishing money, but at the time that kind of arrangement was very common.'

One could argue that on the earlier albums, before each member had found such characteristic voices, the precise point of where an arrangement seeped into composition was not such an issue. But now that Karn, Jansen and Barbieri in particular had developed so profoundly, it's hard to imagine the songs on *Quiet Life* sounding as they do played by any other band. At the time, such financial technicalities were not an issue. The group were excited by the new sounds they were finding in their instruments and by the sympathetic producer who helped to express them. Jansen and Karn especially were like exotic birds that had finally and suddenly learned how to fly.

Punter too was excited by what he was hearing. 'The rhythm section was so unconventional in their craft, being self taught, and trying things in a different way to other taught musicians,' he stresses, 'it meant that the rhythm section was such a part of that band's make-up and how they crafted stuff; you recorded the two of them and just layered everything else on top. It was outstanding, it really was.' Jansen, 'the only natural musician in the group', according to his brother, was not coming into his own alone, but had Karn beside him all the way. 'Steve and I had become each other's biggest critics,' said Karn, 'constantly pushing each other forward to discover new ground.' Jansen: 'I took to drumming pretty quickly and perhaps for some time had a more proficient level of musicianship than the others in the band, but the nature of what we did wasn't about proficiency – in fact the lack of it was what pushed us to explore originality over proficiency. Self-taught musicians tend to do things by ear, so there would be the obvious mimicking of other players in order to understand the skills required, but the technique wasn't handed down and consequently a kind of mutation occurs and perhaps because of that it becomes a natural path to finding your own voice. If you are plagued by technique it's much harder to find it.'

In the autumn of 1979, Japan were less concerned about simply serving up the song as so many other bands would do. In the safety of the studio they were free to explore and challenge the arrangement of a piece to its limit, without ever completely deconstructing it. In contrast to the born again rhythm section and the suddenly sequencer-savvy Barbieri, Sylvian was the most traditional voice – as a writer and literally – within the group. In tandem with Dean's more traditional playing, he would balance out the innovations and eccentricities of the others, resulting in a whole that was unique but recognisably palatable pop music.

The songs were well rehearsed although only 'Halloween' had so far been played live. 'We knew what we were doing by now,' says Dean, 'and we'd worked hard in preparing the songs.' Beside the piano ballads on the album, most of the songs on *Quiet Life* would begin in the recording studio thus: 'I remember us putting the drums down to a click track first of all, and I'd play along with some basic guitar, along with Mick just so the chords were mapped out,' says Dean. 'There would also be a guide vocal.' Jansen: 'Getting a complete drum take was the starting point for tracks with a rhythm section. If anyone else messed up they could drop in but that wasn't the case with drums generally, unless there was an obvious stop point. Usually there would be a sequencer or rhythm box to play along with if the track incorporated one. This was before the days of time code so it wasn't possible to sync machines to a tempo, therefore I would play with a machine and everything else had to be overdubbed without true sync, just trial and error. If there were no strict tempos required then we would perform as a band with a view to getting a good drum take first, then everyone else would overdub.'

This was the first time that sequencers ('the anchor of the song', as Punter put it) had been used on a Japan album and their effect would be paramount in redefining their sound. Barbieri: 'I used an Oberheim 8 step sequencer running the Roland System 700. A sequencer and analogue synth was quite a normal set-up for keyboardists around 1975 to 1982. It was just the latest technology at the time but something new and inspiring for me to work with and quite a feature on that album.' Punter: 'It was a temperamental piece of shit. I knew then that as regards to playing the songs live, we couldn't take that out on tour with us, we'd have to put it on tape.' How these songs would be taken on stage was not a consideration at all at this point; Japan and Punter were falling in love with each other and the studio process for the first time. Once a satisfactory drum part had been recorded, various takes of Karn's bass would then be overdubbed, sometimes direct to tape (foregoing an amp), the ultimate part you hear often being a composite of many different performances. Once the track had the requisite bed of drums, bass and sequencers providing the recognisable structure of the song, the other elementary overdubs – guitar, keyboards and vocals – would be added at AIR Studios. George Martin's AIR Studios on Oxford Street were new to Japan, but a familiar and much loved playground to Punter. 'I loved the whole set up at AIR,' says Punter, 'and they had a studio within a studio there, which was meant for film dubbing but never really took off. I loved it and used it whenever I could. That's where we would finish *Quiet Life*. It had a little vocal booth, where we would overdub guitars too.'

The whole experience of making *Quiet Life*, as it was now known, would always be remembered as one of the happiest times for the band. They had even acquired a band car, a Jaguar that their manager had purchased for them from the famed wrestler Kendo Nakasaki, whose day job was as a mechanic in the Elephant & Castle. 'I'd drive them to the studio every day,' says Huckle, 'about noonish. The mood was high. Sometimes Rich would drive and if we were feeling adventurous we'd let Steve have a go. He didn't have his licence then though.' On top of AIR's mixing desk there could be found doodles by Dean. There was a sketch of a strange being named Alien that marked a faint resemblance to Karn. A photo of the young Elvis had been modified to match Jansen's fringe. The resemblance was uncanny. 'It was Punter who came up with our nicknames,' says Dean, 'and he often remarked at how Steve looked like the young Elvis. He also called Steve "Nancy Boy". I was "Boblet", Mick "Alien", Rich "Doc" and Dave "Big Bad Sylv".' ('For obvious reasons,' added Karn.) 'David was the most serious of the band,' says Punter, 'he was beginning to know what it was he wanted. Or at least what he didn't want.' In turn, Japan had their own nickname for Punter – 'Horace the Hag'. Napier-Bell was rarely there. 'I don't remember him ever interfering, unlike many managers I knew,' says Punter. 'He'd pop in and see how it was going and then pop out again.'

Punter, who was also a drummer, continued to be enthralled by the talents of his new subjects, Jansen in particular. 'The way he inverted beats … I used to call him, "back arsewards"; he would always play something unusual instead of the one beat starting in the obvious place.' Jansen's playing, while always impeccable, had now evolved into a unique blend of swing and sophistication that supplied a deep-pile plushness to the band's sound. Karn's newfound confidence was the perfect foil. After two albums of engaging if flawed effort, Japan's rhythm section as we would know it was finally born on tracks like 'Alien', 'In Vogue', and the title track itself. Punter: 'I would never try to curb their playing. I didn't need to. Mick for instance would bring himself back to the correct point in any song. That went for his saxophone playing too – he was even different as a sax player. He approached things sideways. I never stopped anything they wanted to do because that was part and parcel of them.' Dean and his newfound EBow (a device that gave an infinite sustain to any guitar line) adapted admirably to the more textured approach needed. His playing manages to blur and fade into Barbieri's keyboard textures when needed. Hear how his guitar solo merges into the strings and Mellotrons of 'In Vogue' so seamlessly. On rockier tracks like 'Halloween', his voice is much more acerbic, but never in such a way that it disrupts the flow and panache of the song. For now, despite Japan's growing reticence to rely on the guitar in the studio ('European Son' didn't even feature Dean), Boblet's future in the group seemed assured.

The song 'Quiet Life' itself was an instant classic. 'I remember Dave playing it to me on guitar,' says Dean. 'It was quite simple, just A/D/G etc. but once Steve and Mick got hold of it, it really became something else.' Punter: 'What I remember about the title track is us tuning the bass drum – we tuned it to be in key with the song. I'd never done that before and can't remember how it came about. But it became the anchor to the song.' The attention to detail would produce mesmerising results. 'The middle break in 'Quiet Life' has a left and right alternating synth drum playing along with the sequencer,' explains Jansen. 'This was achieved by using two sensors taped to my knees which, when hit, were triggering some sort of synth.'

'Quiet Life' was the first classic pop song that Japan recorded. It shows off each member's unique skills within a glimmering construct where each part serves and highlights the other. There is no overcrowding. It's at once complicated and accessible. The flawless high gloss sheen of the synths and sequencers mesh perfectly with the buoyant, mutant funk of the rhythm section. The rhythm guitar part is sugar-white Chic, while Dean's solo is haunting, sad and complicated. Sylvian's croon, devoid of all angles and edges, burnishes the song like the chrome fenders of some classic, retro-futurist car. The finger clicks that punctuate the song are the candles on the cake. It is at once groovy and melancholy, bright eyed and mournful, sexy and sad. The vocal refrain of 'Boys' (which actually owes more to Bowie's 'Sweet Thing' than 'Boys Keep Swinging' as has been previously suggested) is countered by the white noise ricochet of Barbieri's synth to beguiling effect. Taken as a whole, 'Quiet Life', sounding like the perfect nephew of later Roxy and contemporary Bowie, would be the most radio-friendly song Japan would ever release. It was the perfect figurehead for the album it heralded.

The last instrument (bar orchestra) to be recorded would be vocals. Sylvian's new singing style would come in for a lot of criticism because of comparisons to Bryan Ferry's vocals, but anyone visiting Sylvian's flat at the time may have been surprised at the abundance of Bing Crosby and Frank Sinatra albums littered around the record player. Sylvian, like Ferry, was in effect attempting a classic croon, seeing the voice as just one more texture alongside the other instruments. It had been a conscious decision to dump his old singing style after the first tour of Japan. 'It was such a strain singing like that so I decided to go back to a more mellow style, a more comfortable range.' There was another reason for the more somnolent singing; Sylvian wanted *Quiet Life* 'to work as muzak, a record that people could listen to intently or ignore'. This would not be possible if sung by the voice of the first two albums: 'All that screaming and shouting just irritates when you hear it and you want to talk while the record is on,' explained Sylvian modestly. Thus, Sylvian was not merely aping Bowie and Ferry's languid style, but adapting his voice to suit the concept of the work as a whole. Of course, it helped that he was a huge fan of Roxy and Bowie – this was a style he could approximate comfortably. Like many of his contemporaries, he had grown up singing along to *Station To Station* and 'In Every Dream Home A Heartache'.

In private though, Sylvian was never as confident about his singing as the end result suggested. Keeping true to the idea that his voice was 'just another instrument', Punter would ladle FX onto Sylvian's voice as he would any other instrument. The results were eerily seductive and perhaps in part an attempt for

Steve Jansen, playing synth triggers taped to his knees, AIR Studios, September 1979
Patti Nolder

Sylvian to mask his lack of confidence in his voice. Throughout his career, John Lennon hated the sound of his singing voice and always insisted on it being treated with a heavy reverb. Punter: 'For the vocal effect on 'In Vogue' and 'Alien', for example, I would have used an Eventide Harmoniser with a very close modulating pitch up and down with a short delay on it, giving it a double-tracked effect when it wasn't actually double tracked. I would then actually double track it on the chorus. That was one of my trademarks. While it filled out the vocal it also gave a weird kind of hollowness to it, but when it came to the chorus it would fill out a bit, because of the actual double tracking. It was a great contrast. I used that harmoniser on guitars, synths, drums … it was a great little gizmo.'

There were musical quotes apparent throughout *Quiet Life* that could be easily referenced back to the music Japan loved. The aforementioned Bowie-aping 'Boys' and the drum pattern of 'Alien', which came from the opening of Roxy's 'Out Of The Blue' were amongst the most obvious. 'They wouldn't exactly say, "Oh we want it to sound like this [Roxy] or [Bowie] track",' says Punter, 'well, maybe they would …' Dean: 'Influences were quite obvious, but I chose to ignore it. It just happens in music.' Songs like 'Fall In Love With Me' (previously the title of a Bowie/Iggy Pop song) did superficially recall the Europop of Roxy/Iggy/Bowie but also evoked the Europe that inspired albums like *The Idiot* and *Stranded*. And, after all, Japan had by now travelled extensively all across that same Europe and also consumed it via books and films. *Despair* was a low-lit, atmospheric film set in post-war Berlin by the German director Rainer Fassbinder, starring the Batt brothers' beloved Dirk Bogarde. The Japan song of the same name, sung in French just like Ferry had done in 'A Song For Europe', could have been the theme song for the film. Then again, the lyrics quoted prose by Erik Satie. Japan were obvious in their influences, but still processed them in such a way that would eventually display an integrity if not an originality all of

Jansen, Karn
Parisian taxi,
September 1979
Patti Nolder

their own. Incidentally, Kate Bush was also recording at AIR and was one of the first people to hear 'Despair'. 'She came in to say hello,' recalls Dean, 'she looked lovely, wearing a leather jacket. She sat down on the floor and we played her 'Despair' at full blast. Once it ended she looked up and said, "Wow! Isn't it big?!"' 'I remember Kate Bush dropping in,' confirms Barbieri. 'She sat cross-legged, listening, and was very complimentary. Very sweet and friendly.'

For many, *Quiet Life* captured the band at their most likeable. In hindsight, they were now at a point between the youthful spunky naïveté of *Obscure Alternatives* and the self-conscious perfectionism of *Gentlemen Take Polaroids*. It would also remain one of their most sumptuous sounding works and this is in part due to their only ever use of an orchestra on 'In Vogue' and 'The Other Side Of Life'. The string arranger on both, Ann O'Dell, was also another solo Ferry veteran. (Interestingly, in contrast to their singer's solo albums, Roxy Music never used strings.) 'I simply don't remember much about my work with Japan, I'm afraid,' says O'Dell. 'I would have met them through John Punter. He introduced me to David, who said that they wanted strings on two songs. Why only two, I have no idea. I remember us talking in a car outside the studio and he was very charming, but that's all I remember.' Karn has stated that O'Dell told him that the inspiration for the parts were his own beautiful basslines, but she remembers it differently. 'Absolutely not! I would never base any arrangement on a bass guitar part. Not at all. The idea is ridiculous.' Whatever the inspiration, the result would be magnificent. Punter: 'I'm not sure if it was my idea to have an orchestra. Maybe it was David's, or both of ours. Obviously, I'd worked with Anne on Ferry's albums and she was extremely talented. She was part of a new breed back then; she was in a kind of Paul Buckmaster vein, but why there were strings on only two, I dunno … just for contrast I suppose.'

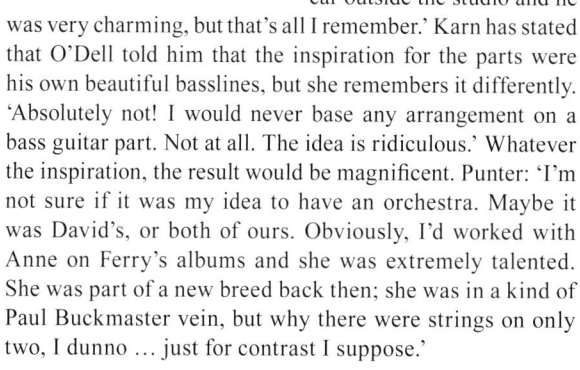

Whatever the inspiration behind the orchestral arrangement, the results spoke for themselves. They added a magnificence to Japan's sound. The orchestra brought out the deepest colours in the songs and added thrilling, cinematic dynamics. They also added a maturity to the work of a band who after all were barely in their early 20s. The 20-piece orchestra enters 'In Vogue' after the first chorus, drifting across the song like fog making its way over a lake towards a château. On 'The Other Side Of Life' they come close to possessing the song during its extended coda. When Sylvian and Dean have retired from the piece, we get to hear the exemplary rhythm section battle it out with waves of string and woodwind. At each end of a bar the music seems to teeter at the edge of a cliff, with Jansen's exquisitely placed fills reining us back to safety. The band had assembled to watch the orchestra bring life to O'Dell's arrangements, which up until then had been merely squiggles on a score sheet. Dean: 'We didn't know what to expect, it was experimental for us, we had no idea what the strings would sound like. We all watched and listened as they played along. It was the first time we got to hear it. It was like, "Oh my God, what is this?!" It was a rush. It kind of gives you a stiffy. You had no idea what it would sound like and then suddenly there was this lushness flooding through all this music you'd been working on.'

Once everything had been recorded, the mixing could begin. This was Punter's forte. 'Punter left the arrangements to us but had lots of ideas and suggestions generally and specifically during the mixing,' says Dean. Punter: 'As far as mixing went, that was my domain. That's where I put my stamp, in the mix. It was very personal to me, I had a way of doing things that no one else did. My drum sound was always referred to by other people as being very "Punteresque". That and the vocal sound.' Punter would usually man the mixing desk alone, with his engineers Colin Fairley and Nigel Walker, while the band – fully made-up and garbed in satin and leather – loitered and smoked on the huge Chesterfield sofa behind him. On occasion, the complexity of a track would call for their input. Karn: 'We'd almost finished mixing the title track, an all-hands-on-deck experience, when John would ask for our help to move the mixing board faders a fraction up or down, or to press certain switches at given moments.' There would sometimes be as many as eight people helping Punter mix any one song. The results were patently worth it. By the time *Quiet Life* was mixed and ready for mastering, Japan were a brand new group. Karn: 'We started taking it seriously when we met John Punter. That had a profound influence on all of us, in that we were suddenly being taken seriously as individuals, as musicians, and he pulled out the best in us. Up until that point we were angry young men trying to prove a point and to go against everything that was current and I think all we needed was somebody to be on our side. And John Punter, who was somebody we'd admired, gave us that confidence.'

In turn, Punter now wanted to work with no one else. He had given Japan his ears and they had taken his heart. 'As the album went on I became besotted with them,' he says. 'I just wanted to become part and parcel of the experience. They also introduced me to a lot of music that was new to me, like Talking Heads, and I introduced them to more classic style pop and rock and it was this mix that made for such a unique album. And I wanted them to sound as good on the road as they did in the studio, so I'd eventually end up going out on tour with them.'

A few songs hadn't made it. The original 'Alien' would never be heard; 'European Son' would surface as a single soon; an instrumental entitled 'A Foreign Place' would be shelved for the time being; another untitled song never even made it into the recording studio. Barbieri: 'I did write a track with David for the *Quiet Life* album that we recorded as a band during the studio sessions but it just failed to get the vote, so wasn't included. Maybe it sounded too close to 'In Vogue'. Mick used exactly the same bass line, note for note, on a track for his solo album called *Weather The Windmill*. Japan's 'debut' album didn't suffer for these exclusions and *Quiet Life* was mastered on 5 November at Trident Studios to the general euphoria of all involved.

The album cover had already been shot. Back in the summer, Fin Costello had photographed the band behind glass for the Japanese release of 'Life In Tokyo'. Fin: 'The cover for *Quiet Life* was shot at my studio in Camden Town. The set we used was for a Violinski [a spin-off group from the Electric Light Orchestra] cover shoot. That's where the glass that David's hand is touching came in. We shot Japan as a lighting test.' In hindsight some would question why only the band's singer featured on the cover. 'Dave had grown in size and was about to take over the whole front cover by putting forward the concept of each member occupying their own panel,' Karn would later write, referring to the gatefold edition of the album. Dean: 'On the first album we're all on the cover. On the second he's at the front and we're at the back. On *Quiet Life* he's on the front. And so on.

Why anyone didn't protest, I don't know.' Jansen: 'I don't remember much about it. The idea of putting the front man on a pedestal was [and maybe still is] a valuable marketing move, but one which ironically may have accelerated the demise of the band.' Dean: 'David was much more focused on this album. And because he was the singer, he was the focal point and so he was the one that the record company and management would go to first. This would feed his ego to a point where he believed he was the most important thing. Just look at the record covers.' The photographer had the last word. 'If anyone is suggesting that ego may have had a part in the decision to have just Dave on the cover, they would be wrong. It was solely a graphic decision. When we saw the pictures it was an obvious choice. There was an interesting use of filter for the cover, which was used a lot in the movies. Harrison filters are made at Paramount Studios in LA for specific effects and I had a set made for me in the 70s. If you look at the vinyl album cover you can see why Dave was used solo on the front. It was the first shoot that really worked to my and Dave's satisfaction and the red jacket was what made it come together so well.'

On 25 November, the band flew from London to play two sold out concerts at the Ryerson Theatre in Toronto. *Quiet Life* had already been released there only eight days previously and apparently sold more than 10,000 copies in the Toronto area in its first week. The band were, albeit briefly, hugely popular in the region for a while. Huckle: 'It was a fairly quick affair, maybe just four or five days. They had had some success over there, so we arranged a hasty couple of gigs and a lot of press/promo type stuff. The two shows were packed out and well received. For some time afterwards we used to talk about the band as being "big in Japan and Canada".'

A new musician had been added via an advert in the *Evening Standard*. Jane Shorter had joined the band on saxophone. 'Jane was a nice girl, quite quiet and rather straight, not so much a prude, just a bit serious and businesslike,' remembers Huckle. 'She had long blonde hair, but was rather plain looking, and didn't wear any make-up off-stage as I recall. I think they had advertised for a female sax player anonymously and she was the only applicant. In truth, she had only been learning the sax for a few months and really struggled in the first few rehearsals. But to give her due credit she stuck with it, and with a fair bit of one-to-one coaching from Mick and John Punter, along with a lot of patience from Dave, she eventually managed to learn her lines, so to speak, albeit in a kinda parrot fashion.'

Dean: 'Jane was very different from us, kind of a New Age, hippy chick. Her joining seemed quite casual. But the fact that she was female was intentional. She was nice enough, but she didn't really add anything unique.' This was the first time Punter joined the band outside of the studio. 'I just wanted to be with them every step of the way,' he explained.

The two Toronto shows, at 6.30 pm and 9.30 pm, sold well. The first show was three quarters full, and the second sold out in three hours, supported by a rockabilly group called The Bop Cats. Japan entered the stage theatrically, enshrouded by a cumulus of dry ice. The audience was enthusiastic, but also confused. Japan's new sound and evolving image was a turn-off for many of the Canadian fans, whose musical affections were rooted in the more traditional rock of *Adolescent Sex* and *Obscure Alternatives*. The reviews were begrudging too. 'The group plodded through their numbers with plodding precision,' said Jonathan Gross in a local paper, 'Japan is a mirror of these shake and bake times, an exaggeration of this facelessness prevalent in this decade's music.' 'Likely to be faceless and nameless in 15 years,' said another. *The Toronto Star*, while still not seduced, had a slightly more insightful line of critique: 'Japan were only using rock to sell their true artwork – themselves.' The writer surmised that Oscar Wilde would have been a Japan fan, but once again the music was dismissed in favour of Japan's 'punk tuxedo' image. Such reviews mattered little to a group who were growing increasingly sure of themselves.

There was a promotional after-show party arranged for the group at the Domino Club on Isabella Street. Fans queued all night on the street to grab tickets and passes given away by a local hairdressing salon. Japan arrived by limo and were interviewed at the party. Aside from the club owner Michael Glower remembering that 'Sylvian looked like a deer in the proverbial fan's headlights', the group seemed in high spirits. When asked if they would consider playing the much more prestigious local Massey Hall, Sylvian grinned in response, 'We're thinking about it.' He couldn't know that in another life, eight years on, he would be selling out that very same venue.

Incredibly, these were the last shows Japan would play in North America. Huckle: 'They never returned because financially any tour would have needed to be tied in with a headline group. They were offered both Queen and The Police, which would have meant being a support act. This was something that Dave was no longer prepared to endure.'

Chapter 5
1980

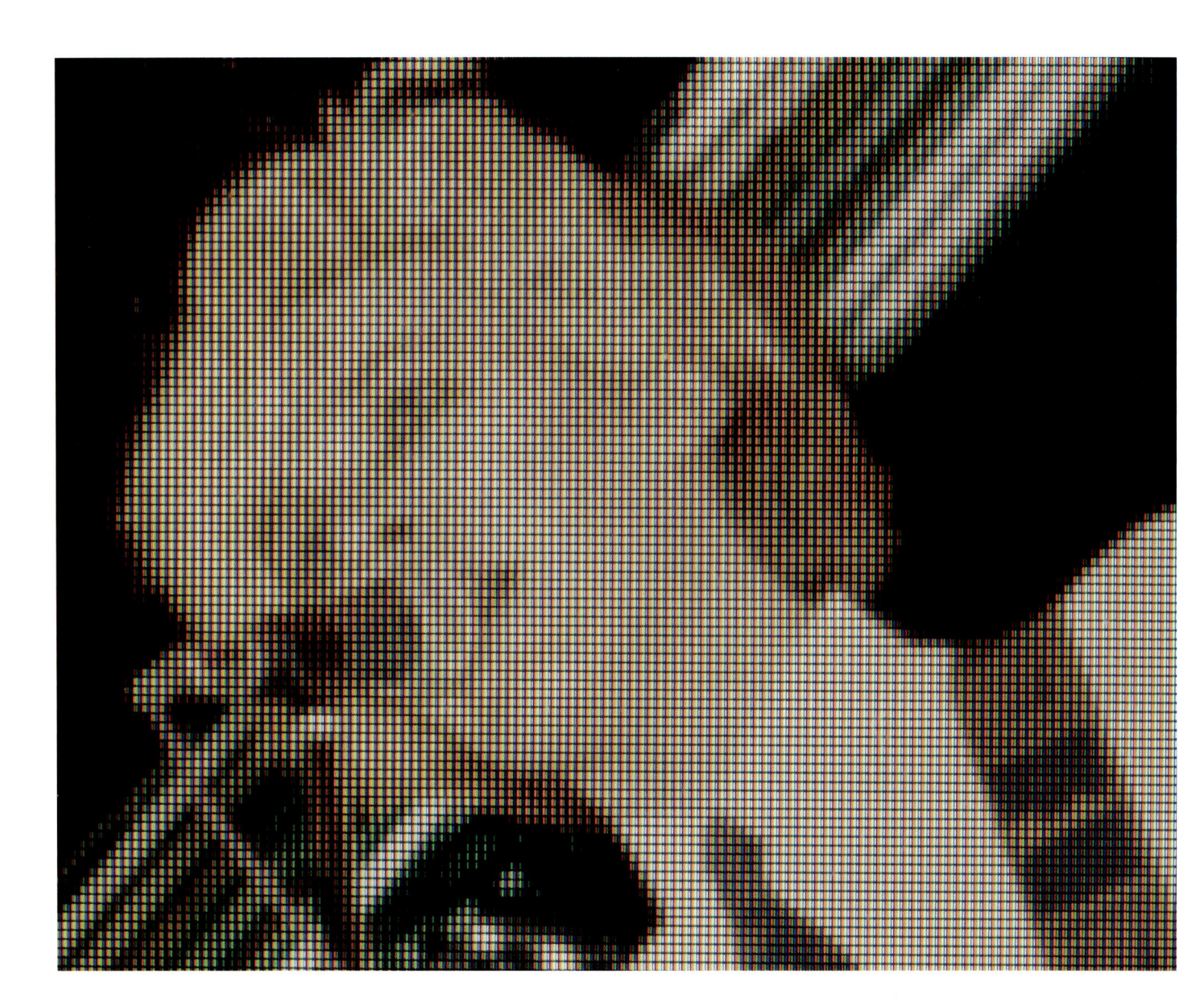

Sylvian
David Sowerby

For Japan, the 1980s had begun with the recording of *Quiet Life* during the autumn of 1979. The rest of the world was merely catching up. Meanwhile, the group were also fleeing their suburban roots, as fast as money and luck would allow. Sylvian was the first to leave, spending the last months of the 1970s in a flat at Wilbraham Place off Sloane Square, lent to him by an absent transatlantic girlfriend. Napier-Bell, perhaps encouraged by the success in Japan, now took full financial responsibility for his investment and this allowed the rest of the group to follow their singer into central London and for Sylvian to rent a flat of his own. The location for all flats (except Dean's, who continued to live at his dad's home in Hackney) was at Stanhope Gardens, an Edwardian square in South Kensington, even then a chic and expensive address. Huckle: 'It was 1980 when they all finally left Lewisham, though Dave had left nine months earlier. Dave was also in Stanhope Gardens a few months before us.' (Jansen: 'I actually lived in Mayfair first with Mick, then Chelsea and back to Mayfair before landing in Stanhope Gardens with Rich.')

None of the band would ever again return to Lewisham for any amount of time. That place was less a home and more a location they happened to grow up in. 'I was never at home in my home town,' Sylvian would explain. 'Maybe that's part of the reason why I [would go on] to experience the world as a hostile place, though much of it was due to my own psychology.' Sylvian was not alone in considering Lewisham to be 'devoid of any redeeming qualities', but it sometimes appeared that he was most affected by it or was at least the most vocal. Deriding the place, he cited in particular the 'village-like mentality of the suburbs that was suffocating. Small-minded, mean-spirited people accompanied by the constant threat of physical danger. But ultimately it wasn't the physical location, but the mindset it tends to breed.' He'd remember leaving the parental home as 'like having a straitjacket removed'. None of Japan would ever 'go home' again.

That January, on the eve of *Quiet Life*'s release, a journalist was allowed a rare audience at Sylvian's 'new apartment'. Or was it? Visiting Sylvian's abode was described as 'taking a trip back in time. Images of Sinatra and Monroe adorn the wall and Bing Crosby looks up from a haze of pipe smoke from an album sleeve on the floor. Elsewhere, Fred Astaire prepares to tap out a Gershwin tune and Lauren Bacall glances invitingly from the cover of French *Vogue*.' Huckle: 'I don't recognise the description of Dave's flat. It sounds a bit like the Wilbraham Place flat, which was mostly filled with its owner's own furnishings. So maybe the journalist is referring to that flat with a few of Dave's belongings mixed in. Or, as was often the case, Connie would dress Richard Chadwick's flat for Dave to use for interviews. Chadwick had a small but modern flat in the Barbican and later a new duplex apartment just off Holland Park Avenue. Hence perhaps the strategically placed albums and pics of Bacall, Crosby et al. A classic case of Connie's smoke and mirrors.'

Further encouraged by his imaginative press officer, Sylvian was encouraged to present a jet-set image that was not quite real, with the singer being described as 'spending most of his time in Manhattan, although still a resident of England'. This was another example of Connie's sometimes desperate attempt to present the group as being something they weren't. The reality was that, physically at least, Japan were resident Londoners through and through, albeit ones who lived in a self-imposed exile wherever they were. The rarefied bubble that Sylvian and, to a lesser extent, the rest of the group strived to live in was seemingly all funded by their manager. 'Early on, all our income was from the record company and SNB's advances,' states Huckle. 'I think they each got £6 a week when Simon first took them on. They were still living with their parents then, but I had already left home and was paying rent from some savings I had. Later, our money went up to £10 a week, then £25, £50 and so on as they got more successful. I think it peaked at £100 a week. Additionally, we had our rent, rates, national insurance stamp, electric, gas and car costs paid as well. So while the cash in hand may have seemed a little meagre, we were living reasonably well considering the undoubtedly large debt that had accumulated, the high cost of running the band and the lack of hits. Remember too, that Japan weren't a band to do things on the cheap. They could have used much cheaper studios, cheaper producers and lived in the suburbs.' The claim that Simon Napier Bell alone continued to fund the band throughout the following years is not a viewpoint shared by members of the band. Huckle's account omits the fact that by now Japan were generating serious income in the territory they shared a name with, and that recording and touring costs were paid for by Hansa and relevant promoters. Barbieri: 'It's worth noting that on our first trip to Japan we played two sold out shows at the Budokan in Tokyo followed by three other big provincial shows. That's close to 40,000 ticket sales. There was also a massive amount of merchandise sold which I'd say generated even more than the tickets.'

The individual members, still barely out of their teens, just went with the flow, feeling lucky not to have to live at home and to be allowed to concentrate on making music full time. However, years later some would question the integrity of

David Sylvian and
Connie Filippello
Nicola Tyson

what was happening at the time. Jansen: 'Things were kicking off while I was still a late teen and although one likes to feel one is in control by that age, many poor judgements were being made, and opportunities lost. To be young and to feel that life is heading very much in the direction you'd intended, one doesn't stop to think about the fact that there's still much of life remaining where that may no longer be the case. Popularity was dismissed as a consequence of making music, which was all the band cared about. There wasn't a business plan. And since making money wasn't our concern, when we finally did, it was then down to the businessmen to do the right thing, which of course they didn't.'

It's important to note than when Japan played a gig – no matter how big or small – none of them received money from ticket sales. The takings were all assimilated into their manager's account. This was standard practice for a professional group, but in time it would rankle. 'There was income from playing large stadiums in Japan and the sale of merchandise,' says Jansen, 'yet very little money in it for us. All the funds went through our management's Hong Kong-registered business address and we were never accounted to nor paid the sums of money one would've anticipated. We were not in control and we were let down – and so the quality of our lives changed very little despite obviously bringing in large amounts of revenue. It defies logic in these more modern times, but we were naive kids breaking out of the repressed 70s, and were concerned only with making music and looking different. Our families were only too pleased to see that we were turning around what was initially a rather worrying indulgence destined to go nowhere, but as things moved forward they took for granted that finances were in hand. Things did move fast, and in retrospect were extremely short-lived in commercial terms, but as friends we had been immersed in the world of making music together since five or six years prior to *Quiet Life*, so from that perspective it felt like quite a substantial commitment by then. Recording a third album and having a budget that afforded us the opportunity to work in a place such as AIR Studios, alongside the likes of Paul McCartney, felt as though we'd travelled very far from those early, dark days of damp rehearsal rooms and total compromise, and yet, despite all that, on a personal level we didn't feel much better off at all. This pretty much continued throughout the life of the band. The paradox of being recognised on the streets yet having no money in our pockets was quite bizarre.'

In their manager's defence, Huckle says: 'It's worth remembering that Richard Chadwick was their de facto bookkeeper, and I regularly saw and discussed some aspects of the books' income and expenditure with him, mainly because I held, and had to account for, the day-to-day cash float. I always felt that Chadwick was absolutely trustworthy in respect of their money, and I'm

Japan at The Venue,
30 January, 1980
David Sowerby

positive he would have said something if he had felt SNB was doing anything untoward.' Beyond the day-to-day vagaries of pocket money and whatever his perceived failings in accounting, Napier-Bell undoubtedly enabled a lifestyle that let the band do the one thing they all wanted to do: make music. After all, it was their manager who had secured their record deal. While Japan were more than adept at making great music and looking great while they did so, it's debatable as to how they would have fared in the business of music alone. And while their manager may have been less than transparent financially, he was at one point their only option. Still, the group were far from well off. Even Sylvian, the sole member of Japan with a publishing contract (via of course, his management's company), received no advances on this deal; this was unusual even in the 70s. It at least meant that for now the group were very much 'all in it together'.

The result of their latest labours was released in the UK on 18 January 1980 (in Japan and Canada it had been released a month earlier at the tail-end of 1979). Reviews in Europe (and of course Japan) were encouraging. Journalists were no longer speaking about Japan's mere potential but the fact that they were now fulfilling it. In Britain the press was less convinced. 'They may seem seamlessly full-ahead European to you,' wrote the *NME* under the pathetic title of 'There's a nasty nip in the air', 'it all sounds slyly studied Roxy Music *Stranded* to us.' Once again UK journalists found it hard to listen to Japan without prejudice, and the fact that Japan's new producer was totally sympathetic to the band was marred utterly by his Roxy Music association. *Quiet Life* made it to number 72 in the UK album chart. Still a major improvement though not a hit by any description.

The group launched the new album with fresh haircuts and sober dress, for Sylvian and Barbieri at least; Karn still rocked a boiler suit like no other bass player before or since. The chosen place was The Venue in Victoria, London on 30 January. The actual location (then owned by Virgin Records, ironically) chosen to present their new look and music was not accidental. Sylvian disliked playing traditional rock venues, and had only done so for as long as he had to. Now Japan were growing in popularity in the UK, their choices were flourishing. They were not big enough to warrant a theatre at this point and Hansa were unwilling to finance such a show but The Venue, with its seated and standing audience, candlelit tables and waitress/cocktail service actually suited the Japan of early 1980 perfectly. Sylvian was certainly more of a cocktail bar person than he was a pub goer and he appreciated his audiences being able to sit down during a performance. Japan were not about dancing, as such.

That night the group sounded enthused by their new material and excited by the new technology that enabled it. Asides from one slightly sour note where Sylvian introduced 'Life In Tokyo' as 'the single that no one saw fit to buy', Japan appeared as happy as they'd ever get on stage. 'They always went down well at The Venue,' confirms Huckle, 'it was one of those rare gigs where everything was in balance.' Karn remembered this gig fondly and as a turning point. 'I remember it suddenly dawning on me on stage, song by song … everyone was applauding, everyone was there for us, and even looked a little like us. The concert communicated something more direct and made up for any journalistic middleman tripe. There's a certain strength to be had from success in one's home town.' There was a begrudgingly objective review in *Melody Maker*: 'The best songs were encouragingly, the newer ones,' stated the critic. "Quiet Life', the new album's title track, is lifted beyond a limp-wristed Bowie tribute by its sharply focused, almost mesmeric, synth patterns which, aligned with the visuals, give way to an eerie fascination.' Japan were still some way off from being unconditionally loved by the weeklies, however. 'The set seemed to go on forever, the absence of variety made irrelevant once the band had locked into continuous motion. It could have been bland, but it was more a pleasantly functional mood music. Even a re-tread of The Velvet Underground's 'All Tomorrow's Parties' sounded unnervingly similar to Sylvian's own songs. And there was the audience, part of the same overlap of home-made camp and beer heads that Roxy Music once attracted, lapping it all up; the same contingent that fall in with the new heavy metal and get called sexually repressed for their trouble. But better sexual ambiguity by proxy than not at all.' Geoff Barton writing for *Sounds* had been a champion for Japan's earlier incarnation, but his enthusiasm, at least for Japan as a live group, was now wearing thin. He described the gig as, 'a curiously inauspicious and purely perfunctory occasion … Japan's LPs are always so rewarding and it's a pity that their gigs so often leave a little to be desired.' The accompanying photos showed off Sylvian's newly reinvented hair to great effect. Even if you hadn't yet heard *Quiet Life*, Japan now looked so different from how they appeared a year ago that they seemed like a brand new band.

A planned three-track single for that January, comprising 'Quiet Life', 'A Foreign Place', and 'European Son' had been dropped in favour of a cover version. Hansa were still not convinced of Japan's commercial appeal. Napier-Bell was under pressure from the head of Hansa to deliver a hit. He therefore told Japan they had to record a cover version of a well-known song. They could choose the song but it had to be a proven hit. 'To my great surprise they agreed,' said Napier-Bell. Still, the fact that Hansa didn't have enough faith in what Japan considered to be their best work hardly helped the relationship. The choice of cover version was unexpected to those who knew little of Japan's background.

'I Second That Emotion' had been a hit for its writer and singer Smokey Robinson when he released it as a member of The Miracles way back in 1967. Such music was part of the staple that Sylvian claimed he had grown up on, but it still seemed like a strange choice for a cover version compared to the more obvious contenders of T. Rex, The Velvet Underground or even Bowie. 'I'm sure David did grow up with Motown, because of his sister,' says Dean, 'but really, he's always been loathe to acknowledge his real influences. In interviews he was reluctant to admit them. Some people don't like to admit being fans.' This was no doubt down to the fact that Sylvian was still looking for his authentic voice and didn't want to be painted by press and peers as merely another Bowie clone, even if in many ways he was now a queerly perfect hybrid of Bowie and Ferry. Other groups were less concerned (The Associates had released an endearingly mangled cover version of 'Boys Keep Swinging' merely months after the original was a hit), but Sylvian was too shrewd and aloof to align himself with idols who were still making important musical statements themselves. To cover Bowie or Ferry et al. would have been seen to be paying homage to or even competing with such figures in some reductive way and Sylvian wanted to distance himself from his obvious influences, not reinforce a detrimental connection that many were making anyway.

In fact, Sylvian was happier to defer to his Ferry influence at this point, albeit obtusely. 'Our sister played to death a very small

Nick Huckle, with Steve Jansen
Keiko Kurata

selection of Motown hits from the 60s,' recalls Jansen. 'I disliked the song 'I Second That Emotion' and could not see the point in a band like ours covering it. I think it was one of SNB's demands upon David for the band to attain a hit, but I wasn't there for that conversation so can't confirm it. In hindsight, it's surprising that David felt compelled to have a go at it, but Ferry had presented a great selection of cover songs during the late 70s and perhaps from this perspective – "if Ferry can do it, it's not uncool" – it was approachable. Thus, to my ears, 'I Second That Emotion' is David's most obvious Ferry-influenced performance.'

Of course Bowie had also released a covers album (*Pin Ups*), but Sylvian was no particular fan of that record. 'I Second That Emotion' would in effect be Ferry's *These Foolish Things* album distilled into one song. Punter, for whatever reason, handed the recording of the single over to his up-and-coming engineer, Nigel Walker. 'I had encountered Japan in the studio while they recorded *Quiet Life,* but didn't know them personally at that point,' recalls Walker, who would go on to work with Sylvian in the mid 1980s. 'However, I had a good working relationship with Punter and had worked as his assistant on many projects and he knew I was ready to start engineering and offered me the chance to engineer 'I Second That Emotion'. Now, I was brought up on a housing estate in West London and it was difficult not to be affected by guys who dyed their hair and wore make-up, even in the recording studio, but when I started to work with them I realised that they were incredibly nice guys, and we began to form a good friendship which lasted for years. I didn't really care what they looked like after that. They were just nice guys.' Huckle: 'Walker was nice too, but a bit odd … he ate only crisps, baked beans and chips as I recall.' Japan's version of Smokey Robinson hardly sounded like the hit Hansa were hoping for. In fact, there were much more commercial contenders on *Quiet Life*. Japan in effect melted 'I Second That Emotion', draining it of all danceable elements, slowing it down to an opium pace over which Sylvian crooned seductively, sounding as if he was waking up while doing so. It was, according to Karn, 'the worst recording we ever made. It does nothing to better the original,

Brian Grogan and Jon Flynn, with Japan flyposters
Martin Grogan

which I love.' A promo video was made at Shepperton and was shown nowhere. The single garnered no airplay. Both Japan and their record company must have wondered at the point of it all.

In the first week of March, with another dead single floating behind them, Japan returned once again to The Venue, this time for a two-nighter. Brian Grogan had been a fan since *Adolescent Sex* and on 4 March 1980, the eve of his 18th birthday, he travelled up from Birmingham to see his favourite band. 'Me and my brother and our friend John got to the venue about 4 o'clock,' he remembers. 'There was no one there, so we tried the door and it was just open! We could hear 'Quiet Life' being played and we thought, "Oh, maybe they're sound-checking," so we snuck down into the venue itself and there they were on stage, but something was odd. The song kept stopping and starting … we quickly realised they weren't actually playing. It was a playback. And this director guy kept saying to David, "Oh, can you do that again?" while these cameramen were doing close-ups of him. At one point the guy said, "Okay, David, now do your dance." But there was no music! There was no playback! David looked so, so embarrassed. The director said, "Just kind of sway side to side and click your fingers, like you're going with the beat." David looked absolutely mortified. But he had a go, kind of swishing to this imaginary soundtrack, while the band behind him just sniggered and laughed. I really felt for him. This went on for two hours and when they finished they went off stage and we were left in the empty venue – me, my brother and these two Dutch girls.'

At this point Japan still had a strong European following that was mainly indebted to the first two albums. As Japan went on to reinvent (or, more accurately, invent) themselves with each successive album, this initial, somewhat innocent following would be lost, replaced by a more mature audience and critical acclaim. With success, Japan would also become far less accessible. But at the beginning of 1980, Japan were still close enough – time-wise at least – to their roots to actually welcome the one-on-one attention of random fans representing home-made foreign fan clubs in their name. Grogan: 'These two girls

Sound check for The Venue/video shoot for *Quiet Life* promo March 1980
Martin Grogan

78

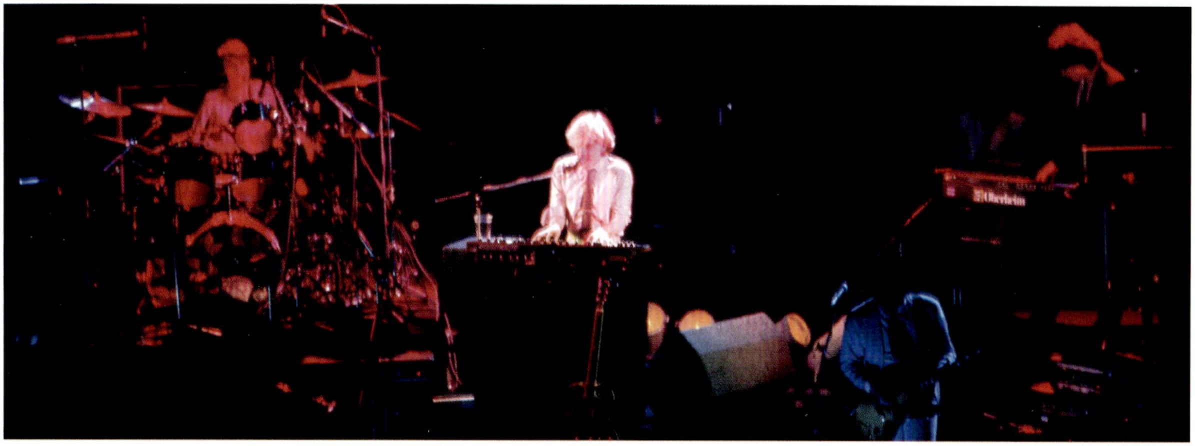
Oberheim
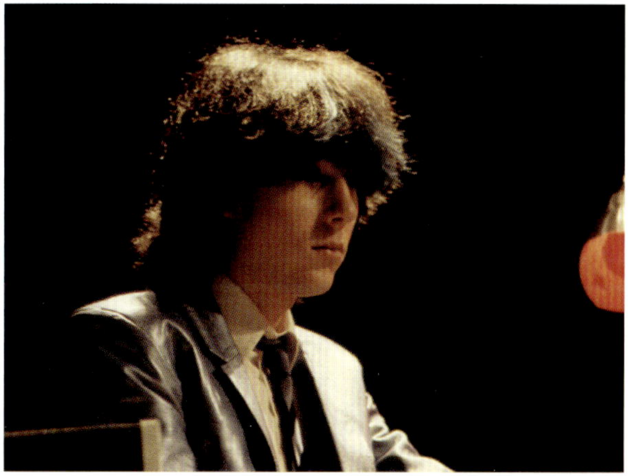
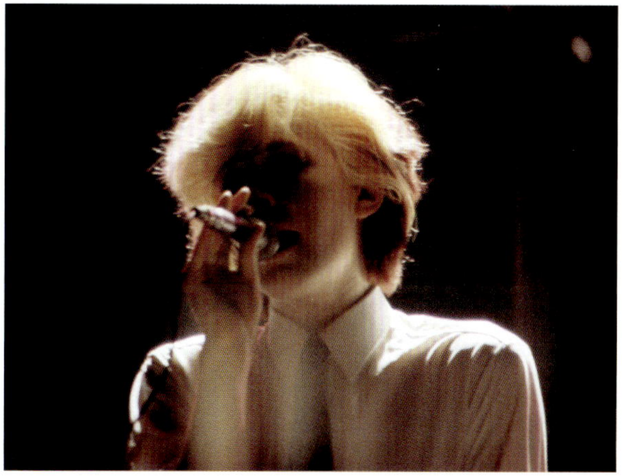
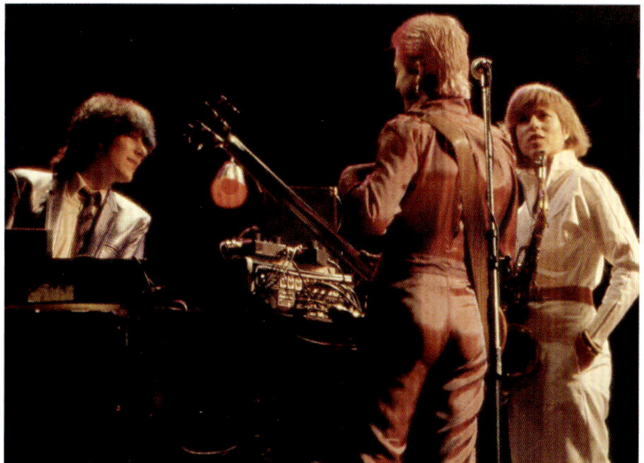
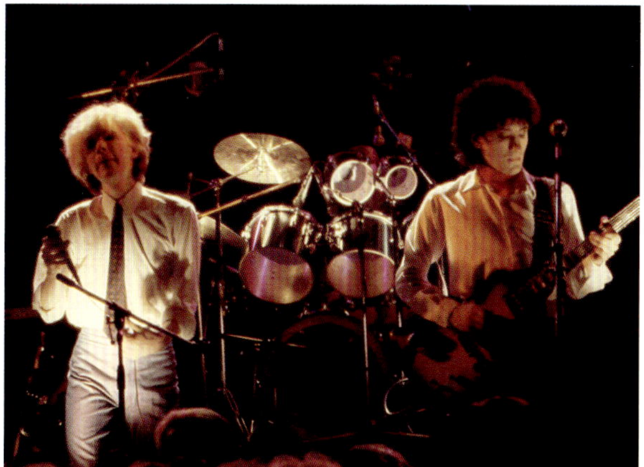

*Performing at
The Venue
March 1980
Jan Kalinski*

were members of the Dutch fan club – in fact they ran it – and had some questionnaires for the band, so we followed them backstage into the dressing room. On the way they told me and my brother that David and Steve were brothers. We were shocked. We had no idea! This was not a commonly known fact! Anyway, we finally knocked on the dressing room door and it opened and there was the band, just chilling out. I was in awe. I just stood there dumb, trying not to pee my pants while the Dutch girls gave them some questionnaires. The band were lovely though, very friendly, and they looked immaculate, just like their photos. David's hair was incredible. I was so in awe of him. He seemed a bit more aloof than the other guys; he was kind of ethereal. The rest of the band were laddish by comparison. We were stood in silence until my brother, who is four years older than me, went up to David and said, "So do you reckon your new album is any good?" I just wanted the earth to swallow me up. But David was good as gold, and said, "I don't think it's too bad, what do you think?" God, I was mortified. But they were lovely and signed our tickets and out we went to Pizza Hut to wait for the gig.'

Japan in concert – and it was now more accurate to describe their live performance as such – were a country mile and then some from the pretty guitar trash spectacle of only a year ago. Sequencers had replaced the guitar nucleus of many of the songs, allowing Sylvian to wander the stage at will, although he was a reticent and reserved performer who stuck for the most part to subtle gestures and insinuation, occasionally offering a fey sway. Angie Usher, who would soon befriend the band, recalls that, 'At

Performing at
The Venue
March 1980
Jan Kalinski

this point he was moving so much like Bryan Ferry that I was embarrassed for him. I still loved them though.' With Punter at the mixing desk and augmented on stage by Jane Shorter's saxophone, the sound was as immaculate as the look. Additionally, the band were in love with their new material and enthused and excited at performing it. 'They were flawless,' says Grogan. 'Just brilliant. The audience were well into it as well. It seemed perfect at the time. The actual sound was incredible.' Punter was so enamoured with the group that he didn't want to let them out of his sight – or hearing. 'I wanted to do their live sound,' he says, 'pretty unusual for a producer, yeah. Of course, I'd done a few Roxy gigs too, but Japan were my first serious venture in that field. It was something that I felt was important for me, working live, with the artist and the audience.'

When the gig ended, the group retreated as always to their dressing rooms where they couldn't avoid the requisite crowd of hangers-on, even if Japan after shows were still a relatively sober affair. Huckle: 'There were lots of regular liggers at the various London gigs and clubs who always somehow managed to show up backstage. Not just at Japan gigs but any of the current bands of the time. Kinda "groupies with dosh" types who like to think they were best friends with everyone. Two members of the then unknown Duran Duran turned up after one of the Venue gigs, but weren't let in. Others were third-rate performers, others higher-end groupies, some just wanted to be in with the in-crowd. Des O'Connor's daughter was part of that group too. Part of my job was to keep them away from the band as much as possible as they were generally considered a bit of a pain. In fact I think word

Japan at The Venue,
1980
Jan Kalinski

Japan at The Venue,
1980
Jan Kalinski

Japan, March 1980
Keiko Kurata

soon got round that there wasn't much point showing up at a Japan gig, because there was no action to be had. Lemmy also seemed to be hanging around backstage at lots of those places too, and it was generally accepted that he did it for free drinks and a chance to benefit from other band's groupies! Nice guy though.' Dean: 'I remember at some party or other, Mick wasn't feeling well and was telling everyone he felt sick. Lemmy very nobly stepped up and offered to put his fingers down Mick's throat to alleviate his misery. I think Mick declined, but Lemmy seemed like a very nice man.'

Quiet Life had again charted in Japan, this time for a total of nine weeks. A respectful appraisal of the group's new more 'serious' music was published in the country's respected *Music* magazine. And yet along with this new respect there would come the beginning of a gradual decline in the pop fervour that had met Japan's earliest incarnation there. There would be a small falling off in both sales and hysteria in Japan for Sylvian and Co from this point on. Not that you would have noticed unless you'd been a witness to the first tour. Pip Robinson was the band's new lighting technician who joined them for the Japanese tour in mid-March. Pip: 'I had just finished a Canadian XTC tour, and tour manager Robbie Wilson with whom I had toured via Bill Nelson's Red Noise recommended me for the Japan in Japan tour. I hit it off with the band and got the gig. My most enduring memory is of just before we landed. Simon said, "Watch this now, when we disembark. You won't believe it." He was right. Getting off the plane, it was insane – all these screaming girls. It was just manic. Unbelievable.' The now familiar UDO security

Japan in Nigata,
March 1980
Keiko Kurata

armed with two-way radios and dressed uniformly in shades and leather jackets were also waiting. 'UDO were a really heavy promoter,' says Jansen, 'very heavy security … too heavy … they're very rough. Basically you don't meet any fans. It's good sometimes though, you need it. You really need it.' Beyond the security, like many others who worked with the band, Pip soon came to realise that the aloof 'look, don't touch' image of the band merely masked a natural shyness and reserve. Robinson: 'The whole band were very friendly and had an amazing sense of fun. They did not seem affected by their fame and didn't seem to take themselves too seriously. David was a hard nut to crack, although always pleasant if not a bit distant. Mick and Steve were easy to get on with and Rob too. Richard was very quiet, a bit shy, but always had a little smile on his face.'

Connie had managed to persuade *Sounds* to cover the Japanese tour. The extensive feature, which would run in the 19 April edition, was a humorous insight into a phenomenon of which few in the UK had any knowledge. 'This is weird,' wrote the freaked-out journalist Lewis, 'sitting here surrounded by 10,000 screaming girls, all aged about 15 or 16 and all of them, in the semi-darkness, looking mouth-wateringly cute with their uniformly black hair and dark eyes. "David-San! Lich! Lob! Meek! Steve!" … the desperate screams, the outstretched arms, the binoculars, the blizzard of paper streamers, are all for David Sylvian, Richard Barbieri, Rob Dean, Mick Karn and Steve Jansen … five tiny figures in the vastness of the Budokan, Tokyo's legendary *Live At...* venue. Nobody in Britain has seen anything like this since the Osmonds'/Rollers' heyday. But here's the really strange thing: the music being played is a

Japan, Osaka,
March 1980
Keiko Kurata

million miles from teenybop. It's haunting, disturbing, frustrated sex, tortured emotions and urban paranoia. A thinking man's band that brings out the screamers? A paradox. But then Japan the band, like Japan the country, is full of contradiction.' Lewis' travelogue again touched on the fact that Japan in person were relatively normal: 'Contrary to their image, the band are not gay, neither are they narcissistic, effete, posey or all the other words that spring to mind. In as much as you can describe anyone with dyed hair and make-up as "ordinary blokes", they are. Except that they are almost frighteningly serious about their music and amazingly self-controlled for a band whose average age is still only 21.' Other insights offered touched upon Sylvian's lack of indulgence in food and drink, 'I rarely saw him drink anything stronger than Perrier water and he rarely ate anything but a piece of plain steak or fish, and usually his diet seemed to consist of small pieces of dry bread,' and that by contrast Karn was enjoying the Nipponese experience more than ever. 'He is the most extrovert, the only one who really wallows in the hysteria which surrounds the band over here, as well as being, according to the rest of the band, a terrible hypochondriac. Mick is wearing a purple shot-silk jumpsuit and white baby-doll shoes, with his hair streaked purple and black and greased back, making him look like some kind of 30s matinée idol gone berserk.'

It was also observed that the band never drank before a show, and that Punter, who ushered the band on stage every night with a spirited, 'Be mega!' achieved an excellent live sound in even the most cavernous venue. 'On many an occasion someone would come up to me after a show,' said Punter himself, who was now routinely made-up each night by Karn,

Japan, Osaka,
March 1980
Keiko Kurata

Japan at The
Budokan, Tokyo,
March 1980
Keiko Kurata

'and say, "Wow, that sounded just like the record," and I was like, "Well, thank you very much, that's just what I hoped to achieve."' 'Punter was great for them,' affirms Pip, 'having a guy like that who was so into them, who cared – it made all the difference.' Japan never would play 'Despair' live but on this tour it opened the show for them via tape before the band themselves collapsed into 'Alien', a clever dynamic strategy that sent the audience's screams into a frothing crescendo.

Much of the show would be spent dodging the gifts and tat flung onto the stage, with Sylvian himself moaning after one missile assault that a streamer had 'hit him in the balls'. Lewis was taken aback by 'the huge, jarring gap between the band's obviously serious musical ambitions and the ridiculously over-the-top, screamy-bopper audience. The pieces just don't seem to fit.' When asked about such hysteria, Sylvian was as philosophical as ever. 'It was much worse last year. I never encourage it,' he explained. 'In fact, if you could read my interviews over here you'd see that I criticise it. But it doesn't worry me too much because at our gigs a lot of kids come through all that and are educated to accept a much higher standard of music. The same kids could go to a Bay City Rollers-type gig and just get lightweight pop, but at least with us they're getting something quite intellectual, musically.' There was hard evidence to prove that not all of the audience were merely there to scream. Among the stuffed toys and candy sent backstage every night, there were also serious musical assessments and critiques. 'Some of the letters we get are critical,' pointed out Barbieri. 'They say, "You played a bum note in the middle of one number," or, "There were two extra bars at the beginning of a certain song." They even write out the notes of the music to show us where we went wrong.' The methods needed to get the band back to their hotel after a show were as fraught and complicated as ever; crew members were employed as decoys, and the car carrying the band made various false twists and turns that would not have appeared out of place in an episode of *Starsky And Hutch*, but it was to little avail. The band and driver inevitably returned to a hotel lobby that was thronged with fans, the majority of whom had also booked into the hotel and were maxing out their room capacity.

The group struggled for normalcy in such situations, attempting to have dinner in restaurants where they were openly lusted after by shoals of adolescent Japanese girls. Lewis reported that the band were aloof to such amorous opportunities, but it wasn't exactly so. Karn, probably the most openly restless and randy of the group, decided one night to follow up on one of the many calls to his room made by a besotted fan. 'I was sick and tired of being treated like a caged animal,' he reasoned, 'and despite the shameless disregard for the rigorous discipline that inhabited our lives, I wanted to be with girls.' Karn thus wandered up towards the room number he had been given via the fire escape. 'I couldn't believe the incredible sight that met my eyes;' he'd recall, 'the staircase was full of sleeping girls.' As he manoeuvred himself through the sleeping throng they began to wake up. On recognising him they erupted into a cacophony of breathless 'MICK!'s. Karn somehow made it to the hotel room where he found, 'Only what I can describe as a harem. There must have been at least 15 girls there.' Karn's carnal desires were squashed however by the strangely muted reception that greeted him there. 'I looked around the room, eagerly expecting them to carry me away, waiting to hear their leader's voice saying, "Please take your pick?" and the unanimous response of "Choose me, choose me!" but instead all I heard was the one question from one or two: "What are you doing here?"' After surveying the scene in awkward silence, Karn eventually left and it was then that the fans' desire erupted, causing the Bacchanalian bassist to call on Robbie Wilson (the tour manager) to bring bodyguards. Once safely back in his room, Karn could only wonder at the psychology behind such behaviour. Was the desire of such fans based on any reality? Or did they only want what they knew they could never have?

In the morning there was more TV. Ironically, in the UK Japan had a hard time getting on television, as their plugger was told by stations that they were 'too visual'. On 14 March the band were interviewed by *Town 5*. Lined up like The Beatles in drag, Japan endured such scintillating questions as, 'Do you have a girlfriend?' and, 'How long does it take to put on your make-up?' Despite such inanities, the band appeared positively joyful, finally having a music they were happy with to mirror their success. On 17 March, a performance of 'Quiet Life' and 'I Second That Emotion' were filmed for the TV show *Let's Go Young* before a seated audience of 4,000. The group appeared confident and still amused by the hysterical reaction with which their increasingly sophisticated music was met. Sylvian's expression was often serene, his made-up features, as Lewis noted, radiating the 'aura of a man totally in charge of his own destiny, a man watching his master plan slowly falling into place', yet within the size eight white jazz shoes, Sylvian was beginning to get itchy feet. 'I'm not really sure what I want from this country,' Sylvian told Lewis. 'Before, I was quite happy to play up to the idea of the teen idol because it was a new experience for me. Now, I'm looking for a way out of that, to lead the kids a stage further because I've moved on.' The song segments that Japan had filmed were due to be aired on the UK's *The Old Grey Whistle Test* if their new single was a hit. In the long run this would prove fortunate as the resultant flop only accelerated their move from a label that no longer knew what to do with them. Meanwhile, Sylvian was more focused than ever. 'I'm not living my life according to someone's idea of how a band should develop. I'm just going through what I feel each moment, each day, and I never plan anything.'

The band travelled to Osaka for the next gig by plane. Travelling by train had become too complicated with fans buying up every other available seat in the carriage. The hysteria did not lessen outside of Tokyo and while for some of the band the experience was still thrilling, for others it was becoming a bore. While abroad, music played a small part in the day-to-day activity of the band. Each gig lasted just over an hour with the rest of the day spent doing interviews and photo shoots interspersed with the occasional business meeting. Meanwhile, the UDO security staff and Japan's crew struggled to keep the band safe, fed and watered. Such a regime must have been frustrating for Sylvian in particular. There was nothing creative about such activities and he admitted that he couldn't 'write on the road', even if he still increasingly pursued solitude when able. Punter: 'David would lock himself away and only come out for the gigs. Mick and I would be cruising the malls being followed by hundreds of fans. But they never got close; there was always a distance, they were respectful. If they got too close you'd turn and go, "Boo!" And they'd all back off. It was hilarious but also quite frightening sometimes.'

Lewis couldn't quite grasp Japan's apparent reticence offstage. Why didn't they ever take advantage of the 'wall-to-wall crumpet' as he himself described it? 'We're all quite introverted,' Sylvian explained patiently. 'As people we're so close that there's no need to talk much. We know what each other is thinking. As personalities we're very stable, so none of this stuff affects us. Besides, if one of us did start taking advantage of it it would bring the rest of us down too much.' Barbieri explained how their personalities bled into the work: 'The *Quiet Life* album, really, is about our lives. We are quiet people. We don't go out much and we're not that much in touch with what's happening.' '[It's] a form of self-expression,' Sylvian continued, 'seeing the things we see, living the life we do and finding a way to express it in music. I see what we do as being closer to a novelist's approach... someone who observes and picks up facts and then writes a story around those facts. That's the way we work and music is only one aspect of what we want to do.'

The tour ended on 29 March in Sapporo. The gig was a near disaster when Dean's pedal board failed four songs in. 'It was a custom-made job,' says Dean, 'and no one had thought to bring another. I just couldn't get it to work and so we tried to improvise with David and Rich doing 'The Other Side Of Life' on piano, but it wasn't happening and we had to call it off.' Karn attempted to explain to the audience what was going on while Japan's crew frantically took it in turns backstage to attempt to fix the malfunctioning piece of kit. Huckle was down about it in particular. 'I always felt responsible for that failure as there was no spare pedal board, not that anyone would have paid for one in any case. They were still very much on a tight budget then.' This incident showed both just how important Dean's sound was to the band and also Sylvian's perfectionism. 'This may portray a bit of an insight into the band's, but particularly Dave's, attitude to delivering their material,' says Huckle. 'Other bands may well have been prepared to "make the best of the situation" and carry on with a less than perfect guitar sound, but Dave always opted to give the audience nothing, rather than an imperfect show. Stark contrast to many of their contemporaries of that time, where the post-punk and new wave of the period was often gladly delivered in a more rough-and-ready style.' The 4,000 strong audience were politely dismayed. 'It was one of the most disastrous gigs ever,' says Dean. Huckle: 'As everyone was so dejected afterwards,

Solid State Survivor by Yellow Magic Orchestra

Simon went out and bought us all Walkmans, then a new and astounding piece of kit which was unavailable in Europe at the time and was even difficult to get hold of in Japan itself, as they were selling faster than Sony could make them.'

Flying home, Karn in particular was deflated at having to return to Britain. 'If only we could stay and work there [in Japan] continuously,' he mused, 'perhaps we'd be able to pay off our debts one day.' On the 36-hour flight back via Hong Kong, where they attended a press conference to celebrate the fact that they'd been voted Best International Band, a lone cassette circulated among the band's brand new Walkmans. *Solid State Survivor* was the latest album by Japanese techno-pop maestros Yellow Magic Orchestra. 'Kraftwerk were already a favourite, but there was something different about this band,' Karn would note, predicting a future friendship between YMO and Japan. '[It] somehow captured the very spirit of Japan. We couldn't believe no one had heard of them abroad.'

Back in London the group were at a loose end. Despite delivering what was undoubtedly their most cohesive, mature and true album so far, Hansa were getting cold feet. While *Quiet Life* had seen a marked improvement in critical reception this was not the Japan that Hansa had signed. There was also the absence of both a hit single and, since *Obscure Alternatives*, an American deal. Hansa did not know what to do with the band and were growing increasingly disillusioned and frustrated. The feeling was mutual. Japan increasingly felt that their record company had no idea of what or with whom they were dealing while the group themselves considered *Quiet Life* as their debut album. Sylvian had not had time to write enough songs for a complete album since finishing *Quiet Life* and it seemed Hansa were in no rush to get Japan back into the studio. So Sylvian mostly retreated to his flat where he listened to his phone ring while the rest of the group practised alone (and in Karn's case pursued sculpture) or socialised as best they could within their narrow social circle. Dean: 'We actually went out all the time. We went to gigs, although not all the same ones. I had my own group of friends and the Japan boys had only each other really, except for Jack Stafford [of X-Ray Spex] and Nick Huckle. They were on nodding terms with Squeeze and The Only Ones because they came from the same area but I don't recall seeing them around much.' The irony was that just as Hansa were giving up on Japan the rest of the world was waking up.

Fin Costello was growing closer to the group and on his way to becoming their official photographer. He now noticed first hand the subtle turning of the tide. 'Like any other young people at that age, the growing-up process is accelerated during those years and as their personalities developed so did their music,' he explained. 'By the time of *Quiet Life* it was obvious to me and indeed many people who had no interest in the image that the music was special. For instance, I was working a lot with Rush and Peter Gabriel during that time and they quite often asked about Japan, especially Mick's playing. Also, Steve's drumming had caught the attention of Neil Peart of Rush. They had come a long way in a few years from the way they were initially marketed as a teen glam band.'

The charts too were looking potentially welcoming. When Japan returned from their Far East tour, the UK singles chart was dotted with sympathetic artists: Peter Gabriel, Martha & The Muffins, Siouxsie & The Banshees, John Foxx, Blondie, and also, at a stretch, if you were feeling perverse, The Vapors' 'Turning Japanese'. Hansa did not have the foresight to see the clues in such chart contenders; they were blind to the validity of such a 'new wave', ideally preferring Japan instead to emulate the other acts that made up the chart that April: Abba, Dollar, Jon and Vangelis.

While the weekly UK music press could still be openly hostile, Connie had scored major kudos in getting the group space in *Vogue* and *The Sunday Times Magazine*. Napier-Bell remembers that the *Sunday Times* coup was Connie's desperate attempt to keep her job. She had apparently proved herself useless as a mere secretary and he was on the verge of sacking her when she begged to be given a chance at PR. Armed with glossy photos of Japan, she made her way to the *Sunday Times* offices where, according to Napier-Bell, in front of the paper's music critic, Derek Jewell, she 'undid the zip of her silver tracksuit, threw the folder of photographs to the floor and lay down next to them. She squirmed amongst the pictures, spreading them around her on the carpet making a collage of sensuality – silver tracksuit, photos, boobs, more photos, blonde hair, yet more photos, Connie's pouting lips – all converging into one image.'

Japan got their five-page spread and Connie kept her job. Derek Jewell was a respected old school journalist and an acquaintance of Sinatra. His major piece on Japan in *The Sunday Times Magazine* in the spring of 1980 was proof of a serious critical shift for the band. Jewell introduced Japan as, 'One of our most talented and unfairly neglected young groups,' and he had the foresight to treat Sylvian as a serious songwriter. 'They have been abused, mocked and under-regarded in Britain,' Jewell wrote, 'the way they look is nothing to do with their music … they are the most original sound to emerge in rock in the last two or three years.' This was a staggering breakthrough for the band, affirming in serious print how the band surely felt about themselves. But Jewell went even further: 'I was reminded of the effect which Paul McCartney and John Lennon had when I first interviewed them in the early 1960s. Japan have that calm, almost magisterial, assurance.' The fact that such a piece made its way into homes that would never have deigned to buy music papers of any sort was paramount. It meant that for once Japan were not victims of the fripperies of superficially hip young journalists whose agenda came before any serious musical consideration. Jewell, in contrast, approached Japan as bona fide contenders. Thus, Sylvian got to mention songwriting influences that had been overlooked by most: Bing Crosby, Cole Porter, Frank Sinatra. Such influences set Japan further apart from their perceived contemporaries and would perhaps appeal to older listeners, like Jewell himself.

In fact, like many UK households in the 1950s and 1960s, Sinatra had been a benign presence in the Batt household when Steve and David were growing up. Jansen: 'I've always loved Sinatra, as both an actor and singer. I so enjoyed *High Society* that I bought the soundtrack on vinyl when I was in my teens. I had *Sinatra Sings Cole Porter* as a backdrop to many a journey in my car all throughout the 80s. That and Bob Dylan.' A photo of Sylvian taken by Lord Lichfield for the piece was even subtitled 'Sylvian: The Face Of Monroe, The Body Of Sinatra'. This was a period when Japan were briefly photographed by high society photographers. Another session with David Bailey soon followed. Huckle: 'I wasn't at the Lichfield shoot. I sat in on Bailey's. As I remember it, he was very quick and professional. I don't think the session took much more than an hour or so. It was at his place in North London somewhere. I was hoping

Marie Helvin would make an appearance, but alas not. Don't remember there being any particular bonding between him and the boys. He was very much in control and directed the shoot with little or no input from them, in contrast to a Fin Costello session, which could take all day and involve Dave and Fin discussing and planning what the end result should look like. Perhaps Bailey wasn't interested by his subjects.' At this time, legendary photographer Angus McBean was also approached via a phone call from Connie, but he declined to take a portrait of Sylvian. With the pivotal *Sunday Times* piece, Connie had come up trumps and the mood at Nomis was high. Delicia Burnell, whose mother worked for Richard Chadwick, was now a full-time member of the Nomis staff. Delicia: 'I was working with Nomis by now. It was like a family. Japan were like a family. Nomis were really behind their artists and they were intimate with them. And that went across the board. The commitment from Nomis was total. That said, Simon came from a very different era. He was of different stock. But he understood the market and was propelled by that. He was professional. Richard Chadwick worked more one on one and Simon handled the bigger picture, broadly speaking. They complemented one another. And Connie was just always there. It was a family affair.'

Sylvian, March 1980
Keiko Kurata

Connie's next move would not be so well judged or received, at least by Sylvian. In May of 1980 she circulated a press release that proclaimed Sylvian had been voted 'the world's most beautiful man'. Such an accolade would eventually become a curse for the songwriter and one that would haunt him for the rest of his life. The title had no basis in truth, although Sylvian was undoubtedly extremely photogenic. He had been voted 'Mr Valentine' in various Japanese pop polls and 'Het of the Year' in a San Francisco gay paper, but then so had many other pop stars and celebrities. The title was a fabrication designed by Connie to get space in *The Sun* and *Cosmopolitan* and their ilk. 'She played the magazines against one another,' said Karn, 'telling each that the other had voted Dave top of their fictitious poll. To *The Sun* it was the *Daily Star* that had voted; to the *Daily Star* it was *The Sun* and so on.' The problem was many people believed such hype and just at a time when Japan were beginning to be taken seriously for their music, rather than their looks. *The Sun* ran an oddly unflattering picture of Sylvian with the dubious quote, 'I like to look good. But I'm not a homosexual. I much prefer sex with girls.'

All this came at a time when Japan were on the brink of making the exquisite sophistication and AOR of *Gentlemen Take Polaroids*. Such press may have made sense two years earlier but at this point it seemed crass and misjudged. Sylvian would later say that having such a title was 'like having a note pinned to your back saying "kick me"'. 'Connie seemed perfectly happy to make anything up to get a story,' says Huckle. 'I remember she once arranged for me – yes, me – to do an interview with a *Sun* reporter about younger men who prefer older women. Apparently she owed the reporter a favour and so said she'd find a suitable guy for the article. Despite my protestations at having little or no experience of older women, Connie said, "Just make it up – they don't care as long as it's outrageous and they can attribute it to a real person," so that was pretty much a modus operandi in those early days. But I think she got less that way as the band became more famous.' Karn: 'Columnists fell for her flirtatious ways and she used the same writers repeatedly, safe in the knowledge she had them hooked and could ask for countless favours, while they felt flattered with egos inflated from so much personal attention.' Huckle, ever the voice of reason, explained, 'It's the case with bands, I suppose, that when they're starting they need a PR person to do whatever they can to get them any press space. Hence it's the more exaggerated or sensational stuff that works. Later, as they become famous, the role of the PR person changes to actually stopping stories, true or false or rumoured, getting to the press – a 180° change of emphasis of the role. Unfortunately, that earlier somewhat dubious stuff sticks.' Napier-Bell remembers Sylvian being 'furious' at such a stunt and demanding that Connie be sacked immediately. Huckle recalls a more measured reaction. 'I think initially when the "Most Beautiful Man" thing happened Dave was a bit chuffed,' he says, 'not realising that it would run and run and run. Having learnt a lesson though he thereafter liked to approve, or otherwise, any press releases, whether from Connie or Virgin.' The rest of the band were indifferent. 'No, I didn't worry about it,' says Jansen. 'It was just the way the PRs worked, the way it will always happen. Dave didn't agree with the ways he'd be promoted, but then it worked, it helped. It's what the PR wanted and that's what they got.' The quote would run forever, still being mentioned 30 and 40 years on, freezing Sylvian's public image in superficial aspic bestowed upon him as a beautiful 22 year old.

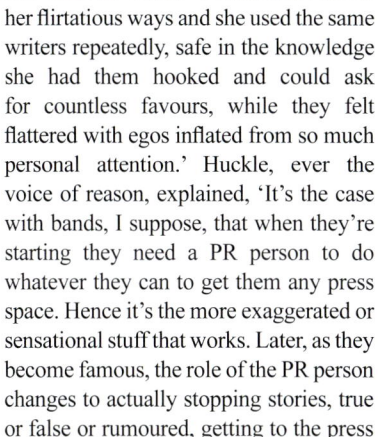

Chapter 6
1980 2

Sylvian, Dean, The Venue March 1980. Sylvian plays Dean's Gibson Firebird
Jan Kalinski

Simon Draper

By the spring of 1980, the tension between Japan and Hansa was coming to a head. Incredibly, there were now no plans for a single to be released from *Quiet Life*, although a wonderful live EP recorded at the Budokan surfaced in Japan and on import. It was also sadly telling that the label had even sent out free copies of the album to select hairdressing salons in London as a misguided promo stunt. Sylvian: 'Ariola never really understood what we were trying to do; they only ever saw Japan as a saleable product because of its image.' Luckily, a much more suitable label was waiting in the wings.

Virgin was a unique, youthful and energetic organisation that was perceived as being as fresh and hip as Ariola Hansa were passé and naff. The move from label to label would be far from smooth however. Napier-Bell: 'Peter Meisel [head of Hansa] told me they were no longer interested in continuing with Japan and would drop them. I went and talked to Simon Draper at Virgin, and he was very interested. Virgin at that time were on the verge of going bust. Draper made moves to sign Japan, and then Trudi Meisel, Peter's wife, and co-owner of Hansa, said Peter had had no right to say the company would drop them, and took legal action against us and Virgin. I had to find the money for a top-level court case and pay barristers etc. The group hadn't a penny. The barrister found precedent for word of mouth termination of contract and Hansa caved in.' Sylvian: 'We knew that unless we settled out of court, the name we'd built up would be lost and there'd be no point in coming back. So we had to settle with them [Hansa] and give them a lot of money, which got rid of the advance from Virgin.'

Most of the band, however, not being particularly business-minded and on a Napier-Bell funded wage of £11 per week, were unaware of the legal details and difficulties in any depth. Still on a high from the creative peak of their latest album and buoyed by massive success in the country of Japan, the mood among the band during the spring and summer of 1980 was high. Barbieri: 'The period between Hansa and Virgin didn't feel fractious. We were quite confident and it didn't seem long before Virgin took us on.' Dean adds that, 'The transition from Hansa to Virgin was not really tense at all. I believe we all thought that at last here was a label that understood more than just the commercial route. After all, on Hansa we were stablemates with Boney M and Amii Stewart. When we signed to Virgin, we were label mates with Magazine, XTC and Simple Minds. By this point there was a more positive idea as to where the band was headed artistically and, as I said, a lot of our favourite musicians and bands of the time were on Virgin, so it felt right. And as a band we felt quite confident, bolstered by finally getting some recognition in the UK.'

Simon Draper was then Richard Branson's number two at Virgin and had been aware of both Japan's progress and their disintegrating relationship with Hansa. 'The 70s were very different compared to the 80s for Virgin,' he says. 'I saw myself as a fan who had the extraordinary luck of also being someone who was able to sign the artists he liked. And that's what happened with Japan. I had actually met Japan pre-Hansa. Simon contacted Steve Lewis who was then A&R at Virgin and the two of us went down to see Japan at a rehearsal room. We thought long and hard about them because they looked really good – really glam – but the music was almost funky – Stevie Wonderish. It was rather like when I first saw Steve Winwood. You saw this young white guy with a big voice – very striking, but, for whatever reason, we passed. I still kept an eye on Japan, then years later Simon came to see me. Their relationship with Hansa was at an end, they weren't selling any records in England. We didn't need to hear demos, it just felt right. David was obviously the leader of the group. Personally he was quite diffident in his manner. And when he wasn't on stage he was more ordinary looking. He didn't come into the office fully glammed-up. He was no Boy George. But he was very strong in his opinions. And we never tried to influence our artists' images. The Human League for instance and the cover of *Dare* – that was completely their idea. You would sometimes get a group who had no ideas, but that wasn't the case with Japan. They had a very strong sense of their own identity. Anyway, I was laughed at when I said I wanted Virgin to sign Japan. No one took me seriously.

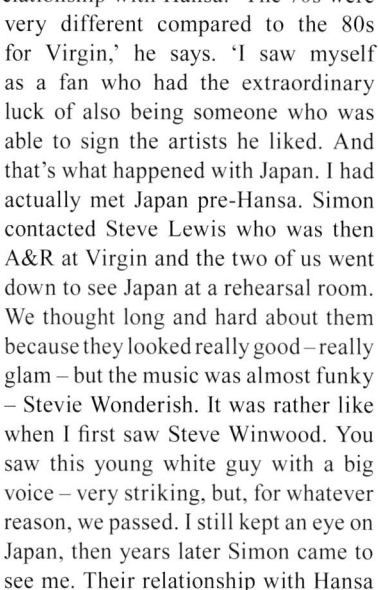

Keith Bourton was the then in-house press man for Virgin. Draper: 'Keith took their three albums home with him on the weekend, smoked a spliff and had an epiphany. When he came in on Monday, he said to me: "I get it. They're brilliant."'
'That's not exactly true,' explains Bourton, 'I was head of press at Virgin and I got on very well with Draper. My office was in the mews opposite the main offices in Vernon Yard. Simon would drop by at the end of the day and we'd talk about music in general; he appreciated my opinion. I remember him coming to me and telling me about the possibility of Virgin signing two acts – Adam & The Ants or Japan. Well, I had no opinion of Adam, but I did tell him Japan were interesting and I already had their albums at home. So we agreed I'd go home that weekend, play the albums and give him my verdict on Monday. So I played them – they'd been in my collection for a while, but I'd never listened to them – and I was completely blown away by *Quiet Life*. I just thought it was a fantastic album. I played it all weekend – couldn't stop playing it and in fact I play it to this day. So yes, on Monday I came in and told him they were great. And yes, I did smoke a spliff or two that weekend while listening to them.' Draper: 'I was interested in my staff's opinion but, at the end of the day, I was lucky enough to be able to do what I wanted, so I did. And in Japan's case the company came round to my way of thinking.'

The convoluted process of extracting Japan from Hansa was soon accomplished with much of the band unaware of the specifics. Stephen Navin, Virgin's lawyer: 'It was a regular deal, as I recall. Not particularly large, but not small either. I dealt directly with Simon and his lawyers; I never had any contact with the band. I know there was some bother with Hansa, but I believe their manager dealt with that, not us, and we paid any advance to him not the group.' Dean: 'We never saw any personal advance. We were just on our regular wage every week. We wouldn't splurge on new equipment when we signed a deal as such. If we ever wanted something at any point, we'd just ask and get it from Simon. Actually, around then I did get a new guitar, a Gibson RD Artist – the first guitar to have active electronics. A really heavy guitar.'

Although Virgin had a much more intimate and homely set-up than many labels, and Japan were pleased to be signing to a label with a cooler roster, there was no specific reaction from the other Virgin bands that frequented the label's offices. 'I don't think there was any particular opinion on us signing Japan and certainly not from the other bands on the label,' says Bourton. 'They were too into their own careers to care. People were more surprised when we signed Gillan actually. We did inherit a Sylvian stalker, too. Connie had warned us about her but we had our own kind of security at Vernon Yard where I, and some of the other boys, would gently persuade those sorts to leave. Maybe it was a mistake not to sign Adam & The Ants, but Japan were a much more "Virgin group" anyway. By that, I mean they had a certain integrity, even though they hadn't been successful. They were different … experimental. As soon as Draper signed them, I would have been given their management's number and arranged to go over and meet them. I met 'em first along with Simon NB and their glamorous PR, Connie at Nomis. I liked the group instantly, but I wasn't sure about Simon and Connie! Actually I ended up quite liking Simon. He was just old school, but Connie ... she struck me as a little rich girl playing at being a PR. She didn't understand rock PR at all. Her idea of making Japan successful was to have Sylvian on the cover of the *Daily Mail* with the headline 'Most Beautiful Man In The World', or whatever.' In some ways Japan were outgrowing Connie. Delicia: 'Marketing was different then, but maybe it was changing too, and Connie was part of what you might say was the 'old guard' of PR. That said she went on to be very successful and still is. She still had integrity.'

The effect that Virgin would have on Japan's career was profound. Finally, here was a label with a progressive mindset, which had signed Japan for what they were and what they could be. Unlike Hansa, they did not want Japan to conform to the latest chart trend. Draper was happy to let them define a trend. This would result in some clashes between the Virgin

Gibson RD Artist

staff and the Nomis stalwarts. Bourton: 'My approach was the exact opposite of Connie's. I wanted to present them as a fascinating, innovative British band and, of course, me and Connie working together, just didn't work. All I knew is that *I* was doing their PR. I didn't particularly get on with Connie – she wasn't my kind of person and I wasn't hers. We had very little in common. I thought her approach with the band was wrong and I discussed this with them. I had a definite strategy and plan, which I shared with the band and they agreed with, so after that Connie took a backseat and I dealt directly with the band. From my point of view, it felt like she kind of just faded out of the picture after six months.'

Despite having released an album only a few months earlier, it felt like Japan had to make up for lost time. Hansa had released no singles from *Quiet Life* and there had been no UK tour to promote it. Virgin were keen to forge a relationship with the band and to capitalise on the growing interest in them. The staff at Virgin were closer to Japan in age and attitude than the staff at Hansa were and they were encouraged to meet one on one with the group. Bourton: 'The very first time Japan came into the Virgin offices, there was an unusually high proliferation of female staff in the reception area for no apparent reason! We'd joke about it. I remember Simon Draper laughing and saying, "Funny how there's so many women in reception when Japan come in, isn't it?"' Huckle: 'I do remember that one of the girl singers from The Human League had a real thing for Dave. She let Virgin know she really fancied him and may even have written a letter to him, which was passed on. I think she came to one of the later shows. Dave showed no interest at all though.' 'He was the prettiest boy I'd ever seen,' Susan Ann Sulley would sigh years later, her love forever unrequited.

Beyond such distractions there was work to be done. Having signed officially to Virgin in August, the band now began rehearsing new material in earnest in order to enter the studio as soon as possible. There was a new approach to proceedings. Dean: 'From *Quiet Life* onward, and on *Polaroids* in particular, Dave's songs were usually played to us as a rudimentary keyboard idea. David would work on a few songs together with Rich at home and then present them to us in rehearsal where we would flesh them out. I seem to recall that we worked fairly solidly on the title track [of *Gentlemen Take Polaroids*] before the recordings at AIR began, more so than the rest.' In its earliest incarnation, 'Gentlemen Take Polaroids' was considerably slower with different lyrics from the recorded version. Sylvian's songwriting – much of it now done at the keyboard rather than guitar, as Dean notes – was evolving and refining. The success abroad and the marked improvement in critical and commercial reception to *Quiet Life* had allowed time for the band's confidence to set like the self-hardening clay Karn was using for his sculptures. Sylvian was now often writing in a classical ballad style that at times verged on the commercial; songs that comprised a traditional intro, verse, bridge, chorus, middle eight, coda. The key to what made Japan unique was that the whole form was then inverted and reborn as something new by Barbieri and the rhythm section.

Tapes of these rehearsals (which were recorded in excellent quality by Huckle on to a four-track recorder hooked up to the mixing desk) reveal that, unlike his band members, Sylvian was still struggling to find his singing voice. Two unreleased tracks exemplify this perfectly. 'Angel in Furs' swoons and sways like a sexy out-take from Roxy's *Stranded*, built upon a melting rhythm section similar to the (as yet unreleased) 'Girls On Film' by Duran Duran. Karn and Jansen seem to delight in punching holes in the traditional structure of the song, while Barbieri's oddly organic timbres provide paths between passages. Dean's EBowed guitar lines, which in places pre-empt the vocal melody of the as yet unwritten 'My New Career', are assured and almost symphonic. The song itself is as good as anything the band had come up with, yet Sylvian's voice is still desperately marred by his Bowie and Ferry schooling. 'Some Kind Of Fool,' complete with the chorus sung wholly in French again (surely a nod to Roxy's 'A Song For Europe') suffers the same deficit. Japan have a fine song elevated by an innovative arrangement with lyrics that are wistful, poetic and touching ('If I say I do/Does that make me/Some kind of fool'), yet the mannered vocals make it hard to take seriously as a whole. 'I agree with the theory that while we were really starting to find ourselves as players, Dave was still struggling to find his voice,' says Barbieri. 'Not as a writer. As a writer he was coming along, but the vocals were still too indebted to our influences. In that regard, at this point, Dave was still a little behind us and the material.'

By the time the next album was actually recorded, Sylvian had found a truer voice so, in theory, both songs could have easily made it onto the finished work, but they didn't. 'I'm not sure why they didn't make it,' says Barbieri. 'They sound like very much of the album, but you just reach a point with a song and you say, "Nah, it's not gonna make it." Perhaps it was contextual and didn't fit onto the album as a whole.' 'I think Dave thought 'Fool' was too close to 'Quiet Life',' reckons

Punter, Barbieri, Karn, Sylvian, AIR Studios
Steve Jansen

Dean. Punter: 'In the studio, David would have toned down any Ferryisms, although I may once in a blue moon pull him up on it. But as far as songs not making it, the band would sometimes say, "Nah, that's not for us," and so David would probably think, "Okay, I'll keep that for myself at some point."'

With a set of songs decided upon, Japan were hurried into AIR Studios once more. Barbieri: 'Of course, we'd recorded *Quiet Life* there and it had been a great experience for us and though it didn't do that well commercially at the time, it had totally transformed the sound and musical approach of the band. I think we had our happiest times during the *Quiet Life* album and we wanted to carry that through with *Gentlemen Take Polaroids*.' Dean: 'I think with *Polaroids* we were hoping to replicate the hugely enjoyable recording experience which was *Quiet Life* by using the same team, but in this regard it didn't work. Ultimately I think *Polaroids* would turn out to be a rather cold, albeit more sophisticated, album in comparison.' Punter, (assisted by the future Mrs Elton John, Renate Blauel) was of course back on board for *Polaroids*. 'The atmosphere in the studio for *GTP* was certainly different from that during *Quiet Life*,' he recalls. 'There were some tense moments, but we still had fun getting the job done.' The album was both an improvement and an extension of *Quiet Life,* with much more attention to detail, texture and depth. The finger clicks on 'Swing' in themselves are a unique delight. Barbieri: 'About four or five of us made this finger click overdub as one take. It was definitely David, Steve and John Punter. I guess a good microphone, well positioned, and the right combination of clicks did the job. John was always keen to add "percussive extras" like finger snaps, hand claps, tambourine etc.'

The album would take two months to complete from start to finish – a comparatively rapid process for such a complex and heavily textured piece of work. With the exception of 'My New Career' and the Sakamoto-assisted 'Taking Islands In Africa', most of the songs were already fully worked out prior to recording. 'All song arrangements were finalised before we started recording,' confirms Punter, 'and the first thing I'd record was Rich's sequencer. The rest of the band would play along to that. Multiple takes would be recorded of each instrument: bassline, saxophone, drums, etc. and the master would be edited from different takes. Additional parts were overdubbed and the vocals done last.' At the time, the likes of Peter Gabriel and Kate Bush were just discovering the joys of sampling, employing the hugely expensive Fairlight CMI to interesting effect on their own albums, but Japan did not follow in this regard. Barbieri: 'We had a lot of gear at our disposal if we wanted – if only on hire – but really I'd say we worked best when there were limitations. [*Tin Drum*, for instance, would feature just three synths and for the most part just two.] Less is often more. We were already experimenting with voice and instrument samples in a way, usually with a cassette machine running through or triggered by the synthesisers. This was about £20,000 cheaper than a Fairlight.'

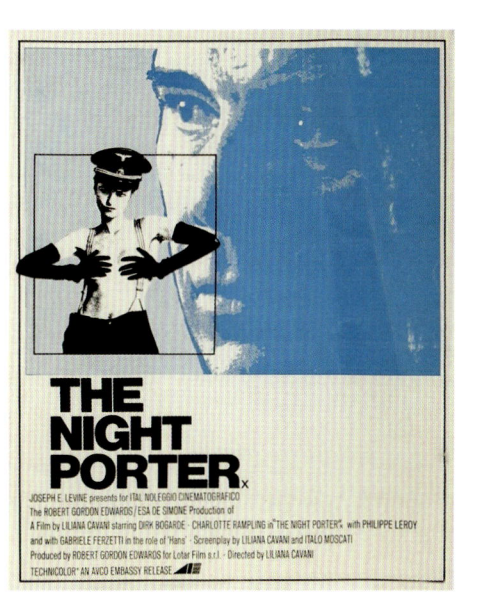

Poster for *The Night Porter*, directed by Liliana Cavani, starring Dirk Bogarde and Charlotte Rampling, 1974

As the album took shape it was obvious that Japan still wore their influences on their sleeve, but were all the more beguiling because of it. 'Burning Bridges' was the cousin of Bowie's 'Neuköln' with added crooning on top. Inspired by the atmosphere of John Hershey's *Hiroshima* book that Steve had loaned to his brother, it would replace the much more traditional sounding 'Some Kind Of Fool', to the chagrin of some. Napier-Bell: 'Usually, if anyone came into the studio and said what Japan were recording sounded like a hit,

David immediately stopped working on it. He was afraid of producing anything that sounded crassly commercial. So we all had to learn – if something sounded like a hit, for God's sake say nothing, or perhaps tell him it sounded a bit "obscure" or "difficult", then he'd go with it.' 'Nightporter' sounded almost out of place on the album, being almost completely acoustic and an obvious reference to the classic songwriters Sylvian had mentioned to Derek Jewell. The title was lifted from a Liliana Cavani film starring Dirk Bogarde (*The Night Porter*, 1974). Like Sinatra, Bogarde was a profound if subtle figure in the Batt universe. 'I think it was *The Servant* which brought him to my attention,' says Jansen. 'I later read his autobiographies and respected his stance on the popular film industry of Hollywood and how he turned his back on all of it to live a secluded existence in the south of France, making European art movies. He was an intriguing character and I felt he would have been a nice presence to be around; whether chatting about nonsense or just sitting in silence, you'd get the sense there was the promise of some insightful knowledge to be imparted. He was humble about himself, whilst paradoxically being quite arrogant towards the fools he'd have to suffer in this world. I liked that. He felt many people were better than him, but he knew where to draw the line. He had standards.' Sylvian openly admired Dirk Bogarde's later work (the art-house explorations of *Providence* and *Despair*, in particular) and has acknowledged that the atmosphere of both 'Despair' and 'Nightporter' were based on the Bogarde films of the same name, although musically 'Nightporter' was obviously a homage to Erik Satie's *Gymnopédies*. As with 'Burning Bridges' and its compositional sampling of Bowie's 'Neuköln', Sylvian once again took an instrumental idea and added lyrics and melody to great effect. Sylvian was open about such influences: 'I was influenced an awful lot by Satie,' he'd admit, 'but I'd milked him dry after 'Nightporter.' People like Satie and Warhol influenced me a lot, but I don't really like their art that much, just the ideas behind it. I adopt their ideas and apply it to my work.' Unusually, both Sylvian and Barbieri would tackle the simple piano part to 'Nightporter' in tandem. 'I think it was just a case of one of us playing the chordal and bass parts and the other playing the top lines,' says Barbieri. 'We may have recorded that together as one take. There was always a rush for the piano and often two people were playing at once.' Barry Guy was a session musician who contributed string bass to the track: 'I remember nothing about the session,' he claims, 'other than they had great barnets.'

After three albums, Sylvian was gaining in confidence not only as a vocalist and songwriter, but also as an arranger and producer. By 1980 he had very definite ideas about how Japan should be presented, visually and sonically. At the very least he knew unequivocally how he didn't want Japan to sound. He publicly denounced their first two albums as embarrassing 'mistakes' and his new-found focus would begin to alienate him from his band-mates. It was no coincidence that one of the newest songs, written in the studio, was entitled 'My New Career'. By now, for Sylvian at least, the work overshadowed everything, including friendships. Dean was not explicitly told that he wasn't much wanted on the album, he just wasn't contacted at all for the most part. 'Weeks went by without him at AIR,' remembers Karn. 'At every opportunity for guitar, someone would raise the question, "Shall we call Rob and tell him to come in?" only to be asked not to, not yet. Rob had, in effect, been banned from the sessions.' As for the rest of the band, while their contributions were more vital than ever ('I reckon we've got the best rhythm section in Britain,' stated Sylvian), there was still friction between the old school friends. 'Disputes followed between Dave and me,' Karn would remember. 'The saxophone arrangements took days to record, with only Dave hearing anything wrong with each layered take. In one instance, [assistant engineer] Colin Fairley sat patiently in the engineer's chair recording one word from 'Methods of Dance' over and over again for three consecutive days.' Sylvian admitted this neurotic obsessiveness in himself and also its detrimental effect. 'I tend to be too much of a perfectionist. I want everything to be that much in tune and, you know, I find that limiting in my music. I've never really been that strict about what they should and shouldn't play. It caused a lot of problems in the studio, not just with the band, but with the producer. I was getting involved in the production side of it as well.'

As usual, once the basis of the track was almost complete, vocals were the last 'instrument' (as Sylvian himself would describe his voice) to be recorded. 'A typical vocal session would generally involve just Dave and me working on a performance,' states Punter. 'Nothing really special beyond dimming the lights was done in terms of creating an ambiance; we just got on and did it.' Sylvian was also keen to bring in outside musicians, perhaps in part inspired by an admiration for Talking Heads, whom he had recently caught live in a small club in Tokyo where they played with an expanded line-up. Dean: 'We were blown away by that show. We were all mightily impressed, David included.' Bowie violinist for hire, Simon House, was duly sought out. Endearingly, Sylvian had attempted to teach himself violin that summer, but soon abandoned the instrument. Huckle: 'I had trouble tracking down Simon House to do a violin part – Dave had heard him on *Lodger* and Mick knew his work from Hawkwind [he had been big on Moorcock and Hawkwind in his post-school days] – but we got him in the end.' House himself recalls nothing of the sessions. 'I find that more and more interesting, actually, to work with other people,' Sylvian commented, 'it was really nice to get outside people working with us and to get their reaction to what we were doing.' The irony of this must surely not have been lost upon Dean who, nevertheless, according to Karn, 'never complained about anything'. Not that Sylvian would have heard anyway. 'I isolate myself from everyone in the studio,' he claimed, intensifying the image of himself as the solitary, maverick purist of the group.

The most important guest on the album was Ryuichi Sakamoto. That summer, Sylvian was formally introduced to the key player of Japanese techno-pop pioneers, Yellow Magic Orchestra, who was recording his solo album *B-2 Unit* in an adjoining studio. *Music Life* magazine brought Sylvian and Sakamoto together for a joint conversation to be published in yet another Japan-saturated edition. This was the beginning of a lifetime friendship between the two. Sylvian obviously saw a similarity in approach between Japan and YMO, citing the YMO track 'Absolute Ego Dance' as an example of where the two groups met musically. In the conversation, the two agreed on the importance of using pure imagery in songs rather than factual specifics. As Sylvian explained albeit obliquely: 'If I write about a town or people, I would write about people I don't know. This would allow me to express my personality.' They also agreed on the potency of cinema as an inspiration to songwriting and as a medium for music to aspire to. 'Take *Apocalypse Now* for instance,' Sylvian told Sakamoto, '"uneducated" people could enjoy watching it as merely a war movie, but people who are interested in the philosophical aspect could take that from the movie as well; various types of people can enjoy that film in various types of ways.' Sylvian was obviously referring to his own musical aspirations here and his goal to make an atmospheric music that worked on many levels according to the listener's personality. In doing so he was aspiring to make a pop music that would outlive its natural lifespan. Japan were already succeeding. The collaboration between Sylvian and his new best friend was manifest in the enigmatically entitled 'Taking Islands In Africa'. Dean: 'I never asked what the songs were about or what the titles meant. It wasn't discussed. I think the lyrics were surreal and contradictory, they didn't really make sense, which is okay as long as they create the right atmosphere.'

With a title in this instance taken from a book of photographs Sylvian had chanced across – 'the lyrics are based upon images I pick up from books, travel and the people I work with, they don't really say anything' – the actual music was composed around a rhythm and chord track that Sakamoto came up with alone. The classically trained pianist wrote the basic parts on a sole polysynth in the studio, with overdubs added by some of the band later. Sylvian: 'Ryuichi played almost everything on that track – that was the idea. When you work with a person you want that person's sound or the atmosphere that person creates to blend with yours in the studio.' Dean: "'Taking Islands In Africa' began with allowing Ryuichi Sakamoto to create a piece from scratch and layering assorted parts in the studio over a few hours, which was a fascinating experience as a bystander.' '[Sakamoto] could turn the pages of his sheet music, smoke, doodle, dial phone numbers, juggle, prepare and eat lunch with one hand while recording the keyboard parts,' commented Karn in awe. (Karn himself would not feature on the track.) Sakamoto himself pointed out that '… Africa' sounded very different from the rest of the material, and rather unlike Japan', but didn't elaborate on what this meant. 'Working with Sakamoto was interesting and sometimes difficult,' says Punter. 'He's a very intense personality and the language barrier sometimes did not help.' Sakamoto at this point spoke almost no English. Sylvian: 'When Ryuichi and I started working together, we had no means of communicating verbally really, there was a language barrier. And all the communication that really worked was musical. He would play something, he'd see recognition in my face and vice versa and we'd move on that level; there was no need for dialogue.'

The resultant sound of the album, built layer by layer like a watercolour painting rendered in acrylics, was polished, dense, buffed and panoramic. Aurally, there was not a hair out of place. The same could not be said of its personnel. Rob Dean was ultimately to bear the brunt of his band's new direction as his continued absence proved. Musically and even aesthetically there was obviously now little place for him in the Japan of the 1980s. His Bolanesque look had fitted in with the previous decade, but he struggled to fit in now either visually or musically. 'It was true that I found less space to create on *Gentlemen Take Polaroids*,' he affirms, 'and although I'm not sure how much I was aware of it, my own creative goals were drifting apart from the rest of the group, which in turn made it increasingly difficult to come up with parts that I was happy with. The band was moving more towards electronic music with YMO, Eno, and Kraftwerk as perhaps the strongest influences and a distorted guitar was feeling more intrusive than complementary on a fair bit of the material.' On some of the tracks it's hard even to identify anything as sounding like an actual six string. 'Guitar-wise during this period, the heaviest influence was Fripp's work, which often sounded decidedly *un*-guitar-like,' explains Dean, 'and as a result I used a good deal of EBow as I had on *Quiet Life,* but to me this felt quite limiting. I recall trying in vain to introduce an acoustic guitar part at one point.' Tellingly, in retrospect an acoustic guitar would have sounded completely out of place on the album.

Clearly, Dean and Sylvian were no longer on the same page. Sylvian: 'With Rob, the basic thing was that on *Polaroids* and even *Quiet Life,* I felt I was holding him back because I had specific ideas for the guitar and I kept imposing them on him all the time. It would take hours in the studio, because I'd be pushing him maybe a little against what he'd want to do. It came to a peak on *Polaroids* as Rob played on only about four tracks.' The early 80s UK pop music scene would be notoriously anti-guitar, EBowed or not, and Dean now struggled to find any footing in a group he'd been a member of since the mid-70s. 'But I'm not sure how much pressure I felt coming from Dave,' he argues. 'I think the pressure was all mine. Robert Fripp was an influence because he had transported the guitar into the 80s in a staggeringly inventive way and really it was hard even to come close. I grew up with the influences of the melodic artistry of The Beatles, the folk-tinged work of Fairport Convention and the sheer power of bands like Cream. I was not particularly fond of Fripp's work in King Crimson up to this point, but the contributions he made to the work of Peter Gabriel and Bowie just floored me. But ultimately I didn't really want to emulate anyone. To be honest, I wasn't entirely in love with the direction Japan was moving into and so naturally it became a struggle.' 'I can remember Dave's expression of frustration,' recalls Huckle, 'as he stood behind the desk attempting to get his ideas across to Rob in the recording booth.'

Polaroids, while pivotal, would prove to be Japan's tensest album so far. Involved in every aspect of the album from the songwriting to the artwork, the singer would often introduce a cover version into proceedings solely to alleviate Sylvian-dominated sessions. In this case, another Motown gem 'Ain't That Peculiar' (and previously, 'All Tomorrow's Parties'), but when the atmosphere got fatally heavy, there was always the pub. Japan were not clubbers or pubbers by nature, but the combination of work stress and their fondness for their gregarious producer (who would go on to run his own pub in Canada) and the centrally located AIR resulted in the unlikely scenario of the quintet hanging out at the local alehouse. 'Because John Punter was so well-liked,' recalls Dean, 'and we had bonded with him so strongly, the notion of us visiting the local seemed more acceptable. Also, over the time we had recorded at AIR we made friends with several of the staff and so it seemed logical to pop down the pub to relieve some of the stress. In our time with John, both on and off the road, it was fairly normal to be in a bar somewhere laughing and joking and David was no exception, although I wouldn't say that he particularly would be as relaxed as the rest of us. He was always very aware of his public persona.' Punter: 'There was the local pub [The Duke of Argyll] where you would share a beer and a chat with John Cale for instance and yes – we even got David to that pub once or twice!'

Previously, Japan had attracted much hostile attention in public due to their made-up appearance, but now, when compared to the Steve Stranges, Marilyns and Boy Georges of London, they were hardly noticed. 'Rarely would there be any negative comments by this time,' says Dean; 'I believe that our appearance was actually rather sober in comparison to what was currently around us.' Even the studio itself was more of a social hub than most. 'With the set-up at AIR it would have been very difficult not to interact socially with other musicians,' confirms Barbieri. 'Invariably, there would be conversations upstairs in the cafeteria at any hour and one would always be chatting to folk in the foyer or along the corridors. Occasionally, this would result in invited "listening parties".' Dean: 'Studio time was never entirely exclusive; it wasn't a closed set as it were, other than when vocals were being recorded. I think it occasionally helped lighten the intensity of the recording process when we had visitors. The record company would drop in from time to time, including Mr Branson himself on one or two occasions.'

Across the hall from Japan, Duran Duran were recording their first album. 'I do remember Duran Duran showing up to pay their respects to the band,' remembers Nicola Tyson, friend and photographer of Japan. 'I remember them piling into the studio, a bunch of awkward lookalikes – they were nobody at the time and it was a big non-event!' 'I remember them hanging around,' says Dean. 'We knew they were listening in and taking notes. We were probably a bit aloof.' Duran, and in particular John and Nick, were huge fans of Japan. Karn: '[Previous to meeting at AIR] Rich and I got a cassette from a band who wanted us to produce their album, and it was a band called Duran Duran, who we'd never heard of. We listened to the tape...' Karn was not taken with what he heard at the time. 'So we wrote back and said, "Sorry". We found that it sounded so similar to us that they wanted us because of who we were and not that they thought we could do anything good with it.' Barbieri: 'Duran Duran were very pleasant the few times we met them, but suffice to say we didn't really like the tape at the time and ultimately passed on it. You couldn't help but mix with other groups really. It was quite incredible working in such a small building with all these artists making their albums. Whilst making *Quiet Life,* Kate Bush visited our studio, and Paul McCartney had studio two on almost constant hold. He asked if we needed any guitar on our album. He and Linda were very nice people. We also met Michael Jackson. That was ... weird.' Punter: 'There was always some socialising at AIR, mostly with Paul and Linda McCartney, as Linda was a huge fan of the band.' Work-wise, Barbieri's outstanding memory of recording the album was, 'John Punter doing a mix. It was a hilarious process. In those days there was no recall on the desks or flying faders, so the mix had to be done manually with all hands to the deck, so to speak. All the level changes, external FX sends and mutes had to be done manually. He liked to take this job on solo even though we, or others, could assist. So we would watch from the sofa behind him as he wheeled himself in his chair from one side of the desk to the other in a "Basil Fawlty" manner, working up a sweat at the controls like a man possessed.'

Outside of the studio and their private lives, Japan presented a very un-rock and roll image to the public. For instance Sylvian, then a committed smoker, would never deign to appear on stage with a glass of water, let alone a single cigarette. Yet this was the 1980s, and sometimes, if only in order to put in extra time at the studio, like everyone else in the music industry Japan indulged in illegal substances from time to time. 'I think coke entered everyone's lives in those days,' says Barbieri. 'Not just the artists either. But Steve never indulged. A wise decision!' Twelve-hour days were the norm, and if the group had more stamina than their producer, they could carry on with a night shift engineer, with or without the aid of substances. Karn: 'You know the old idea that cocaine goes hand in hand with being a musician and working late at night? I don't think that's true at all. I think you lose your sense of judgement completely.' Dean: 'It was an extremely insular group, but I wouldn't call it a particularly sober one. It was a very close unit socially and it was rare that any outsider could penetrate that, but there was a good deal of fun and laughter, a side that the public rarely, if ever, got to see. In particular, Mick and Steve could be very entertaining when on good form.'

Fun and laughter aside, tensions continued to arise. Halfway through the sessions, the situation was judged to be so taut that a change of environment was needed. Japan and Punter consequently relocated to The Townhouse in Goldhawk Road. It was here that the album was completed. 'My New Career' was written ad hoc in the studio, its title possibly lifted in part from a recent film. Sylvian was a frequent cinemagoer, but watched TV sparingly. 'I try to use TV only to watch films,' he once said, 'but you have to be careful, or you can easily end up watching any old rubbish.' He may or may not have seen *My Brilliant Career*, a movie released in art house cinemas in 1979, but he would have definitely heard Bowie's 'A New Career In A New Town.' Like many of the more uptempo songs on *Polaroids*, Karn's bass on 'My New Career' is a sinuous delight; a sensuous, rubbery counter-melody weaving lushly through the entire song. Karn: '[It] took us one day to write in the studio. I much preferred it to another ballad.' 'Methods of Dance' also had its origins in film, and was definitely a result of Sylvian's late night Kensington TV habits. Based on a BBC documentary of dance choreographers working in New York, lyrically it references Bowie and Roxy explicitly: 'Then out of the blue ...' sings Sylvian on the chorus, going on to quote Bowie in the verses with, 'Sense the doubt' and 'Speed of life' etc. Musically, the influence came from further East. Dean: 'If there was any direct reference for *Polaroids* as a whole, it was YMO's *Solid State Survivor*. The influence of YMO on 'Methods Of Dance' is clearly evident, but the percussive elements in particular take it a step further. I think both tracks represent the band as a unit at its strongest during that period.'

The cover version, 'Ain't That Peculiar', (Peter Gabriel had also released a live version of this tune from his 1977 US tour) was to be the group's final foray into Motown. Barbieri: 'This cover reflected David's listening tastes, I guess. Not mine. I was never into Tamla, but it was nice working the electronics into these songs.' Japan's version of the Marvin Gaye standard is more an *inversion,* taking the song apart and rebuilding it via an indecipherable code. On first hearing it sounds like it's being played sideways. Sylvian: '[Our] rhythm section are very adaptable; they've got such a characteristic style that whatever they play immediately becomes Japan.' Motown founder Berry Gordon's and Marvin Gaye's reactions are sadly not on record. Barbieri: 'If they did hear our version, I'd bet they would've been pretty shocked. It's an interesting interpretation. It was never apparent to me where the one in the bar fell. Steve created really inventive percussion parts. I think it's the strangest track on the album.' It's perverse to think that a cover version replaced 'Angel In Furs' or 'Some Kind Of Fool', but the choice was deliberate. As Sylvian explained: 'The idea was for it to loosen up the feel of the album. Some people thought *Quiet Life* was too perfect.' The Motown cover explicitly proved that Jansen and Karn were now a uniquely powerful combo who could be counted on to turn the most basic chord progressions into something utterly alien. 'It was great seeing Mick and Steve work together,' says Barbieri, 'I wouldn't say they ever had "chops", but they just played these unique parts. So original. Of course, we had respect for each other and we afforded each other space to express that.'

For Sylvian, the making of the album was apparently quietly traumatic. 'I was going through many musical changes,' he explained. 'I wanted to get away from *Quiet Life* but still felt very attached to it ... unusually for me. Things were getting very strained halfway through *Polaroids*. We had to take a break.' Dean confirms that 'the working process for *GTP* was somewhat different from the albums that preceded it, in that some of the material was created and constructed in the studio rather than in rehearsal, and David was probably more in charge than before. He wanted to move further away from the obvious Roxy Music influence, which pervaded his writing on *Quiet Life*, but ultimately I don't really think he succeeded. It may be that *GTP* was created a year too soon.' Unlike Hansa, Virgin had complete confidence in the band and Japan were left to their own devices in the studio, with neither record company nor manager dictating any concession to commercialism.

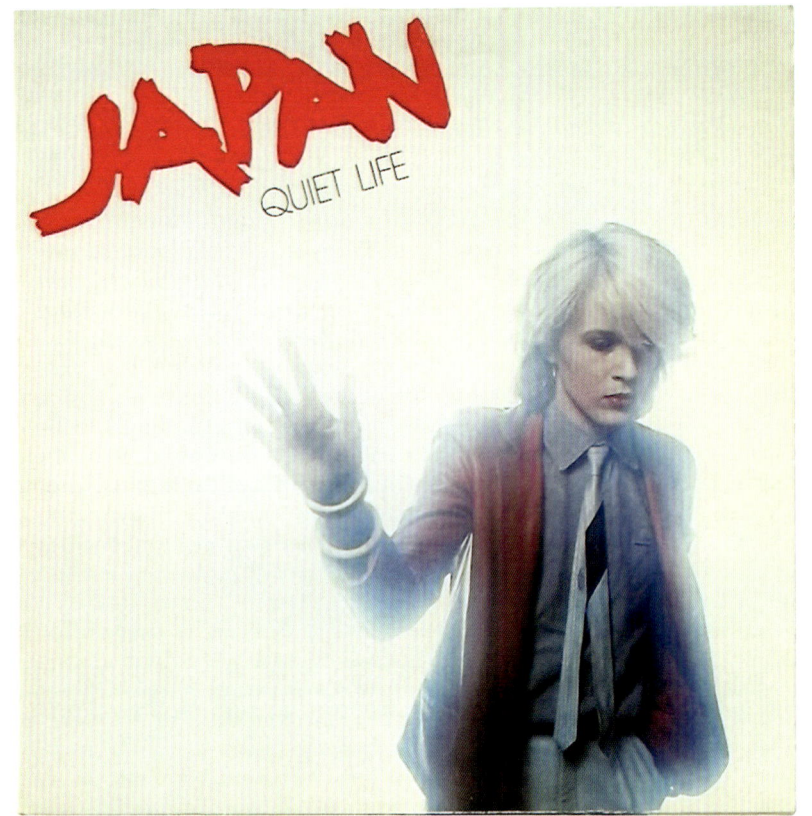

Still in his early twenties, Sylvian had a surer sense of himself and his work by now than ever before. This would not lend itself to the constraints of a band set-up for much longer, but for now there was work to be done. *Gentlemen Take Polaroids* would be mixed, mastered and packaged as quickly as possible, with Virgin rushing to meet the Christmas market. Bourton: 'When they delivered that album we were all completely blown away by it. It was a big step forward we thought. It gave them a distinct identity, but we still weren't sure about the viability of getting songs from that album on the radio. Through touring with them I'd come to have a better idea of how their music was being received, but at this point, although we loved the album, we weren't sure how it would go in the singles market.' Sylvian was as ever self-critical: 'I don't think it's the best thing we've done. It was a very hard album to make because there was a lot of strain in the studio … feelings between members of the band weren't too good, because I was putting limitations on them, because I was after a certain sound. I've never done that before. I'm happy with how it sounds – the thing is that I was growing out of it before we'd finished it; we worked on it for too long. I'd already begun to pull away from "muzak".'

Dates were booked to promote the album and Virgin launched an inventive ad campaign ('Music For Adults Only') that would eventually get the album just outside the Top 40. Even as the group were starting to show cracks, they were finally on the way to real success. 'By the time the album was mastered,' remembers Napier-Bell, 'Dean was no longer a bona fide member of the band. His leaving seemed an inevitable situation. He came from north London, all of them from south London. But he'd fitted in pretty well and even adapted himself to wearing make-up offstage and all the other things David required of them. His leaving was obviously the beginning of the end of the Japan we'd worked so long to break.'

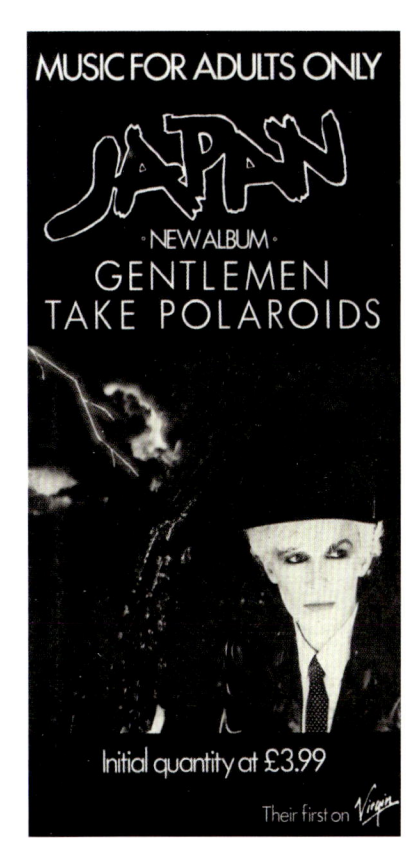

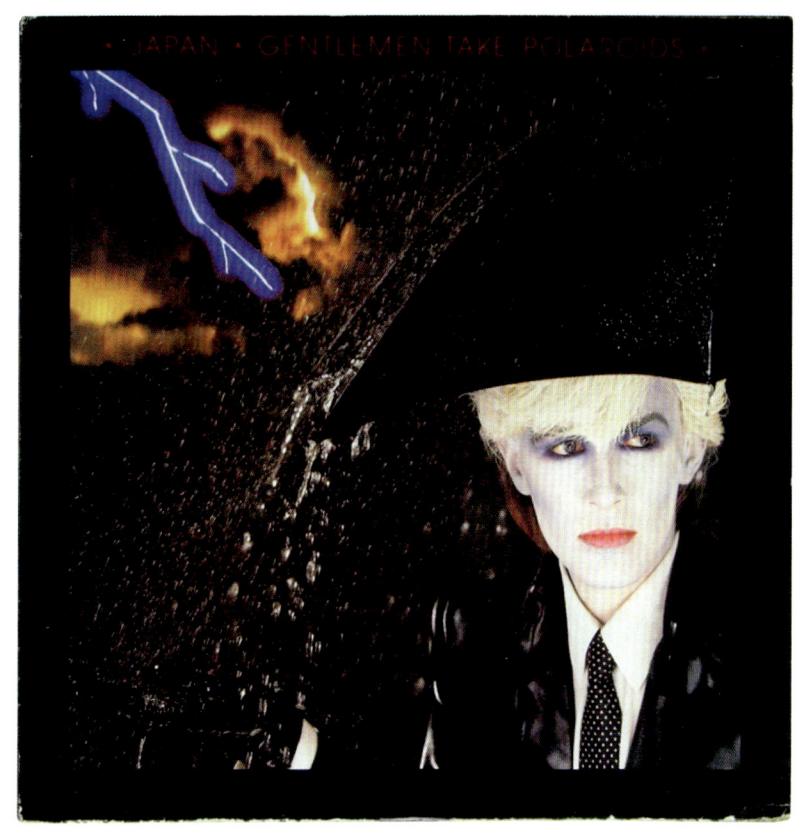

In October, the title track from the album was released as a gatefold double single. The second single included a first for the band – two tracks credited to Japan members other than Sylvian. Barbieri: 'I already had the basis for 'The Experience Of Swimming' written, and just allocated myself some time in the studio on my own. I recorded it all in the small Studio 3 at AIR with my gear set up behind the mixing desk. Mick played some oboe in the middle section. Dave titled my track.' A second instrumental, 'The Width Of A Room', was Dean's debut. 'I'd never submitted anything to David for him to write to. I was always working on stuff at home, but just for myself really. But at this point, we were told the B-sides could be for us. I think David was under enough pressure to write stuff as it was, so maybe that's why we were invited. I wrote 'The Width Of A Room' on guitar but I wanted to do it with keyboards. David wanted it on guitar though, so I started doing it on electric. But I felt it should be done on keyboards. And we went with that in the end. A kind of film theme thing. I was happy with David putting a title to it as I couldn't think of what to call it.'

The single charted at 60 and was received well, particularly in the clubs but still, as Bourton predicted, it received little airplay. Bourton's attitude towards press, however, was paying off. 'I got them on the cover of *Smash Hits* and that was a big breakthrough,' affirms Bourton, 'we were trying to get them away from the perception that they were mere poseurs and we did it eventually. I wasn't trying to get them into *Jackie* magazine and the like, but then few Virgin bands went that route … maybe The Human League. Japan had serious musical ambitions and I wanted to get that across. They were trying to make music that was distinctive and I think they had started that with *Quiet Life*. And now the serious press were just beginning to take them seriously and that included style magazines like *The Face*.' There was another futile foray into videos, with two films made for the title track (which would be filmed during the sound-check of their November Lyceum show) and 'Swing'. The videos were at least tastefully done compared to their garish predecessors and, in 'Gentlemen Take Polaroids' particularly, Sylvian gave great face. Dean: 'Our videos never seemed to really come together. And it was random. I've no idea why we made a video for 'Swing'. Making videos was something foisted upon us; we had no agenda as a band for them. And they were so tedious and expensive to make. The live performance ones were okay. You just went through the motions. As long as there were no fantasy sequences … as a medium I hate it. It invades upon the song and never enhances it.'

Released in November 1980, *Gentlemen Take Polaroids* was Japan's biggest hit album in the UK to date, although it would take another six years before it went gold. It would spawn no bona fide hit singles but was hugely influential and, more importantly, it set Japan up for their one real masterpiece, *Tin Drum*, to be released almost exactly a year later. It also distanced them once and for all from the Japan of *Adolescent Sex*. Yet despite the massive growth in their fan base, Japan were still considered by much of the UK press as a joke. 'Japan's current sound is one long, diffuse outtake from Roxy Music's *Flesh And Blood*,' summed up the *NME*, a verdict shared by all the major weeklies with *Sounds* titling their review, 'Music for out of work hairdressers'. 'Roxy Music in drag,' belched another. Yet the group had always worn their influences on their sleeves. 'Originality is so overrated,' a 21-year-old Sylvian had quipped a year earlier, and Japan were the epitome of a group who had grown up in public. *Polaroids* was an assured statement that reflected both Sylvian's new-found sense of purpose and the rapid evolution of Japan as self-taught musicians. Of course, the UK was far from the only market. Although *Polaroids*, like *Quiet Life*, would not get a domestic release in the US, there was still Europe, Japan and Australasia to consider. In the latter territory, legendary Australian TV personality and music lover Molly Meldrum plugged the album on his hugely popular *Countdown* music show when it was released there in the first months of 1981. 'Let's have a look at a group that I think are fantastic,' drawled Molly, holding up the striking album cover for the TV camera. 'I loved them a couple of years ago when everyone said, "Ah, the guy can't sing and they're absolutely rank," but this album here is really starting to take off in quite a few charts around Australia so watch out for 'em.'

The cover of the album alone, taken by Stuart McLeod, was an instant classic, portraying Sylvian as a Helmut Newtonesque artifice that channelled Dirk Bogarde from *The Night Porter* via the emergent New Romantic movement. The cover picture was one of the few visual concessions Sylvian ever made to fashion. Fin Costello wasn't convinced by the concept enough to believe that he 'could do it justice'. Nicola Tyson took the back cover portrait on the roof of AIR. 'I worked closely with Japan during that period. They were all gentlemen actually, as I remember it. The refinement wasn't a pose.' Tyson and Sylvian in particular became friends. 'David was an important muse for me,' recalls the photographer. 'There was a creative connection to the friendship, although theirs was a different world and medium – the wrong one for me – and I wasn't involved *at all* in any of their creative composing moments other than hanging out at some recording sessions a bit – quite boring if you are not a musician or an engineer. David was a perfectionist.'

Sylvian was fond enough of his new friend to give her the expensive Antony Price jacket he wore on the sleeve. The jacket was a size 36, proof that Japan were also very thin.

Contact sheet of Japan at the Duke of Argyll pub, London circa *Gentlemen Take Polaroids*
Nicola Tyson

Sylvian's Antony Price Jacket, which he gave to Nicola Tyson
Courtesy of Nicola Tyson

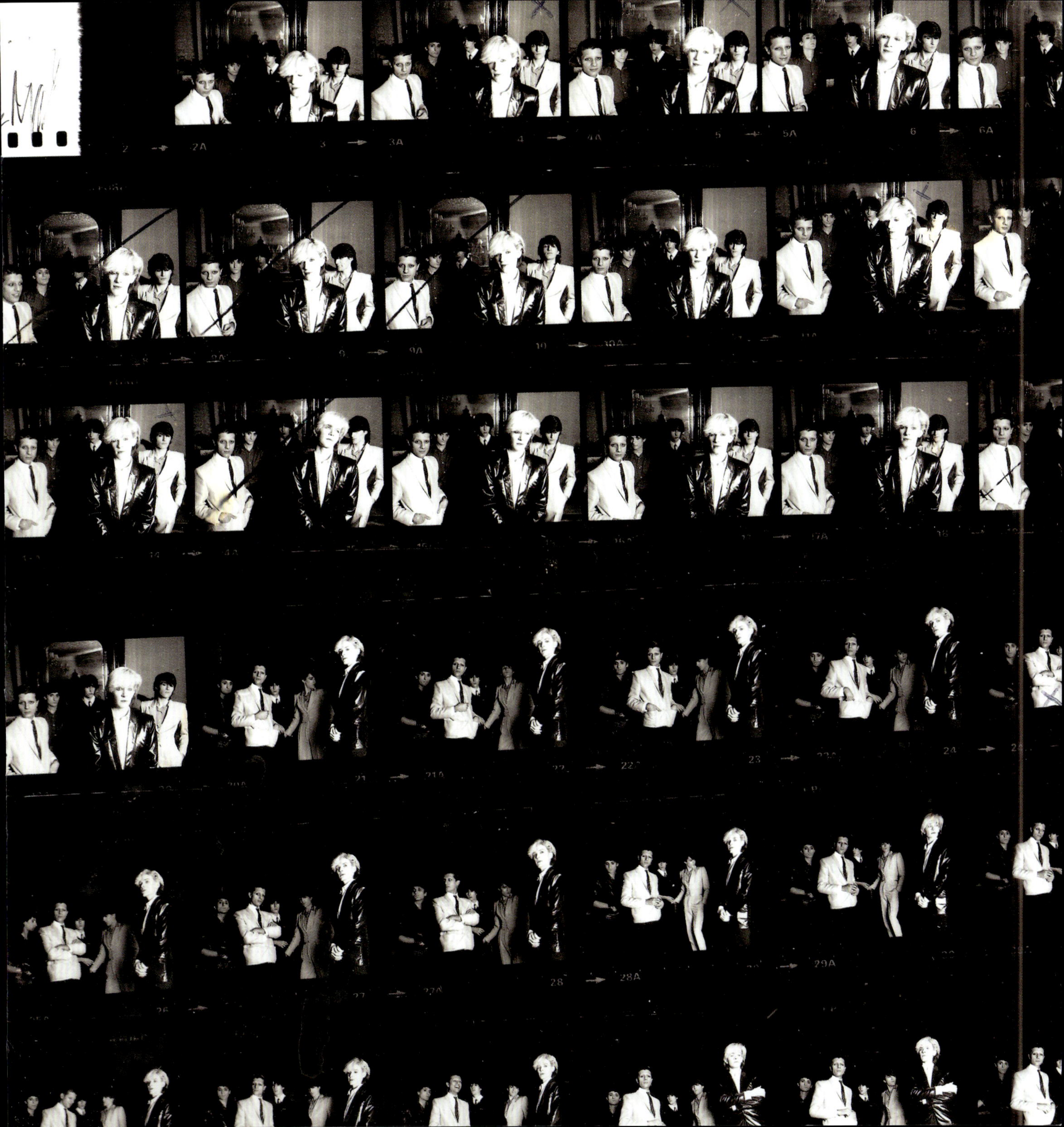

Huckle: 'Yes, there was an understanding amongst them that keeping reasonably thin was a good look. But there was no structured effort in that direction. They lived off burgers and chips while in the studio, for example. I think Steve and Dave were naturally thin. Steve of course burnt it off through drumming, Mick had made a great effort to lose weight after leaving school and loved his food [he did cook] but like all of them, I think, just kept it all to one main meal a day interspersed with the odd snack. Dean: 'Yes, there was an unspoken rule that everyone in Japan had to be skinny. I remember we did a photo shoot and I was wearing a shirt that made me look like I had a pot belly – I didn't – and David rather disparagingly pointed it out.' Mick, although an excellent cook and food lover, relied on his nervous energy to keep slim. Dean: 'Mick would eat and work late at night and his body found its rhythm. He never snacked. He created food to eat. I always thought Mick was maybe anorexic.' At home, David, in his purist fashion stuck to breakfast cereal, toast, soup, and Gitanes, popping out late at night to shop at Europa Foods in Earl's Court. Band image was obviously important to him. 'I sometimes lost control over demos, but never on how we looked,' he'd admit.

The cover of *Polaroids* was a self-conscious nod to the New Romantic/Futurist movement, which was exploding in the UK. Although Japan had all the credentials to be forerunners of such a faction, they typically saw themselves as a cut-and-style above their perceived peers. Mick Karn: 'Certain bands were beginning to be classed together that had little to do with each other, such as Adam & The Ants, OMD, Spandau Ballet, collectively tied together by the slender threads of fashion. Perhaps I was missing something; I wasn't exactly paying attention to current trends.' Japan were now finally becoming trendy, and professionally the relationship between them and Virgin was blooming. Bourton: 'I'd go directly to them rather than through Nomis. I got on very well with David in particular.

We'd socialise every few weeks and go out for a Japanese meal together. He wasn't at all how he was perceived. He was very straightforward, basically a south London lad. He had no airs or graces and had a wicked sense of humour.'

Within a year, Japan had found the right producer, label … and hairdresser. The burnt-out peroxide fringe that Sylvian sported on the cover of *Polaroids* was the last time Mane Line would tend to his hair. From now on, Japan's follicular needs were tended to by one Allan Soh, a Chinese friend of Napier-Bell. Soh had started as a fashion designer, but had tired of the sewing in solitude and had moved on to designing hairstyles for The Kinks and rich housewives. 'I think it's the hair that can really make a group,' says Soh. 'I was the guy who really defined David's look. When Simon introduced me to them they had this long, straggly hair and it was me who cut it shorter and really started that look. After this I had many fans and clients coming to the salon asking for the same cut. When the group sat down, I first suggested highlights and for it to be layered rather than just long and bleached. Of course, David's natural hair was dark brown and I didn't like that. I liked the blond look.' Soh would sculpt the defining Sylvian haircut that the singer, to his ultimate chagrin, would become most famous for. Soh: 'When he found his style he stayed with it; he had that look for a long time.' Some detractors would see Sylvian's hairstyle as either being a peroxide version of Ferry's flick or a Monroe version of Bowie's soul era wedge cut, but Soh claims sole credit. 'No, Bowie wasn't particularly an inspiration. I think my inspiration came from myself; I just came up with ideas like doing the hair with chopsticks and using horse urine to bleach it and so on. I approached a haircut like sculpture. I didn't think about it too much; I just went in and did it. I had a basic training; my mother was a hairdresser a long time ago. But I just moulded the hair, as if it were clay.'

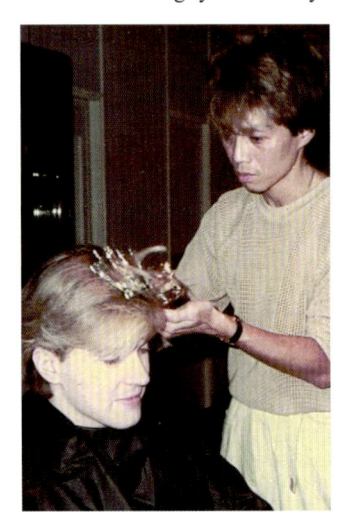

Allan Soh and Sylvian at Soh's salon, Knightsbridge, circa 1982

Sylvian was Soh's pet project, but the hair wizard had varying relationships with all the members. 'I remember Simon bringing Japan over to the salon for the first time; I soon got to know them all individually. I was in Paris at the time and at first they were resistant to me doing much with their hair, which was very, very long. But slowly they came round and I was able to modernise their image.' Soh had apparently met Japan before their initial makeover at Mane Line as seen on the cover of *Quiet Life*, and Mane Line would occasionally deal with hair matters in tandem with Soh up until 1981 when Soh became the band's full-time hair stylist. 'As I got to know them as people, you found out what they really wanted. David and Mick came the most often,' Soh recalls, 'then Steve. Steve did his hair on his own mostly, at home. They didn't have to come every day. Normally, if you cut it well, do a beautiful cut, then they can manage it themselves. Getting the colour right too – that's important – but if the cut and style are right then it takes care of itself. Mick used gel and David used hairspray. Of course, if it was a photo session then I would be there to style it for that to make it perfect. I wouldn't prepare for every concert, but for a live concert the rougher the cut the better I think. But the secret was in the cut not the product. David could swing around and it would just fall naturally back in place. David had the best hair I think. When he came to the salon he would sit with the other clients, but he was very quiet, quite reserved.' Soh could be proud of his art. Over the course of a live show, under hot lights, Sylvian's 'do' would barely deviate from its immaculate conception from the first song to the last.

On 16 October, the band attended a YMO show at the Hammersmith Odeon. Just as Sylvian had bonded with Sakamoto the previous summer, now Jansen forged a friendship with Yukihiro Takahashi, drummer and programmer with the group. Takahashi: 'I think Ryuichi introduced me to Japan around 1978-79, and I remember meeting the band for the first time backstage at a show in London. They were still very young then, and I was struck by the contrast between their glamorous visual image and their sound. That's how much their music fascinated me. I did feel an immediate affinity with Steve's drumming. This feeling grew stronger when he started playing in sync with the computer, but it's hard to explain precisely why. What I can say with certainty is that his meticulously calculated and sophisticated drumming style felt very familiar to me. Aside from his abilities as an instrumentalist, I also found myself relating to his entire stance towards musical composition and programming. In all the years that I've known and worked with him, this feeling hasn't changed one bit. I'm reminded now of when Steve told me, not long after we first met, that the first time he saw me play was when I was drumming in Sadistic Mika Band in the 70s and we opened for Roxy Music. Steve and David were still in their teens at that time and, for some reason, I still remember him telling me this.' Jansen's approach to the drumming and percussion on *Polaroids* had evolved to great effect. He was a musician finding both his voice and his brand, and he now used Tama drums exclusively. 'Tama had a pretty high profile in stores at the time and were quite reasonably priced,' says Jansen. 'I wasn't aware they were made in Japan at first, but that was a bonus. Becoming popular over there meant good support from Tama and subsequently an endorsement. They make good drums.' *Polaroids* contained no ride cymbal and little in the way of traditional crash cymbal, if at all. 'I didn't like using ride cymbals by the time we'd started on *Quiet Life*. I think I associated them with heavier rock and they opened up the sonics of the kit too much. Similarly, I felt the overuse of crash cymbals was too heavy for the direction we were heading in. The Chinese crash cymbal I started to use sounded very similar to white noise. The metal being a lower grade made the sonics more dull, very trashy and brief, with little sustain, but did a great job of adding dynamics. I purchased a range of them from a Chinese instrument shop in Shaftesbury Avenue called Ray Man as they weren't readily available from Western cymbal makers.'

Sylvian and Jansen backstage at a YMO concert

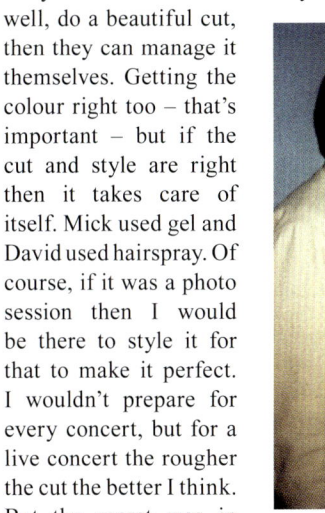

Jansen's progress could be heard in the group's final show of the year at London's Lyceum on 27 November. Although Sylvian complained of having to play live at all, he recognised the important effect doing so had on Japan's studio life. Sylvian: 'Because we did very few performances then, we couldn't let go of *Quiet Life*. From that perspective, performing is quite important. All the emotions that came with recording the record are still in you, and the only way to get them out is by performing, so that you don't care so much about it anymore. You need to be able to take distance from it. You need to grow away from it if you ever want to be able to begin with something else.' The show itself was massively oversubscribed. Draper: 'The success we had with them happened fast; it wasn't as difficult as I'd thought it was going to be. I remember the turning point clearly. Soon after the release of *Polaroids*, Simon Napier-Bell came and asked me for tour support. "I need £12,000," he said. "Okay," I said. "But it's for one show,' Simon said. I mean, to use a whole year's tour support for one show? But then soon after he came to me and told me: "I don't need your money. The show is sold out four times over."'

Yet still the critics bitched. 'Teeny bop transvestites … are the pits and Japan are the favourite victims of faggot-baiting now that Bolan is dead and no longer an embarrassment,' raved *Melody Maker*. 'Of course, his mincing and mascara have been forgiven/forgotten in dewy-eyed retrospect, but not so Japan, who continue to pollute our public auditoriums with their paint, powder and poofy hair-dos … A conveyor belt of sound without climax or depth, beginning or end, fronted by David Sylvian who, for all his Ferry mannerisms, can't match the man for vocal or visual style.' Such fatuous, politically incorrect ramblings must have been more frustrating for the band rather than hurtful. 'We did feel like a lot of the press were against us, even then,' says Dean, '*Sounds* were okay, but *NME* hated us. Being called 'poofters' or whatever had no effect on us at all.'

The concert was nevertheless a public turning point for the band. As the ticket sales proved, they were now becoming independent from a reliance on press approval, and another step forward came that December when Japan finally made their debut on BBC2's *The Old Grey Whistle Test*. This was a major opportunity for the band and they met it perfectly. They appear confident, professional and, at the same time, peculiar and intriguing. Dressed for a clerical job on Mars, lush of barnet and thin as sticks, they show no obvious emotion other than a total commitment to their craft. Sylvian intones otherwise seemingly meaningless lyrics with utter sincerity and earnestness. There is no smiling, nor are there any unnecessary gestures, even during the risible introduction by presenter Annie Nightingale. Japan are sincere about what they do and they want you to take it seriously or not at all. *The Old Grey Whistle Test* was a highly respected and reputable music programme and one of the few TV music shows Japan watched at home with any regularity. Dean was still an official member of the band and the tensions of *Polaroids* seemed to be put aside for now: 'It was a big deal for us, yeah. It was a respected show. We kind of felt like we'd arrived.' The choice of songs performed was telling too; 'Swing' and 'My New Career', while among the least obscure songs from the album, were still hardly Top 40 contenders and the latter allowed Sylvian to join the band as a fellow musician, sat at his Prophet studiously drawing out chords as he crooned. Dean: ''My New Career' was one of David's favourites from the album; I think he felt like that's where he should be going.' The appearance also allowed us to hear what Japan actually sounded like live, with Dean's massive Gibson much more audible than on record. 'Live, I was able to get the guitar parts louder,' says the guitarist, 'that was always a beef for me – that the guitars were too quiet on the records; they were buried. Guitar dynamics can give a song more muscle, but on record, mine were always a bit low in the mix I thought.'

Once again, Japan had ended a year being barely recognisable from the group that had begun it. Since *Adolescent Sex* they had struggled within the Zeitgeist that ebbed and flowed around them. With the 1980s now finally dawning, they would go on to define it.

Backstage at *The Old Grey Whistle Test*, 1980
Nicola Tyson

Chapter 7
Art and Parties

Sylvian would say in retrospect that one of his main goals during the Japan years was that of 'self sufficiency'. Presumably, when Japan had established themselves, his 'dear friends' would enjoy a similar independence. During those first few years of the 1980s, such a position seemed not only possible, but inevitable.

From 8 to 20 December 1980, Mick had his debut sculpture exhibition at Hamilton's Gallery in Mayfair, his interest in sculpture prompted by the chance viewing of a shop display in Germany in 1978. On returning to the UK he had immediately tried his hand with the medium. 'I've never been able to draw or paint, and that's as far as art went in school,' Karn would recall. 'I don't know what it was that made me buy the clay; it was while we were on tour when I bought some in Birmingham. And I started thinking of what to make with it. At that time I was really into hands; I was amazed how valuable they were – to me especially – what would I do without them? When I got home from the tour I started making a hand [eventually entitled 'Satchmo']. I sat up all night doing it, and it just wasn't working out at all, and by then the clay was virtually hard, and I just squeezed it into a little ball. In the morning, it was the shape it is now – it looked right. But not until I screwed it up! That gave me the confidence that I could make something.'

John Russell Taylor was a writer and art critic for *The Times* and would help facilitate the show. 'I first met Mick at a dinner hosted by Roy Miles [a major art collector and dealer at the time],' says Russell Taylor. 'Roy was at his height then and Japan were becoming quite big too. Roy hunted celebrities.

Japan at The Venue, March 1980
Martin Grogan

Mick Karn at home with his sculptures
Richard Barbieri personal archive

Mick's work was interesting and sort of in tune with the times. I'm not sure if people would have been interested if he wasn't a pop star but his work had something. I remember being sat with Mick and Roy in the back of Roy's Rolls-Royce. Roy's hands were all over Mick, but he took it well. My impression of Mick was that he was very sane and "in control"; I liked him. I was surprised, pleasantly so, at how straightforward and direct he was for a pop star. It might seem that the showing of Mick's sculptures in a West End gallery would be very exceptional. At the time, remember, Japan were becoming big business, and Roy loved to stuff his openings with [often dubious] aristocrats and celebrities, which then meant sportsmen and rock stars. I remember that Connie brought them together – I think she was doing publicity for both at the time – and it would have been to their mutual advantage, particularly for Roy, in engendering publicity. As for the sculptures themselves, "promising" would be a fair estimate, I think, and no one said any more. I wrote something for the show, but remember catalogue introductions and such tend to be taken with a pinch of salt anyway, not because people assume the writer is puffing up his subject for money, but because he is presumed to be a mate of the artist, and therefore necessarily biased. Note that I would write like that for an invitation card, but definitely not in a review for *The Times*. I don't remember anything at all about the rest of the band.'

Karn himself felt a little sheepish about his show or at least the publicity he was getting. 'I couldn't help but feel guilty,' he'd remember. 'Have you any idea how difficult it is for an artist to get themselves in the prestigious [*Sunday Times*] Atticus column? Yet there I was, short-cutting and elbowing my way into the art world without a care for the artists that had been struggling for years to achieve the same.' The publicity did its work. Huckle: 'Loads of people showed up – for the launch party anyway – mainly because of the Japan connection, but no one bought anything. I'm not even sure that Dave went. Steve and Rich certainly did. My impression of how the others viewed his sculptures might be wrong. No one was an art or sculpture expert. But then this art critic guy [Russell Taylor] publicly stated that Mick had talent. So Mick being Mick and easily led, as I suppose anyone might be at that stage of life, convinced himself that he had a greater talent than was actually the case. In my own opinion, Russell Taylor only praised Mick because he wanted to get into Connie's knickers, and having bigged Mick up couldn't back away from it.' Russell Taylor: 'Who could forget Connie?! She was extremely … picturesque. Vivacious.' Huckle: 'And so all these so-called art professionals, and non-art types, went along with it. The Hamilton Gallery guy just thought it was a way to make a buck and keep on the right side of Taylor, who eventually seemed to try and distance himself from it all, as Connie's publicity machine took off. As for Dave, who I believe, had a bit more of an artist's eye, he was polite about it all, but never seemed overly enthusiastic. The result was that everyone encouraged and supported Mick without really knowing much about the world of sculpture and the arts, or where Mick's stuff fitted into it.' As Huckle says, Karn's bandmates were more intrigued by their bassist's extracurricular activities than impressed. Barbieri: 'I did like Mick's sculptures. Every time we went round his flat there would be a work in progress. Some were quite grotesque in style. In later years they were more "classic" and demonstrated he had studied and understood the muscular and skeletal structures of the body. He was also quite obsessed with vaginas it seemed.'

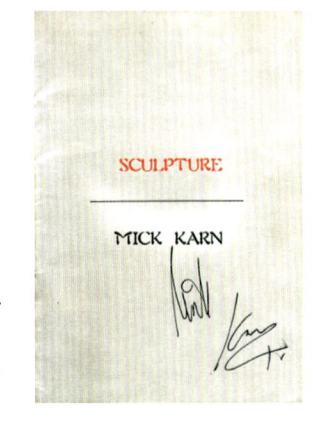

On the opening night at Hamilton's, Gary Numan, then at the height of his fame, was introduced to the band by the ever-networking Connie. 'Darling, I want you to meet Gary Numan,' she cooed to Karn, 'he's a big fan of yours.' 'I wasn't familiar with any of his work,' Karn would confess, 'apart from the single ['Cars'] that had been played to death.' Jansen, Barbieri and Karn were polite to Numan, but slightly bemused. Although to the readers of *Smash Hits* et al. Numan and Japan represented more or less the same thing, in actual fact their motivations were far apart enough for the group to see Numan as a slight oddity. 'He wasn't an artist we were listening to other than by chance,' affirms Karn. Then again, the fact that some saw Numan as 'weird' was something the band could relate to. Barbieri: 'He did seem a bit weird, but then people said that about us. As with many other artists, I've come to appreciate how great some of his work was.' Both Numan and Japan were socially isolated mavericks who had grown up working class and shared similar musical influences, so it was not surprising that Numan, vigorously prompted by Connie, attempted to befriend the band.

A childhood friend of Numan's, Nick Robson, recalls that, 'Gary and I grew up listening to the usual suspects – Bowie, Lou Reed, Iggy, and Roxy Music – but we were also impressed with the bands that followed later in similar genres – Ultravox and, of course, Japan who we saw as "the new Roxy Music". I remember first meeting some of the members of Japan at Gary's house in Wentworth – this would have been late 1980 – and noting the lipstick on the mugs of tea in the kitchen. This was quite odd as I knew there weren't any girls in the house on that day. It was just funny I guess. I don't recall if it was the whole band or just David Sylvian, Mick Karn and one other member, but it may have been all of them on that day. Gary had taken them up in his plane one Saturday and I don't think the flight was David's favourite trip. I was a huge fan of the band and the normality of meeting them over a cup of tea did steal some of the lustre and magic from their identity. However, they were still this quiet blend of unique, intelligent, and interesting individuals, the likes of which I'd never previously encountered.' This was a rare occasion for the usually socially insular Japan. Huckle: 'Yes, they hardly ever mixed with other bands and the like. They didn't do the New Romantic clubs or anything like that

Cover of Mick Karn's *Sculpture* catalogue
Keiko Kurata

either. I do remember some of Duran coming to see them at a couple of shows. They were polite to them, but didn't encourage friendship and if you went through any of their record collections back then you would be most unlikely to find any Human League, Visage, Culture, Spandau, Duran, etc. I think someone had a Heaven 17 album, but that was probably a freebie from Virgin.'

On a later occasion, Numan and Karn met at an after-show party at London's Legends nightclub where [future friend of Sylvian's] Mark Wardel observed them in the cordoned-off VIP area chatting to one another. Numan helped himself to spoonfuls of sugar from their table as he and Karn discussed co-writing together. Numan would also suggest co-writing with Sylvian, but unlike Numan's flying career, the Sylvian-Numan friendship would never take off, but there *was* an instant rapport between Karn and Numan. The two were interviewed together for *Music Life* at Christmas 1980. During the conversation, Numan explained how he now needed a new band as his were then on the verge of splitting up. Karn was already committed to playing with Numan who explained that, 'I'll need a drummer, but I can't ask Steve Jansen as that would mean I was just replacing Dave and that wouldn't be so good.' The two also spoke about getting together in Japan during Japan's next tour there (this would result in a gross comic misunderstanding) and Karn reflected how similar Numan's and Sylvian's thinking was in some ways. Whether this was true or not, a Numan-Sylvian collaboration would never transpire, but before the end of the year Numan invited Mick into his Shepperton studio to try out some musical ideas. The sessions went well. 'It was extremely easy to work with Gary,' said Karn. 'It was my first work outside of Japan. He gave me complete freedom, some of the album being completely improvised in the studio, and he kept some of the first takes, so I couldn't be happier.' This marked the beginning of Numan's infatuation with Karn. From this point on he would attempt to instigate a close friendship with Karn, the bass player being the reluctant recipient of what would turn out to be lost affections in a room.

In February 1981, the band began their *Polaroids* tour. With just one date in London at the Hammersmith Odeon, which was recorded and broadcast by BBC Radio 1, the rest of the tour took place in Japan.

This first appearance at Hammersmith was a milestone for the band. Huckle: 'I do remember being really chuffed when they played that first ever show at Hammersmith Odeon. It was the place where as teenagers we went to see all our fave acts. So actually to see them playing there to a full house of star-struck fans was pretty impressive. Incredible when I think back to those days at The Rock Garden playing to an audience of Rob's girlfriend and a drunk.' This was also the first tour where the band used tapes. Pre-recorded elements were not used to hide deficiencies in the live performance but to augment the songs themselves, as the studio versions of the songs were so complex. 'The reason we often replicated live what we'd recorded in the studio, right down to the tiniest detail,' affirms Jansen, 'was partially because we'd worked long and hard to find what we considered to be the correct pieces of a musical puzzle, and subsequently felt it couldn't be deviated from without causing a problematic ripple effect.'

Japan were by now an experienced and formidable live group. Had they chosen to, they could have played as a power trio and still pulled it off. (There were rumours that this is precisely the line-up Karn secretly wanted.) They were however less concerned with the bogus notion of 'authenticity' in their live presentation than they were with playing the songs as they felt they should be heard. After all, as Jansen says, Japan laboured hard in the studio to create the most evocative and definitive version of any song that they could. Their recording process was not about recording live versions of songs; in effect, Japan were bringing the studio experience to the live stage and not the live experience to the studio as many of their peers still did. Their producer was still manning the mixing desk. Punter: 'I had the tape [with the pre-recorded elements] next to me at the mixing desk, and I also had a back-up tape running in sync, so it was obvious to anyone who could see; it wasn't something we were trying to hide. It was basically the sequencer track because the sequencer itself was crap.' 'People always said Japan had a great live sound,' Sylvian would admit in a rare expression of professional pride. In essence, Japan were setting up a kind of mobile laboratory/studio wherever and whenever they played. 'That's basically it,' says Nigel Walker who would go on to replace Punter at the live desk later in the year. 'They wanted it to sound close to their studio recordings when they played a concert. They weren't interested in improvising.'

The foundation stone for this approach was their 20-year-old drummer. Jansen had the unenviable task of playing along to a click or percussion part on tape, which in turn was synced to pre-recorded elements on reel-to-reel tape; the rest of the

Japan performing in Shizuoka, 15 February 1981
Keiko Kurata

band then played along with Steve. Thus, if Steve missed one beat or dropped a drumstick and stumbled, it was not only the drum part that would suffer, but the whole song would skid out of sync. Jansen never missed a beat. 'No, he never did,' says Dean. 'He was great that way. He was like a human metronome. And he didn't even feel pressured – he was confident, he got a kick out of it.' Jansen: 'When we first started using tapes it was very primitive. I still used fold-back wedges to monitor the band and myself, but in the headphones I would have some form of rhythm track – I think it must have been either a rhythm box or a sequencer of some sort – and in the other channel were the various overdubs that would come and go throughout the track – chorus, backing vocals, saxes, more sequencers, additional percussion etc., all from the original recordings. These sounds were also sent out front of house for all to hear. Consequently it was important not to miss the start point otherwise certain overdubs intended to enter at a given point would end up appearing in the wrong part of the song. Sometimes it happened and this was usually due to improper vocal entries or solo lengths, in which case I had to try to relay to everyone where we ought to be in the track and, if that failed, just ignore what was in the headphones. It was simple for John [Punter] to dip the fader on the recorded sounds so the audience wouldn't hear them, and he was very good at recalling all the bar lengths and therefore he knew when things were going wrong. It didn't happen often I have to say.' Barbieri: 'As for mistakes on stage – there are always mistakes and usually the audience doesn't notice. With Japan it was the discipline of executing the recorded work on stage that took precedence. No real improvisation was going on.' Such rigidity would eventually become a problem for Sylvian at least, who as it was found the mechanisations of touring increasingly numbing. 'I just don't enjoy going through the motions,' he would explain, 'touring is done mostly for the band's benefit.'

At the beginning of 1981, the group were just beginning to perfect the cross-pollination of live and studio techniques to great effect. Barbieri: 'There were a lot of keyboard parts on *Quiet Life*, *Polaroids* and [later] *Tin Drum*, many of them of a sequential nature. Without the MIDI programming facility we have today, these patterns and sequences were played or controlled by analogue step time sequencers. Playing just one of these parts live would mean you couldn't also play all the other elements. Analogue sequencers didn't have memory so couldn't be programmed for the next song in a matter of seconds. We decided to record and put all sequenced or constant keyboard parts on tape, so with things like 'Life In Tokyo', 'Quiet Life' and 'Methods Of Dance' the sequencer is on tape and, with a click, went to Steve's monitoring. A few other elements like brass were on tape as well.'

Japan shopping in
Osaka, February 1981
Keiko Kurata

Either for budgetary or aesthetic reasons, the group were ultimately reluctant to expand their onstage personnel via session players à la Talking Heads even though Sylvian had mused about doing just that in recent interviews. Barbieri: 'If the music contains a lot of elements, then you either end up with a seven-piece band or you put some on backing track. I can't see the point of using tons of hardware on stage, so that you can just press a button that plays the sequences. You may as well have it on backing track because there is no human interaction going on with that part. It's best to concentrate on playing as many of the performed album parts as possible.' Jansen: 'It was a discipline, but one I felt was a great challenge and got a kick out of pulling off. If anyone ever noticed a red light on top of the PA system (of course they didn't), I can explain that was triggered by a switch near my left foot, and was an indication to John that I could see everyone was ready for him to start rolling the tape.' It was obvious that having a session saxophonist on stage with the band added little upon which tapes couldn't improve. Jane Shorter had not been invited back for this tour and went on to join The Thompson Twins. John Punter, besotted with the band, temporarily put his recording career on hold to become Japan's full-time live sound engineer. The band, along with crew and Nick Huckle, flew to Japan for the tour, once again via the cheapest, most gruelling long-haul flight.

Despite their profile and success in Japan, the band still travelled as if they were a fledgling new wave group on a home-made indie label (which, actually, Virgin was), sharing rooms and with little time set aside to recuperate, socialise or go sightseeing, although they did manage to catch a Talking Heads show in Japan on the *Remain In Light* tour. 'It was incredible,' says Dean, 'we were all blown away by them, David included.' By now, Sylvian disliked playing the enormous, reverb-laden Budokan and the novelty of being a pop star and a heartthrob was wearing thin. As such, tours of Australia and festival appearances in the UK and Europe were rejected. Japan's current set list still included older songs, although the days were numbered for these refugees from the first two albums. Dean: 'We always did small tours. Even in Japan we only did three weeks. I wasn't ever sure why. The set list was chosen in order to please both an audience and the band. Old songs would have to be able to be rearranged in order to fit in with the newest songs. 'Obscure Alternatives' was a very atmospheric song anyway, so could be easily rearranged to fit alongside the newer material. And no, it wasn't a drag to rearrange songs; it was actually fun – well, for some of us, anyway. And remember – we didn't have that large a repertoire. That was another reason for revamping the older songs.'

Japan also had their very own celebrity stalker on this tour: Gary Numan. Perhaps disorientated by his rapid and recent

Far left and centre: Gary Numan arriving in Japan, Spring 1981
Keiko Kurata

Right: The Batt brothers go walkabout, Japan
Keiko Kurata

rise to fame and suffering from as then undiagnosed Asperger's syndrome, he had become infatuated by the band to the extent that he had flown himself and a bodyguard over to Japan to follow the band on tour. The group were given no forewarning and were simply surprised to notice him a few steps behind them wherever they went, often sitting a few rows behind on the bullet train. Sometimes, feeling sympathetic, they would let Numan travel with them from gig to gig on their bus. Numan himself would explain his trip years later: 'They vaguely invited me to guest with them on their Japanese tour. I managed to locate their hotel by ringing around and I met them there the following morning while they were having breakfast. They seemed surprised to see me and there wasn't much conversation, so I felt a bit awkward. Then they said they were going to get ready, so off they went to their rooms. Suddenly I noticed them running out of a side door and climbing into some waiting cars.' Numan recounts that he followed them to the station and onto a train and eventually had to buy tickets to their Budokan gig where, 'right up until the theatre doors opened I assumed it was all still going to happen.' What exactly he thought was supposed to happen is a mystery. Karn: 'There were never any plans to have Gary join us on stage. I wonder how he could have thought that at all possible as nothing had been rehearsed musically or vocally … it was all a bit of a mystery as to why he was in Japan the same time as we were,

often appearing on various journeys we were taking and sitting separately behind us. I sat with him briefly on several occasions as he made no attempt to approach us.' Dean: 'You know that's the first I've heard about him expecting to play with us live on tour. I'm pretty sure it must have been just in his own head, unless he'd spoken with Mick about it drunk in some club somewhere – Mick that is – since I'm sure the general consensus, had there been one, would have been in the negative.' Barbieri: 'I can only imagine that somebody gave him a reason to go to Japan with us on the same plane and stay at the same hotels etc. Maybe something was meant to happen, but didn't. I can't believe he just followed us to the other side of the globe because he wanted to.'

Numan would still be telling variations on this story 30 years later, seemingly sincerely believing that he and Japan had agreed to perform in concert together and that he had been 'blown out' at the last minute. Short of jamming – the last thing either act was predisposed to do – it's mystifying as to what Numan had in mind. Dean: 'What can I say? He's an odd one. He can hardly say we legged it – he was with us for a good week or so I think, on the bus. He was at every sound check. I think I felt a bit sorry for him and felt that someone ought to try and communicate since he'd come all that way, although him having a personal bodyguard was a bit off-putting.' Huckle: 'I have no recollection of him

Japan performing in Kyoto, 23 February 1981
Keiko Kurata

Numan on tour bus with Sylvian, Karn and Simon Napier-Bell Japan 1981
Keiko Kurata

being there at all. As the person responsible for backstage access, who stayed in the same hotels, ate at the same restaurants and travelled in the same planes and bullet trains etc., I can't believe I wouldn't have noticed a small Numan chap being there.'

The shows themselves were the usual success, although some onlookers noted that Japan's singer sometimes seemed to be going through the motions. 'If I had to act, I wouldn't do it,' countered Sylvian, 'that's why I don't do tours for a long period of time. There are nights when we play and I don't do anything except just stand there and sing; I feel the audience might be getting a bit bored, but then I might be a bit bored doing it so what would they prefer to see – me putting on an act just to please them or me singing the songs as I feel them that night? I can only do exactly what I feel. So many people misinterpret the way we do things; they feel it might be a bit pompous, but it never is.' From the wings, Huckle was sympathetic: 'In those days you toured as the main means of promoting your album, so being a pragmatist Dave did what he had to do in terms of touring, but only as much as he considered productive and could be kept on the right side of tolerable. Also in those days the technology around live shows was relatively primitive, expensive and often unpredictable or inconsistent. This did not suit Dave.'

The earlier songs still played from the first two albums were often only recognisable from their titles and lyrics – 'Adolescent Sex', for example, had been filtered through the rhythm section's best deconstruction filter – and were much more effect and synth saturated. Sylvian sang with little love for the original melody even if the band themselves remember it otherwise. Jansen: 'I don't think we did much in the way of revamping. What we did do was usually not so vastly different, but we would each try our best to breathe new life into certain songs that we felt weren't up to scratch or that we might have seen a way to adapt to our more current style of playing at that time.' Karn adds: 'Every time we tour, we try and change some of the old ones that don't sound right.' It wasn't just Sylvian who had wearied of the early songs. 'It is just so hard to work up a feeling for songs on the first two albums,' explained Barbieri, 'so we try to make them more interesting.' According to Karn, these jittery, start-stop hi-energy remodels of old tunes were still more fun to play than the more regal sounding new material, claiming that on one occasion, 'Steve actually fell asleep during 'Taking Islands In Africa'. 'Jansen concurs. 'Yes, that song was immensely long and uneventful rhythmically. To say it dragged on would be an understatement. I did fall asleep during that song, just the once though, right to the point where I managed to catch myself before falling off the stool. A momentary lapse.'

Sylvian, as ever, refused to second-guess his audience or his bandmates and put the work before all else. 'It's not what people want; it's what we want to do. If you can't play them with any feeling, there's no point in playing them at all.' Barbieri was in agreement: 'It's very hard to think of what people want all the time. You can only think of what you want and then after that maybe give consideration to what other people want. It sounds selfish, but it's the only way you can do it.' Aside from Karn, who was a natural and mesmerising performer, so far as the rest of the band were concerned, Japan were an entertaining live act only by default. 'I don't think you should ever compromise,' explained Sylvian, 'we compromise between the four of us and the producer, and that's as far as it should go, and we have real problems as everyone has their own ideas about how they want to hear something, so if you start thinking about the audience as well…'

With the Japanese tour behind them, there was time for a brief break in Bangkok. Punter remembers it as a partly idyllic experience: 'We were actually stranded in Thailand, on Pattaya beach, for a week. We had first class accommodation, all paid for by the promoter because he'd fucked the date up. We'd arrived on the Friday to play on the Saturday, but the gig was actually the *following* Saturday, so we had this beautiful hotel and were out in the sun on the beach, enjoying free cocktails and so on – and David never came out of his room! For the whole week he stayed in his room and the only time he came out was to play the gig. It was bizarre. It was like, "Really?" Maybe he was writing all the time, but it was weird. An extreme experience because we had a week off in this beautiful place and he never spent any time with us.' Karn also noted Sylvian's gradual self-removal from the group at this point. 'David was beginning to isolate himself from us,' he'd recall, 'and he didn't attend Rob's 25th birthday party either.' Delicia Burnell, now a permanent fixture at Nomis, reasoned that, 'David was always self-referencing. He was much more introspective than the others. Maybe that goes with being the lyricist? Next to his "existentialism" Steve and Mick were jesters, but even they were pretty introverted compared to "normal" people.'

Back in London, Japan were welcomed by their new label. The staff there were pleased with the sales and reception of *Polaroids* and were keen to take the group to the next step as soon as possible. Everything was in place to do just that. Draper: 'In 1981, I acquired a larger stake in Virgin as a holding company and consequently I had more authority. I also had a lot of credibility with Richard [Branson] and my staff and so if I felt a group were high quality, like The Penguin Café Orchestra for instance, and I liked them personally, then even if they weren't selling that much, as long as they were selling *enough* and I liked them – as with Japan – then they could continue on the label. I was answerable to no one but Branson. And it was a lovely feeling, especially so later in 1983 when we became a very successful, powerful and rich company. But before that happened, most of the other staff at Virgin and I were motivated by just loving records. And we loved Japan.'

Consequently, on Friday 29 March 1981, the band assembled at Basing Street Studios once again with John Punter. 'John had shaved his beard off,' remarked Jansen in his diary, the producer losing the face fuzz presumably the better to accommodate the occasional make-up he now wore. Dean, although still officially a member, did not partake in the sessions. This decision did not seem to raise any eyebrows within the group (and it would have been impossible to notice in Karn's case). All thought was towards musical progression. Barbieri: 'The purpose of the session with John was to record a double A-side single: 'The Art Of Parties' and 'Life Without Buildings'. It would sound very different from *Polaroids* and was most likely us searching for a new approach.' This was a rare excursion for Japan into something more uptempo and hopefully commercial by default. The group's approach in the studio was free and open. Jansen: 'I think 'The Art Of Parties' would have been written on rhythm guitar, and we would have undoubtedly played it to death in rehearsals until each member came up with a part. I'm unable to recall any brief prior to starting *any* Japan song. I had spent so many years playing one-on-one with David on rhythm guitar, since we were about 12 and 13 years old, that I just did what I

Karn attempting to sink Punter's boat, Thailand 1981
Richard Barbieri

would feel inspired to do. We had a way of latching on. I didn't need direction, as I pretty much took the initiative with what I was going to do and no one in the band was a greater critic of what I was doing than myself. In hindsight, I think that 'Parties' was probably a case of me syncopating with the funky guitar part, which I think David was originally seeing in the long term as a brass arrangement. We used to really enjoy albums like Michael Jackson's *Off The Wall* and perhaps there was some element of that going on. It was being written as a single, so I think there may have been a priority to come up with something that might get people moving or achieve some radio play.'

It was still academic as to who actually 'wrote' the songs, although on the forthcoming sleeve of the single there would be a new credit, abandoned thereafter: 'Written and composed by Sylvian/Arranged by Japan'. At the time Jansen would explain that, 'Who did what was never an issue because each person through their role is equally as important as the songwriter, so it never became a big deal – the fact he [Sylvian] was actually writing the songs. He doesn't order everybody around. What he does is to give a general direction to most of the stuff we're doing – some of it he doesn't. Stuff like 'The Art Of Parties' he didn't have a direction for, but mostly he knows the basic idea of what he wants, then he leaves it up to us. It starts from me and Mick, to bring the song together from the roots. So there's no dictatorship; it's not like that at all.' The song would showcase the rhythm section most explicitly with a

Sylvian doing vocal takes for 'The Art Of Parties'
Steve Jansen

drum pattern that seemed to have no beginning or end and was danceable despite itself. 'It isn't a particularly difficult drum part,' Jansen would say modestly, 'it's very linear and the hands are simply playing sixteenths but moving around the kit to stress different beats on different drums. I was keen on going light on the downbeat [where a bass drum is almost always to be found] and this created the rather unusual sense that the rhythm track is drifting.'

'Life Without Buildings' was even more startling, and at first listen almost Sylvian-less. Jansen was for once the lead instrument and the sound of his drums was queasy, propulsive, aggressive, disturbing and seductive. They even *sounded* odd. Jansen: 'The tom sounds on 'Life Without Buildings' were created by doubling the toms with a low synth sound to provide a bend note. Each tom had a different synth note played with it. I did my best to play them in sync, but I could hear flamming, especially in the intro. The toms, and I think the drum ambience mics, were also processed through a harmoniser to give the kit more of a slur [also to be heard on 'Ain't That Peculiar']. You can hear this on the toms, but it's also quite predominant on the hi-hat because it really affects the top end as it rings quite a bit.' Sylvian takes full credit for the song, despite singing only a few lines halfway through during the song's breakdown, although he does contribute keyboards throughout.

Unless you checked the credits it would be hard to notice Dean's absence. Jansen explained his omission: 'Rob's input was at a time when guitar riffs and technical solos were the order of the day, but we'd left all that behind after *Polaroids*. There was less need for a player with capabilities beyond that which David could provide. Also, Rob didn't really have the patience to fine-tune a performance, which made him a little different from the rest of us, so I think these two factors are what prompted his exit.' Barbieri: 'It wasn't so weird not having Rob around since on *Polaroids* he was becoming less involved, through no fault of his own; it was just a case of the keyboards and synths becoming more dominant in the writing, arranging and overdubbing process.' Punter, however, was taken aback at the absence of Dean: '"Where's Boblet?" I'd asked, "Oh he's not playing on this one," Dave told me.' Punter didn't know it then, but soon he would be excised from the band too. 'We'd formed a very close and comfortable working relationship with John after completing two albums together as well as live touring with him mixing out front ... perhaps too comfortable,' says Jansen. 'I believe we went into these ['Parties'] sessions

together as a natural progression of that relationship. However, during the subsequent writing process of the material for *Tin Drum* I think it became apparent that change could be a good thing. I believe we wanted to find an alternative to conventional, safe production values. But saying that, the 'Parties' sessions went smoothly – in particular the exploration of ideas for 'Life Without Buildings'. We were liberated by the fact it was to be a B-side – it was sort of a licence to indulge. We explored some of the concepts that were of influence at that time – albums such as *My Life In The Bush Of Ghosts* by Byrne and Eno and, prior to that, *Movies* by Holgar Czukay. Both these albums utilised the placement of audio from sampled sources [via tapes] playing out like scenes from a movie amidst predominantly instrumental tracks. We, rather timidly in retrospect, tried it out on this final session with Punter and although it wasn't to any great effect, it was probably the first buzz we'd felt of transforming a track by incorporating scenes from an outside source. The imagery it created took us outside of our own creativity and that was the purpose, I think. Also, here we were focusing more on the recorded sound itself as opposed to leaving it up to the producer, which consequently led to spur-of-the-moment ideas steering the music.' The result would be more of a footnote to *Gentlemen Take Polaroids* than a preface to *Tin Drum*, while occupying a space in Japan's discography all of its own. The sound was more acoustic or perhaps organic even, especially in its electronics, than anything previous or to come. 'Life Without Buildings' in particular seemed to embody the dust and clay apparent in the Frank Kobina Parkes poem 'African Heaven', an extract of which Sylvian chose to print in the forthcoming tour programme:

'Give me some drums;
Let them be three
Or maybe four
And make them black –
Dirty and black:
Of wood,
And dried sheepskin,
But if you will
Just make them peal,
Peal.
Peal loud,
Mutter.
Loud,
Louder yet;
Then soft,
Softer still
Let the drums peal.'

The band themselves were very happy with the recordings. 'It remains, for me, one of John's best works of production,' Karn would say. Mixing of the two tracks finished on 24 March. Simon Draper came down to the studio to listen and was impressed although not overly hopeful of any instant commercial breakthrough, but this was not an issue. 'I expected it to take time. There was no rush,' he says. Aside from the forthcoming *Oil On Canvas*, this would be the last true studio work the group did with John Punter, although the producer himself wasn't aware of it then. 'We could all hear the similarities between *Quiet Life* and *Gentleman Take Polaroids* and that's not meant as a criticism but, for us, moving forward always meant changing everything that had come before,' stated Karn. Punter's replacement was already on the periphery. Barbieri: 'Previously, while we were recording *Polaroids* at AIR Studios, a man called Steve Nye was engineering Sakamoto's *B-2 Unit* album in Studio 3. We were very impressed with the overall sound, and also with Ryuichi's creativity on the Prophet 5. At some point after the 'Art Of Parties' sessions, I imagine David decided to approach Steve Nye with regards to the new album. I can't remember any of us not being happy with John's work at any point, but possibly because the music we were working on in rehearsals was becoming more abstract and experimental, we most likely felt that a change in producer was a good idea.'

That spring, on the streets of London, Japan were finally becoming fashionable. In the UK, they had been considered a foppish, confused joke for so long that even the press department at Virgin was taken aback at the sudden turnaround. 'Almost overnight, magazines were treating them with respect,' remembers Bourton, 'they deserved it, but it was almost a shock at first.' One music publication even predicted that 'The Art Of Parties' would make number one. This turnaround was no doubt in part due to the vagaries of fashion.

The New Romantic movement had begun in London in late 1979 and was peaking in 1981. A glam reaction to the spit and speed of punk, the Blitz Kids who comprised the movement worshipped Bowie, Ferry, Kraftwerk, and a European ideal steeped in glamour, elegance and decadence, the make-up was heavy and an ideal of artificial beauty was its zenith. Visually, with their expansive hair-dos and self-applied make-up, Japan fitted the bill even if in fact they had little interest in, or actual connection to, the movement. Karn at the time noted: 'It was very painful to notice that the things we've been doing with so much devotion for such a long time weren't recognised until the Blitz movement suddenly became fashionable. That gave us a bitter feeling, especially towards the press. I think we've been influential, especially as individuals; I hear people drum like Steve, and my bass-playing is being copied. You shouldn't make it bigger than it is though; it is a fact that people are being influenced all the time.'

Mark Wardel

Japan were far too aloof, shy, insular, and self-referencing ever to belong comfortably to an outside group or movement. At this point they were still socialising together, mostly at home. 'Yes, we generally just used to chill around our flat,' says Huckle. 'A little puff, a little coke, and some sake and/or brandy. There were occasions of group giggling, usually when Mick was there and was telling a story about some predicament he'd got himself into. Dave could giggle with the best of them if the mood was right.' This isn't to say Japan were complete hermits. Dean was still a cinema fanatic and Mick was increasingly to be seen at opening nights and launch parties.

Even Sylvian, self-appointed glam pariah that he was, was making new friends. Mark Wardel was an ex-Liverpool art school student and had gravitated towards the London club scene in 1979, becoming friendly with designer Antony Price who had introduced him to the in-crowd – the international jet set comprising mostly art world figures, pop stars and independently wealthy heirs and heiresses. Wardel also mixed with the Blitz Kids, the ultimate gaggle of wannabes who would in many cases (Boy George, Steve Strange) become exactly what they aspired to be. The movement's philosophy was manifest in the clubs themselves. 'It was "Dictatorship on the door, democracy on the dance floor",' says Wardel. 'You could be in the Embassy Club and you'd maybe see a window cleaner who looked the part dancing with the Duchess of Argyll or the flower seller from Piccadilly sitting with Rod Stewart and Britt Ekland.'

Where did Sylvian fit in among such a scene? Although he was the son of a brickie, he certainly looked the part, and thanks to his exclusive publishing deal with Napier-Bell and Virgin he was becoming financially independent. He also travelled enough to qualify as jet set, yet was reticent socially and chose his friends carefully. Wardel was also blonde and made-up, resembling a taller, much more dramatically handsome version of the Warhol ideal. 'I'd seen David around,' he says, 'and I guess because of the way we looked, which was similar and quite striking, there was a connection, but he was always quite reserved, especially in public. He was very cool and always looked great. He came across as this rather elegant figure, who you would only very occasionally see out and about. People thought he was snooty, but then they also said the same about me, although we were in reality hiding behind shyness and I think if you're well dressed and projecting a strong look, that can often be perceived as aloofness. I know that some of the Blitz luminaries could be quite bitchy about him, but then he never frequented Blitz. I mostly saw him at art openings or places like Legends or the Embassy Club. His personality was completely different from any of the Blitz habitués although we were all to varying degrees vain – it was the era's drug of choice and we all shared a work ethic, even if for Steve Strange, say, that work was more to do with ambition for its own sake. David's interests were more intellectual by comparison.' Wardel had first properly encountered Sylvian at a rare live event that the latter had deigned to attend in the VIP enclosure at Wembley Arena for a Gary Numan concert that April. 'We had been on nodding terms before then at various places, but this is probably when we really spoke properly for the first time. David was there with Mick and Richard, but I got the feeling he wasn't really into the Numan show and wasn't there totally of his own volition. There was another concert the following week that I was going to – someone like Hazel O'Connor – and I said, "Maybe I'll see you there," and

he replied, "Oh God no, absolutely not." He wasn't into that whole scene at all. I hit it off with David, but not the rest of the group particularly. David and I had a slightly similar look as I guess we were drawing from similar reference points, but we also had similar personalities and interests. I'm convinced that the fact that I was a painter and not a musician was important as, had I been the latter, I don't think we'd have become friends at all. He was very interested in art and the Warhol ethos at that time, as we both were. I don't think he had that many friends but I found him easy to get on with and he had a great sense of humour. I wasn't intimidated by his celebrity as I was by then quite used to mixing with famous people. Socially the dynamic was obviously in his favour as he was so busy with the band and travelling a lot; I'd wait for him to call me and we'd maybe go out for dinner and rarely, if ever, to clubs. I'd go to his flat or he'd come to my studio where we would sit and discuss art and music etc. Occasionally I'd visit him at the studio when Japan were recording or rehearsing and maybe take some Polaroids or something, but I didn't really ever go to clubs or parties with him – it wasn't that kind of friendship.'

On 28 March, while the new single was being mastered and pressed, Karn was introduced to Japanese photographer Yuka Fujii. Eleven years older than Karn, Fujii had in fact photographed the band in her role as staff photographer for *Music Life* magazine back in 1979, but had apparently made little impression on Karn then as it was only now that he'd recall meeting her for the first time. Fujii, who had previously been partner to Chick Corea, was now employed by *Music Life* occasionally to host 'tea parties' in London for their readers. It was at one such event that Steve and Mick, shepherded by the ever diligent and sociable Connie, spent the afternoon at the Metropole Hotel signing autographs, smiling and posing for photos and attempting hesitant small talk across the long tables with a gaggle of Japanese girls. Karn and Yuka hit it off instantly. This would be Karn's first serious relationship. 'We began spending more and more time together at my flat,' he'd recall, 'losing all track of time until morning when she would leave.' Yuka soon moved in with Karn. 'It was the first time I'd ever lived with anyone,' he'd say, 'it gave me a sense of completeness and maturity.'

On 1 April Sylvian officially told Dean that he was no longer part of the band. Typically, 'he [Dean] took it well', noted Jansen in his diary. Dean's leaving felt natural. Huckle: 'I just think they outgrew him musically. When he first joined back in 1977, or whenever, he was the better musician. By *Polaroids,* the rest of the guys had caught up, but more importantly were keen to experiment and push boundaries, whereas Rob seemed, to me anyway, to stay where he had always been creatively. He was a great guitarist, but stylistically I think he became removed from Dave's vision for the band. At that time they were becoming far more keyboard/synth orientated, experimenting with non-standard rock rhythms and so on. I think Dave was looking for a guitar presence that didn't feel or sound like your standard rock guitar part. As far as I'm aware, Rob leaving was purely musical. As I mentioned previously, it was clear during the recording of *Polaroids* that Dave was getting very frustrated that Rob couldn't "get out of the box" stylistically. He wasn't able or willing to play outside of his established playing style. There was many a growl and "ARRHHHH" from Dave, when despite trying to describe a feel/emotion/rhythmic idea/etc. to Rob from the control room he would revert back to his comfort zone. I suspect that Dave may have been pondering the Rob situation for a while before *Polaroids,* because he undoubtedly would have begun to wonder during the preceding rehearsals. It must have been really hard for Dave but, ever the pragmatist, he would have felt that Rob remaining in the band risked a stagnation of their musical development as a whole.'

Dean took the news gracefully and was himself tired of the situation. 'It felt like David would say something and we'd all just agree with him,' he remembers. There was no protest from the rest of the band. 'I really don't know how much the others were consulted about the decision, but I know it was a hard time for them all, as they did all get on so well,' says Huckle. 'I can't remember there being any arguments between Rob and any of the guys during the whole time he was in the band. But he did appear to take it very graciously. He would still hang out socially with everyone for a long time afterwards and showed no bitterness against anyone. Nor did any of the band to him.'

Dean: 'Despite what Nick Huckle says, I personally recall David's frustration over a guitar part during the recording of Gentlemen Take Polaroids on only one occasion and this was concerning the song 'Some Kind Of Fool'. I was actually as frustrated as David, because it was a song I was particularly fond of yet struggled so much over. I eventually created and recorded a part, chordal in structure, that I was happy with, but not long after the song was dropped altogether. In regard to other songs on the album, the parts for 'Swing', 'Gentlemen Take Polaroids', 'Ain't That Peculiar' and 'Methods Of Dance' were established before the recordings took place, together with the other ditched track, 'Angel In Furs'. As far as I can recall I did not even attempt guitar parts on the remaining tracks which I knew as well as David, did not need them.

'I disagree with Mick's statement that I was "banned from the studio". There were certainly not weeks on end when I was not in attendance. I recall being there but not participating for long periods. Often though, I would leave the sessions early and go to the cinema nearby. By this time the cinema consumed me. There was barely a week when I wasn't haunting one arthouse or another. I spent a fair amount of time at the studio but felt that there was no point hanging around the cafeteria playing Space Invaders while days were spent recording saxophone parts. I'd be there, quietly reading a good deal of the time. Perhaps because for long periods my input was, to say the least, minimal, Mick remembers it as such.

'Something that I have not disclosed to anyone until now is that I was actually aware of the sessions for 'The Art Of Parties' that I was not privy to (thanks to an opportune encounter with one of Air Studio's engineers in Oxford Street one day). He was surprised to see me because he knew that at that very moment the band were in Basing Street studios with John Punter and unbeknownst to him he was informing me of it. So I knew what was coming and it was something of a relief when I got the call from David. Rather than a confrontation, I had decided to wait and so by the time it arrived I was in a good place in my head with it. As I have said before it was quite a release. The final tour I was happy to do, knowing that there would be a fitting end.'

'Everyone loved Rob,' says Barbieri. Dean: 'I went over to one of their flats and they played me 'The Art Of Parties'. I said, "Oh, it sounds great." I had no problem with it.' Sylvian suggested in the press at the time that Rob would be pursuing photography. 'Nah,' says Rob, 'he was just pulling things out of thin air. But there was no animosity. It was the end of an era for me. I've always been quite logical about things like that. I just let things take their course. They had a party for me at Mick and Yuka's place and made me a cake with a plane on it. [Dean was due to fly to the States soon.] We were all still friendly and I'd still hang out with them.'

'The Art Of Parties' was released on 1 May. The packaging was luscious, with photos by Jansen taken in Karn's bedroom, but looking like the group had somehow parachuted into the set of Coppola's *Apocalypse Now* for the night. 'I took the photos of the band for the 'Parties' cover after returning from Bangkok,' says Jansen. 'We wanted to look sweaty and unkempt which was a bit of a departure for us. Maybe because it was me taking the photos, we felt comfortable risking a bad outcome. I've no idea what it has to do with any art of any parties.' Sylvian again channelled Warhol on the cover, wearing prescription-free spectacles, a Walkman and a camera over a Walmart workman's shirt. The combined package was Japan at their Pop Art prettiest.

The Art Of Parties Tour began on 7 May in Nottingham, with tickets priced at between £2 and £3.50. Sylvian sported a military-look suit on hire from Antony Price and the tour was the first outside of Japan to have its own programme. The crew arrived at Nottingham Rock City at 4.30 pm to set up. Travelling in a luxury bus whose laminate interior gave off the smell of stale vomit, the band were supposed to head directly to their hotel, but in typical Japan fashion they were delayed, apparently somehow getting lost on the motorway. The soundtrack to this journey, via the in-bus tape player, was Strauss. In an *NME* interview conducted at the hotel, the journalist noted Sylvian's curt behaviour towards Dean when he asked if the guitarist was to be included in the accompanying photo shoot: 'Dean: "Do you want me in this photo?" Sylvian: "No, you stay here!"' Dean was stoic: 'I wasn't shocked by that, no, although I do remember it. I'd already left, I suppose, so I was just fulfilling my obligations.'

The tour was ostensibly to promote 'The Art Of Parties', but there was no promo video made for the single and no one seems to remember why. Jeremy Lascelles: 'Now that's a very good question. I honestly can't remember the answer though. Were we hedging our bets as to the real commercial viability of the band? Or was David a reluctant participant? Whilst we absolutely believed in the band and their artistic aspirations, it is possible (and I can't be certain of this) that we weren't absolutely convinced that they had the big hit song. It was, after all, a very singles-dominated market at that point.' Keith Bourton: 'It wasn't considered *de rigueur* at this point in the music business to have a promo video for each single release. Although, having said that, Virgin did try to do just that at the time. I'm not sure if it was down to the band's reticence or us at Virgin who wondered about the viability of the single getting to radio. The tide was certainly turning for Japan in terms of media acceptance.' Indeed, 'The Art Of Parties' was Japan's highest charting single yet in the UK, reaching a respectable 48 and an appearance on *Top Of The Pops* was duly offered for 12 May. Sadly, a football match overran on BBC1 and the programme was cancelled. Most of Japan would have cursed their luck as they played Edinburgh that night. The venues outside of London were medium sized, but it was obvious that the group were making new fans by the week.

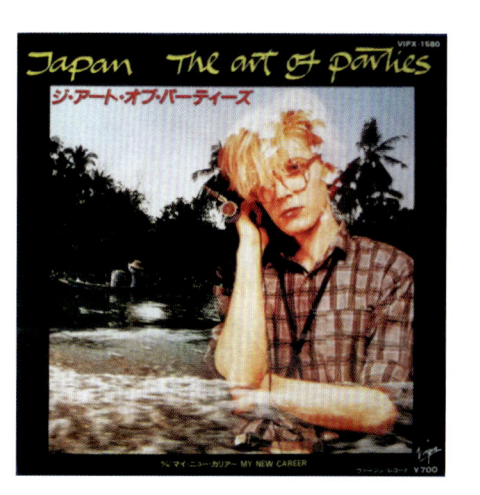

David Rhodes would soon go on to play with Japan, but was then finding his feet as Peter Gabriel's guitarist. He happened to hear 'Parties' and offered a musician's appraisal of Japan's new direction: 'I just love the rhythm. There's a nice double thing on the bass, going away from the bass drum. It was lovely to take, what was then, a very black feel on the guitar – Chic were very big at the time – it was like somebody playing a Nile Rodgers guitar part but a white boy doing it. It doesn't have the grooves that Rodgers or Chic get yet it still has its own very specific power, and again with Steve's drumming, the patterns he builds, rather than just doing a normal dance beat.'

Dean was still performing with the band and still on the wage meted out by their manager and wasn't treated as a guitarist for hire in any way; had he been, he would have been paid more. Everyone knew this would be Rob's final time with the band after being a member for six years. Despite the increasing crowds, sold out venues, the slow conversion of the press and the imminent commercial success, the guitarist himself remained typically stoical. 'No, I didn't feel bitter or excluded,' he says, 'I felt that we had already achieved some recognition in our home country anyway. We were well established. Just the fact that we could play the Rainbow and sell out The Venue and tour generally meant we were doing well. Okay, we weren't doing

Top Of The Pops every week at that point, but we were doing well. And it felt logical for me to leave.' As Dean prepared to exit, another associate was about to enter Japan's circle.

Angie Usher was a young, glam Londoner with a Bowie habit. 'I first saw Japan at the Camden Music Machine years before. I just thought they were amazing. Looked amazing. Sounded amazing,' she says. 'A few years later I moved up to London from Essex and by that time I was friends with the DJ Mark Moore [S-Express], and he got us tickets to go see Japan at The Venue. This would have been 1980. They were now the "new" Japan if you like. And I was completely hooked, as was Mark. He was a huge fan too and more than that he just loved all kinds of music. He had the biggest record collection I'd ever seen. Anyway, at this time I was working at the British Diabetic Association in central London. And in the mailing room there on one of the filing cabinets, someone had scratched "Japan – Mick and Steve". And I was like, "Wow, someone else is a Japan fan who works here," and my boss said, "No. That was them. They worked here. They weren't interested in the job at all. They hated the job and all they wanted to do was make music." So when I told him they had he was like, "Wow! Really? They actually did it?"' (For the record, Steve Jansen never actually worked at the company.) Usher: 'Our friends were in a band called Modern English and they were supporting Japan on *The Art Of Parties Tour*, and we slept on their hotel floors so we could see Japan for free every night. We were at an after-show in a club in Leeds and I saw Japan sitting with their security, kind of cut off from the rest of the party and I said, "Can I go and talk to them, because I used to work at the same place as them?" And the bouncer was like, "No, no, no," so I just ignored him and pushed past and sat down with them. And I said to Mick, "You know where you used to work, behind Oxford Circus – that's where I work." He was like, "No way!" And that's how we became friends.'

Steve Walker was keyboard player in support band Modern English and a friend of Usher: 'I was a fan of Japan already. I'd enjoyed watching them grow from being this glammy rock band into this futurist ideal. They really were considered the prettiest boys in the business and that whole "most beautiful man in the world" shtick must have been a real burden to bear. I think it got on David's nerves. But he was a striking looking man, no denying that. They were a touch aloof at first but as soon as you got to know them they were just the boys next door really. Very nice guys and they treated us well. We shared the same agent, ITB [International Talent Booking], and the tour was arranged through them. Of course, in those days you had to buy onto a tour too. We did half the dates, and then a band called Wasted Youth did the rest. We were happy to be supporting; they were a band of our liking and they weren't a million miles away in sound. The tour opened our eyes up to how it could be for a band – being constantly photographed, mobbed by cute little Japanese girls … they were in demand. And even though they hadn't actually had a hit in Britain at this point you could feel it was only a matter of time. It was coming. Steve was particularly impressive; a lot of drummers were anti-tapes, anti-drum machines, and for some the studio was one thing and playing live another, but he used the best of both worlds. We didn't have a lot of money at the time so some nights we couldn't afford to stay in a hotel and had to drive home from the gig, so we saw no backstage drinks or after shows really.'

The tour ended with two nights at the Hammersmith Odeon, and Dean would not play with Japan again. Usher: 'I felt he was the outsider. He was never as comfortable as the rest with the make-up. The rest of them lived near each other and he was off on his own in Hackney. I just got the sense it was never a permanent thing for him.' Marina Muhlfriedel (Hansa): 'I was disappointed when Rob left. I thought he could have adapted and brought more to the sound. But David was increasingly into a minimalist ideal, so it seemed to me, and a big part of that was the oriental influence. He understood the idea of "negative space" and that extended to the album covers and maybe even band members.' With Dean now due to move to the US, in the UK Japan were as big as it was possible to get without having had a hit.

Japan at debut
Hammersmith
Odeon concert.
Sylvian wears
Antony Price
Jan Kalinski

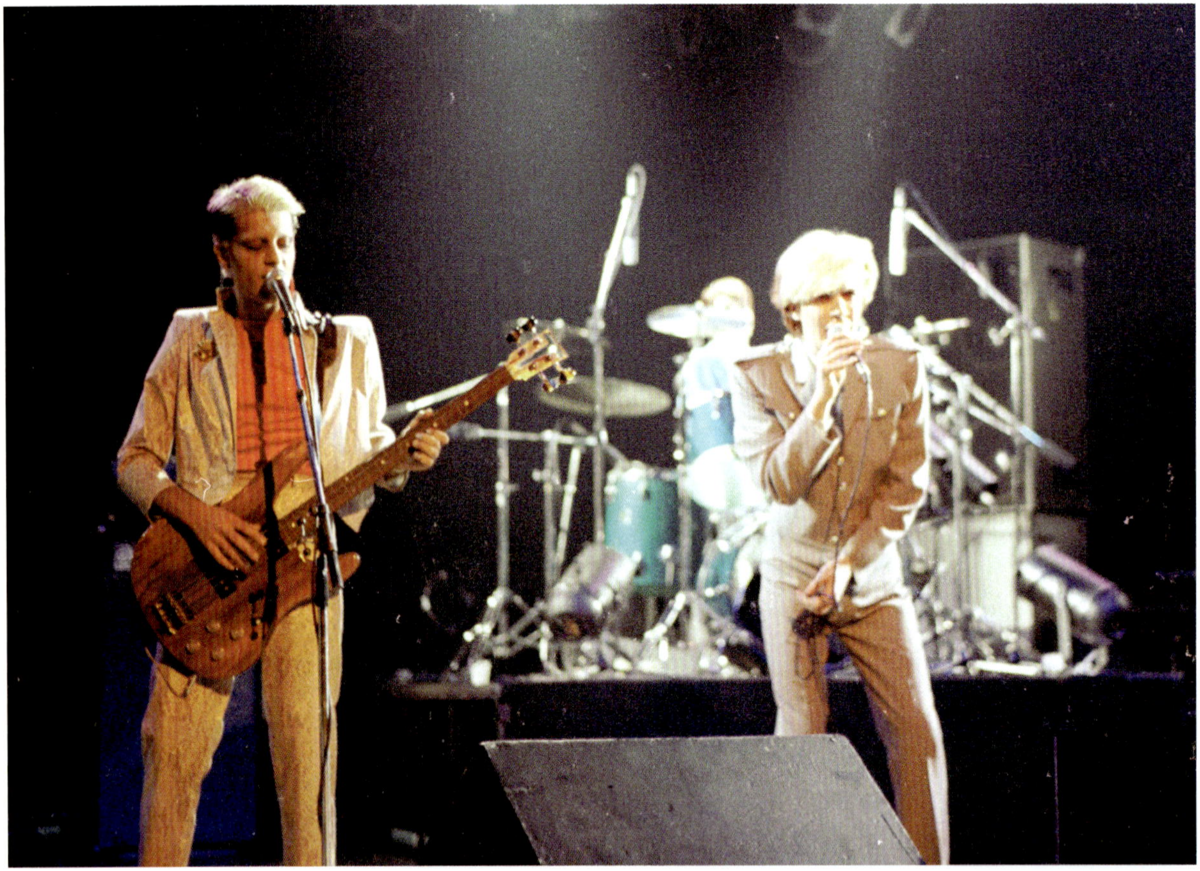

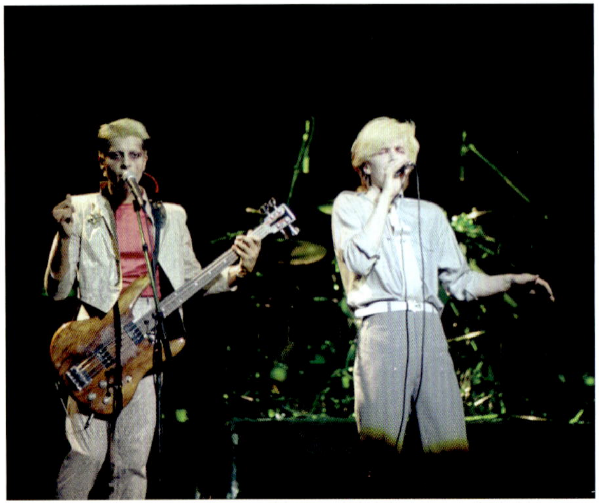

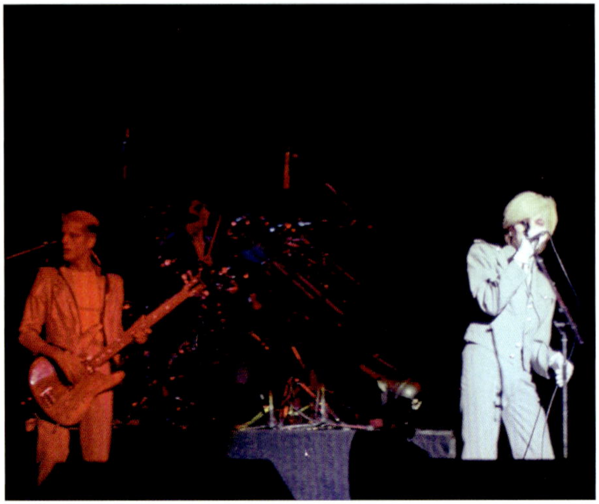

Japan at the
Hammersmith
Odeon
Jan Kalinski

Chapter 8
The Tin Drum

Steve Nye,
Ryuichi Sakamoto,
AIR Studios, 1980

The Manor Studio,
JacoTen

The last week of June in 1981 was the coldest summer spell in England since 1835. On a Sunday afternoon, beneath slate grey skies, Jansen, Barbieri, Sylvian and Karn, along with their new producer Steve Nye, were driven by stalwart Nick Huckle from London to Oxford. Situated in the village of Shipton-on-Cherwell, just north of Oxford city and set in a ninth century manor house, The Manor was Britain's first residential recording studio and the then jewel in the crown of Richard Branson's blooming Virgin empire. Since 1970, the cast of clients it had so far housed was as impressive as it was eclectic and included Mike Oldfield, John Cale, Sandy Denny, XTC, Van Morrison and PIL. Set in 35 green acres, with its own lake, the recording studio it housed was state of the art and with enough on-site lodging to house up to 40 musicians. It was within this quasi-rural setting that Japan would begin to record their final, least pastoral sounding work ever.

Jeremy Lascelles: 'Virgin owned both The Manor and Townhouse Studios so we obviously always tried to make sure they were fully booked, and so if we had a group signed to us who were due to record, our preference would be for them to use either of those studios. Of course, if the band or their producer insisted on using another studio that would be fine. The only issue that would bring up would be if either of our studios was empty because, say, of a cancellation then Richard Branson would phone me up and say, "Do we have any bands recording? Get them out of where they are and put them in our studios!" That could cause problems, but didn't happen often because The Manor and Townhouse were very successful. Very few bands needed their arms twisted to go and work in those studios because they were great studios. Obviously we'd charge our bands to use our studios and that would go against their recoupable debt and no, we didn't give our own bands discounts either.'

The group arrived somewhat squashed in a Ford Granada late that afternoon. 'I think Steve Nye had been there before, because I recall him confidently giving directions as we approached Oxford,' says Huckle. Indeed, Nye was familiar with both The Manor and its unique hierarchy of accommodation. Rooms ranged from a grand master suite to poky servant's lodgings. 'There wasn't a fight over who got the master bedroom because I don't think anyone knew about it until we arrived on that first afternoon!' says Huckle. 'So Steve Nye got it. He obviously knew about it beforehand, but kept quiet on the journey and made a dash for it as soon as we got out of the car. I remember him shouting back something like, "You better hurry, guys, or the best rooms will be gone." Then everyone else realised what was going on and there was a bit of a dash up the grand staircase to get the best remaining rooms.'

Back in London, the relationship with Punter had become too cosy, too domestic, unchallenging; for the band at least. 'No one told me why I wasn't wanted for *Tin Drum*,' he says, 'I just didn't get the call. Then I heard my old engineer Steve Nye was doing it. I was a bit upset, I admit.' This was not the first time that Punter had had to make room for his one time apprentice. 'John had partly trained me up only to see me being asked to take over engineering Roxy Music and also co-producing Bryan Ferry,' says Nye. 'Although I had played no active role in those decisions, I can see how John may have taken the progression in my career as a personal snub. It was never thus. By the time I had been asked to work with Japan on *Tin Drum* after John had put in so much effort to facilitate their progress as a band, I think it could well have been the last straw. Things were not the same for John after that.'

The man who had now bagged the best room in the house was dark haired, bearded and heavy set and, like Punter, a chain-smoker, albeit of French cigarettes, Gitanes (Punter had favoured Players). Nye was then an upcoming producer and also an established member of the Penguin Café Orchestra for whom he played Rhodes Piano. His blokey appearance (compared to Japan) belied an acute musical sensitivity and history that placed him in the perfect position to produce Japan's ultimate album. Nye had worked his way up through the ranks at AIR Studios 'pretty much straight from school in 1971, a year after the Oxford Street studio had opened,' he remembers. 'I had wanted a job where I could listen to music all day and I got it.' Throughout the 1970s he had worked alongside names like Bill Price, Jack Clegg, the famous Beatles engineer Geoff Emerick, Spike Milligan and most notably (in Japan's case) Karlheinz Stockhausen. 'The studio became practically my whole life,' says Nye. His eclectic background ensured that he was able to record anything and anyone superbly. 'During the mid-70s I got my toes wet engineering adverts, backing tracks for *Top Of The Pops* and other such training sessions whilst still assistant engineering with some of the great artists of the time such as T. Rex, Procol Harum, Roxy Music, Stevie Wonder, Wings etc. By the late 70s I felt experienced and confident enough to be engineering albums on my own, again with an amazing variety of artists and producers including Chris Thomas, with whom I had the wonderful experience of recording people like The Pretenders, Roxy, Bryan Ferry, Pete Townshend. It was then I met and worked for John Punter.'

It was at the decade's end that his first specific step towards working with Japan would occur. 'I had already worked with a curious band from Japan called the Sadistic Mika Band and at the end of the 1970s I worked with a certain Ryuichi Sakamoto from Tokyo, the likes of whom I hadn't heard before. Wall-to-wall synthesisers, drums, bass, rhythm parts, melodies, and most importantly, sumptuous atmospheres – the lot. I already liked the techno-pop of Kraftwerk, but this had more emotion to it. I fell head-first right into it. By 1980 we were finishing recording and mixing Sakomoto's first solo album, *B-2 Unit*. What a delight! I became a huge fan. These new sounds enabled a whole new world to be created. I felt at home. This is what my training had been leading up to. But now what? Ryuichi went home to Japan and that was that. I don't remember being aware that the singer in a band called Japan, who John Punter was producing in the next studio at the time, was inspired by Sakamoto and had written a track with him called 'Taking Islands In Africa'.'

Nye and Punter were at this point more than acquaintances, but not quite friends. They were chummy colleagues with the slightest riff of competition between them. 'I had been assistant to John on many albums over the years, and I knew he had co-produced Japan's *Quiet Life*,' says Nye, 'and he had apparently taken them under his wing. John relished the father figure role and was thrilled to have produced their then new album *Gentlemen Take Polaroids*. I think it was the first chance John had to work with a band relatively early on in their career that he felt he could guide to further success. Unfortunately, they seemed to want to go in a different direction. Although *Polaroids* was recorded next door and a lot of my engineering pals had worked on it, I don't remember spending much time in there, if any. Indeed, to my best recollection, it wasn't until they approached me to ask if I would be interested in recording and co-producing their next album that I formally met them. I am only guessing, but I would imagine that my work with Ryuichi and Yukihiro, whose work they admired, had something to do with their decision. I was largely unaware of their style and musical tastes other than it was a bit more pop-oriented than the kind of work in which I was interested. As I came to know them and work with them I soon realised there was more to them than I had presumed.'

B2 Unit by Ryuichi Sakamoto

Neither Nye nor the members of Japan would remember their first meeting, but the relationship and rapport between them felt natural and was instantaneous. Nye shared with them a talent for concentration, detail and for seeing the work through, no matter what. Barbieri: 'Steve Nye was pretty quiet initially and some might mistake him for being moody, but he had a very dry sense of humour and an aura of confidence. Unlike other producers/engineers, he wouldn't be put off by endless programming either. His attentiveness matched ours in that and many other respects.' This was fortuitous. While the New Romantic movement shimmied around them, Japan had no desire to become a part of any fashion, past or present, that might jump-start their career to the next stage or the commercial breakthrough that so many were anticipating – and, in their manager's and record label's case, counting on. Indeed, their pop days, insofar as any one would recognise the term then, were over. 'It's a strange feeling when you finally reach the place where you'd always striven to be, like a plateau of solitude,' Karn would muse. However, in following both their instincts and a music that was much less obviously accessible, Japan were about to reinvent early 1980s pop and consequently become more popular than ever.

The origins of *Tin Drum* had begun in London's Chinatown. 'Yuka brought the first Chinese records home,' says Karn of his then live-in girlfriend, 'which filled my head with unknown sounds, and it was only a matter of weeks before they were circulated around the band and we were all hooked.' The albums that Yuka had purchased were on sale exclusively from Chinese supermarkets around London's Little Newport Street and Gerard Street. 'They had generic titles like *Chinese Orchestral Music, Songs From The Himalayas, The Shamanism* or *The Gamelans Of Bali*,' remembers Barbieri. This was the kind of music that you would hear playing in the background at any authentic Chinese restaurant and 'it was the unusual instrumentation that left us wondering at how the absence of guitars, drum kit, synthesisers and anything else familiar, somehow still produced commercially driven music,' concludes Karn. The albums were passed among the members of Japan. Outside of the hermetically sealed confines of Sylvian's apartment, Adam Ant successfully channelled equal parts Bolan, Bowie and Morricone. Old Sylvian favourites Michael Jackson and Smokey Robinson were also charting high. The only recognisable element of any of this current music that would surface in *Tin Drum* would be the occasional echo of the Burundi-style drumming that Ant employed. In his case, such percussion owed more to the twin drummer set up of 1970s glam acts like Gary Glitter than it did to any ethnic influence, despite the costumes.

The group were now united in their enthusiasm for music that none of their peers even knew existed. This would provide the catalyst for Japan's breakthrough. Karn: 'Previously every member of the band listened to different music. Steve and I especially to African music, Richard to electronic music, and all those things came together on *Quiet Life* and *Gentlemen Take Polaroids*. Those albums got a very balanced sound, a sound in which everything was perfectly in place. After *Gentlemen...* this began to bore us. Before *Tin Drum,* none of us appeared to be well informed about the latest developments [in pop music] because we all had been listening to the same music, which was Chinese music.' Jansen: 'At the time, I wasn't listening to much mainstream pop and even knowing Paul McCartney well enough to greet and chat to him along the corridors of AIR Studios, amicable guy that he is … I think I was at that deluded point of feeling that nothing else mattered. I'm not sure if that's a healthy or terribly unhealthy state of mind, but it was all part of an insular state of being which I'd carried with me since leaving school.' Nye would now become the fifth member of this insular state. 'My manager did the deal with Virgin. I was on a fee for each track and I got points on the album too,' says Nye. 'I was a bit finicky about what I did work-wise; I preferred to do the more musical things. I didn't want to do Kajagoogoo for example, because it's hard to get on with something if you aren't into it.'

Although barely familiar with each other, Nye and Japan were now cohabiting at The Manor. 'At first blush they seemed a bit quiet and serious,' the producer would remember. 'It's not unusual for a bunch of lads that have known each other for so long. I think it's quite common to be a little distrustful of someone who could have some control over what happens to you, even if just in the short term, especially when it comes to one's creativity. It's possible they considered that I might be cut from the same cloth as my predecessor [Punter], having been taught by him, so to speak. Out of them all, I think most people found that Mick, bless him, was the most approachable at the beginning and that was the case with me. He was less guarded and more relaxed it seemed.'

Japan had rehearsed many but not all of the songs they were due to record. Rehearsal tapes from 10, 11, 15 and 16 June show Jansen and Karn in particular struggling to agree upon exit and entry points of songs like 'Still Life In Mobile Homes' to the point of exasperation. Jansen: 'That was six rounds, I come in on eight.' Karn [sounding impatient]: 'It's *four* rounds, then six rounds.' Jansen: 'Rubbish!' Such stresses were a part of any serious band's make-up and such efforts were more than worth it. It was essential, especially with this innovative new material, that the groundwork was paved before entering the studio. As Jansen explained, 'We usually have a certain amount of the songs arranged before we go into the studio and once we get in that's usually the most spontaneous part.' Nye: 'There were no demos and we made no plans. The only remit for me was to get the album done as efficiently as possible since the budget was so tight. I believe we were allotted six weeks in total to get the album delivered. Had I known what was in store in terms of the complexity of the tracks, I may have been daunted by the prospect, but I was blissfully unaware and that was a blessing.' Nye was not particularly familiar with Japan's previous recordings and didn't make any effort to listen to them in preparation. As a result, Nye 'had not formed any opinions as to their strengths and weaknesses. As it turned out, I don't think there would have been much to gain in this particular instance, since *Tin Drum* was such a unique album and not really comparable, which I'm sure was the way Japan wanted it anyway.'

Track allocations for the song 'Still Life In Mobile Homes'
Steve Jansen

After a restful night in their variously tiered bedrooms, Japan awoke on Monday 22 June, to begin their chef-d'oeuvre. That first day mostly involved the setting up of drums, microphones and any other instruments that would be needed at this stage. 'Most of their equipment came down in a van with one of the regular "man with a van" guys we used,' remembers Huckle. 'Other bits and pieces were hired in as required and usually delivered by the Maurice Plauquet company. I remember on this occasion we rented a marimba and various bits of percussion and a Prophet V.' The setting up of equipment and sound levels on that initial day had exhausted all concerned, but they still attempted a start. 'In the evening we tried to get into working, but for some reason we couldn't quite get the song 'Talking Drum' worked out so we left it for the night,' recalls Jansen.

By the Tuesday, some actual recording had been accomplished, with the drums and bass to 'Talking Drum' being completed. At this point the song was mooted to be Japan's next single with 'Canton' as the B-side. Sylvian would always see 'Talking Drum' as a personal favourite and as the key track to the album. Jansen's drums were vital in this respect. Throughout the album, Jansen's drumming is more expressive and yet in some ways more deadpan than ever before. Each beat and each *hit* sound exquisitely thought out as if the drummer had programmed himself before recording the track. Unlike 'Talking Drum', some of the drum tracks on the other songs on the album would combine a mix of real playing and programmed drum sounds. In addition, Nye would add FX to the drums as they went along. 'On 'Talking Drum',' he states, 'a lot of the sound comes from the room it was recorded in. That big stone room at The Manor had a great ambience, a natural reverb. Then, when you feedback the harmoniser I added to it you get a weird, unnatural sound. But I would only use the harmoniser on the *ambient* drum mics. Then I added a noise gate, which cuts off the

Karn with saxophone and angklung in background
Steve Jansen

reverb and makes it sound even more unnatural and I'd add a harmoniser in *stereo*. So the left-hand side is pitched down and the right-hand side is pitched up. It adds a queasy feeling to the drum sound.' Whatever the methods of drumming, *Tin Drum* is far from devoid of feeling; on 'Talking Drum' itself, Jansen is almost aggressive in his authority, even as the drum pattern seems to deconstruct and reconstruct itself as the song moves forward in zigzags. Their actual sound suggests a slight vertigo; a disturbance of the inner ear. Usually the drums and bass for the whole album would be set in place first before attempting overdubs, but instead – perhaps because it was a planned single – Japan decided to complete 'Talking Drum' as soon as it was begun. Karn added his bass immediately after Jansen finished. 'The rush to finish it as we went along,' says Nye 'could also have been down to Virgin wanting to know what they were getting as soon as possible.' The resulting rhythm track was a proto-funk scaffolding strobed with odd-angled grooves and holes with plenty of space left for Barbieri and Sylvian to interject their meticulously programmed synth lines.

Gavin Harrison, a world-renowned drummer who would one day go on to play with Barbieri in the band Porcupine Tree explains the rhythm section thus: '[They] fascinated me. They broke all the rules; there was no sort of "follow-the-bass-drum-with-the-bass" Motown style or putting the snare drum on the 2 and 4. They just made up weird, quirky rhythmic patterns where Mick would play between Steve's notes. Steve is a very stylistic drummer, but he's very, very simple. I don't think he's ever played a hard fill in his life, and he would probably tell you that he can't. He came at drumming like a photographer, or somebody who's not a drummer. Pretty much any drummer I listen to, I can hear where they're coming from; I can tell their historic path. Steve Jansen might as well have stepped off another planet. I couldn't understand where he got any of this stuff.' Jansen was never particularly keen on theorising his playing, but did at least attempt to explain some influence at the time. Jansen: 'I've always admired [Yukihiro] Takahashi since I saw him in the Sadistic Mika Band [supporting Roxy Music] years ago, and he struck me then as being a really good drummer. Then when I heard he'd worked with YMO, I was convinced. He has influenced me – he's about the only influence I can pick out.' Takahashi and Jansen would go on to become firm friends and decades later Takahashi would return the compliment: 'I did feel an immediate affinity with Steve's drumming,' he says. Karn and Jansen were the (drum and) base architecture of *Tin Drum*, but it was an architecture that showed its skeleton on the outside, an aural equivalent of the Centre Pompidou in Paris. This was a startlingly unique basis for a pin-up pop band in their early 20s.

Working around the clock on Wednesday 24 June, Japan began recording the planned B-side to 'Talking Drum'. 'All was going well until we started work on 'Canton',' Karn would remember, 'and the Travis Bean bass began to let me down.' The problem was that on this particular track the bass part required Karn to rub the aluminium neck 'quite frantically, sliding notes continuously in one small area, and the heat generated from my hand was enough to bend the metal out of pitch'. As a result, Karn would have to leave the bass to cool down mid-recording, which was interrupting the flow of the session and the tight schedule imposed upon them by Virgin. The ever-resourceful Huckle phoned round and had located a local bass manufacturer, Wal Basses, who invited Karn into their workshop. Thus Karn, due to the pure luck of Wal having a workshop in Oxford, switched from Travis Bean to the bass that would become his signature. 'The Wal worked perfectly on the first take,' says Karn; it was the beginning of a beautiful relationship. Soon after, Wal would make Karn a custom-built bass with a Brazilian mahogany core and African tulip top, adding humbucking pickups and an active pre-amp. With this problem overcome, both the bass and drums to 'Canton' were soon completed. 'Mick and I nailed it on the fourth take,' says Jansen. An unusual looking instrument was found under some tarpaulin; constructed from bamboo and the height and width of several feet, the unknown instrument was an incredibly fortuitous find. The unique sound it produced by rattling peas within the bamboo suited the pentatonic Orientalism of 'Canton' perfectly. That Friday, Karn and Jansen recorded the 'bamboo rattles' that duplicate the piece's main melody. It was a two-man job. 'The two of us had to duck and dive in all directions to avoid hitting each other,' recalled Karn of their playing of the instrument, 'a synchronised choreography full of grunts and groans from stretching to reach the appropriate tubes.' 'Watching them play that,' says Nye, 'was comedy.'

With the foundations of two tracks laid down, the shape and direction of the album were beginning to reveal themselves. Sylvian: 'We started with 'Canton' which was the first thing we recorded along with 'Talking Drum' and we just decided that they worked so well we'd arrange the rest of the album around the same ideas.' Less than a week into recording, the two main men at Virgin – Branson and Draper – arrived to check on the progress. 'We would visit them during recording,' says Draper; 'they were very self-contained and sure of who they were, but it wasn't a closed set. They were very confident of who they were musically by now, but there was no sense of us or Virgin being cut off or alienated.' Later that day on Thursday 25 June, Simon House, who had previously played violin on 'My New Career' and the unreleased 'Some Kind Of Fool', arrived to add his arabesque contribution to 'Talking Drum'. He would also double the melody part of 'Canton', but this wasn't used in the final mix.

Tin Drum was a different recording experience from previous Japan albums, both in content and context. The Manor was a world unto itself and one Sylvian wouldn't return to until 1986. 'Virgin were always trying to get him to record at The Manor,' says Huckle, 'but after his initial experience with *Tin Drum,* he wasn't into it for some reason.' Sylvian was a self-confessed hermit and it was perhaps the communal living aspect of the studio that didn't agree with him. Nye: 'The Manor was residential, so we were together for meals and after work for a beer or two and a game of snooker, but usually tiredness would put you quickly to bed.' Huckle: 'Unlike all their other albums where I spent most of the time in the control room, at The Manor there was tons to do if you weren't recording. Steve, Rich, and I spent a lot of time playing snooker in the games room. They also had a great lounge with a VCR and loads of what was then the latest thing – videos! Dave barely left the studio as I remember, apart from mealtimes. There was a huge kitchen where everyone assembled for meals. We had home-cooking for a change unlike the McDonald's fare we lived on at AIR.'

The Manor even came with its own menagerie. Barbieri: 'There were two giant Irish Wolfhounds at The Manor, Willie and Bowser. They used to come inside the studio for biscuits, but couldn't stay long because the warmth caused arthritic problems for them.' Huckle: 'Yes, I remember the giant Wolfhounds that just seemed to sleep all day. Then there were the swans. There was a hysterical moment when Mick, in his inevitable fashion, managed to upset the swans in the lake, and was chased across the expansive front lawn by a giant, irate swan flapping its wings wildly. I think Mick did claim he'd caught a nip on the bum. A few of us were watching, doubled up with hysterics, from the games room.' Nye himself was a refreshing, down-to-earth presence. 'He would seem to eat a vindaloo every day, which resulted in much breaking of wind,' laughs Barbieri. Jansen: 'He was proud of his flatulence. He'd do so and say, "Right, now get out and walk!"' Barbieri: 'He would also pinch our arses as we went up the stairs, but he was incredibly sensitive and tasteful when it came to artistic matters. A great musician, with perfect pitch I think, and very open to our ideas, however abstract they might have seemed. I consider him the fifth band member on that album. He had the patience and creativity to cope with some quite demanding sessions. It was intense at times, but we still had fun. That's the weird thing with making albums. You take it so seriously and put every creative ounce into it, knowing you'll never be able to change anything once it's completed. Yet on the other hand, at times you can be joking around so much, you're nearly incapable of recording an overdub.'

On Saturday 27 June, Japan awoke late and started final overdubbing on 'Talking Drum' at 2 pm, which was mixed by midnight. They then did the rest of the overdubs on 'Canton' and finished mixing this it at 10 am the following Sunday. This was the first Japan song to be co-credited to Jansen as a writer and, indeed, the drums on 'Canton' are a lead instrument, propelling the track forward before all else, almost dominating it. 'Steve wasn't a particularly loud drummer,' says Nye. 'He didn't play hard, but didn't play soft either. The sound of the room had a lot to do with it. His patterns were so unique, he would never play anything that was just "straight" and that was a relief to me, after years of recording straightforward drummers.'

There were no gigs booked that summer and any offers that came in were refused. The only focus was to write and record the new material. Japan's approach was more meticulous and yet freer than on any previous album. For some this was down to a feeling of having nothing to lose; apparently Karn did not see much of a future for the band beyond the next year. 'We started from the feeling that this would become our last album, so we only did what we felt like ourselves,' he'd reason, '[it was] very spontaneous, and that put the frame for the whole album. That's the strange thing about *Tin Drum*. It was made on instinct.' Karn was hinting at the pressure exerted upon the group by label and management that if they did not secure a commercial breakthrough soon, then they would be dropped. Sylvian, seemingly aloof from such considerations, never saw this as a factor. 'There were always worries that we would be dropped by our record company,' he'd explain years later. 'There was always that threat of being dropped, but I can't ever say it affected my attitude to the writing of the music.' Huckle says that, 'I'm not sure whether Virgin actually could have just dropped them because they had a three album deal. But having lived under that threat almost since day one with Hansa, I don't think the guys took too much notice of such threats by that time.'

Karn was also possibly considering a solo future, his confidence empowered by recent session work and the fawning reaction to his exhibitions. He and Sylvian were their least close during the recording of *Tin Drum*, with the bassist absenting the studio when he was not needed. Sylvian, on the other hand, never left Nye's side and when he wasn't contributing to a mix or recording vocals or guitar he was alongside Barbieri programming synths. Karn and Sylvian were fire and earth, the former with his outgoing, humorous personality, precocious sexuality and love of the hash pipe; the latter quieter, not given to demonstration, his humour rarer, dryer and more refined and his use of drugs confined to the occasional toot of coke to keep him focused and working long into early morning. In company, Karn invited you into his world and entertained you there, while Sylvian stood aloof but coldly charming, neither courting nor rejecting your friendship. When these two elements worked in harmony, as on stage, the effect was uniquely beguiling and dynamic; in day-to-day life, less so. 'Making that album strained relations within the band considerably,' Sylvian would recall. 'We were beginning to close off from one another, which meant that we couldn't give musically to one another. There were differing ambitions, and I was at odds with the band. They were also very dependent on me to write material.'

Sylvian would often speak of the pressure he felt in having to come up with an album's worth of material each year. The

Barbieri, Sylvian, Nye, Regents Park Studio
Steve Jansen

problem was, of course, a matter of qualitative not quantitative control. Sylvian was capable of bashing out songs at will but such songs rarely meant anything to him and consequently he was unable to muster enough enthusiasm to record them; he wasn't in the habit of mustering enthusiasm for anything. Even wonderful pieces like 'Some Kind Of Fool' had been abandoned because their author had not sufficiently believed in them. Possibly because of this, *Tin Drum* would be the first album to feature co-writers, with Karn and Jansen being officially recognised as composers on three of its songs. Unlike all the previous albums, there was no surplus material begun and abandoned, and no outtakes. The group used everything they had. *Tin Drum* was the first Japan album properly to use space and sometimes even silence as an instrument in itself. In fact if Rob Dean had been replaced by anything, it was silence. Guitar on the album was so minimal that Nye can't even recall recording any. It does of course feature on 'The Art Of Parties' and 'Still Life', but on the former, the guitar tracks were used from the previous Punter sessions.

With Dean now gone (although he did visit The Manor, sporting a beard before leaving for America), the group were a more efficient and finely honed unit. 'Although I do think they lost something when Rob left,' says Punter. 'He grounded them in a way and his more traditional playing allowed them to go further afield as it were.' Relationships in the band were generally amiable, although as they were all much more confident in themselves and their instruments, they were also becoming more independent. 'We'd learnt to stay out of each other's way,' opined Karn. 'There was much more individual time allocated to working alone with Nye, instead of everyone passing judgement on each other's work.' 'David tried to keep a very loose rein on Mick,' Huckle would explain, 'he didn't want him doing too much outside of the band, but he would be pissed off when Mick had been smoking too much hash and would turn up late for a session with his eyes all bloodshot.' Although Sylvian would later remark that Karn's role was that of 'a session musician' during the recording, Nye says that, 'I don't recall any palpable tensions in the studio and certainly no bickering that I noticed, so mediation was never required. Anyway, I don't see being "schoolmaster" as part of my job description. If there were any conflicts going on, then the participants were certainly professional enough not to allow it to manifest in the work.' Huckle: 'It generally felt like there was a high level of creativity and confidence among the guys. There was a different atmosphere from the previous two albums – it was much more workmanlike, which was partly down to Steve Nye producing; there was less larking about and he had a drier sense of humour than previous producers.'

Further rehearsals of the new material began on 10 July for a period of three days and then again during the last week of July into the first sunny days of August. Nye was present at the latter, taking notes. Between rehearsals, Sylvian would continue to work alone on material at home, presenting it to the group during the intensive rehearsal periods at Nomis. The Nomis studio complex in Hammersmith was by now a commercial concern; a melting pot of successful names and faces of the time. Japan, however, didn't mix. 'Everyone who was anyone was there during that period – Police, The Jam, Adam and his Ants, Haircut 100, Graham Parker, David Essex,' remembers Huckle, 'and they were always kind of mingling during breaks in the large reception/relaxation area over coffees. However, Japan would avoid them by using the back stairs to and from the SNB office on the second floor and slip in and out of the building almost unseen. Not out of arrogance or rudeness, but from shyness. Mick perhaps would have been an exception to this, but had he lagged behind to chat he'd have been chastised for holding everyone else up.' Although down to a four piece, Japan were now at their most formidable and Karn alone would have been a key player in any group, continually expanding his arsenal of instruments and bringing something new to the sonic table. On 3 August, he and Jansen took a trip to Ray Man, a music shop in Chinatown, where he purchased a dida. 'I kept hearing a shrill but melodic sound on some of the records in Chinatown that I guessed was probably a reed instrument; it doesn't follow Western scales and a lot of the notes had to be found by squeezing the reed with my lips or blowing harder, instead of fingering alone.' The early 80s pop scene in Britain was infused with cod Oriental musical flavourings and pseudo pentatonic piddling – the aural equivalent of soy sauce with fish and chips – but what other groups were seeking out the source and adding arcane, authentic Asian instruments to their work? And which groups would have someone as talented and versatile as Karn to play such instruments? Japan were now an utterly seductive anomaly, the most beautiful looking freak in the pop circus.

On 5 August the band met with Fin Costello to shoot the initial photos for the cover for the, as yet, only half-finished album. Karn's version of events concerning the photo shoot for *Tin Drum* casts Sylvian in a questionable light. He recalls that the singer arrived at the shoot ahead of schedule, presumably to dominate proceedings. 'He had, behind our backs, arranged an alternative time for the session to begin,' reckoned Karn. Nevertheless, a full band photo session was duly shot which Sylvian would reject and, according to Karn, go so far as to put a needle through the negatives of any Barbieri pictures of which he didn't approve. 'I don't remember that,' says the keyboard player, 'but I know that Dave didn't like the suit I was wearing so we had to do them again.'

Jansen's diary notes that Sylvian didn't like the look of either Barbieri or Karn in the photos and thus asked for a reshoot at a later date, but no one except Karn recalls the needle incident. Fin Costello: 'I don't want to get into a dispute over how the *Tin Drum* cover came together, but I will explain how it came about. I had a large number of books of photographs in the waiting area of the studio, one of which was Marc Riboud's *Visions Of China*, which was shot in China in the 1950s. There were several pictures that David saw in it, which we discussed. Coincidentally I had been building a set for an Ozzy Osbourne shoot, which looked like the Chinese peasant rooms in Riboud's book, so I called David and suggested a test shoot. Mick and he came over that afternoon while the plaster on the set was still drying and we developed the shot there and then with them and my assistants Denise Richardson and Tony Harrison. The props in the picture are all from my kitchen except the poster of Mao, which we bought from Chinatown for 50p. Mick cooked the rice, which we ate while Tony developed the film (2 roll HP5) and made contacts. I still have the contacts and there are no pinholes in any of them, just chinagraph marks on the selected frames. The rest of the band were *always* going to be on the back cover in another shot based on an image from Riboud's book [a photo of a divorce court]. Incidentally, technically it was a bit of film/chemical trickery to get the 1950s look in the texture of negative as the original type of film used by Riboud [orthochromatic film] was no longer available.' Whatever the due process, the cover image would become a classic. It represented the music perfectly with Sylvian and the group as glam tourists in a contrived scene that was faked so sincerely it was almost more authentic than the real thing. The epitome of modern Western pop music. When he was later accused of *Tin Drum* being nothing more than 'cultural tourism', Sylvian, rather than take such an accusation as an insult, instead responded thus: 'Of course it is. That's obvious. But it led us to invent instrumentation. And that, as kids, is an exciting development.'

The next day the band reassembled at Odyssey Studios near Marble Arch in central London to resume recording. 'It could be a bit of a drag setting everything up every time we moved,' says Nye, 'but then again it kept us out of our comfort zone, which was a good thing.' The group rarely all turned up at the same time. Outside of the studio there were still the ongoing day-to-day duties of interviews and photo shoots to be getting on with, many of which increasingly involved Sylvian and Karn only. Sometimes the recording sessions seemed to operate on a shift system, with different members working on separate parts at different times that occasionally overlapped. Barbieri sometimes sat programming in the control room with headphones while the painstaking process of assembling the drum parts took place or while Sylvian did a vocal.

On 6 August Jansen began building up the drums for 'Cantonese Boy' piece by piece, working solo in Karn's absence until 4 am. When the day's studio session was over he continued to work back at Stanhope Gardens, programming a Linn drum part until 6 am. He worked with headphones. 'Steve also had a Simmons kit set up at home to practise on,' says then flatmate Huckle, 'and it's fair to say the neighbours didn't like it.' The work ethic on *Tin Drum* would have impressed Chairman Mao himself. An excerpt from Jansen's diary reveals the agonising attention to detail and the hours well spent:

07.08.81 ODYSSEY STUDIO. MICK WASN'T READY SO CAME IN LATER – I DECIDED TO RE-DO THE DRUMS ON 'CANTONESE BOY' BECAUSE THE SNARE WAS BUZZING TOO MUCH – TOOK A FEW HOURS – STARTED ON THE BASS – I THEN DECIDED THERE WAS ONE BASS DRUM BEAT THAT WAS TOO OUT OF TIME SO RECORDED THE DRUM TRACK AGAIN – DONE BY 11.00PM – MICK STARTED AGAIN ON BASS – BUT HE THEN DECIDED TO ALTER IT – SO INSTEAD I PUT DOWN THE LINN DRUM BASS DRUM FOR 'STILL LIFE IN MOBILE HOMES' – THEN STARTED RECORDING REAL HI-HAT AND SNARE WITH THAT.

08.08.81 – FINISHED PUTTING THE SNARE TO 'SLIMH' – MICK RECORDED THE BASS ON 'SLIMH' – FOLLOWED BY 'C BOY' – FINISHED AT 4.00AM.

09.08.81 – MICK FINISHED HIS BASS ON 'C BOY' EXCEPT FOR THE CODA – I PUT THE OCTOBANS AND CODA FLOOR TOM ON 'C BOY' – MICK THEN COMPLETED THE CODA BASS PART – STARTED ON KEYBOARDS – FINISHED 5.00AM.

Sessions continued at Odyssey for the next week, with more foundations being built for 'Still Life In Mobile Homes' and 'Sons Of Pioneers', the only Japan track ever to credit Karn as co-writer. After initial difficulty (Jansen had a problem finding a suitable pattern for the track which was solved when he switched to beaters instead of sticks), the bass and drums to '…Pioneers' were quickly completed. This was one of the most original pieces of music Japan recorded. Aside from the title, which could be traced back to the name of a 1930s American country and western group (The Sons Of Pioneers) it was hard to link this piece with any of Japan's obvious musical influences. Although Karn would claim that he did not begin composing seriously until 1982, this was not the first time he had offered a bass line for consideration by the group. Huckle: 'Mick would sometimes play something in rehearsals and if it was rejected he'd simply say, "Okay! That's another one for the solo album then."' '…Pioneers' was unique sounding, hypnotic and trance-like. It laid out an unfamiliar sonic terrain for the listener and like the group itself you either got it or didn't. Sylvian: '[You could say] 'Sons Of Pioneers' is just a bass line over and over again with just a few things thrown on top. It will bore you if you don't like the feel of it or you don't, for want of a better phrase, get into it, but that applies to all of our music.'

On 13 August, Japan and Nye moved once again to the less expensive Regent's Park Studios. ('A distinct lack of home comforts,' noted Jansen in his diary.) A 24-year-old Phil Bodger was there to welcome them. 'I was the house engineer, the tape op. Any band might bring in another engineer as well as producer, but I came with the studio. I'd invariably make tea. Regent's Park was about half the price of AIR. It would have been classed as a budget studio. I got the impression that they were on a budget and had to do things fairly cheaply. There was talk about that. I remember them coming down for the very first time because they all turned up in full make-up. That was quite striking. I knew who they were vaguely, but I didn't know much about them. I was really into YMO at the time, so there was a connection. They were impressive looking … their make-up was great, they looked great. The studio was in a basement, quite a small room. They came with Steve Nye who brought a quarter inch tape just to test the monitors. I remember Nye was a bit abrupt. I asked him if I should set the tape machine up – pretty dumb question, admittedly – and he didn't say anything, just looked at me with a disdainful expression, kind of like, "Of course! Don't ask, just do it." It was an odd room; heavily carpeted and very dead sounding.'

The varying studios and their respective acoustic qualities would work in the album's favour, adding subtle colours to the recording. Nye: 'I liked the heavily carpeted rooms at Regent's Park. You can hear that "dead sound" perfectly on some tracks.' Bodger was impressed by the dedication and skill of a group who many still regarded as faux musicians simply because of their appearance. 'Their commitment was obvious,' he says. 'They were completely focused. I'd get in about 10 o'clock and open the studio up, set up the desk. Steve Nye would come in after that and then the group would drift in. I'd fix them a coffee. We'd do a 12-hour day, breaking for lunch; I'd get a sandwich for us all from a shop across the road. Jansen and Sylvian weren't the easiest people to get along with, although Steve was friendlier than David. David was a little bit odd, very detached. I think I barely spoke to him. They weren't overly friendly. Rich was nice, but incredibly shy. Hardly said a word. Very quiet. Steve Nye was the same as David in that he was detached but also, as I've said, he blew hot and cold. One day he'd be fine and another day very moody. But you know, aside from being a producer he was a fantastic engineer, trained at AIR. I remember him telling me about working with Frank Zappa, who was a huge hero of mine. And the idea of this very English engineer working with Franz Zappa, who only worked with the best, kind of proved Nye's credentials to me. He was obviously a brilliant engineer and they were all well into it.'

Bodger was one of the few outsiders allowed a glimpse into Japan's insular, workaholic world at this time. 'The warmest one was Mick. He was lovely. Mick made the sessions fun. When he was doing his bass parts he cracked a lot of jokes, but apart from that it was hard work. Whatever David went on to say, Mick didn't appear like a "session player" to me at all. He seemed very much a part of the band during those sessions. He was the most charismatic member too. He'd often play from the control room, straight into the desk rather than through an amp. And I'd be sat next to him operating the tape machine. That was an experience. He was unique and impressive and quirky.' Bodger was obviously used to more traditionally rock and roll clients, but Japan had never fitted this archetype and were in the studio to work, not socialise.

There were few visitors during recording and little inclination to party afterwards, as Nye explains: 'While we were in London I had an hour's journey straight home after the sessions and an hour back on the train in the morning, so there was little time for anything but work, travel and sleep. There was not much in the way of socialising apart from the odd sake-lubricated visit to a Japanese restaurant. The levels of concentration for me were intense during the sessions. I always strove to do my best, as I believe I owed it to whoever I was working with to match their level of commitment and professionalism in order to achieve the desired result. That is not to say it was a chore, just the opposite. It's a joy when you love the music and admire and respect the musicians.' The minimalism of this new material Japan were recording actually called for more effort. Sylvian: 'We worked much harder on these arrangements simply because they're so sparse; everything had to have the perfect sound for this or that line and it had to do just the right amount and no more because we wanted to leave it as barren as possible. We didn't want to clutter it up like *Polaroids* where there were so many underlying things you don't actually hear those that just work as texture.'

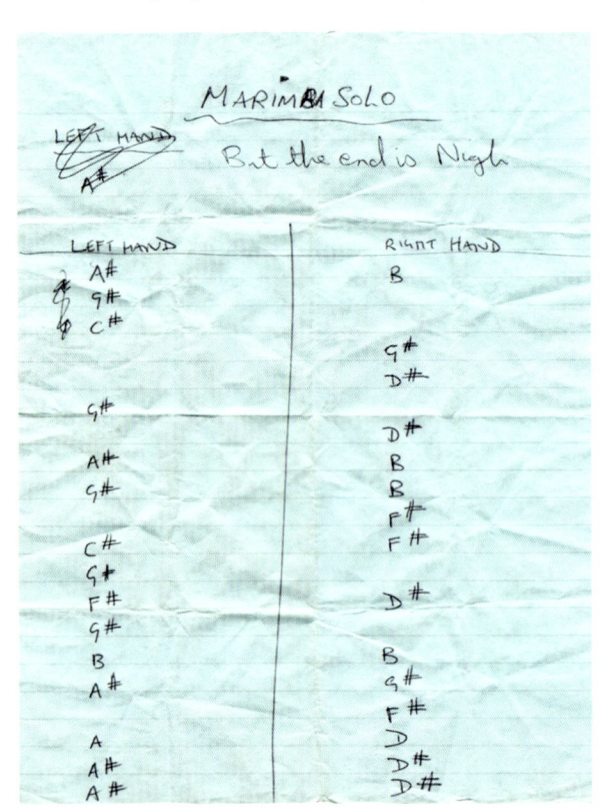

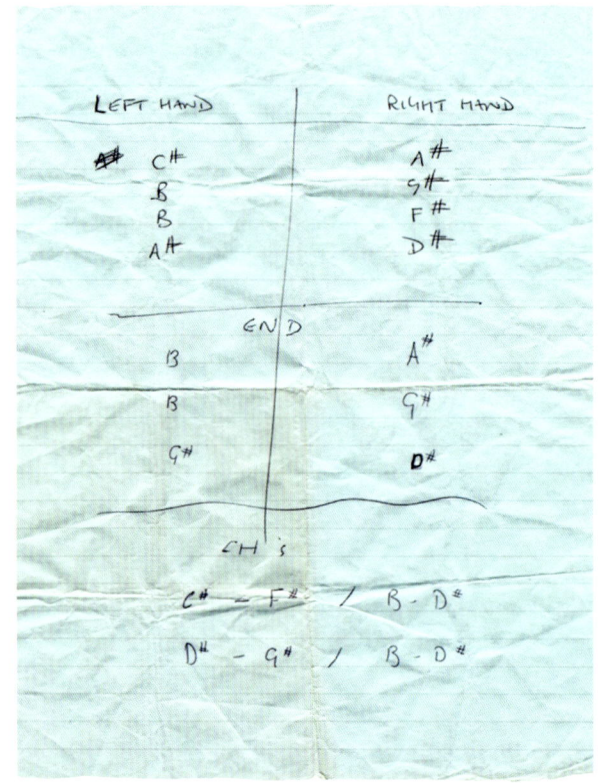

Original annotation for Jansen's marimba part in 'Ghosts'
Steve Jansen

Such was the nature of this stripped down music that it was difficult for the ordinary listener or even other musicians to work out exactly where these songs on *Tin Drum* came from. It was hard to imagine any of them, with the exception of 'Ghosts', being written on an acoustic guitar. This would form part of its appeal. Japan themselves were discovering the album as they created it. It was even hard to hear a traditional triad chord played anywhere on the album; they were there, but far from obvious. Nye: 'There are many chords on *Tin Drum*. Rich happened to mention that he and David used to tune their second oscillators to a fourth or fifth interval, thus providing a harmony of sorts, just played monophonically.' Of course, Karn would sometimes play chords and Jansen's drums were uncommonly musical, but this new music was as far away from *Adolescent Sex* in its arrangement as London is from Bali. 'Despite their glam image, I wasn't surprised that they could play,' says Bodger. 'Steve and Mick stood out, but they were all good. Rich basically sat in a corner with a synth and headphones on. The genius of his programming to me was that the sounds he created sounded like real instruments. From my point of view – as someone who worked with loads of different bands in a short space of time – it was very impressive and it was very different.'

If *Tin Drum* was pop music, then the phrases, parts and the sounds used were shockingly unconventional. Sometimes it seemed as if Karn in particular would overstep some unwritten musical boundary – but he never did and neither did Nye have to curb his playing. 'I never heard any bass parts prior to actually recording them,' says Nye, 'I remember spending time with Mick one-on-one recording some of the bass parts and they are treasured memories. Mick was always fun to be with and working with him was no exception. We all know what a great, innovative player he was. Technically and musically he was of the highest order and, although he took his playing seriously, it was always undertaken with such joyous panache and freedom of expression. It doesn't get any better than witnessing Mick Karn transform a track with his trademark sinuous creations so effortlessly executed.'

On 14 August work began on a song called 'Ghosts'. It would take a while for this track to take shape, but it was instantly apparent that it was something special. Time was used efficiently, however, and another song, 'Visions Of China', was attempted simultaneously with Jansen and Karn struggling to find a working rhythm part in an ante-studio. Meanwhile, in the control room, Sylvian, Barbieri and Nye began building the foundations for what would become, for many, Japan's greatest song. Various synths (although no more than three at any time) were set up around the room, some anointed with an ashtray or, for the sugar-hungry Nye, chocolate digestives. Sylvian and Barbieri had spent hours programming these keyboards, laboriously searching for the correct sound for each phrase for each part of the song. Sylvian: '*Tin Drum* was a wonderful challenge to work on. Richard and I were stretching ourselves enormously in terms of programming new sounds. We only used a Prophet 5 and an OBX and tried to emulate fictitious musical instruments. It was really hard work, but it was worth it.' Despite the incredibly rich variety of synth colours, Barbieri and Sylvian used only the aforementioned Prophet 5 and OBX, and some Roland System 700. Barbieri remembers: 'We took such care over each individual sound that we got quite paranoid about all sounds being new and different. My big influence on that album was Stockhausen, especially the abstract electronic things he was doing in the late 50s. Listen to a track like 'Ghosts', for example, and you'll hear all these metal-like sounds that hardly have a pitch, yet subconsciously suggest a melody.'

There was no fanfare or announcement heralding this new ballad. It was introduced to the sessions as simply one more track to be recorded, as Nye recalls. 'I knew absolutely nothing about the song until we started recording it. I imagine we started with some SMPTE time code and a rhythm box [later removed] of some description. Obviously without bass guitar and drums it was always going to be a bit different.' It would be a cruel irony that the song which would go on to be Japan's most respected and successful song in terms of chart placing would not even feature Karn. But no one was thinking of that then. Nye continues: 'The first musical part we recorded was the synth-bass drone part of Dave's. We had to leave plenty of space on the tape before the bass notes began to allow room for Rich's intro sounds. The long sustained bass note in the bridge before the second verse was a bit of a mystery to me at the time, but it was early days.'

Barbieri and Sylvian sometimes played the same keyboard simultaneously, hip to hip, while a Gitane-smoking Nye looked over his shoulder at them to cue the track on tape. 'Next were the three rhythmic "stab" chords at the beginning of the chorus part of the song [Dave again] and the answering "churchy" organ chords from Rich,' explains Nye. 'That's the first familiar sound we hear on the track, somehow warm and comforting amidst the unnerving strangeness. Steve's marimba part was added at a later date. I think this is when the melody and lyrics made their first appearance.' Working tapes of the song – recordings made in the studio as the piece was developed – reveal different lyrics from the final version. Sylvian originally sings, 'When the room is quiet/ The day is dead and gone/And I feel like walking'. However, even while the lyrics are in flux the structure of the song is already firmly in place and there is absolute conviction in the voice. It's as if Sylvian knows that in 'Ghosts' he has finally found the voice he has been working towards since 'The Tenant'. It would also point a way forward for him personally and thus chime as the keynote in Japan's demise. All of this lay in the future. Such notions were not yet an issue at Regent's Park Studios in the summer of 1981.

Even hardened professionals like Nye, who had previously worked with many 'highly esteemed' artists, couldn't help but be taken aback by the power of such material. 'That vocal,' says Nye, 'when David first sang it as a guide … There are times when the first time you hear a singer put the vocal onto a track it is a moment of complete transformation. A revelation. Unexpected and instantly recognisable as something special. I remember recording Bryan Ferry singing 'Love Is The Drug' for the first time on a completed backing track to which we had hitherto all sung "pirate tunes". Suddenly it was a different track altogether. 'Ghosts' was one of those occasions. Spine-chilling. Not a *scary* spine-chilling, despite the ghostly connotation, but an emotional one. A beautifully constructed melody and a lyric that touched something deep inside. I remember thinking,

Barbieri, Sylvian with Oberheim OB-X
Steve Jansen

Top: Sequential Circuits Prophet 5

Above: Oberheim OB-X

"Bloody 'ell, this is really something."' It wasn't in Nye's nature to be awestruck and, after this initial jolt, through a fug of coffee and cigarette smoke, work continued apace. 'Okay, that's the song,' says Nye, 'now it's time for the decorators to move in. So then we go to Steve with his hands full of marimba mallets, well two in each hand to be more precise. I don't remember if he played them like that, but it looked good anyway and, as we know, Steve always looked good. It's a tricky thing to have to play musical notes when you're used to just hitting things, but Steve came up with a great part for the solo and after a while he mastered the instrument and also played, for him, the slightly easier rhythmic parts in the choruses. To be fair, Steve was not a stranger to the piano, but although the keys are laid out the same on a marimba, they're huge and you have to play each note separately with a mallet so it's a bit tricky at first. The way Steve played it, with a slight feeling of awkwardness, gave the part a kind of fragility and demented, childlike quality which, to me, greatly enhanced the unsettling atmosphere.'

Jansen no doubt appreciated working with such an open-minded producer, one who did not baulk at the drummer effortlessly moving from drum stool to keyboards and onto marimba, (although it should be noted that this was the case since the band began working with Punter). 'Working with Steve Nye you got the sense you were in some sort of boot camp together,' says Jansen. 'By this I don't mean to imply he was strict and bound by routine; on the contrary he was quite laidback despite the constant filter-less Gitanes and strong black coffees. I mean that he had expectations. There was a standard of musicianship that needed to be maintained. He would mock any shoddy playing, much to the amusement of those not playing. He was very focused and serious about the discipline of getting things right, but not in a regimented way, more with the attitude of, "Well, you're the musician, you really think that's good enough?" And when inspired moments arose he would genuinely enthuse, by his standards. He was a real musician's musician and loved to explore all possibilities as though there were better things being overlooked by leaving efforts unchallenged. I think Steve showed us that. I can recall that when I came up with the marimba solo on "Ghosts", he was really engaged with where I'd stumbled to with the melody, but I just couldn't figure out where the ending ought to go, so he was making suggestions from the control room through the headphones, until I said, "Please come out and show me what you mean," which he did. That solo was subsequently tagged with the moniker, "the end is Nye". I reckon he was in it for those moments and that's where he really came into his own. Being a musician, his input on that level can not be overstated.'

This sums up the very real group effort that went into *Tin Drum*. Roles were, to a point, liquid, and everyone involved was utterly committed and enthused by the work in which they were involved regardless of traditional roles or ego. Once the bones of 'Ghosts' had been established, attention turned to its exquisite sonic detail, a glacial mosaic rendered exclusively by Barbieri's and Sylvian's synths. Aside from the marimba and eventual vocals, nothing on 'Ghosts' was acoustic. And yet the synth patches themselves sounded like real live instruments, albeit as if taken from an orchestra found upon an abandoned spaceship in the Gobi Desert. 'And this is where the fun really starts,' says Nye. 'I don't recall the complete order of play, but there followed a sprinkling of sounds including Richard's masterfully programmed and mysterious cascading, ghostly sound that leads into the first bass note, which he tells me he played with just the touch of one key. It appears throughout the piece at various times and significantly adds to the atmosphere. This sound proved a little technically challenging in that it contained a very strong harmonic peak which made the needles hit the end stops on the sound meters and over-excited the chorus effect unit. I believe that with today's technically advanced, computer chip-driven technology it would have been more successfully dealt with. An "if only" moment with the benefit of hindsight. One aspect of the recording of this track that presented me with a technical challenge was noise in the form of hiss. The track is very sparse and quiet at times with no cymbals or loud guitars to cover it up and, with everything being recorded analogue, keeping the resultant tape-hiss to a minimum required great care and attention. Another factor was the sounds. The way the analogue synths had been programmed and the very nature of the sounds and effect processors of the time meant that there was inherent noise in the systems themselves. Often the sounds were of quite low levels which meant that further amplification in order to achieve better signal-to-noise ratio in the mixer and on the tape ironically introduced even more noise.' Nye didn't see such factors as setbacks, merely problems to be solved in pursuit of a common goal. Some days were better than others. 'I always felt that one could tell if things were going well in the studio on a day-by-day basis by how humorous Dave's mood was,' says Huckle. 'He became far more thoughtful and slightly removed when things were a bit "bogged down" or not going to whatever vision he had for a song.'

As 'Ghosts' came into being, appearing to grow out of air like some cryptic crystalline formation, the in-house tape op was hypnotised and a little confused. Bodger: 'I'm sure the noises that begin 'Ghosts' weren't a Prophet. They came from a little computer someone brought in. The reason I mention it is that we spent all day trying to record it. It took ages because we were recording to tape and the noise was so dynamic. It was really difficult to record it without distorting and it was also making these noises at random, so it was a matter of catching a random noise that sounded good in the track. It was some kind of early home computer, I'm sure.' Barbieri: 'No. All the sounds on 'Ghosts' were from synths; a Roland System 700, Oberheim OB-X and Sequential Circuits Prophet 5. My System 700 was just a side cabinet with no keyboard, so perhaps this is why he was confused.' Barbieri was the strong and (near) silent key component on this track. Just as Sylvian had finally come into his own as a singer and writer (the two would be indistinguishable on this particular track), the keyboard player had finally found his musical apex. Nye: 'Let me take a minute here to say that Richard's patient and studied programming of his synthesisers is very underrated in my opinion. He, along with Dave would spend long periods of time in the studio just exploring their chosen synthesisers and effects, searching for sounds. One on the left speaker, one on the right, completely isolated from each other in concentration, literally pushing the envelopes to find that special unique sound that would broaden the soundscape and achieve the desired effect. I would hear a sound begin to develop into something interesting only to be suddenly abandoned, possibly saved on a preset, maybe not ever to be heard again. Also, Rich had a great ear for melody and used his self-taught musical abilities to their fullest potential. He didn't allow his untrained technical dexterity to hinder his knack of finding something special. There was no Keith Emerson or Rick Wakeman overplaying here; less is more. Just as Steve and Mick defined Japan's sound, maybe more noticeably to most, Rich's contributions in sound, rhythm and melody were equally important in creating the band's unique identity, along with Dave's vocal and creative synth work.'

Questioned about why he and Sylvian used so few synths, Barbieri explains that 'when you know a lot about the architectural process within a synthesiser, you can programme pretty much any sound you want'. Techniques which Sylvian and Barbieri used included the use of pink and white noise from analogue oscillators, which led to the characteristic breathy nature of many sounds heard on the album, and the programming of much movement into the sounds, courtesy of effects like modulation, stereo panning and reverb. These effects were generally included in the sound themselves. It is important to note that *Tin Drum* was pre-digital. 'With analogue synths, you're working with a pure wave form,' explains Barbieri. 'You start with a purity that you can affect as you go along.' Barbieri was keen not to take all the credit. 'David was/is an amazing synth programmer,' he explained, 'and should get much more credit as such for *Tin Drum*.' Sylvian himself was aware of who played what. There seemed to be no ego involved in such decisions. Every painstakingly achieved part, every performance, was there to serve the song. *Tin Drum* was fat-free. A rare and expensive aural sushi overseen by a man – Nye – who would take as long as was needed.

'Richard and I produced the majority of the electronic sounds on that album,' affirms Sylvian, 'and it was very laborious work. It would send producers, engineers and musicians into states of complete boredom [laughs]. They had to take long breaks because we'd be in the studio tapping away at keyboards, programming and looking for these elusive sounds that we wanted to get to. What was enjoyable was delving into the sonic nature of what we were working with and really breaking up those arrangements into these kinds of mini-electronic scores. The recording process was very restrictive and incredibly laborious, but it was a very exciting period, because that's when synthesisers had become much more affordable.' Sylvian was correct. In some respects, 'Ghosts' was a mini-album in itself, a miniature symphonic score rendered in analogue synth. Their producer seemed far from bored by the effort involved and relished the construction of the song. Nye: 'So, one by one, these freshly-mined gems would be added to the scenery, bringing the whole alive with their other-worldliness. Some rhythmic, some melodic and some just purely sonic treats like Dave's ethereal sounds that flit across the stereo as if out of and into another dimension; *now* the long bass note makes sense. One of the brightest gems for me was Richard's beautifully-voiced contrapuntal melody in the second verse which plays so well with the vocal melody and adds a further level of ghostliness to the piece with its slowly fluctuating pitch and unusual phrasing, appearing again in the solo section to equally great effect. Another part I especially liked was Rich's high floating synth melody in the second half of the later choruses. All these diverse musical events combine to form the intricate and well-crafted whole.' Karn would remain absent from the track and so was perhaps able to appreciate it more because of this. '[It's a] beautiful track,' he would state, 'with emotionally charged lyric writing.' No one remembers why Karn didn't contribute to the piece. 'It wasn't discussed,' says Nye. 'Maybe he just wasn't there.'

These intensive working conditions suited Nye and Sylvian in particular. Certainly there was nowhere else the latter would rather be. Still, to all appearances, a single and 'keen' (in his own words) young man living alone with no particular responsibilities outside of the group, work was Sylvian's life. Virgin however, like any other record label, had deadlines to meet and wanted this new album in the shops as soon as possible. As far as Sylvian was concerned, sleep was something that just got in the way and was to be avoided where possible. 'Dave used coke in the studio to remain awake and focused,' says Huckle, 'but I don't think there was really that much about, compared to most of their contemporaries. In the studio there would be the odd gram floating about, shared over perhaps a 12-hour period, and on many days there was none at all because no one really had a "guy you could call". We usually hoped the engineer or tape op could source it, but it certainly wasn't Fleetwood Mac. The use of coke in the studio was very moderate compared to most rock and roll groups, I would have thought. And Steve Jansen never ever partook. Mick liked his hash, but in my time with them I didn't ever think of anyone as having a problem with coke in terms of a reliance or an addiction. More that it just gave a shot of confidence and burst of energy when required.'

Sylvian was always open about his non-recreational use of the drug. 'Cocaine was a facilitator. It didn't bring out the best work in me and it certainly affected the tone of my voice when I sang,' he would reflect. 'I did use coke just to enable me to stay awake for long enough to produce work and to fulfil a day's commitments in the studio.' Unlike other groups, the use of such a drug was purely practical and, outside of the familiar confines of AIR, discreet. Bodger: 'I don't remember there being any coke around at Regent's Park. At the end of the session Mick might skin up, but not while there was work to be done. Nye: 'I avoided any stimulants at work apart from caffeine, nicotine and curry. Not necessarily in that order. Alcohol was never an issue in the studio and governance of a group of hard-working, intelligent people like Japan was completely unnecessary.'

Ensconced in the studio, the outside world rarely mattered. Commercial considerations, chart placings, pin-ups, magazine features, videos, meetings with Connie and Simon ... all were just a necessary annoyance while the group concentrated on the music they had striven for so long to achieve. Bodger: 'Simon Napier-Bell never came into the studio, although I remember them speaking to him on the phone. The only guy that came in was Fin Costello. I remember him showing them all pictures. He was obviously very close to them and they had a real interest in how they looked, but apart from that and Yuka visiting – whom I also thought was odd by the way – it was a closed shop. Just work, work, work.' Their manager was never particularly interested in making his presence felt while his artists were working and this suited Sylvian just fine. 'I had to find another, less commercial way of working,' he would sum up, 'which was why during the recording of *Tin Drum* we kept Simon as far away from the studio as possible.'

With the exoskeleton to 'Ghosts' successfully erected, work on more traditionally structured songs continued. Bodger: 'I remember for 'Visions Of China' spending about a day and a half just getting the drum track with Steve sat behind his kit with just a click track. That track was all about toms. Steve would, as I recall, play to nothing but a click. No guide bass or guitar. He seemed to have the whole song mapped out in his head. And in those days, of course, you couldn't chuck it all into a computer and chop it up, quantise it etc. You could edit different drum takes together but not different drum parts. It would all have to be in time. That wasn't that unusual if you were a good studio drummer. The parts were kind of repetitive.' In this instance, Bodger was correct in his recollection. Amazingly, Jansen did indeed record the drum parts to this song solo: 'It was written around the rhythm track which is why it was credited as a co-write,' he says, 'I recall working through ideas quite intensely in the studios for this track, mapping out the song structure, and when it came to recording the drums I wouldn't have needed anything more than a guide vocal with a click track. David would have probably recorded guide vocal with rhythm guitar for his pitching, but I wouldn't have needed the guitar, it would only have gotten in the way of accurate timing. This particular song has a shuffle, the amount of which would be open to interpretation, so it would have made sense for me to determine that without anything else. I believe Mick hadn't quite arrived at the definitive version of his bassline, so he wasn't playing along with me. All other parts were then subsequently developed around the rhythm track.' 'Visions Of China' would replace 'Talking Drum' as the choice for next single. The mechanics of who wrote it would haunt Karn for the rest of his life. Referring to his melodious bassline which leads the track, Karn would state: 'Ask someone in the know to hum 'Visions Of China' for you, quickly, before they have time to think about it. What melody are they humming? I know which one comes to most.' For whatever reason, such issues wouldn't be dealt with at the time. Perhaps it was already too late.

Overdubs continued through to the end of September, with Nye and the band upgrading to AIR Studios on 14 September. A sign of life went on outside of the studio. The group attended the opening of Karn's new restaurant venture at the October Gallery on 21 August, where the Penguin Café Orchestra performed. (The group's leader, Simon Jeffes, was one of the few visitors to the studio during the making of *Tin Drum)*. There were further photo shoots. Jansen took Yuka Fuji's portrait at Stanhope Gardens on 29 August for what would become the cover of the 'Cantonese Boy' single. Soon after, according to Sylvian's wishes, Costello re-shot the band for the back of *Tin Drum* on 8 September. That same day, while driving from the studio, Karn and Jansen were stopped by police in a random check. Jansen notes in his diary that, 'Mick was searched, but they didn't find his stash.' It's interesting to imagine what would have happened if Karn's hash had been found. Japan's public image if their bass player was faced with a possession of drugs charge would have undoubtedly shifted. For better or worse, it's hard to say. But knowing how close Mick had come to being splashed over the covers of the red-tops would have surely strained Sylvian's nerves in particular. Later that month, the Hansa re-release of 'Quiet Life' entered the UK chart at 39. This was Japan's first ever release to crack the UK Top 40 and yet amidst the work in hand, the ensuing visit to *Top Of The Pops* was merely a blip amidst the relentless recording schedule.

With most of the tracks in an advanced state of completion, Sylvian was able to begin recording vocals during the Regent's Park sessions. 'There was no particular ritual involved,' says Nye, 'unlike with Bryan Ferry. When I recorded Bryan singing, he wouldn't want to be seen, probably because he liked to perform the song as he sung. But with Sylvian, I saw him sing everything through the glass. He stood – I wouldn't allow a singer to sit because it closes them up – and he had no props other than lyrics and his cigarettes. It was pretty straightforward. We'd sometimes use effects, but mostly these would be added later. We did try a vocoder on 'Ghosts', but it wasn't happening. Sylvian sometimes had a tendency to sing flat, but I'd work with him, to the extent that at the end of a vocal session my throat would be all constricted because subconsciously I'd been singing along with him in sympathy.' Sylvian himself was always purely pragmatic regarding vocal duties. He would rarely talk about needing the 'right vibe' and, unlike other singers, never needed to be buoyed by brandy or inspired by incense. His approach to vocals was detached almost to the point of being clinical; it was sometimes as if he thought of his voice as just another sound. 'There's a style that I've kept to, obviously, but the voice is just like an instrument,' he would explain, 'for instance, if you use synths you've got so many variations of sound you can use, but you have to develop a sound that becomes your character so that when people hear it they don't just hear a synth, they hear something they relate immediately to you. I think the voice works on this album. To be honest I haven't concentrated on my vocals at all, I've been much more interested in playing.'

Some critiques of Sylvian's singing style would accuse it of being bloodless, mannered, clipped, stilted and emotionless. But it was this very lack of expression that lent them their power. And after all, on an album as economical and perfect in its construction as *Tin Drum*, space was paramount. At times, even the spartan use of electric guitar was almost intrusive. Sylvian would grow as a vocalist and in time retrospectively criticise his vocals of this period, critiquing the 'artifice' he heard in particular. Then again, there is a saying that one reveals themselves most by the choice of mask they wear, and anyway *Tin Drum* is an album all about context and the period in which it was assembled and, on those terms, Sylvian's vocal contribution to it approaches perfection.

Unlike most albums, some of *Tin Drum* had been mixed as it was recorded. The bulk of mixing, however, took place once the final vocal had been done on 'Ghosts', which was also the last song to be mixed. The onus of this final work was predominately on Nye. 'I also did all the engineering on *Tin Drum* myself, except for the content previously recorded for 'The Art Of Parties',' he explains, 'so I would set up the mix and the band would come in later on and make their individual comments and suggestions, which I would then implement, or not, as the general census dictated. It is fair to say that Dave probably had the lion's share of comments and overall control. The songs were, after all and for the most part, his work and that is a common situation for a singer-songwriter in a group. On the whole though, the band were on the same page musically and decisions were largely democratic. Enough care had been taken during the recording process sound-wise, that very little tweaking was required, apart from some spatial effects such as reverberation, echo and delays etc. There was some effects-processing added at the mixing stage, but the work that we had all done during the recording meant that everything sounded pretty much the way we wanted on the master tape. There was some equalising necessary since we had recorded in several different studios, but the songs themselves were sufficiently different in character that it all seemed to blend together well. All the mixes were done manually – this was pre-computers. If I ran out of digits with which to adjust faders or tweak knobs etc., then band members were commandeered to make additional adjustments, with some sat next to me at the mixer or, when we ran out of room, from behind the desk over the top. All hands on desk! The trick was not to give a musician a fader that controlled his own instrument, for obvious reasons! Steve was especially adept at this because of his impeccable timing. This "performance art" was fun, usually producing slightly different outcomes in each take resulting in the need to edit all the best bits together to create the master. No wonder we were there all bloody night. Final word? TAXI!!'

Of course, mastering the record was the final word. On 1 October, after an all-night mixing session, Nye and Sylvian took the master tapes to Utopia Studios to cut the record. Perhaps because they were no doubt in a state of exhaustion, they later considered the results as unsatisfactory. On listening to the acetate over the following days, Nye requested a re-cut. On 5 October, they returned to Utopia and the painstaking construction of *Tin Drum* was finally completed and delivered to Virgin. Sylvian: 'The making of *Tin Drum* got totally out of hand. It was taking a long time. The record company had a budget they were trying to make us stick to, and we'd gone over it. There was a phone call to the studio from the head of the company saying, "It's gotta be finished tomorrow." I said, "It'll never be finished tomorrow." He said, "Then that's it. You're not gonna have an album. Just stop work now." We were calling each other's bluff. I told him, "Then you won't have an album to release and you just wasted £70,000. You might as well give us a few more thousand and get an album." That did it.' No one else remembers such specific pressure. Simon Draper: 'I don't remember it being a particularly difficult album to make, especially compared to other albums we were involved with. And we were extremely happy with the result. Everyone at Virgin thought *Tin Drum* was quite brilliant.'

Outside the world of *Tin Drum*, the IRA were still bombing London and the CND were marching en force. *Brideshead Revisited* had just begun its TV run, bringing another Sylvianesque blond fop, in the shape of Anthony Andrews, into UK living rooms. In the charts, Toyah, Adam Ant and Laurie Anderson were all riding high, the latter with her odd minimalist hit 'Oh Superman' boding well for Japan. But by now, Sylvian and company were no longer chart outsiders anyway. By the first week of October, 'Quiet Life' had peaked in the UK charts at number 19. The future, finally, looked wide open for Japan. No one knew it then, but the group had peaked too. 'There was no awareness that it would be their last album while we were making it,' says Nye. 'Nor did it manifest itself in the work being done.' With a bona fide hit on their hands, Napier-Bell's phone was ringing off the hook. Virgin were thrilled and motivated by the new album they had to sell. An extensive December UK tour was booked. Japan's cache as actual musicians was on the rise and they were reaping the respect of other groups, while finally becoming fashionable. Thanks to their *Top Of The Pops* appearance, they were at last pop stars in their home country. What could go wrong?

Plenty. Japan would never make another album.

Chapter 9
Burning Bridges

Steve Jansen with billiard cue, Japan
Richard Barbieri

On 10 June 1981, at their manager's sumptuous west London studio/office complex, Japan had begun rehearsing the material that would become *Tin Drum*. By 22 June they had relocated to Oxfordshire to begin recording with Steve Nye. The group and their new producer were unified, focused and enthralled by the work in hand. A bearded Rob Dean stopped by The Manor to say goodbye before moving on to the US. Having found their direction in 'Talking Drum' and 'Canton,' the group returned to London for more rehearsals at Nomis on 10 July with Steve Nye making notes. No gigs were considered during this period and promotional activities were kept to a minimum. Japan were now in full work mode, discovering a new musical path as it materialised in front of them.

Outside this heavy work schedule, there was still time for a social life. Angie Usher: 'I was now getting to know them properly, and one night we all met up in Chinatown, without Dave, and we had the biggest laugh. It was just a brilliant night in a Chinese restaurant, just non-stop laughter. In person, I noticed that Steve was the most striking to look at. Just incredible cheekbones on this beautiful face; really, really striking. Without Dave they seemed more relaxed and fun; Dave was more conscious of his image if you like. But without him they were just normal blokes – except when they went on stage. Then they became these completely different people and I was always stunned by that transformation. They all had girlfriends as far as I knew; I was just their mate. But compared to other people in bands I knew they weren't lads. They didn't go out clubbing much or on the pull. This was partly because they weren't into boozing and drugs particularly. But I did think it odd, with David in particular. He'd spend so much time making himself up and looking brilliant and then just stay at home … it was strange. Mick was the one I became closest to. I'd spend hours in his flat, talking, listening to music sometimes while he worked on his sculptures; we were so close that for a time he was like my best girlfriend, although this would come later after certain events had played out. Anyway, after the Chinese meal I went back to Steve and Rich's flat which they shared with Nick Huckle. I slept on the sofa bed in the lounge. Steve gave me a kimono to sleep in. Their flat was like something out of *Men Behaving Badly*. The bathroom was broken and the whole place was kind of grotty. But they were really good fun.' Usher had befriended the group at a time when they were becoming less dependent on one another both socially and musically; they were, as much as it were possible within their rarefied environment, growing up.

That spring, just prior to the *Tin Drum* sessions, Karn once again visited Gary Numan at Rock City Studios in Shepperton to contribute further to what would become the *Dance* album. Numan wanted to include both Karn's saxophone and bass playing on the album, which would also feature Rob Dean's EBowed atmospherics alongside Connie rambling seductively in Italian on one track, 'Boys Like Me.' Numan would confess that, like pretty much everyone else who met her, he was utterly seduced by Connie, although his infatuation would remain unconsummated. The sessions began with 'She's Got Claws' and Karn, long used to the painstaking approach of his alma mater, was surprised at Numan's casual approach. 'This was the first time I'd played with Gary and the first time I'd played purely spontaneously, and it made me want to do the rest of the album,' he'd recall. 'With the sax riff I was just waiting for that part of the song to come up, and while I was waiting I was just playing around with the sax and Gary actually kept that take as the riff. He kept everything, even the tuning up at the beginning.' Karn was also somewhat bemused by the drum takes. 'On 'A Subway Called You' we spent at least a day getting the right drum takes and the drummer [Cedric Sharpley] just sat there with Gary standing over him directing him when to hit the cymbals. I thought this was just a run-through, but when he finished he said, "Okay, that's it," and there was this poor drummer struggling to pay attention to him and he never even got a second chance.' Karn favoured this track at first but had lost interest by the time it was mixed when Numan, in Karn's opinion, 'just turned it into a poppy tune'.

This was Karn's first recording experience outside of Japan and he impressed the Numan coterie with his untutored musicality and reptilian style. Nick Robson, friend of Numan's and a Japan fan, was in attendance: 'When I watched Mick Karn performing on the other side of the glass of the control room, he had this mesmerising method in his playing of both sax and bass. He was not only a unique instrumentalist but he emitted beauty from his whole being in a very sensual and soulful performance. I know that Gary learned so much from watching Mick play fretless bass and became a pretty damned good player of the instrument himself.' Unlike the painstaking methods employed by John Punter, with Numan as producer Karn was unsure at times if they were actually recording a take or not. Dean also noted Numan's lacklustre approach. 'It was all one or two takes. I didn't think it was very good. I also remember that Gary – mid-sessions – kept going out to his car to listen to *Polaroids* for inspiration.'

Karn and Numan had by now become friends of sorts, but would later fall out. Nick Robson: 'I have never heard Gary speak disparagingly about any member of Japan. I do believe though that Sylvian and Gary were never meant to be close friends, but Mick and Gary did share a similar sense of humour and appreciated each other's musicianship.' Karn, however, was growing increasingly perturbed by the intensity of Numan's attentions. 'I felt like I was being chaperoned on a date that had gone on too long,' he recalled. 'Plans for the next date being made before I'd had time to know how I felt about him, when actually all I did feel was uncomfortable.' Huckle: 'Gary was not the kind of guy we would ordinarily hang out with. I remember racing Mick and Gary down the A4, with them in Numan's big American Trans Am and me in Japan's Granada. He was very into his boys' toys.'

Back at Shepperton, 'Slow Car To China' was the last track they'd record together. Karn: 'Gary was talking while standing next to someone else and not really paying attention to what I did, and I was standing there feeling a bit stupid, so I asked the engineer to play me the song really quietly and record what I was going to play. He did and when the song finished the machine broke and I just walked out of the studio and never went back. I never even heard what I played until much later so it surprised me that Gary chose to leave all the mistakes in.' Karn would also note that when it came to do final vocals, Numan would change the original melody to complement Karn's bass part. This, in effect, would constitute a co-composition but, as usual, Karn's contributions were treated as no more than session work and so yet again he was denied both a writing credit and subsequent royalties. One track – the jokey B-side, 'Bridge? What Bridge?' – was apparently even released without Karn's knowledge and without any payment to him. This belied the song's playful origins. Nick Robson: 'The recording of that song was the funniest time I ever had in any studio. Thereza Bazar and David Van Day [from Dollar] were there and the session was also attended by Karn. Mick was a very funny guy and he and I started to do a kind of black version of the song in the control room while Gary was singing a guide vocal. Gary saw us in hysterics through the glass and wondered what was going on. When we explained what we were doing, he decided that this was how the song should continue and so four or five of us ended up adding the "blacker" vocal elements that are on the song. I can't recall the song entirely, but I believe my line at the end of the song "Hey, where is this bridge anyway?" was how the song got the title, 'Bridge? What Bridge?' That was just one of those incredibly funny evenings where all seriousness was put to bed.' At the end of the sessions, Karn walked out without saying goodbye.

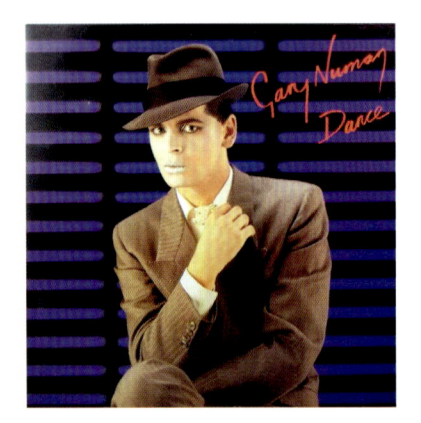

For a while Numan assumed they were still friends and was publicly grateful for the musical input. 'Mick's style was different from anything I'd done before and definitely helped me to move on and change the style of music I was doing,' he'd say. The resultant album, *Dance*, was definitely Japan-esque. Although not without a strange and gimcrack charm, it illustrated by comparison just how much work went into Japan's albums. Karn's contributions were confident and inspired, but lacked the precision and definiteness of his playing with Japan. *Dance* also lacked the intricacy of Barbieri's programming and the authoritative eccentricity of Jansen's drumming and percussion. It also suffered from lack of an actual producer. For better or worse, the songs sounded as if they were composed in the studio hours before they were merely engineered and recorded, rather than being rehearsed and produced. The vocals, and even the lyrics, sounded like what they were – first and second takes – while the synth parts were one-fingered and the FX-laden drum machines lacked subtlety. Despite this, the music had an intense, troubling, catchy allure. Numan also had the edge over Sylvian hook and melody wise but ultimately, compared to the group of which Numan so obviously wanted to be a member, *Dance* lacked sophistication. Still, it was much more commercially successful than Japan's albums, and made number three on the UK chart. Not that Japan were concerned, as Sylvian barely considered Numan as competition. Huckle: 'Dave didn't rate him at all.'

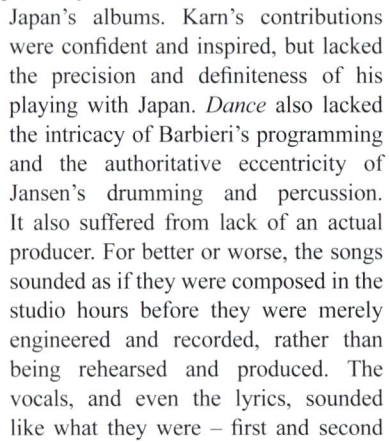

Karn would actually review *Dance* in *Zigzag* that summer and its less than enthusiastic timbre would put the final kibosh on his and Numan's friendship. Numan, oddly, would claim that Karn had been paid to write the bad review. For Karn, the fracture was a relief. 'I think he may have become

The October Gallery/
Penguin Café
Keiko Kurata

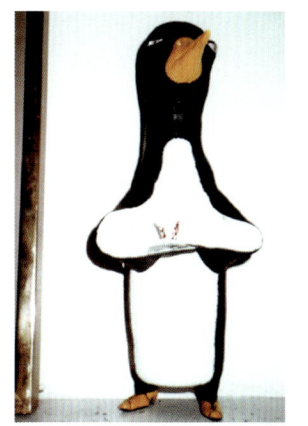

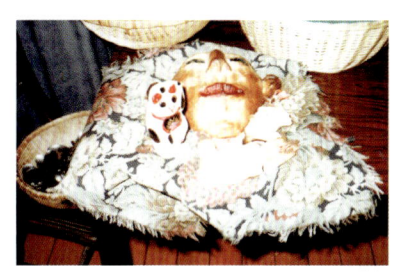

a little obsessive about me, or us,' said the bassist, recalling whole days spent with Numan in cars, planes and at Numan's parents' and girlfriend's homes. 'It left me wondering if he had any other friends, or anything else to do with his time,' mused the bassist. Dean: 'On the Gazza side, he's not really the sort of bloke you could imagine being close friends with – he's not very deep, and possibly Mick felt he was trying to get a bit too close and was realising his shortcomings. He was clearly embarrassed when the whole joining us on tour thing in Japan happened and I don't think David was very amused.' Perhaps referring to this incident, a lyric on Numan's track 'My Brother's Time' reads, 'Like someone in Japan who just lied'. Nick Robson: 'I'd say that they appreciated each other as artists, but were never ideal soulmates. As men and musicians, they/we all grew up listening to the same music so there was an obvious thread there, but I would say that Japan as a group were much more art school than Gary, who I think was very much more down to earth in private.'

Sylvian was never overly comfortable about Karn taking his trademark bass playing elsewhere. Huckle: 'It may be true that Dave felt he sometimes had to keep a bit of a rein on Mick artistically and creatively, in that Mick would get involved in a lot of non-band related activities. And as the band "leader" Dave obviously would have wanted to ensure Mick's non-band stuff wasn't to the detriment of Japan's stuff.' However, it was hard for the naturally gregarious Karn not to spread his wings. At this point, almost all his interests were met with commercial opportunities. That spring, along with his live-in girlfriend Yuka, Mick began running a restaurant/café at the October Gallery in Holborn. Christening the venture The Penguin Café after the Simon Jeffes band that Japan so admired, Karn was able to mix sculpture with cooking, offering sculpted finger biscuits as the main attraction. The venture was a modest commercial success, but Karn opined that 'it was the hardest I'd ever worked', and surely at a point where his energies were needed elsewhere. Karn himself admitted as much: 'It came and went in no time. It was opened properly, lasted 10 months, but I stopped it when we began doing the *Tin Drum* album, as I couldn't be cooking during the night and recording during the day – no time to sleep! – which is probably why it took me so long to record *Tin Drum*. So it was just an impossible situation and something had to go.' Sylvian and Barbieri contributed a soundtrack to the space, recording instrumental pieces at home on a four-track recorder. *Music For The October Gallery* aka *The Penguin Café Tapes* would never be released commercially. 'The music was very Eno,' says Barbieri, 'and very rough, quality wise.' Karn and Yuka's multimedia culinary venture was not to everyone's taste. Angie Usher: 'I went of course and ate something and got the worst food poisoning. so I said to Mick, "Who cooked that thing I ate with the kidney beans in?" and he said, "Um, Yuka," so I said, "She's fucking tried to poison me!"'

While Karn spread himself across London and Oxfordshire, Rob Dean was living in LA and playing with Marina Muhlfriedel's band, Vivabeat. Marina: 'We'd been going through some issues with crazy management, labels, etc. and I decided I really had to take a stab at it, so I called Rob and asked if he'd be interested in playing with us for a while. And we were completely shocked when he said, "Yes." He then married a friend of mine called Spock – purely for green card purposes.' The two remain married, on paper at least, to this day. 'It was fun to begin with,' recalls Dean, 'living a new life. I watched a lot of TV.' While Dean had made the flight to LA, he had missed the boat in terms of Japan's eventual success.

That September Hansa re-released 'Quiet Life' as a single, and remarkably it picked up airplay. 'Quiet Life' was the first single of Japan's actually to be playlisted by Radio 1. Jansen recalls being awoken by a phone call from Barbieri on 22 September with the news that the single had entered the chart at number 39. This was surely the moment the group had waited years for and yet the reaction from them was muted. Speaking just prior to a thorough flan-flinging on the UK's anarchic kids' Saturday morning TV show *Tiswas* a few weeks later, Karn could muster little enthusiasm when asked about Japan's long awaited UK success. Dressed in lime and sounding down, Karn could only say, 'We were disappointed at first, but then it's like a negative feeling in the end. We don't care if it happens or not. We don't mind it but, as I say, it's a complete blank feeling. There's no excitement, no feeling, just blank. Not even bitterness.' When pushed by the puzzled TV presenter, he faked acquiescence. 'We're glad it's happening. Yeah. Excited, I suppose.' Bourton: 'It was a bit odd for one of Japan to do *Tiswas*, but Mick was less discerning about what he'd do publicity-wise. He also had a different relationship with Connie as he liked her and the rest of the band didn't particularly, so she'd tap him to do stuff that David wouldn't. Mick may even have done that show to annoy Dave.'

Of course, Japan were at this point consumed by the new album they were working on and, after all, 'Quiet Life' itself was two years old. 'It was an edited version too,' explains Barbieri, 'and we weren't into any edits on our tracks.' If the group weren't exactly celebrating, then their current label Virgin were livid. Lascelles: 'It really pissed us off. It was incredibly irritating. I'm not sure if we went as far as considering legal action, but we were really pissed off.' Bourton: 'We had a few arguments with Hansa. We felt they were exploiting all the hard work we were doing. They were cashing in on their own failure. But there was a flipside – we had the band and they didn't. So ultimately we were able to exploit Hansa's success, ironically.'

The promo video for 'Quiet Life', filmed at the time of the single's original release in early 1980, finally garnered some UK TV airplay, marring Japan's newer and more mature image only slightly. Any frustration at this recycling of the past lay within the group and Virgin. The make-up and hair had been refined since this video was filmed at The Venue in early 1980 and more suitable clothes could now be afforded, but the group were still recognisable as cosmetic pop candy. The public and powers that be – TV and radio producers, magazine editors – were finally happy to accept Japan. Behind the scenes the group were maturing by the week and refining a new sound that would quietly revolutionise their approach. 'Quiet Life', although still oddly sophisticated and couture for the time, sounded guitar heavy and feyly romantic compared to the emergent *Tin Drum*. But however sophisticated or complex they were becoming, Japan were still basically a pop group and unlike some of their peers were not bogged down by political agendas that would prohibit them from playing the game. The Pop Group and The Clash had both invented politically worthy reasons not to appear on *Top Of The Pops,* but surely there was no reason for Japan not to appear. After all, they had grown up during the show's golden age and had sucked up Roxy Music's, Bowie's and Bolan's appearances on the Thursday night 40-minute pop programme as much as Ian McCulloch and Boy George had.

On 23 September, Japan were duly summoned to appear on the programme. The day before had seen the band at AIR Studios, interrupting their *Tin Drum* session to fake a new recording of 'Quiet Life' for their appearance on *Top Of The Pops*. This was par for the course according to the Musicians' Union law of the time. The band went through the motions overseen by an MU representative and then continued work on 'Visions Of China' once they'd left. The band worked through without

Filming the 'Quiet Life' video
Martin Grogan

sleep until it was time to leave for the programme, but there was just one problem. 'David didn't want to do it,' remembers Huckle. 'I dropped Rich, Steve and Mick off at Television Centre and went back to collect Dave. He had decided he didn't want to do it as it was "old material." I called SNB who rushed round to Dave's and eventually he persuaded him that he must do it, and he did.' Barbieri doesn't recall this incident but says, 'I can quite believe that David initially refused to appear. He didn't like any aspect of the live experience or performance really.'

Despite the fact that such an appearance would mean promoting Hansa material, Napier-Bell and even Virgin had a right to be exasperated at Sylvian's reticence. Yet Virgin were at least sympathetic. Bourton: 'David didn't want to do *Top Of The Pops* in the same way as he didn't want to appear in any of the tabloids. That was the cause of the major haemorrhage with Connie – she was asking him to do things like that and I was telling him not to and he was agreeing with me. But then we had to force a lot of our acts to do *Top Of The Pops*. The worst thing about that show was that you had to be there at 9 o'clock in the morning and sit around trying not to get drunk or take too many drugs, although Japan were the band least likely to drink and do drugs it seemed to me. I never saw any evidence of it and we never even discussed it – unlike other groups I went there with. But nevertheless, actually appearing on the show could be quite a bore.' A reluctant Sylvian was duly driven to do the show. The band was initially introduced by DJ Simon Bates as 'a brand new band', a description Sylvian wasn't happy with. Huckle requested a different introduction from the DJ and got one. Suddenly Japan appeared in living rooms nationwide. 'We were the only band that week who had never been on the show before,' said Karn. 'We didn't know where the dressing rooms were or where to stand on the platforms during rehearsals. It was all new to us.'

Japan's debut appearance on a truly popular UK television show would divide opinion in classrooms up and down the country. Kids either loved or loathed them. The actual experience, for Japan, who were finally filmed for broadcast at 8 pm, was underwhelming. Huckle: 'I remember being surprised at the first *Top Of The Pops* we did at the way they had this large studio with several stages on it, but only about 25 people as an audience that was just shuffled around from one stage to another. It wasn't what we'd imagined.' In the clip, Sylvian plays the game and deigns to sway in an understated manner, while forsaking any attempt at miming the song's guitar parts. Mick, Steve and Rich are stoic. The band come across as expensive, posh, slightly eccentric, and aloof, and look as if they'd rather be somewhere else. The song belies its age, sounding fresher than many of the other songs sharing the charts with it. Most of all, Japan look like total naturals, despite themselves. Once they had finished their filming they didn't hang about. Huckle: 'There wasn't a lot of mixing with other acts. In fact I don't remember them going to any green rooms as such; they mainly stayed in their own dressing rooms, but that may be just because I was busy elsewhere with band gear or otherwise. I remember the odd face dropping by their dressing rooms on occasion just to say hi, that sort of thing, but never the other way around. I don't think any lack of mixing was out of arrogance or snobbery, merely a combination of shyness early on and later, habit. They were after all a very insular band. Dave became much more adept at the social graces thing as time went on. And they were all always friendly, charming and likeable when approached in those kinds of situations, but just not that bothered about making the first move. I do remember that whenever they did *Top Of The Pops*, or any TV I suppose, they would insist on doing their own make-up, much to the annoyance of the Beeb's make-up girls.'

Sadly, no one had bothered to tell the producer of the song about its success. John Punter found out by an uncanny chance: 'I was on tour with [heavy rock group] Nazareth,' he'd remember, 'and had just had a shower prior to the gig. I was sat in my hotel room and *Top Of The Pops* was on. And this is the truth – I actually thought, "I wonder what it would be like to see Japan on *Top Of The Pops*?", and at that moment the DJ actually said, "And now, with 'Quiet Life', it's Japan!", and I went, "What?! Amazing!"'

Japan had been rejected in the UK for so long that they had become used to it, even comfortable with the fact. Yet now, overnight they were being invited onto the kind of TV shows that only a year previously their PR had been desperate to get them onto. In effect, 'Quiet Life' was a Trojan horse that Japan could use in order to promote their newer more esoteric material. As such, although having already outgrown such a mindset to some degree, Japan were happy to play the pop game at last. On *The Oxford Road Show* that November, Japan performed 'Quiet Life', 'Cantonese Boy' and 'Visions Of China'. Sylvian in particular seemed more than happy with this state of affairs, smiling at the lookalikes in the audience grinning back at him.

Mark Wardel: 'I had dinner with him when he came back from doing *The Oxford Road Show*. He was in a real buoyant mood about it all. He was happy. He moaned about having to do 'Quiet Life', but then he moaned about having to do a lot of things. I think he was happy that 'Quiet Life' was a hit out of all the other possible Hansa singles.'

Finally, in the UK, Sylvian had become a bona fide pin-up. It was ironic that now Japan were finally finding their musical voice, the public and media were becoming infatuated with their looks. 'I am *not* very attractive,' Sylvian told *Flexipop* that December, somewhat unconvincingly. 'In fact, I feel quite the opposite. But I know my faults and if you know your faults you can make the best of what you are.' It was like 1978 all over again. 'A bit of make-up helps,' Sylvian continued when pressed for beauty tips, adding that, 'they [my parents] often used to try to persuade me to change my appearance for the sake of a peaceful life. I'm not sure how they feel about it now. I know they enjoy my success, but I don't know whether they use my work as an excuse for the way I look.' For many in the UK, 'Quiet Life' and the accompanying glut of press and TV appearances that appeared in its wake was an introduction to Sylvian's world. Compared to the more down-to-earth patter of UB40, The Specials and even Duran Duran, Japan seemed like a bunch of reclusive fogeys. 'I've always yearned to be independent of other people,' Sylvian said. 'I was very much a loner as a child. And I still am. Often I do nothing for days on end but daydream. I sit perfectly still on my settee without ever turning on a stereo or a television. The phone rings endlessly, but I don't answer it. If I go to a nightclub I find the quietest place to be, where I'm least likely to be approached by other people. I've only been into a pub once or twice. I feel so vulnerable when I'm surrounded by lots of people in an open space. It only takes that one little act – wearing make-up – to make the world around you seem to change drastically. People react to you so strangely. It gives you a different outlook on life. It makes you grow up. Nowadays I don't dress up as flamboyantly or wear as much make-up as I used to. I still get remarks on the street though, only it doesn't worry me any more. If a guy had to put on make-up in the morning before going to work it would take another hour or so to get ready; it would be impractical, but I have the time to do that. I suppose I'm lucky.'

To many of their critics such trite interviews only reinforced the opinion that Japan were nothing but poseurs – a damning indictment for some in the Thatcher-ravaged UK of the early 1980s. It was true that none of the group, unlike their contemporaries, was particularly political either in private or publicly. Some years on, Jansen would explain his attitude as unchanged: 'I've never managed to tolerate politicians. To me, there isn't much that separates the characters that enter the arena of politics even though they feel motivated by different values. It's all a bit of a game and a club. But it's the economy that ultimately decides the fate of all things, not votes. Voting rarely concerns the bigger picture as it's more to do with people's own backyard. I get by without affiliating with any "team" because I genuinely feel the outcome will be overall the same for the country. It's almost as if politics in this country is about splitting hairs. It needs to be more radical to get my interest.'

In 1981 Jansen and Barbieri were very much in the background. Inevitably, during this first flush of commercial success, the magazines naturally homed in on Japan's singer. Thus, it was Sylvian's public personality that by and large would set the template for Japan's image as a group of dour and humourless individuals. In reality, Japan enjoyed a laugh as much as anyone. This would never come across in the media 'because it wasn't really something we could comfortably present to the public,' explains Jansen. 'Perhaps certain inhibitions were a result of a combination of shyness and lack of confidence, and therefore there was a need to be guarded. You play the part and rise up to the occasion of doing interviews, but if it isn't in your nature as a person to be public then there's only so much you can do. If you look at a band like The Beatles you can see how they enjoyed the interaction and were relaxed enough and honest enough about who they were to come across as endearing and good humoured. We were the polar opposite. We had buried our true selves within a public image, which was a vital form of expression, a liberation and an escape from

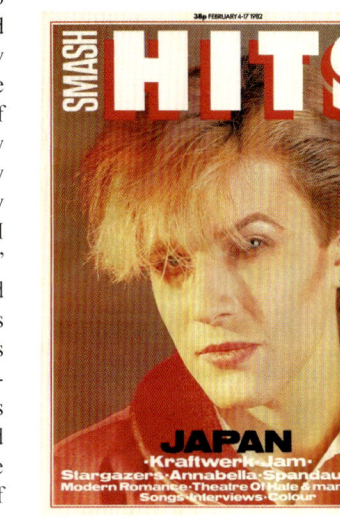

Smash Hits, February 1982

the oppressive 70s. It wasn't then possible to jump about like comedians, as that would have looked even more absurd (or maybe not, who knows?). Regrettably though, the plentiful good laughs were resigned to behind the scenes only.'

That September, Japan were advertised as being the headliners for the Daze Of Future Past Festival in Leeds. Dean: 'I was in LA by then, but Simon phoned me to ask if I'd do this festival, but then I never heard anything again.' This was because the band pulled out shortly after the first press adverts appeared. 'SNB was in negotiation with the promoter about Japan headlining and the promoter went ahead and advertised before they had agreed fees or signed any contracts,' confirms Huckle. 'The Cure had similar issues and also pulled out.' Initially, Napier-Bell had expected the group to be excited at such a prestigious billing, but instead was met with blankness. 'It was an important meeting, a showdown,' Karn recalled. Apparently Simon stormed out of the studio saying that as soon as the next album was finished both he and Virgin would be dropping the band, but this only focused the group further. Now that they had won over the public it seemed to be part of their make-up that they had to have someone to fight against, not that Japan were ever the type of group to play festivals, as headliners or otherwise.

Much more frustratingly, Hansa released a new compilation album that month with the telling title of *Assemblage*. Comprising tracks from *Adolescent Sex* onwards, the album was an instant and steady seller, peaking in the UK at 26, seemingly causing much frustration for Japan and Virgin alike. Yet in actual fact, the album's track listing had been approved by Sylvian, Karn and their manager; no doubt they were making the best of a situation that was out of their hands. An early acetate was also sent to the *NME*'s Paul Morley asking for his input before the final track listing was approved. However, Japan weren't unanimously loved by the press at this point, with one weekly summing up the album as 'a fart in a mortuary'. The record-buying public, at least those who had only recently become aware of the group, were no doubt confused by the album's content. For anyone familiar only with the Japan of 'Quiet Life' or 'The Art Of Parties', hearing 'Communist China' and 'Adolescent Sex' for the first time must have made them wonder if they were listening to a completely different group. Confusion was compounded further when that October, Virgin released the first track from the *Tin Drum* sessions, 'Visions Of China.' Interestingly, the single was released only in the UK, Spain and Australia, with Sylvian and Jansen giving their first televised Australian interview from AIR Studios with Molly Meldrum for his *Countdown* programme. The single was not released in Japan itself.

Virgin had undoubtedly lost some of their momentum to Hansa. Bourton: "'Visions' was the single we all thought was going to be big and actually we were reasonably happy with the chart placing [32].' The single, backed by a Steve Nye remix of 'Taking Islands In Africa', picked up only moderate airplay and next to the Roxy-Bowie swagger of 'Quiet Life' sounded thrillingly avant-garde or difficult and obscure, depending on your viewpoint. Meanwhile, *Assemblage* was selling well without any promotion by the group and, in effect, the Virgin Japan were now in competition with the Hansa Japan, but there was at least a video to promote the bona fide new single. Directed by Steve Barron, who would go on to direct *Teenage Mutant Ninja Turtles*, the 'Visions Of China' promo was Japan's first attempt at employing a narrative within a video, based on a storyboard by Sylvian. The group, however, were underwhelmed. Jansen: 'As people we were very much inspired by movies and so I don't think any of us particularly felt that this cheap-looking video medium was a very fulfilling and interesting one to pursue. Budgets were ridiculously small and directors' ambitions, with the advent of tacky special effects, invariably too large, so the result was never destined to be anything of much quality. 'Visions Of China', with its back story, was attempting to be conceptually abstract, but cheap production values and lazy concepts certainly made it utterly fail artistically. To be fair, the industry was still learning its trade and sadly for us we were the performing guinea pigs alongside performing dragons. I've no idea who came up with that concept, but it's no leap of the imagination, is it?'

On 13 November, barely a couple of months after being mastered, *Tin Drum* was released. It was met with unanimous praise and instantly rose to number 12 on the UK chart. In some aspects, this was a perfect time for Japan to release it. After more than three years of consigning Japan to a critical and commercial wilderness, the press and the public were finally coming round. In interviews, Japan were no longer by default on the defensive as had been the case since 1978. Reviews were not only kinder, but perceptive. Although the lower-tier pop magazines such as *Jackie*, *Patches,* and the like could lap up the group's photogenic good looks and leave it at that, in addition, Japan were now being taken seriously as musicians and composers by the "serious" press.

With the release of *Tin Drum* the *NME*, for instance, finally got the band. 'Japan,' wrote onetime doubting Thomas Paul Morley, 'could be as great as the smile of genius on David's face claimed they were.' In a half-page review, adorned with an oddly unflattering portrait of Sylvian, Morley went on to theorise about the new brilliance of the group, concluding, 'Japan – now – have to be taken seriously; there's no other way. Be haunted by 'Ghosts' and hear what I mean.'

At the same time, Hansa were muddying Japan's clarity of purpose with old releases, and the inter-band friendships were not as inclusive as they had been, although this was often the case with Japan once an album had recently been completed. 'You always think,' said Sylvian, 'when you've just finished an album – should we bother carrying on?' It seemed to be a habit with Sylvian that after each album he would consider breaking up the group. All involved were now aware, however, that *Tin Drum* was a peak, its producer included. 'I was pleased with the album,' says Nye, 'and it was satisfying to have produced something new and different sounding. I never read the music press, so I don't know how it was initially received, but what made me feel the most proud was the complimentary comments from my peers, fellow producers and engineers that I respected. As time went by, it was also very gratifying to have artists approach me with offers of work because of my work with Japan. Commercially it is always gratifying to receive gold albums or any awards for your work as it is a direct reflection of how well the album was received by the record-buying public as, after all, that is who we make albums for.'

The success of *Tin Drum*, and of course 'Quiet Life', meant that interview requests were at an all-time high. The group were now put into a position where they would have to explain to curious journalists why a band called Japan had made such a Chinese-sounding album. 'A lot of those things were tongue-in-cheek and were taken more seriously than intended,' explained Sylvian, referring to the musical and lyrical references to China on the album. 'I think the humour – if you can call it humour – is so slight that it can be confused sometimes. For me, 'Cantonese Boy' and 'Visions Of China' were just fun … and maybe slightly cynical; parodying.' Barbieri: 'It's not really a Chinese album, but it's got a lot of Chinese influences on it. We just like working with different atmospheres I think. We are interested in a lot of places we haven't as yet been to. It was just that whole period in Chinese history that seemed to interest us most – the Mao period.' Sylvian denied that there was any actual Maoist message on the album. 'No, it's not political at all,' he reasoned. 'It's based on the image people have of China, or that we have of China. To me time is irrelevant. If someone mentions China to you and you don't know that much about it you get all different periods coming to mind; it's hard to fit all the pieces together and that's what it was like in the beginning. It was loosely based on the music and images; it's nothing to do with politics, because you're walking on a thin line when you deal with something like Chinese traditional music, as so many times it's been interpreted by Western people that it's become trite. The idea of working on Chinese-based music has been done so many times that everything has come over cheaply, and the ideas have never been pushed that far, which is probably what you think about 'Canton', but for us it's worked well and Japanese and Chinese people who have heard it actually thought it was taken from original music, so it must have worked to some extent.' Jansen: 'As musicians we perpetually struggled to avoid conventional technique and attempted to find a voice. There was indeed so much focus on this, yet I think musically we weren't really equipped to make it truly work, and that's why an album like *Tin Drum* sounds so odd, and to my ear awkward. Maybe in retrospect that's a good thing considering it was essentially created by a pop band and attained the success of a pop album, yet isn't remotely pop music – a real one-off – but that doesn't necessarily make it listenable or musically proficient. Musically, *Tin Drum* was very much the sum of its parts.' Whatever *Tin Drum* actually was musically, it was a commercial and critical hit, a classic album that would remain in the UK chart for the best part of a year.

Unlike Wire, Bauhaus or Roxy Music, none of Japan had ventured into further education or art school. But by 1981 Japan *were* an art school. Alongside Karn's growing reputation as a sculptor, Jansen too was beginning to commit seriously to photography and would soon be exhibiting his prints. What other band had a rhythm section whose work appeared in galleries? Meanwhile, there was a tour to consider and Japan needed a guitarist. David Rhodes *was* from an art school background. 'I was at St Martin's on the foundation course and I didn't start playing in a band until I was 22,' he explains, 'and within a year I was doing Peter Gabriel's record and I was more into noise and non-playing.' Indeed it was Rhodes' work on Peter Gabriel's *Melt* LP that had caught the ear of Japan. Barbieri: 'I can't remember how we approached him, but there weren't any other names in the hat for the job, so he was first choice I guess. At that time the only reference point for us would've been the third Gabriel album. All the other good stuff he did with Gabriel and Talk Talk came later.' Rhodes: 'It was an odd time for me to join them. *Tin Drum* was obviously an accomplishment – very well made, beautifully constructed. I knew that record best although I'd been aware of Japan before that. I was sent a bunch of tapes and I agreed to do it. So I sat down with the tapes and played along basically, just learnt the songs. It was more about learning the songs than guitar parts, as on some songs it wasn't necessarily obvious what the guitar should do. Where the guitar part *was* obvious – you learnt it.'

Dean's musical presence in Japan had eventually become a very subtle yet distinct one. His parts were often EBowed and so treated that they were sometimes hard to tell apart from Sylvian and Barbieri's keyboard parts, yet the very fact that they *were* guitar parts – and played by Dean in his own specific style – meant that if they had been dropped from the mix, their absence would have been obvious. Rhodes wasn't just stepping in to fill your common or garden guitarist's jazz shoes; his approach would be as sonic as it was musical, something his art school background had equipped him for even if in terms of actual equipment he and Rob were dissimilar. 'I don't think I actually even had an EBow,' he recalls. 'I didn't get one until after the tour. But I was into pedals and enjoyed making funny noises, so learning the actual parts was the troublesome bit for me.' Next on the agenda was a haircut. 'I had long hair, so I thought I'd better get that seen to. Japan's appearance was obviously a big thing for them, but I think it was more about "us against the world" than merely narcissistic. Anyway, I went to a very nice man called Keith at a salon called Smile on King's Road. He said, "Hmm. Yeah. Let's make it look like you're growing out dyed hair." So I had it cut and just the ends of the hair bleached. He said, "It'll look like you're kind of just leaving the band." I then bought some nice clothes. No one told me to do this, and it wasn't so much about fitting in as about not sticking out.' Rhodes now looked and sounded the part, adding another splash of blond to the picture. Barbieri: 'We got along absolutely fine. He seemed a very positive and easy-going guy and he was great at playing the right parts with the right sounds. He probably didn't get to express himself that much with a lot of the material as most of the parts were written in stone.' Jansen: 'He seemed to be quite guarded as a person, but his guitar work was good for us; I was impressed with his input at the time.'

The mildew-rotten chambers of Kilburn were by now a vague and grotty memory – a symbol of dues paid – and the other David turned up at the gleaming new Nomis rehearsal complex to start a two-week rehearsal. Here, Rhodes got to observe the band close up: 'They were obviously close and as an outsider I had to look for a way in. They were very supportive of me but not overly friendly, even to each other. They had a weird way of relating to one another and to the world. They were a bit cool. As a player and a hired hand, you had to hold your ground while winning people over at the same time. I did play hard and "on it" back then and I remember David suggesting that I didn't need to jump into parts so much. So if it went from an instrumental to a verse he preferred it to trail off rather than stop abruptly. I didn't work from chord charts, or even notes. I just winged it. My set-up was a Roland JC 120 amp, a delay unit, an MXR with a nice old Strat – a pretty pink one – and an Eventide Harmoniser. We rehearsed everything that we played live. No extras. It was very specific.' Sessions were daily and at a civilised hour. 'I don't think they liked getting up too early and I said I wanted to finish at nine each night, so we started in the afternoon. I had just split up with a girlfriend and was living with a mate in Brixton and I wanted to get back before the pub closed.' Japan would not join Rhodes for a pint, 'but we got on. Steve and Mick were unique players, on the *Tin Drum* material in particular. On some of the older stuff, the disco type stuff, it was pretty straight by comparison, but on the newer stuff Steve was playing very stylised things and Mick was filling in the holes. I wouldn't call it powerful exactly, but the effect of what he was doing with Mick was very unique, quirky.'

Rhodes was less enamoured by the management. 'I thought Napier-Bell was a bit creepy. Not my kind of guy. Flashy, cigar, big car. Very clever, but motivated only by cash. But then I didn't really get to know him. I liked Richard Chadwick, however; I liked his vibe. He was a gentle soul. David seemed to like having him around too. I myself had a hopeless manager at the time and so as far as what I was paid for the Japan tour I was shafted. My manager didn't really know the score and that was taken advantage of. We negotiated through Nick Huckle and he must have known the score … and you *never* do that to people.' It seems this was another example of what Napier-Bell exactly *did* do to people, even those close to him, in this case using the relatively naive Huckle to negotiate with Rhodes a deal that was advantageous to one person only, who wasn't in the group. Par Can would again operate lights on the tour: 'Huckle was a nice guy, but not really that on the ball. He

Markus Innocenti and Edward Arno, the set designers for the *Visions Of China Tour*

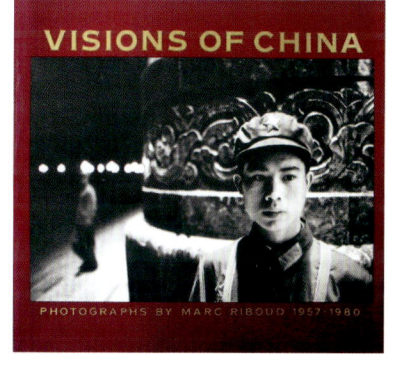

Marc Riboud's *Visions of China* book

was thrown into the deep end and learning as he went along.' Barbieri: 'It's difficult when a friend ends up working for you and I'm sure we abused that friendship along the way, but I hope he still has some fond memories of those days.' Angie Usher: 'Simon didn't like outsiders, even other musicians. He didn't want anyone influencing "his boys." And what you have to remember is that although you didn't think it at the time, they were so young then, and malleable.'

The forthcoming *Visions Of China Tour* would be Japan's biggest yet in the UK, and their third that year. The group were riding a rare wave for any pop group – they were now commercially successful, critically respected and fashionable. As such it was planned that the tour should incorporate a lavish stage set that travelled with the band from venue to venue. The designers chosen for this job were Markus Innocenti and Edward Arno, two hip and happening set designers who worked as partners and even dressed identically. Markus Innocenti: 'We came to Simon's attention through Virgin as we'd done some work for Simple Minds. We were given *Tin Drum* and then met with David and listened very carefully to what his ideas were. David was the band's voice, and he had the greatest say. What we came up with was a kind of English music hall version of a Chinese village. The drum riser was big – it almost came up to David's head and had an opening in its front that someone could walk through. The stage was covered in cloth and had a paving look, but it had to be really taut otherwise Mick couldn't do his shuffle. There was even a ladder that David could climb up in order to sing from a raised platform, but he wasn't keen on that idea. There was a small bridge and behind it all a projector screen. This was very important to David, as he wanted to project actual visions of China onto it – stock footage of China we got from the Chinese embassy. The whole thing was a huge, theatrical deal.'

Par Can: 'The lighting, co-ordinated by our boss Pip Robinson, was very specific and there were slides too [some images from Marc Riboud's *Visions Of China* book]. The lighting was set up to look like a fan, an oriental kind of thing – six white lights. It was very impressive.' Edward Arno: 'They were intense people, or David was, or maybe the situation was. David was very self aware, to the point that it was almost weird. I remember one meeting we had with him in this very spare room and it was like everything was arranged just so for him. You felt like you were a walk-on part in the "David Sylvian Story". It was almost funny. I mentioned this meeting to Mick; I said, "Is he always like this?" and Mick said, "Yeah, and that's one of the reasons we love him."' Innocenti: 'Of course, we were made to feel that Simon was doing us a favour by letting us do this gig. He got us incredibly cheap. I got on with Mick best. Richard was quiet but a lovely guy with a core of steel, I thought. Steve was a sweet guy and all the girls loved him. David was very aloof. I wondered if this was in part because I became so close to Mick.' Arno: 'Mick and I became *very* close as the tour went on. Anyway, we listened to David's ideas and went away and had the set built. We thought the band were going to be very excited by what we'd come up with.'

After two weeks at Nomis, in early December the band assembled at Shepperton Studios for a dress rehearsal, where the Chinese-influenced set design was finally assembled and on display. Exhibiting behaviour that was becoming a pattern before an important live event, Sylvian seemed to panic on entering Shepperton, declaring that he 'hated' the set and promptly walked out again. Innocenti: 'We turned up for a dress rehearsal and David freaked out. He said, "It's all too much! It's not what I wanted at all!" I tried explaining that we had no lights on it and that when it was lit it would make all the difference; lit, it would have looked stunning. We were due on tour in two days, and I couldn't believe he was saying this. I suddenly realised there was something going on in the band that I wasn't privy to and I put it down to nerves. Anyway, David kept going on, "I hate it! This is not what I wanted," and so on. I persuaded him to let me light it, just a bit, and the rest of the group were blown away by it – "Oh, it's awesome," and so on, but David wouldn't budge.' Karn: 'I've known him for about 11 years and he's very easily influenced by anything anyone might say; it stays in his mind. The week before the tour started, he did an interview with one of the papers and the guy who was doing the article said how dated he thought the whole rock scene was and that it was pathetic the way we were trying to make it stay alive by using things like slides and stage sets, and Dave agreed. I think that's what put the spark in his mind and a week later he wanted to do the tour with no lights at all, which would have been a total contradiction of what we had planned for four months before the tour. I think it's a great weakness not to see something through that you've decided upon.' Barbieri: 'We eventually lost a lot of money when it was decided the stage set construction wasn't right and a new one had to be rebuilt.' Karn: 'The set was completely taken over by Dave and designed by Dave, so if there was anything in it he didn't like, then it was his fault. When we turned up to rehearse the weekend before the tour started, the set was much bigger than anyone ever saw; it had towers in the top where I would be playing saxophone, Dave would be singing 'Ghosts', the others were at the bottom, and there was a roof over the whole thing. All the lights were theatrical lights especially designed for the set; you can't use them on a normal rock concert, so Dave would have been letting down all the lights people as well, not to mention the fans because he just refused to do the tour in the end.'

Innocenti and Arno were shocked, but pragmatic. Innocenti: 'Another meeting was arranged between me, Arno and the group. It was like walking into the middle of an argument. David kept on saying that he wasn't prepared to tour with that set and there was talk of cancelling the tour. Mick looked sullen and annoyed, Steve was embarrassed and Richard was furious. He was the most confrontational with David. And it suddenly seemed to me that David was using the set thing to sabotage the band. He was trying to distance himself from them.' Karn: 'That whole night was spent arguing with Dave, everyone arguing. It came to a stalemate where he said he would not do the tour with that behind him, so that left Richard, Steve and me in the position of saying, "Alright, we won't do the tour if it's *not* there," which would have been really childish so we didn't do that, we said, "Okay, you can have your way again, we'll do the tour without the set," because we just couldn't let all those people down.' Karn recalls this crisis happening within 24 hours but others involved recall it playing out over a number of days. In Karn's version he states that the band argued all night on the eve of the tour, with Sylvian offering the ultimatum: 'It's not my decision anymore; either the stage set goes, or the tour is cancelled. It's up to you.' Karn was, understandably, 'livid', telling Sylvian: 'Have it your way, but get this straight – I can't carry on like this, you're impossible to work with, and it's just not a band any more. I've had enough.' Karn states that this was the point that Japan broke up, while not mentioning that he had already aired plans to make a solo album, thus breaking, according to Sylvian, an 'unspoken agreement' that none of the members of Japan would ever record solo while still part of the group. Karn says that the arguments raged until early morning, leaving only a few hours left to pack.

When he returned to his flat to do so, Yuka was of course waiting for him. She apparently cut short Karn's justified grumbling with the shocking words: 'I will be moving out while you are on tour and moving in with Dave.' Karn was, of course, devastated. 'I hadn't only lost my companion and partner, I'd also lost my best friend.'

Innocenti: 'That was an interesting time on many levels. There was huge tension in the band at that point, particularly between Mick and David. The Yuka thing just brought to light a deeper tension that had simmered for years. Mick told me that he and David had been incredibly close and that something had happened and they'd stopped being as close. Mick felt he had disappointed David in some way.' Arno: 'As I became close to Mick he told me that the reasons for the tensions between him and David went back to a specific event that had happened in the very earliest days of the band.' Innocenti: 'It was obviously a great time for them professionally, as the tour had sold out, their album was a hit and they were on the brink of realising their dreams. In the heat of the arguments, I felt that not only was David separating himself from the band, but was also trying to separate himself from pop music itself. The rest of the guys had given their whole lives to this and now David wanted to walk away from it. The feeling I got from being in that room was that David was saying 'fuck you' to his friends in a very selfish and arrogant way. It was like, "I'm the artist and you're just the band." Richard was incandescent, because maybe he understood this more than anyone else. He was shouting at David, "You can't be serious, what are you thinking of?" and at this point I decided to side with the band. At that final confrontation David was looking strained, but wasn't giving up, like a little kid who was determined to get his way no matter what. Rich was rigid with anger. I tried reasoning with David again: "You've got to see it fully lit. If you don't use this set then technically you've got a problem." I was bullshitting to a degree, just trying to persuade him, and I remember in the middle of this he just gave me this cold, icy stare. At this point Rich jumped in, "Maybe we can use *some* of the set." Arno then chimed in, "Yeah, we can remove bits and pieces, this and that," and finally, finally, David said, "Okay."'

So began the 'Shit Tour' as the band would ever refer to it. Although everyone involved, from the soundman (Nigel Walker) to the guitar roadie, knew that something was amiss within the group, the specific reasons as to why were unclear. According to Karn, he did not speak to anyone during the first few days of the tour and even Jansen and Barbieri were at first unaware of the Yuka situation. As the tour progressed, it was Karn not Sylvian who apparently told the two what had happened. Jansen was sympathetic, up to a point. 'Obviously the Yuka effect was significant but not decisive in the band's demise. I was spending a lot of time with Mick during this period and he was quite happy in the knowledge that Yuka and David were spending time together a few doors along at Stanhope Gardens where we all had apartments, as he seemed to want to reclaim his space. To be completely honest, I was surprised that he decided to make such a big deal of it, but over the years I recognised that he would suffer a cyclic pattern of rejecting partners, pushing them away, then once they're gone being very upset over the loss. I watched it happen a few times afterwards and even pointed it out to him on a few occasions, so that particular event was a result of Mick's pattern, David being a bit of a recluse and not putting himself in a position to meet new, unconnected females, so no doubt feeling a connection that worked for him. And Yuka? Well, I can't speak for her, as I've no way of knowing what was in her mind at that time. But as I say, this wasn't the cause of the band's split, which was occurring regardless, but it perhaps inflamed the underlying clash of egos between the two more emotionally unstable members of the band.'

Angie Usher: 'There was no sign that it was going to happen and I think that's what hurt Mick. It was so unexpected. I think too, it was a way of David attempting to destroy Mick.' Huckle: 'I just can't buy into the idea of Dave getting together with Yuka in the way he did in order to dominate Mick. It seemed to me that Dave's interest in women waned somewhat as the band became more successful, as they would kind of become a distraction. At first it was obviously very flattering having lots of women interested in you, but it quickly became too much of a hassle. One thing that was very apparent is that Dave, unlike Mick or Steve for example, never once indulged in the groupie thing when touring. When he did have girlfriends, the relationships were always short-lived and invariably with women who were significantly older than him. I think today they'd be known as cougars. None ever got to move in with him or he with them. Yuka was almost certainly the first woman he really bonded with in that way and had a proper relationship with. I think that letting Mick know when they did was just down to the unfortunate timing of events. They couldn't tell him much beforehand because their relationship wasn't yet at that point, and to tell him after or during the tour could have made it look like they'd been going behind his back for longer. I think Dave genuinely believed that the relationship between Mick and Yuka had all but broken down anyway, and that Mick would not be as hurt as he was.'

Indeed, Sylvian and Fujii would stay together romantically for a decade and they remain friends to this day. The irony of the situation was that it was such an un-Japan like event to happen and yet one that would forever haunt their legacy. Sylvian was a pop star who always strived to maintain privacy in his personal life and yet soon would be publicly known as the 'cad' who stole his best friend's girlfriend and broke up the band. The true reasons behind such an incident will forever remain private but it does seem, according to those who were there, that Sylvian considered the seven-month relationship between Fujii and Karn as already being over. Sylvian himself would speak sparingly of the incident, only saying, 'I can't explain the whole situation completely because it would mean delving very deeply into Mick's private life and I don't see that I've got the right to do that.'

Somehow the sold out tour began as planned on 7 December 1981 at the Cornwall Coliseum in St Austell. For the first few nights it was touch-and-go if the band would get it together. Mark Wardel: 'I remember I drove down to Cornwall with Simon Napier-Bell for that first concert and backstage Simon kept telling me he had to stop himself from telling me to get on stage in case David went AWOL because he thought I looked like a cross between him and David Rhodes.' Ultimately, there was a job to do and the livelihood of many people – roadies, technicians – depended on this tour. John Punter was otherwise employed, so his engineer Nigel Walker stepped in to do the sound confirming that, 'I think the basic idea was to reproduce the sound of the albums as close as possible in concert. So it made sense for the band to take a studio guy on the road with them to mix the sound.' Jansen was also using a

Karn, Jansen, Sylvian, Rhodes, Visions Of China Tour
David Sowerby

mostly electronic kit for the first time, opting for a Simmons Kit over his usual Tama, although he did augment the set-up with the occasional acoustic drum, 'because it seemed like a cool idea at the time,' he says. 'They were minimal and at the forefront of a new technology; however, as it was an infant science it was hard going. The sounds weren't very stable, and there was no recall so all the knobs had to be manually set. The pads themselves were made of riot shield plastic and with their lack of yield caused hand joints to swell.'

Meanwhile, Rhodes was still adapting to the strange eco-climate of the group: 'We didn't go for a meal or anything before the first date, so we hadn't socialised at all. It seemed a bit weird to me but it seemed like they had their own world ... maybe they thought *I* was weird. We got in the van that first morning and that was weird too – dark and dingy – and I didn't find out why for a few days. When we got to the venue the set was there, which looked more like a tea house than a pagoda, but it was okay. I still had no idea what had happened, but it all seemed very subdued.' Innocenti: 'On that first date there was hardly anything of the set, just a few risers and so forth.' Par Can: 'That first sound check was delayed because Mick was so distressed although we didn't know why then. We were actually told, "This might not happen." Some serious talking had to be done for it to do so and that talking went on right up until the band walked on stage.' Miraculously the concert went ahead and, despite a few dirty looks between Karn and Sylvian, the audience were none the wiser of the behind-the-scenes grief.

Rhodes: 'After the show we went to our hotel and I thought, "God, I need a beer," and Mick said, "I'll be down in a little bit." I had a few drinks with the crew and Rich and Steve. And then Mick came down about two in the morning and he just looked like a peacock. He'd cleaned himself up and put on tons of make-up and was dressed beautifully. I thought it a bit odd that he would make that effort for a small hotel bar in Cornwall at that time of the day. As the tour went on I found out that Mick and Dave had fallen out badly and it was awkward.' Par Can: 'After a show, if we were hanging

Visions Of China Tour
Jan Kalinski

out, if David was there Mick wasn't and vice versa. We weren't sure why.' Usher: 'I really felt for Steve because he was torn between his brother and Mick, who was his best friend in the band.'

Offstage, Sylvian and Karn avoided each other as much as possible. Innocenti: 'The next day Mick wanted to travel with me instead of the band. I was driving the set in a truck. I was a little bit bemused by this but, of course, said okay. It was snowing and a hard drive, but Mick kept me company chatting away. During the tour, David didn't mention the set to me again and he kept to himself. So we gradually began bringing back more bits of the set each night. By the time we got to Hammersmith, the whole set was in place.' Huckle: 'Actually, the whole set was never in place. Dave wouldn't have the bridge put up, even by the end. It was a really hard job to keep that tour on the road … Dave and Mick were barely talking, and if they did it was a vitriolic argument. At several points one or other of them wanted or threatened to stop the tour. A lot of it of course was in the heat of the emotional moment! But sense prevailed. It's a credit to Rich and Steve that they kept the two of them from walking off by reasoning with them about being unfair to the fans, crew and everyone else involved. Poor David Rhodes must have been a bit shell-shocked. I think SNB showed up at the Leeds Queens Hall gig to try and steady the ship, but unfortunately Yuka also showed up at that show, which didn't help, though I think she did give Dave a lot of support which helped dissuade him from walking off.'

As bits of the set were added, a kind of strained equilibrium settled on the tour and other more day-to-day stresses were allowed to manifest. Par Can: 'There was no catering on that tour and meals were supposed to be organised nightly for the crew. Huckle panicked a bit and dropped the ball. Instead of a proper meal, a whole lot of McDonald's turned up. The boss of the road crew, Simon, saw this fast food and freaked. The whole lot went across the room. When Huckle came in, Simon pinned him against the wall and one of the other guys took Huckle's wallet out and took out 50 quid and said, "Right,

*Visions Of
China Tour
Jan Kalinski*

we're going for a proper meal and we'll be back before the show," so we went and had a curry. It was a hard lesson Nick had to learn.' 'I don't remember that,' says Huckle in his defence. 'I remember having caterers from day one, the same as on the previous tour. One hot meal per show after soundcheck. I think he's probably referring to the odd occasion when perhaps some of the crew missed the main meal because of gear arriving late as the weather caused a real problem with transport that winter.'

When Karn and Sylvian weren't on the verge of duelling and Nick Huckle wasn't being assaulted by the crew, the occasional lighter moment was allowed. 'Me and one of the other members of the crew were sat in our room after a show listening to a Kenny Everett tape – his Captain Kremmen,' remembers Par Can. 'Mick and Steve must have heard it and came in saying, "That's really cool, who is it?" so they came in for a drink and the barrier came down. I remember talking to Mick about his first ever gig in Newcastle and I told him, "I was there!" He was amazed. By the end of that night we were like a band of brothers. They were then much more confident about suggesting things or raising issues with the lighting and set. But I never socialised with David or Rich. If I did it would have brought us even closer together. Steve and I talked about photography. I would set up my Canon and photograph the band on stage and Steve would give me tips.'

It also helped that the audiences on the tour were at capacity and utterly besotted with Japan. At the Manchester Apollo on 13 December, two future members of a band called The Smiths were in attendance. 'I always loved Japan,' remembers Andy Rourke, 'but when I saw them live [with Johnny Marr], Mick Karn stole the show for me with his Chinese slippers and magical dance moves; he was almost like a mime artist! My first bass happened to be a fretless bass, so of course Mick's bass playing had me mesmerised. His bass playing had a massive effect on me; I would learn all of his bass lines verbatim. This guy was a fucking genius! He really helped me raise my game when it came to playing bass.'

Visions Of China Tour Jan Kalinski

Far right: Japan with competition winner Julie Bray

Despite such rare occasions of levity and the crowds being at their most appreciative, both the tour and, indeed, Japan would never truly recover from this most recent fracture. Like a salve applied to a boil, success seemed to bring out all the underlying toxins and tensions that had been building up within the band in the preceding years. 'It was fascinating actually, to witness such tension,' says Innocenti, 'because usually that kind of thing goes on behind closed doors and yet because we were involved, being the set designers, we were dragged into it.' The dominant bugbear was of course 'Yukagate'. Jansen: 'That was more agonising than working with the Simmons Kit. It was a massive elephant in the room. It was painful to witness and I felt terrible for David and Mick. There were hours of tight-lipped tension until something small was said and things would erupt between them. One such time occurred after the show in Leeds, so we decided to have a group discussion back at my hotel room. The conversation between the four of us was getting pretty heated as David and Mick continued to bicker, while Richard and I found our patience wearing awfully thin. When the phone rang to say that the winner of the fan club drawing competition was downstairs waiting with her parents, we all had to go down and put on a smile.' Indeed, there is a photo of the group meeting competition winner Julie Bray that shows only Sylvian managing to muster a pained smile for the camera, while the expressions of Karn et al. show men who, beneath the make-up, can barely contain their fury.

Huckle had of course been witness to such rows from day one, but even so was upset by the new intensity of the disagreements. 'There were two levels of argument,' he says. 'Firstly there were those held in company, say in the studio, or in offices and dressing rooms etc. These tended to be fairly lightweight and probably only a notch or two up from a heated debate. Then there were those that would take place in more private surroundings, often in the car or someone's apartment. These could become really heated and loud, with nothing held back and much use of – not so much heavy swearing – but what was, to me, often quite hurtful language. But they never turned violent. Most arguments were between Mick and Steve, or Steve and Dave, or Mick and Dave, or a two-on-one combination of those three. It was a demonstration of the strength of their friendship that all these arguments were soon forgotten or put aside and within a short time everyone would be back on good terms again. Nor can I remember any argument causing a gig to be cancelled or prematurely ending a studio session, but it came close on the "Shit Tour". Still, by around halfway through the tour things became a bit more manageable with Dave and Mick agreeing to keep away from each other apart from onstage and during any PR duties, and the remainder of the tour settled into a routine, albeit a rather moody one. Ironically, they were going down really well with the audiences and doing some great shows.'

Live reviews began to appear in the weeklies and were almost all positive, praising in particular the set design and the 'high-tech sheen of the Japan sound and lighting'. Rhodes: 'The lighting guy had done something with the lighting, put a little slit of light onto the stage in front of me, but he hadn't told me about it. I've since learnt a bit about stagecraft, i.e. when there's a light you step into it, but I didn't know that then! So what was meant to happen was that the neck of my guitar was supposed to be lit up, but all you could see was the end of my shoes.' Par Can: 'Well, to do the lights properly, you've got to know the music. If you don't, you can wing it, but you still need a sense of timing and you need to be able to keep a beat. You just have to watch the drummer's left hand, the one he hits the snare with. It'll always come back to a four even if someone like Steve, with his particular style of playing, could make it tricky.'

Rhodes, having no personal investment in the emotional life of Japan, was able both to keep aloof from any arguments and to offer temporary companionship for Karn. 'It was kind of an odd tour, going round England at that time of year,' he says, 'but one of the high spots was going to a Turkish bath with Mick in Newcastle. I'd never done that before, and afterwards we went on to do the show and, you know, those "scuttles" Mick usually does ... well that evening he was just standing still, drained, as he'd got so hot!' Par Can: 'Newcastle was my home town so I had a lot of friends waiting to see if I could get them in, but I just couldn't and anyway I was so busy as we were really up against it time wise to load everything in. I was doing a job, not hanging out with the band; I was working. Anyway, that night we in the crew finally heard what had happened – how the tour was almost over before it began. When we heard about what happened, we thought it was a pretty shitty thing for David to have done. Mick's problem was that usually in this situation you could leave and get away from it, but he couldn't as he had to be on stage every night.'

The tour must have seemed never-ending, for Karn in particular, as the band made their way through some of the heaviest snow Britain had seen in years. Rhodes: 'I remember the drive from Newcastle in particular. It was snowing; filthy weather. We were driving to Scotland. There were abandoned trucks along the motorway. The driver had to put diesel in with the petrol to stop it freezing and it stunk. We arrived in Edinburgh in the middle of the night. The heating was broken and it was the coldest night in years.' Rhodes at least was finally warming to his temporary band. 'Mick and Rich had a kind of catchphrase,' he recalls, 'they used to say it when we were going to a loo at a motorway stop or whatever. I'd just go to a normal urinal and do my business and they'd go to cubicles and each of them would say this independently of each other: "I'm a cubicle man myself!"' The tour moved on through Scotland and back through Birmingham and Brighton with Karn steeling himself every night by putting the audiences first. 'So many people knew there was something wrong,' he'd reflect, 'and they kept asking us every day what it was but what really upset me was that the actual fans were picking up on it and people would come up to me and say, "What's the matter between you and Dave?" because we were giving each other dirty looks on stage, which I wasn't even aware of.'

The tour ended impressively with five sold-out dates in London at the Drury Lane Theatre and the Hammersmith Odeon. The sense of relief that the band had somehow made it this far was tangible. Par Can: 'I went into the dressing room on one of the last nights to have a drink and David was there of course, getting ready in the full-length mirror, and we were chatting. And just before he went on, I got a hug! Fuck me, I got a hug! He was uncharacteristically smiley and happy. He was either high or in love!' Despite the personal differences, Japan were approaching a peak in terms of their live performance even if, for Rhodes, the shows still lacked a certain something. 'There was very little in the way of improvisation,' he says. 'It was very measured, very dry musically and maybe even a bit dry emotionally. Sylvian was so into his world and the shows weren't very giving.' This, however, was part of their appeal and the aloofness portrayed on stage was perhaps more of a reflection of insecurity on Sylvian's part. 'I remember at one show,' says Edward Arno, 'I overheard David, just before he went on, say to some girl or other, "Do I look okay? Do you think they'll laugh at me?"'

It was also true that Japan were mainly interested in focusing on the music onstage rather than entertaining the audience, although Karn himself was a born performer. The resulting 'look, listen, but don't touch' stage persona was also one finely tailored to the fashion of the day. Rhodes: 'It suited the time, certainly. One wonders if they would have gone further if they'd been a bit looser. For myself, I was quite still on stage. There was the set all around us which felt like the focus, moody lighting, and then there were Mick and David of course, whom the girls loved to look at. The whole thing was so stylised. Sylvian didn't seem to enjoy it and that's just the way it was.'

*Visions Of
China Tour
Keiko Kurata*

By the last few dates, the show was closer to a theatrical performance than a pop concert. At the Drury Lane shows the curtains of the stage rose slowly as the band played the opener (and closer) of the set, 'Canton'. The lighting was deliberate and subtle, the sound immaculate. At his most expansive, Sylvian wandered the stage as if crossing a tennis court back and forth, casual, unruffled, often smiling and only occasionally reaching out to make contact with the outstretched fingertips of the audience. Each member played their part of the musical jigsaw with panache. Only a sometimes glaring Karn provided any real movement and friction. At the final Drury Lane show, Sylvian introduced the encore with the words, 'We're in love with you,' and the feeling was mutual. After two encores, the band were gone, leaving the backstage tension to manifest itself in two curiously violent incidents: one fan who attempted to make contact backstage was apparently 'kicked in the face' by a security guard as the group's van sped off, and a journalist had his finger broken while being deterred from entering a dressing room.

Obviously, with things the way they were between band members and with Yuka occasionally appearing, there was little inclination to party. Rhodes: 'I don't remember anyone ever coming backstage except for members of "the organisation". It was quite odd.' Angie Usher: 'In all the time I knew them, I never went backstage. Dave just made you feel so unwelcome. After the gig, a few of us would congregate on the actual stage as they were unloading the gear, but that's as far as any party went. And yet, Steve had such a dry sense of humour, although you'd never guess unless you knew him. Richard too. David – I don't think he was ever happy being a front man.' Potential groupies were given increasingly short shrift. 'There were beautiful women around,' says Par Can, 'immaculately dressed, but the band hardly gave them the time of day. And the women who followed Japan were beautifully made-up and seemed so posh. They were Princess Diana and Jerry Hall types. You could just see that they'd taken the time, even if the next day they were going to work at Tesco or whatever.'

By the time of the final show at Hammersmith Odeon on 27 December 1981, Virgin were convinced that Japan were finally going to be massive. 'I was with them a lot on that tour,' says Keith Bourton, 'and I'd be stood by the mixing desk and clocking the audience. The band would always ask me what it sounded like and how it looked. We were trying to decide what to put out next as a single and of course the last possible candidate because of its dirge-like pace would have been 'Ghosts'. But when we played Hammersmith, the place went absolutely ape-shit when they played that song. It got a good reaction on the whole tour but in London particularly it got a massive response. The very next day there was a meeting to discuss what would be the next Japan single, and that's when the idea of releasing 'Ghosts' first came up.' Virgin didn't yet know that the band they had recently signed was more or less over. Innocenti: 'By the end of that tour, my opinion on the set thing was again that David used it, as a decoy almost, as what he wanted to do was to separate himself from what Japan were becoming – which was a successful pop group. For the rest of the guys it must have been like finally getting married and then finding out that the other person didn't want to sleep with you on the honeymoon.'

Chapter 10
Voices Raised in Welcome

Autographed photo dedicated to *Music Week*, Hong Kong, December 1982
Music Week Archive

Letter to Cathy and Claire, *Jackie* Magazine 1982

1982 was Japan's year off. It was the first year since 1976 that the band did not record an album together. Writing, recording, releasing and promoting an album every year was pressure enough for any band and the *Visions Of China Tour* had worn everyone's patience Bowie-thin. By now, Sylvian and Karn could barely stand to be in the same room together and Jansen and Barbieri were exhausted and frustrated by the constant tension. Perversely, this was also the year when Japan would peak in popularity; in the UK it was the year they 'arrived'. *Tin Drum* was selling steadily and both their Hansa and Virgin singles were charting. Japan were finally in demand. In the UK there was now barely a music magazine printed that didn't feature the group in some way. The letters pages of *Smash Hits* and *Noise* were littered with the fawning rhapsodies of teenage girls obsessed with Sylvian in particular. 'His wavy hair and sexy eyes make me want to cry,' wrote one besotted teen from Bradford. In Fred and Judie Vermorel's *Starlust: The Secret Fantasies Of Fans* (written in 1983 and published two years later) there would be a long, disturbing passage detailing the surreal dreams of one Japan fan that only made one wonder at the type of fan mail now arriving at Nomis.

Fan obsession aside, by 1982 Japan were finally respected, commercially successful, and in vogue. They were also the best looking band of the year, a perfectly photogenic bouquet next to the lumpen clump of New Romantic wannabes, and more seductively inscrutable than the pop porn of Duran Duran. Japan now dressed in casual designer suits, with their Allan Soh hairdos processed to perfection and their make-up subtle and extremely flattering. Throughout 1982 magazines would acquire a certain class and cachet just by putting a picture of Japan on the cover. However, behind the scenes, they were barely functioning as a group and for the first few months of 1982 the heartbroken Karn was scarcely functioning as a person.

In addition, despite the flash image, and although they were making a reasonable living for musicians, Japan were hardly rolling in it. Angie Usher: 'Their public image was glamorous, well off, luxurious even, but it wasn't the reality. For instance, if you took away all the sculptures and art from Mick's flat, it was so grotty, especially for the area.' Karn could be forgiven for a lapse in his housekeeping as he was still processing the events of the previous December. 'I began to understand that what had really taken a beating was my pride,' he would state. What hurt Karn most was the loss of Sylvian as a friend and the resultant disharmony of a group that had been a family to its members since their teens. 'I spent a lot of time with Mick after the "Shit Tour",' says Usher. 'I was keeping him company. He needed it. Just talking, listening to music. We smoked opium one time as an experiment, but it wasn't a regular thing. He was in a lot of pain. He felt like he'd lost two important people in his life. There was a framed photo of him and David above his bed; he really had considered him his best friend. After the Yuka thing he didn't take that picture down, but he just didn't sleep in the bed any more. He slept on a sofa bed in the lounge. He was so, so depressed that I was actually worried for him.'

Karn was dragged from his flat in the last days of December and put on a plane to attend an exhibition in Tokyo at the enormous Parco department store where both Karn's sculptures and Jansen's photographs were on display. Jansen: 'It was a one-off event to combine the interests of Mick and me outside of music. I'm not sure how it came about, but Parco invested in projects such as these in their gallery space, strategically

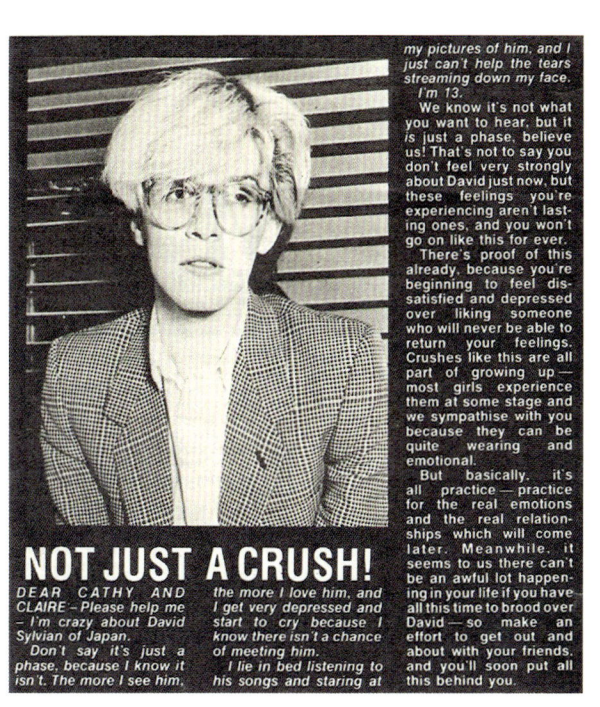

Art Of Parties exhibition, Parco, Tokyo
Keiko Kurata

placed on the top floor, inevitably creating some level of custom. It came at a good time, as we'd just finished the UK tour and it was a good departure from performing and working together as a band, while still maintaining the public profile. Mick and I went to Tokyo with Richard to attend the opening of the event and to spend the New Year there reassessing the fallout of recent events and allowing the dust to settle.'

The situation in London wasn't helped by everyone living in such close proximity. Karn had a room with a view and that view was of Sylvian and Yuka's living room. This was obviously not a vista he would choose to contemplate. Sylvian at least was tactful enough to depart. 'After the *Visions Of China Tour*, Dave decided to move,' says Huckle, 'so he, Yuka and I drove around looking for flats. We saw this incredible place opposite the Royal Albert Hall. It had this huge living room but it was all done up in this Indianesque type decor – very red walls – and he didn't like that, didn't think red was a very good vibe. This was before he got into joss sticks, obviously. So we settled on this place on the top floor of Elm Park Mansions on Park Walk, Chelsea, which he rented off an American guy.' Sylvian was now free to move one step closer to his goal of self-sufficiency and explore the first serious romantic relationship of his life without Karn as a neighbour.

Sylvian and Yuka would live together on and off for the next few months before settling down together for the duration. Despite Sylvian's ascendant fame, in some ways they were just another young couple. Usher: 'I'd see Dave and Yuka in the supermarket occasionally – Europa Foods in Fulham, which was so overpriced. Dave would kind of grimace in acknowledgement when he saw me, but would never actually deign to say, "Hello". Yuka was more friendly. When I first met him I thought it was shyness, but as time went on I got a sense that he thought he was superior.' Huckle: 'He was quite happy popping to the local convenience stores in and around South Ken and Fulham. They tended to stay open late at night around that part of town, so it was easy to avoid the crowds. He wasn't a cook or anything so only ever bought basic necessities: milk, coffee, ginger nuts and the like, and fags of course. He smoked Gitanes in the main though, unlike Mick, only moderately.' Sylvian was now a bona fide pin-up in the UK and such shopping excursions were not without their surreal moments. Sylvian: 'Someone came up to me in a supermarket once and said, "Cor, you're the best David Sylvian lookalike I've ever seen!"' Meanwhile, Karn left Tokyo and headed straight to Toronto, disastrously hosting the CFNY Radio Awards. 'It was the most nerve racking thing I've ever had to do,' he'd shudder in memory, 'never again, and I'm sure CFNY thought so too.'

On 7 January, 'European Son' was re-released. As the band were in no position forcibly to halt the release of their Hansa material, they decided to make the best of it. Master tapes were duly transferred to AIR Studios where Steve Nye was at the desk. 'Mick updated his bass parts on 'Life In Tokyo' and 'European Son',' confirms Nye, 'and I also remixed seven-inch and 12-inch versions of those two tracks plus 'I Second That Emotion' and 'All Tomorrow's Parties', which were all re-released as singles. My brief was to make them sound like the recently successful Japan of 1982, I guess. I tend just to mix them as I hear them anyway.' Mark Wardel was in attendance at these sessions. 'They were remixing 'European Son' for some reason and didn't seem all that enthusiastic about it. I love phased sequencers, so I was kind of saying to David that I would love even more of it on the track and he was laughing and saying that they had plenty of it already and kind of jokingly putting the level super-high for me.' Sylvian was not enthusiastic about these re-releases, but neither was he angry. 'It really all depends on what it is they decide to release; 'cos it's out of my hands, I really have no control over it,' he philosophised. 'I can't say I like the idea … it interferes with what we're doing now and it gives people the wrong impression of what we are actually doing, but it's out of our hands.' 'European Son', already previously released and owned in several formats by the Japan fanbase, nevertheless made it to number 31 in the UK singles chart. Perhaps mercifully for Japan there was no accompanying promo video to embarrass them.

Meanwhile, Virgin were excited and inspired by the prospect of Japan and, unaware of the behind-the-scenes stresses, were considering a bright future for their investment. Jeremy Lascelles: 'Obviously, anyone who had heard Japan's music could hear their influences – Roxy, Bowie etc. In fact Bowie was everywhere in other people's music at that time, but by *Tin Drum* they'd stopped being beholden to those influences. They had become truly innovative and it's their greatest work. They were, particularly for the era, truly ground-breaking by not just sticking with the standard pop format. They could have chosen to push the edges, discover their own voice and make something even more original out of that. I'm not sure why they weren't doing so at that point. I don't personally remember any friction. If I had been there in person, maybe, but I don't remember us being aware of any grief. You know, record companies are commercial entities whilst trying to be nurturing of creative forces so there are bound to be difficulties. There is a schedule set in place as a company needs its records to come out at a particular time and you can get a bit panicky if that looks like it's not happening. You try not to impose such pressures on a group, but those concerns are quite real. As far as early 1982 and Japan were concerned, Virgin were very hopeful.'

At Nomis, the mood was less optimistic. The band had been booked onto *The Old Grey Whistle Test* that January but, on returning from Canada, Karn had gone AWOL forcing the appearance to be postponed. This was the first time in Japan's history that such an event had occurred. While Karn was eventually located and pacified by Richard Chadwick, Sylvian was more in demand as a 'personality' than ever and he presented a calm, unruffled persona when on Friday 29 January he appeared on the BBC Radio 1 review show, *Round Table*. His fellow guest panellist was Robert Palmer who revealed on air that he was a major Japan fan. 'I think it's modern soul music,' Palmer said, demonstrating a deep musical cognisance. 'When David sings, all you can hear is this emotive thing behind it; it draws you into it entirely.' Palmer, who had been recording professionally since the early 1970s, now proved that the musical old guard was beginning to accept and appreciate Japan's music. His statement was a prescient sign that many were finally beginning to recognise the soul behind the pristine image. Palmer even ordered a bottle of champagne live on air for him and Sylvian to share. Yet the affinity was not as strange as it seemed; both men were progressive in their musical aesthetic and shared a love of soul music and Motown. 'It's not surprising that he and David hit it off,' says Keith Bourton, who had arranged Sylvian's appearance on the show. 'I know they got on and enjoyed a drink together after the programme.'

The musical offerings on the programme could hardly be to Sylvian's taste. For someone who was then immersing himself in the music of YMO and Toru Takemitsu, and who was just about to buy his first Derek Bailey album, Sylvian ('a spokesman for modern youth', according to the programme's producer) was diffidently unmoved by the sounds of Nick Lowe, Fun Boy Three and Hank Marvin. Even Talk Talk's 'Mirror Man' with its remorseless Simmons kit trudge and flanged fretless bass, while superficially on the same page as Japan, actually only illustrated how far Sylvian and Co had come with *Tin Drum*. Only the skewed melodic hysteria of The Associates' 'Party Fears Two' struck any kind of chord. 'I liked it. It's very unusual. The lyrics are very unusual,' said Sylvian in approval. (Sylvian had recently revealed that his doctor had advised him to smash plates to alleviate tension and so he probably related to the opening lines of the song about smashing a cup). Billy Mackenzie – The Associates' eccentrically operatic singer – would also enthusiastically attend a Japan show later that year.

Meanwhile Karn (and a fleeting Steve) appeared on the fledgling children's TV show *Number 73*. Usher: 'I drove down with them to Maidstone to do that awful show, with their guitar tech Lionel driving. I was really ill on the way; I felt very, very sick and Mick said, "You'll be all right." We got down there the night before filming and Steve and Mick said, "Let's go for a curry," and I almost threw up at the mention of it. But I managed to make it to the restaurant and pushed a few vegetables around the plate, but we had such a lovely, lovely time – such a laugh. When we got to the studio the next morning Steve saw the whole set-up and said, "I'm not having anything to do with this," but one of them had to do it, and because Mick had to make sushi on air – I don't think Steve could – Mick had to do it.' Jansen: 'I felt like someone on a BBC visitor's pass observing just how shit it is to work on children's TV. I went along for moral support, but I don't think either of us knew quite what to expect as the briefing would have been purposely vague. Perhaps Mick had agreed to prepare food as that had always been a passion of his and maybe he hoped to get that across. But unfortunately, this was a shockingly produced children's TV show, not *Masterchef*.' Karn's presence on the programme is indeed stilted and uncomfortable as if he'd misjudged the measure of it. 'Mick and Connie would often collude in the name of "any publicity is good publicity",' explains Jansen. 'For that you need your standards set low and your expectations high, otherwise you wouldn't bother. I guess it would have been better if he'd managed to be more ironic about the content but, due to his passion for food, maybe that wasn't an option, and consequently resulted in him trying to be taken seriously on a show that's not taking anything seriously.' Of course, this was not the first humiliating TV exercise Karn had suffered. 'I was in Birmingham the year before when Mick was flanned on *Tiswas* and when he came back to the hotel he was infuriated by it. So angry,' says Usher. 'None of them wanted to do such shows but they all felt they kind of had to. Connie was trying to make them mainstream.'

The first months of 1982 also saw Karn and Jansen, along with Bill Nelson, contribute to the albums of various Japanese artists. First up was Akiko Yano's (Sakamato's wife) album, *Ai Ga Nakucha Ne* at AIR. Karn: 'I had some problems when I did the Akiko Yano album. I got a cassette of the songs and went through them thinking, "He [Ryuichi] is gonna love this."' In the event, Ryuichi did not. 'What I was doing just wasn't on,' explained Karn. The bassist would have to re-record his parts according to Sakamoto's directive. Sylvian even did a rare duet with Yano on the brief lullaby of 'Goodnight', the track subsequently being used on a Japanese radio advertisement for Seiko watches. This was followed by work with Japanese singer-songwriter and ace guitarist Masami Tsuchiya of the band Ippu-Do, again at AIR and with Jansen, Karn and Bill Nelson in attendance. Around this time there was supposed to be a launch event by CBS for YMO, Ippu-Do, and Sandii & The Sunsetz, but it was cancelled due to the outbreak of the Falklands War. Sandii and Makoto Kubota of the Sunsetz did make it to London, however, and began the basic tracks to what would become the *Immigrants* album.

Japan the group seemed to be creating a wave of interest in the UK for all things oriental. This fascination with Asian culture, and in particular for Japanese and Chinese motifs, peaked in the UK during 1982. While confined mostly to pop culture, if you were under the age of 24 it was simply cool to wear sleeveless T-shirts with obscure Chinese lettering on and to have the Japanese import version of any 12-inch single or album, complete with requisite 'obi strip' over the dreary UK domestic edition. Even Hollywood would express this with the release of Ridley Scott's *Blade Runner* that summer. This lavish adaptation of Philip K Dick's classic novel *Do Androids Dream Of Electric Sheep?* depicted a future city that was one part New York, two parts Tokyo, with a Vangelis soundtrack that instantly became a favourite of Barbieri. 'I remember three or four of us went to see *Blade Runner*,' says Huckle, 'and were so impressed by it that we went back to see it again the following night.' The film even had its blond anti-hero in the form of Dutch actor Rutger Hauer. Being artificially blond was the peak of cool in 1982 and if you were peroxide with a Japanese edge – all the better.

Sylvian's explanation for this interest in the East was that, 'Musically it's fascinating because it hasn't been explored before by bands over here or in America. It's looking for a new way; you get stuck in a groove … there's only so many influences you can pick up on here or in the US so it's nice to pick up on influences from the East and see where you can take them, with a totally different attitude to the people who live there.' As to the rash of American and British groups playing pentatonic scales on top of 12-bar blues progressions in a clumsy attempt to weave oriental signatures into their otherwise cod Western schlock, Sylvian remained academically aloof. 'It depends how they do it. I don't like the way they do it for the sake of it being fashionable to do it.' Karn himself was less enamoured with the Japanese take on Western pop. 'Japanese people can do some things very well. No matter if they make cars or music, technically it is always safe and sound,' he reasoned, 'but they are looking down on their own tradition and up to England and America. When they hear something which they like, they'll make something that looks like it to give themselves the satisfaction that they can do it too, just as well as the English or Americans. You could call that recycling, although they won't look at it that way, because they've been doing it for centuries.'

The US and UK labels were hip to this new oriental vogue, and Epic and Alfa (via CBS) shared staff for the launch of Japanese acts in the UK, although there would never be any real commercial breakthrough, and in hindsight the UK interest was a novelty. Sandii: 'I liked the energy that was coming from London at that time. I liked Simple Minds, Culture Club, The Slits and I loved Grace Jones' 'Nightclubbing'. I was interviewed by *i-D* magazine and *The Face*; they seemed to be into all things Japanese too. David Claridge, who ran the Great Wall Club in London, came over to Japan and interviewed me too. People in London really seemed to like my *Eating Pleasure* album, which Harry Hosono produced.' Karn was not convinced of this Japanese-Anglo hybrid: 'It has no depth,' he reckoned. 'You can listen to it, but after that you've heard enough of it. The sound is all right, a lot of clever things are happening, but there is no surprise. Everything fits decently together. When Japanese people hear something they want to copy, they can only copy the form, not the feeling. This is why a lot of Japanese pop music is so empty, which is a pity, because if they would make their own music, they could also give it their own feeling.'

Even as Japan hibernated musically, Karn was more in demand than ever as a session bassist. That spring he travelled to Paris at Robert Palmer's invitation to work with French singer Marie Léonore. 'Doing sessions with other people is one of the most frightening experiences,' confessed Karn. 'Robert Palmer asked me to go over to Paris, but I was so scared. When I'm that scared doing something new, I like to jump in the deep end and go all the way, so what I like to do when I'm nervous is ask if they'll let me warn them first that I won't know what notes to play if they tell me so I'm to go ahead and put the bass down on the track without having heard the track first, and see what happens. That worked pretty well with Gary Numan, he kept the bass I did first time, and it worked with Robert Palmer, but all the other keyboard players had to change to play my notes! But once you do that, it gives you the confidence that you need.'

Behind the scenes, Japan and their manager decided to book one last tour for the end of the year. For Japan, this was a way of consolidating their success into some much needed fiscal currency. Meanwhile, Napier-Bell was convinced that the success of the tour would persuade the group to stay together, but Karn was by now chomping at the bit to record the solo album he had first conceived the previous winter. 'We realised that the band was beginning to become successful and if we did want to do any solo projects we'd have to carry on with Japan, otherwise Virgin wouldn't let us do anything on our own,' he explained that spring, 'so the band isn't splitting up, but there's definitely a feeling that as soon as anything better comes up we're taking the first chance we get.' Virgin were not thrilled to read such statements in the press. Simon Draper: 'It was around now we first started hearing rumours of them splitting up. Disaster! By now we had a name, a brand, and when you've achieved that you always want to make use of it, but they had little interest in that. We expected them to be a commercial success and they were, but they could have done a lot more.' 'I could see that there was a rift that was deeply entrenched at that point, but we didn't consider them to have split up,' says Jeremy Lascelles. 'We knew that was a possibility but hoped, especially when *Tin Drum* was such a success, that they would have stayed together, that they may change their minds. They were still involved with all the promotion for the album and singles, *Top Of The Pops*, TV … they still did all that. I was a fan by then and would go to see them live. They had gone from not being cool, a kind of Hansa joke, to being the coolest band around, and really good musically too. It was quite a transformation. And I was like a lot of people who had had this perception of who they were and had turned out to be wrong, and subsequently I revised my opinion.'

Virgin, a label hosting acts such as Simple Minds, Human League, and Magazine, was at the time a new species – a label as cool as its bands. Unlike Hansa, Sylvian and Co felt comfortable dropping into their offices at Vernon Yard. Bourton: 'Yes, Japan weren't strangers to the building although I don't remember any other Virgin acts being particularly interested in them. Bands on any label just don't tend to interact. They would have been too into their own careers. Except if that group had girls in them – then they would invariably be in love with either David and/or Steve! When David came in and was being fussed over by numerous members of female staff, he was very cool about it, if not embarrassed. Steve dealt with it a lot better than David did whereas David was much more retiring. He was far too private but also very good-natured and just tried not to let it affect him too much.'

Tin Drum was selling steadily but had so far birthed only one low-charting single, 'Visions Of China', so it was time for another release. The choice was at first controversial, even at an enlightened label like Virgin. 'I really pushed for 'Ghosts',' says Bourton. 'At a meeting in December, I told Simon Draper, "The song that is going down unbelievably well live is 'Ghosts'. I think if we took a real flying jump we could release it as a single," and everyone looked at me as if I was insane, which I understood. The one person who backed me up was Jeremy Lascelles. People were worried because the vocal was so down – it was a dirge.' 'Keith was obsessed by that song,' confirms Lascelles, 'he just kept playing it and playing it, but Simon [Draper] was the boss, the MD, and it just so happened that, at this point, he was on holiday! And we were just saying, "We've got to put this out as a single. Everyone who hears it has a phenomenal reaction to it. It's gotta be a single!" And so we made the decision to do it without deferring to Simon. This was the days before email and mobile phones and, when he found out, he said, "You're off your fucking rockers!" but we got it out there. It was a brave thing to do by a brave group.' Sylvian had already heard the song on the radio by chance. 'I knew then, when I heard it, it was a hit,' he'd say at the time. He was right. Sylvian did not see the song itself as being particularly obtuse – it was the arrangement that gave this impression. 'I persevere with ballads or love songs because that's the most classic form in pop music, so I thought if people understood the form I could take more liberties with it,' he'd say. 'Maybe 'Ghosts' is still the best example. A lot of the abstract painters used the portrait as a foundation to work from; it gives everybody a way in.'

While the single was pressed and artwork assembled, there was the rescheduled *The Old Grey Whistle Test* to attend to, which was now booked for 4 March. Karn was still not a happy camper. Huckle: 'Mick had locked himself in his flat, refusing to go. SNB and I were outside his place for about an hour talking to him through the letterbox and trying to coax him out. Eventually time ran out so SNB asked me to kick down his door, with the aim, I assume, of forcefully dragging him to the studio. Needless to say, I managed only to damage the door's paintwork a little and bruise my shoulder, but Mick did then open the door, really pissed off that it might be broken, and SNB took him into the kitchen and had words with him. We then drove to BBC TV Centre with him still in a major sulk. 'That performance,' says Barbieri, 'was a bit weird. I think Mick and David were in conflict at the time and we had two extra people up there with us [David Rhodes and Sakamoto] so it felt less like a band. Mick just sat on stage during 'Ghosts', which he didn't play on. I'm not sure why he didn't play some harmonics, which is what the rest of us were doing. I think he made a point of being on stage but not playing to annoy David probably. David had previously been keen to involve Ryuichi more with the band and having him perform a track with us on *The Old Grey Whistle Test* was just another step. Generally, when an outside musical influence or personality was introduced into the band, it strangely diminished it in my opinion.' Nevertheless Japan's performance is confident, soulful and glacial. Sylvian remains seated throughout and seems oblivious to his one-time best friend who during the first number simply sits waiting the song out. In this incarnation, 'Ghosts' is more organic than the recorded version, fuller and more passionately delivered by its singer. 'I felt that was the only time while I was with them that Sylvian loosened his grip on things,' says David Rhodes. 'They all seemed to admire Ryuichi a lot and he is a lovely guy and I felt it made things easier. Sylvian just let him do what he wanted and he fiddled about and I enjoyed him being there because it suddenly felt like you could make a few more noises and interact more.' Usher: 'Mick looked so isolated in those clips. He was so sad behind those sunglasses. Whenever I saw Mick and David in the same room together they never spoke to one another, but even before that I got the impression that David was apart from the other three.'

Next to the iceberg drift of 'Ghosts', 'Cantonese Boy' seems insanely pop by comparison with Rhodes's funky guitar part sounding as if it had been transplanted directly from Duran's 'Girls On Film'. This would be the last time Rhodes played with Japan. 'I always wondered if I was a bit neat for them,' he'd say in hindsight. 'Well, not wild enough, in the way, say, Masami was, with a lot of Adrian Belew-isms, a lot of noise, and again Rob had always been a noisy player. I'd bumped into Rob a few times; he was a nice guy and I think he'd done a great job. I met him after my Japan experience and we went out and got drunk. I really liked him. Generally, I got on best with Mick, although not to the point where we'd keep in touch. Steve and Richard were less guarded than Sylvian. I remember talking to Mick about dreaming of shit. He told me that Freud said that symbolised money. What did I learn from my time with them? It was interesting. The *Tin Drum* material was great and it was a pleasure to play on that. I found the earlier material a bit less challenging; it felt lighter and had less flesh on it. I would have been happy to work with them in the studio because I find playing great fun, but by then David had felt it had run its course.'

Sylvian was in fact recording at the time. Sakamoto was in town to work with him on a one-off single at Martin Rushent's Genetic Sound studios in Reading. Immediately after the band's appearance on *The Old Grey Whistle Test*, they began recording ad hoc in the studio with Nye as producer. Sylvian: 'It was the first time that I had worked with Ryuichi Sakamoto properly; we both went into the studio and started writing there and then and the idea was to come up with something interesting.' 'Bamboo Houses' came together first but was deemed to be 'too much B-side material' according to Ryuichi's then translator, Peter Barakan: 'Sakamoto had only a few days in the UK and the pair struggled to come up with a more typical A-side.'

After Sakamoto had returned to Japan, Sylvian and Nye laboured on, editing and mixing the riffs and parts laid down with Sakamoto. Lyrics to 'Bamboo Music' were completed at the last minute with vocals being added almost at the mixing stage and The Penguin Café Orchestra's Simon Jeffes was also invited to contribute Ebowed guitar. Nye: 'Obviously, David was aware of my involvement with the PCO and Ryuichi had collaborated with Simon Jeffes in Tokyo on a Penguin track called 'Heartwind', and I remember Dave attended one of the PCO concerts in Tokyo, so there was an obvious connection there. I didn't recall Simon working on 'Bamboo Houses', however Steve showed me a photo from those sessions of Simon playing his Gretsch guitar using a violin bow with Dave and Ryuichi looking on. I think Rich especially was a fan of the PCO and had also seen the band live.' Jeffes's contributions would not make the final mix. 'There's always a chance that it isn't going to turn out exactly as you planned it,' explained Sylvian. 'When I finished 'Bamboo Music' I couldn't say that I was 100% pleased with it, but that was partly because of the circumstances; we were only together for about six days and it took me ages to finish the thing after Sakamoto left. As time goes by, I enjoy it more and more, simply because the song has so many things about it that I would like to improve on. I always find that songs that I'm pleased with at the time of finishing, I never go back and listen to them again as there's no point – but with something that you're not totally sure about you find that you get more attached to it as time goes by.'

Jansen was contributing drums and percussion to the sessions and was dismayed at the time it took. A few years earlier Japan were recording entire albums in the same time it now took Sylvian to record two songs. (additionally, the extended studio costs would presumably be added to the group's debt and not to Sylvian's alone). 'It seems to take more and more time,' said Jansen of the recording, 'I thought it would be quicker, but we're always looking for getting more out of it. I've been working with Dave on this thing for Ryuichi and it's taken three weeks. For a single, it shouldn't be allowed, but that's the way it's been because of the way we work now. We don't just go in the studio and put down the first thing that sounds good, we listen to it and make sure it's going to stay sounding good, which you can't do in an hour, you have to live with it, which isn't cheap. But that's the way we get results.' The result was no great departure from the Japan sound. 'I've always written the stuff for Japan and normally I've directed it as well, so obviously something that I did is going to sound close to Japan even if it's a solo project,' Sylvian would reason. 'I don't think that's a bad thing, although I suppose it's true that you should try to get away from what you were doing previously. However, that single was planned while Japan still existed and Sakamoto and I had wanted to work together for over a year. I'm in no hurry to break away and prove myself as a capable solo artist. I don't actually differentiate between that single and Japan's stuff.' What this said for Sylvian's opinion of Karn's contributions to the band was obvious.

The Karnless 'Ghosts' was released on 12 March. The cover of the seven-inch portrayed a meditative Sylvian, (looking slightly more anxious on the 12-inch), in an infra-red photograph by Jansen taken on the roof of Stanhope Gardens. 'Ghosts' was a pivotal release for Japan and Sylvian in particular. The quality of the song was inarguable whether you liked the group or not. It was a classic ballad delivered with a startling arrangement and such an unusual chart candidate that some initially regarded its success as that of a novelty song. It would be Japan's defining moment musically and one that, alas, did not feature their bass player. The success of the song commercially only strengthened Sylvian's personal convictions about where he was headed. Sylvian: 'I guess working with Japan, the band was uncomfortable working with the quieter material. They always wanted to do something a bit harder, something they could get their teeth into. I was being more and more drawn to these quieter compositions, and when I got the positive response to 'Ghosts', and that being something of a breakthrough to me as a writer, I realised, "Well, I can pursue this avenue and it's okay," as every album doesn't have to have these power pieces on them. And so I think I naturally fell into that style of writing because it so much suited my own nature.'

The B-side of 'Ghosts' was a 'live' version of 'The Art Of Parties', which ditched Rhodes' solo in favour of a Sylvian overdub. This version actually features three guitars with only Rhodes' main riff remaining. 'That's definitely me playing the bulk of 'The Art Of Parties', the main groove and the distorted drop,' says Rhodes. 'The solo is someone else, as is the rather feeble little groove part that comes in near the end. Actually, years later I was working with Ross Callum and he said, "David, on this track we're gonna go for an 'Art Of Parties' vibe. Now you won't know that tune but …" I had to correct him, "Actually Ross …"' This unique version of 'Parties' was originally due to be part of an album. Huckle: 'I have this memory of booking the studio around then for a week for mixing. I recall the guys going in with Steve Nye, but then Dave not being happy with either the recording or perhaps the performance itself, and so "accidentally" wiping the 24-track tape so as to prevent Virgin mixing it themselves, because I think Virgin had loaned them some additional money on the basis they'd deliver a live album from the tour.' Nigel Walker was engineering: 'We mixed the song together at Island Studios. I think I recorded it at Hammersmith Odeon using the Island mobile studio. John Punter was mixing the sound in the Odeon, so I got the job recording the concert. In those days groups would often record concerts without a clear objective. All I remember about that session is that the mixing desk at Island had long metal switches to open and cut the signal to each channel and I had recently nearly lost two fingers while dropping a heavy bit of gear and my arm was in a sling. I foolishly used my damaged fingers while working and opened up my stitches, which made a bit of a mess.'

Japan's *Top Of The Pops* appearance for 'Ghosts', filmed when the song charted at number 42 on 18 March, is in its own way a classic of the era. The home-grown special effects

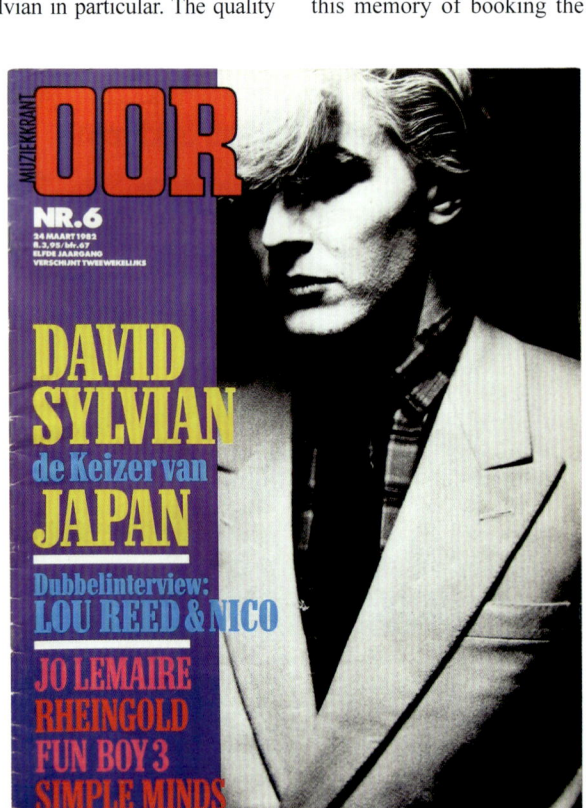

Sylvian on cover of *OOR* magazine, March 1982

Sylvian with fan post Top Of The Pops appearance

applied by the in-house editors work despite themselves. Sylvian abandons any pretence at performing by dispensing with a microphone all together. The group, Karn included, miming to Barbieri's keyboard parts, are tranquil, stately and beautiful, letting the song and their hair speak for them. Huckle: 'The guys were pleasantly surprised by the broadcast and weren't aware of the melting effects until seeing the actual transmission the next day. The visual effects were probably an afterthought by the producers once they got it into post-production. And yes, it was a bit more effort than the Beeb typically spent on *Top Of The Pops* effects for that time. It was after all a rather static performance, by necessity. They hadn't done a video for that single – I don't think Virgin thought the investment was worth it – but I think overall it ended up being one of their best TV performances of that mimed, quick turnaround type.'

An old associate followed them on the programme with his new 'Music For Chameleons' single, something of an echo of what Japan once were. Gary Numan: 'Japan were there performing their 'Ghosts' single and no one at the programme liked it, and the technicians were taking the piss out of them for being so pompous and full of it. Halfway through their performance I had to walk on to another stage to prepare for my bit and half the people at least left Japan to come and stand by me. The *Top Of The Pops* crew had to round people up and push them back towards Japan again, otherwise it was going to look a bit empty.' Huckle: 'It was par for the course for BBC stage-hands/technicians to snigger and take the piss out of the acts on the show, particularly the more exotic or unusual ones. I saw that behaviour at all the episodes of *Top Of The Pops* I attended, not just at Japan but more generally – unless it was Status Quo, which kind of defines your typical Beeb technician of the day. The audience at *Top Of The Pops* was never large and it was always the case that they were being pushed and herded around the studio so as to fill the camera shot. Generally they were a more teeny-bopper 15/16-year-old schoolgirl bunch, who would undoubtedly prefer the run-of-the-mill superficiality of Gary Numan to the more inventive and ground-breaking depth of a Japan performance.'

Everyone involved with the single was elated at its success. Nye: 'Its strengths? Its originality and longevity. Its failures? That it didn't get to number one.' Bourton: 'It exceeded even my expectations. It was a left-field choice and was either going to sink or swim – and it swam and then some. I've always been proud of being involved in that decision, but I did have the advantage of seeing how it was received live.' Lascelles: 'Its sales were double anything Japan had sold previously, at least.' The single would be Japan's most triumphant moment. 'Ghosts' – a rhythm-less, moribund construct of a song about self-doubt and anxiety – made existentialism seem erotic and silence sound sexy. It reached number five in the UK singles chart.

By 1982, the New Romantic movement in the UK was already dying out. Although never a part of such a faction, Japan were still often identified as such. Ultimately it would prove to be yet another fleeting fashion they would survive. Japan were, however, now surrounded by groups who took bits and pieces from their musical vocabulary: half-hearted attempts at fretless bass, hysterical Simmons kit thumping, 'atmospheric' keyboards, stilted, pseudo-baritone singing. 1982 was even the year Roxy Music delivered a Japan-esque sound with *Avalon* (there had been an overlapping in the two groups contemporary sounds as far back as 1980, as 'The Same Old Scene' and its B-side, 'Lover', indicate), but with the success of 'Ghosts', Japan were more than ever above it all, as their producer observed. Nye: 'I have to say that I concur with Mick Karn's observation when he said, "Certain bands were beginning to be classed together that had little to do with each other, such as Adam & The Ants, OMD, Spandau Ballet, collectively tied together by the slender threads of fashion. Perhaps I was missing something, as I wasn't exactly paying attention to current trends." Nor was I.

I had not really spent much time listening to other bands. Certain things would grab my attention, but I never kept up with the scene. I preferred to plough my own furrow. I was naturally aware of the comparisons drawn between Roxy and Japan, but by the time we were recording *Tin Drum* I think any such comparison was tenuous at best. To this day, I don't think Japan had any competition at the time. Take 'Ghosts' as an example; in my opinion, only someone of the calibre of Bowie or Gabriel could pull off such an adventurous and original song. Generally acknowledged as being unique, they were then, by definition, in a class of their own, much like the best of the progressive bands of the 1960s – who were all creating their own original sound nurtured by the more far-sighted record companies of the time, which allowed bands to make several albums before pulling the plug through lack of commercial success at the first attempt.'

By the spring of 82 America had once again taken an interest. For the first time since 'Life In Tokyo', Japan had a licensing deal in the US with CBS/Epic. That March they released a compilation entitled simply *Japan*, comprising songs from both *Gentlemen Take Polaroids* and *Tin Drum*. In addition, a flexi-disc featuring 'Life Without Buildings' – hardly Japan's most commercial sounding track, although perhaps that was the point – was given away free with *Trouser Press* magazine. Although Sylvian was offended by the Frankenstein approach that the American album employed, he took the opportunity of a trip to New York to promote the release. He would go so far as to dismiss the album release in an interview with *Trouser Press*: 'I'm not happy with it,' he said, 'I didn't like the idea of splitting up two albums.' At this point, some were still hoping that Japan would tour the US and that *Tin Drum* would earn a domestic release there, but neither would ever happen. Sylvian himself must have known that the group had no long-term future and such a trip, which he took with his manager and Fujii, was more akin to a short holiday. 'Number one albums and hits in the States…' Sylvian would reflect a few years on, 'these things already seemed unimportant when Japan split up; I'd already lost that.'

Sylvian was chaperoned in New York by Susan Blond, onetime Warhol superstar, and by now head of CBS. Aside from an awkward interview on MTV and some low-key magazine interviews (Japan would never be accepted by *Rolling Stone* magazine), her first remit was to introduce Sylvian to his long-term hero, Andy Warhol. 'I remember David because he was so attractive and also a real artist,' recalls Blond, 'so I knew Andy would love him. Anyone I liked I would take down to the Factory, which was then at 860 Broadway. I believe David had his girlfriend with him. He was very beautiful at that point in time and Andy was smitten with him. In fact Andy would have always wanted to look like David. Andy was never really good-looking, but so wanted to be.' Warhol filmed Sylvian wandering around the Factory and interviewed him for his cable TV show although the material was never broadcast, and resides in the Warhol archive in Pittsburgh. Sylvian and Warhol later met for dinner at The Russian Tea Room and Sylvian was not disappointed by the encounter: 'I met him recently in New York,' he would recall a few weeks later, 'when I did an interview for *Interview* magazine, plus an interview for Andy's cable TV show. You know that image he portrays, that of banality, like going along with everything that you say, everything's great and wonderful? Well, he's not really like that, you can tell that there's something deeper than that. Most people have the impression that he doesn't speak very much, that he just responds to people's questions in that "yeah, great" manner, but really he talks quite a lot and he's a very interesting person.' The two artificial blonds got on to the extent that a musical collaboration was planned although, like a similar venture planned with fellow New York resident Quentin Crisp, nothing would come of it. Warhol would shed some light on this a few years down the line in an interview with *The Face* magazine:

The Face: 'Are you still working on some lyrics for the group Japan or did that all fall through?'
Warhol: 'Oh, what is his name? David something.'
The Face: 'Sylvian!'
Warhol: 'Yeah, oh, what happened to him?'
The Face: 'He hasn't done very much for ages.'
Warhol: 'Oh really, why? He was so cute. God, he was so cute. I really liked him a lot. He's not doing anything? Why not? Does he wear make-up?'
The Face: 'God, yes, he wears tons! What did happen to the lyrics?'
Warhol: 'Well, because he went back to England and then he went to Japan, it was sort of hard for us to get together. Anyway, it was only going to be one line.'
The Face: 'What was the line?'
Warhol: 'That's what we were having trouble deciding.'

From New York, Yuka and Sylvian flew directly to Tokyo. Again, the purpose of the trip was merely a break, although there would be the inevitable photo shoots and interviews to

Jansen touring with Yukihiro Takahashi on his *What, Me Worry? Tour*
Keiko Kurata

mark the occasion. Typically, Sylvian would end up working as he was once again introduced to Sandii and the Sunsetz, who were then building on the tracks they had begun in London at the beginning of the year. Sandii: 'I was really into New Orleans music and Hawaiian music, but when I heard *Tin Drum* I was really drawn to their talent. And then we were playing a concert in Tokyo in the spring of 82, and David and Yuka came to see it. After the concert David said, "What are you doing in October? Would you like to support us in Britain?" Of course, I was very surprised and honoured. It was the first time I had met David properly and he was very sweet and gentle; to me he looked like a poet – very artistic and beautiful. He was funny, too, typically British. I loved him instantly. He looked very "real". Some people said his look was merely make-up, but I didn't feel that way. He had a star's aura – an artistic one. The way he looked at things, the way he spoke, it all had a poetic sensibility. He listens very carefully; he listens with his heart. We were recording *Immigrants* at Alfa Studios in Tokyo and David visited us, and I don't remember if he offered to contribute to the sessions or if we asked him, but we needed some lyrics for a melody and he actually came back to the studio and did a guide vocal and I asked him if he would sing with me and he said, "Oh, sure," but we were a bit worried about management and label issues, with him singing with us, but he said, "No, no, never mind about that. I like to do what I want to do and I'd like to help you out." He was very quick doing his vocals – in two takes. I had no problem singing in his phrasing. We loved the way he sang. In fact my partner at that time, Makato, used to do a good impression of David. The way David sang, he made the words caress you; it was like, "Wow!" We used everything he gave us, there were no outtakes.' Sylvian would later say that following *Tin Drum* he encountered something of a writer's block and, while his lyrical contributions to 'Where The Fire Still Burns', 'Illusion' and 'Living On The Front Line' were palatable enough, they are also among the most pedestrian writing he ever committed to tape.

Before leaving Tokyo, Sylvian met up with his brother who had been touring as drummer with Yukihiro Takahashi on his *What, Me Worry?* tour that June and July. Takahashi: 'Steve has played with me on a number of my solo tours in Japan over the years. I have a lot of memories and stories from these tours, but I can't say I've ever felt annoyed by the fact that, no matter how much we drank, he always looked great the next morning! There was one time on our first tour together in 82 when he drank so much after the last show that he missed his flight back to London the next day; we were all much younger then.' Jansen shook off his hangover to film a promo clip in Tokyo with Sylvian and Sakamoto for 'Bamboo Music'. The single was only a minor hit in the UK that summer, but for Jansen the experience of working with Takahashi was an important one. 'I'd had my best year to date during that lay-off between Japan tours' Jansen would reflect, 'spending much of it in Japan touring with Takahashi through the summer months and extending my stay… I think I was there for three months in total and lived so well, paid better than at any time with Japan (because it didn't go through SNB). I really was enjoying the variety of the job for once and feeling very independent of the band.'

1982 was the year that all of Japan's efforts from the previous 10 years came to fruition. Each member was now in demand in a remarkably wide range of territories. While Sylvian dined with Warhol in New York, Barbieri received a request to produce a Swedish group called Lustans Lakejer, who were indebted to the British new wave musical stylisations of Magazine, Joy Division, and Ultravox and by now were sounding and looking like a perfect hybrid of Japan and Duran Duran. Their main writer and singer was Johan Kinde, a young fop obsessed with the peculiarly English notion of expressing youthful disaffection with an elegant glamour. Kinde: 'We were all extreme fans of Japan. Our label was small, but they also owned the label that put out Abba so we were able to convince them to approach Richard and know that they could afford it. In fact they may have suggested it, as we wouldn't have had the confidence to do so, but we loved the sound of the Japan albums, so the head of our label Stranded Records approached Richard and, to our amazement, he agreed.' Barbieri was intrigued enough by the band's 'Diamonds Are A Girl's Best Friend' single to agree to meet the band in Stockholm that spring. 'We had dinner,' says Kinde, 'and he was very nice; we got on. By coincidence the Human League were in town and we ended up partying with them. When he returned to London we heard soon after that he wanted to do it and we were very happy.' Barbieri: 'I'm sure I wasn't the first name on their list, but probably near the top. They admired Japan for sure. I was very keen to produce.' Kinde: 'It is odd how we didn't approach John Punter or Steve Nye in fact, but back then there was such a huge gap between the Scandinavian music scene and the rest of the world – apart from Abba, who were international – that it was amazing to get anyone from the UK to work with us. In particular, we loved the synth sounds on *Tin Drum* and I think that's why Richard's name came up.'

Barbieri moved to Stockholm for three months that summer to work on the album at Abba's Polar Studios. Although he had never actually produced an album at this point, his naturally studious and meticulous nature meant that he was a natural. 'I loved being in the studio, even more so when others were doing their parts,' he'd recall. 'I kept a close eye on all the equipment and what the engineers were doing. It was all fascinating to me. Though I was never anywhere near accomplished enough to engineer a session, I felt I could articulate in a musical sense my ideas and opinions within that environment.' At Barbieri's request, Nye's engineer Nigel Walker flew out to assist the keyboard player. 'It was the most enjoyable time for me,' continues Barbieri. 'I think it was the first time I'd been to Sweden. Quite surreal. It was very weird to finish a long day's work in the studio and discover it's still daylight, while you walk to a nightclub after midnight. The guys in the band were cool and we got on pretty well. The material was very much in the Japan ballpark and with some Duran Duran thrown in, so it was very much of its time.' 'It was a thrill for us,' says Kinde, 'and we were all very happy with the work – the whole band – which can be unusual.' Barbieri was charmed by the group and relieved to be away from the stresses of studio work with his own group. 'We were working in the more modest studio two at Polar,' he remembers. 'There were two nice sessions going on in the main studio below while we were there – Phil Collins

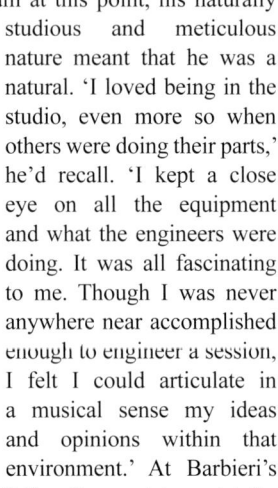

The Barbieri-produced Lustans Lakejer, Polar Studios, Sweden

was producing a solo album for Abba's Anni-Frid and then Steve Lillywhite was producing Joan Armatrading. It was a very well-equipped studio; we had an early sampler, but we didn't really experiment enough with that. Everyone just kept going back to the preset of a woman having an orgasm.'

This was perhaps in anticipation of a visit by Karn, who had been staying with his new girlfriend Orly Kroh and Rob Dean in LA. Dean remembers Karn's visit being a lot of fun, with the bassist on one occasion taking acid before a supermarket trip. 'I remember Mick tripping in the middle of an aisle,' says Dean, 'sitting down and crying out, "Orlllllly," in a really forlorn, funny way.' Once Karn had slept off his chemical adventure, he made for Sweden. Barbieri: 'I sometimes try to drag friends into sessions and I knew it would be fun to have Mick come out for a few days. It's always good to have a new flavour added to the pot and we thought saxophone would work nicely in a couple of places. It's also a good idea to bring in a new personality when you've all been stuck in a studio together for weeks on end.' The group were doubly thrilled at this late addition. Kinde: 'Mick was just as nice as Richard in person, but he looked more like a rock star. He flew to our studio in Stockholm direct from LA; he walked in and he had this fantastic suntan and looked like a million dollars. He was flamboyant, kind and charming. It was my favourite three days of the recording while he was there. He was fantastic at rolling joints as well. We were in his hotel room once and while he was talking he was skinning up this three paper spliff and just being really funny. He told us that when he still lived at home, he was in his parents' house alone one night with a face mask on (a cream to cleanse his pores) and he was in a kimono. The face mask had hardened to a kind of stiff, actual mask and he's sat there in his bedroom playing his bass acoustically. Suddenly, he hears a noise downstairs and thinks, "Are my parents home early?", then he realises it's burglars in the house and they are coming up the stairs! So, with his long red hair, dressed in a kimono and with a white face mask on he goes out to confront them. He squares up to them on the landing and screams, "What the hell are you doing here?" and as he does this the face mask cracks and begins to crumble off. The burglars saw this, screamed and ran out of the house. Anyway, by the time he had finished this story he had made the biggest spliff I'd ever seen, a giant Jamaican thing ... what I guess you would call a "Camberwell carrot". The sessions were a blast for us and we were deeply happy at the result.' The Lustans Lakejer album, *En Plats I Solen* (*A Place In The Sun*), is charming and extremely listenable in any language. The Japan influence is obvious, particularly in some of the drum patterns, but this works to the record's advantage and the album would eventually go gold in its home country. A version sung in English would be released under a different group name, Vanity Fair, with Barbieri helping out on the translation of lyrics.

While Japan's individual members flitted about the globe, Virgin naturally continued to recoup on their investment by releasing a third single from *Tin Drum*. On 13 May, 'Cantonese Boy' was released in an assortment of formats (seven-inch, double seven-inch and 12-inch), recycling various old tracks as B-sides. The single peaked at a respectable 24 and once again came without a promo video, although there was a magnificently stilted *Top Of The Pops* appearance, where the group obviously looked as if they'd rather be anywhere but there. Where Japan did want to be that year was in the recording studio – just not with each other; or, to be more specific, Karn and Sylvian did not want to work together. Karn had first raised the idea of recording solo just prior to the 'Shit Tour'. Karn: 'While we were recording the album [*Tin Drum*] in October, I decided that because I don't enjoy recording that much (it's thinking about the music too much), that I would like to record a solo single using different musicians. It didn't mean that I wanted to leave Japan, it was just a little experiment that I wanted to do. I would pay for it all myself and if Virgin didn't like it, then I couldn't care less 'cos I'd done what I'd wanted to do. I suggested it to everyone and they weren't too happy about it because Virgin were interested and wanted to release it, and the others felt that if it was successful then people would be coming to the concerts even more to see me rather than Rich and Steve. They were quite upset and the argument they used against me doing it was that friendship had always come first in anything we had ever done and, if for no other reason than that, I should wait another year or so until the rest of the band were strong enough to be in the position to do the same, so I let it go; if it meant that much to them, it didn't mean that much to me.' Thus Karn had put off his debut solo recording session until everyone in Japan felt comfortable with him doing so.

That time arrived in the summer of 1982. Interestingly, Karn broached the idea of a solo album with Simon Draper directly rather than going through his manager. Virgin agreed to finance an album on condition that there was a potential single, and there was. Karn had heard Iva Zanicchi singing 'Testarda Io (La Mia Solitudine)' in Luchino Visconti's *Conversation Piece* movie and had fallen in love with its wistful, Latin melody. The song was originally written and performed by Brazilian megastar Roberto Carlos, (who was intriguingly drug lord Pablo Escobar's favourite singer). Despite having little faith in his singing voice, Karn now decided to adapt the song using his own lyrics. Once satisfied with his version, now entitled 'Sensitive', Karn wanted to record the song as soon as possible. Ricky Wilde, son of 1950s rocker Marty and brother of the then hugely popular Kim, was chosen as the producer. 'Jeremy Lascelles called me and asked if I'd work with Mick,' remembers Wilde. 'Being a massive fan of Mick's I said, "Yeah, I'm definitely in." I did love Japan, but I also loved what Mick did with Gary Numan. Everything I heard him play was fucking excellent and I just wanted to be a part of it. Of course, when I met him he was a lovely man as well; I was taken aback by how lovely he was. First time I met him was at Sarm Studios, which was weird, as normally we'd meet up before that but I only remember meeting him for the first time in the studio.' The session booked was for an A-side and B-side only. The languidly demonic 'The Sound Of Waves', its title borrowed from a Yukio Mishima book, would appear as the latter.

Speaking volumes for the relationship between Karn and Sylvian, Barbieri and Jansen were also invited to contribute. 'Steve came in and he was great, lovely guy,' says Wilde, 'but instead of live drums we wanted to go with a movement rhythm computer, which I'd used on Kim Wilde's second album. But it was a nightmare to use, a dog. Timing wise it was slightly early or late and hard to sequence, but in the end we got it working and we both loved the sound of it. We used that for snare, bass drum and toms and Steve played hi-hats and cymbals over the top of it. I didn't know in advance that Steve wanted to be involved, as I thought it was a Mick project, so when Mick suggested Steve and Richard come in, I was happy but surprised.' If Virgin were happy with the Wilde/Karn collaboration, then a full album would be given the green light. The two worked quickly, as was Karn's wont, and Wilde was impressed. 'Watching him play was mesmerising. It really was something. What's weird is that it looks like he's a beginner. His hands are really clumsy, but then you listen to what he's playing and it's just amazing how he does it. There are no frets, obviously, but he was getting the tuning with ease and I couldn't work out how he did it. The vibrato he got, he'd use his whole hands not just his wrist; it looked wrong, but sounded so right. It really was amazing to watch. To this day I've never heard anyone play that way. He was a one-off, unique.' Karn was confident in the studio and didn't verbalise his insecurities, especially where singing was concerned. 'Recording his vocals was very laid-back,' recalls Wilde, 'I don't like spending ages recording vocals and if someone isn't feeling it, I don't want to push it. But with Mick it was very organic. Once we had enough of a backing track I suggested he give it a go and he was like, "Yeah, sure." It was a very, very easy process, and we tracked the vocal as well, which usually is not an easy thing to do if you're not an experienced singer, but he got it straight off. It was very quick and he was very relaxed. Very easy. We did about five takes and chose the best. It was a lovely experience.'

Delicia Burnell, still working for Nomis and future girlfriend of Karn, says that, 'I don't think Mick thought that singing was his strong point. He was happy to sing, but it wasn't as natural a medium for him as other media. He could pick up any instrument and get a sound out of it, but when it was just his voice I think he felt more vulnerable.' Karn was more than talented in other respects. 'At one point,' says Wilde, 'he said, "I've got an idea to try a sax solo", and I said, "Okay, who should we get in?" and he said, "I'll do it." I was like, "Oh, okay." I never had any idea he could play sax! So he got his sax out and I wasn't expecting much but I guess he had it all planned out in his head because we got it in two takes. I was like, "Is there no fucking end to this man's talent?" I was gob-smacked.' 'Sensitive', however, would appear as an obvious contender as a single compared to the rest of the album. Its B-side, 'The Sound Of Waves', was much truer to the rest of the album and to where Karn's head was musically that summer. ''The Sound Of Waves' was a lot of fun,' says Wilde, 'I'd worked with Kim on her albums and in particular I'd done a backward guitar solo on her single 'Cambodia'. So while we were working on 'The Sound Of Waves' I said to Mick, "Hey, it might be interesting to turn the tape over and record some reverse stuff over it, to get some kind of ghostly, atmospheric stuff." He said, "Great, yeah, let's try it." So we turned the tape over and turned the bass up and the bassline had this beautiful new line, which became a brand new track, 'Lost Affections In A Room'.'

Virgin were impressed enough by the Wilde/Karn sessions to agree to finance an album, which for reasons no one now remembers now was done with Colin Fairley at AIR. 'I don't remember why I didn't do the album,' says Wilde, 'but it doesn't bother me. Also I had no idea 'Sensitive' wasn't a Mick original. How strange. His choice of listening and influences were right out there.' The lyrics to 'Sensitive' were so bold as to be potentially embarrassing. 'We never discussed lyrics,' says Wilde, 'I had no idea what Mick had been through with David and he never brought it up. I went out with them, with Mick, Steve and Rich but no one ever talked about that.' Deli: 'It was written after and about the break-up with Yuka. It must be very hard when the two people you love the most go off like that. Quite a betrayal.' 'Yukagate' had finally gone public in April when Karn had bared all in a *ZigZag* interview where he went into embarrassing detail regarding the rift between Sylvian and himself. Wilde was oblivious to the Japan politics and was only sad he never got to hang out with the whole group. Wilde: 'They were lovely people and I thought, "Oh, I'm bound to meet David too at some point," but I never did. I was going out with Steve's ex at this point, Patti Nolder, and we'd all go out together. We were all friends and Richard was hysterical; I mean you look at a photo of him from then and he's got a face on him, but at the time he would make me cry laughing. But then, in the 80s it was all about pouting.'

With Wilde moving on, sessions for the rest of the album continued at AIR with Fairley and Karn producing, and other familiar accomplices were called in. David Rhodes: 'I was asked to come in and contribute. I got the impression he was just fiddling about; it didn't feel like he really knew what he was doing. It was all done very quickly. But again, it was like carrying on from *Tin Drum* where every instrument was playing a little part and having a kind of conversation with one another. I thought it very canny.' Angie Usher, a complete novice as far as professional recording went, would contribute ethereal vocals to 'Trust Me'. Usher: 'I think Mick had just heard me singing around his flat. I also used to do an impersonation of Yuka's singing, kind of screeching. He played me the track and asked if I was up to it. I said, "Sure." The studio was dark and full of smoke. All I remember is drinking endless cans of coke and smoking while we did it. I wasn't paid, no. It didn't feel professional at all, just like we were doing it for a laugh.' Fresh from Sweden, Barbieri was also a welcome guest at the sessions. 'Mick asked if I would programme up sounds for him to play on his solo album,' he recalls. 'I gave him my Oberheim OBX synth to use. Mick had written all the parts and wanted to play everything, so I tailored the sounds to suit the track and his playing style. A lot of it had a Turkish, Greek, Arabic flavour. It was actually really nice hanging out in the studio without the pressure of having to come up with ideas and instead just listening and programming sounds.' Other visitors to the AIR sessions included George Martin ('Reminds me of when I was working with John Lennon,' quipped the Beatles producer) and Richard Branson, who was less impressed, fidgeting while Fairley and Karn played him some finished tracks, until he dragged the bass player into another studio where Mike Oldfield was recording. 'Now *that's* what instrumental music *should* sound like,' the tactless Virgin boss told a hurt Karn.

Titles was completed that August, recorded, mixed, mastered and delivered within 28 days. 'Sensitive', despite some encouraging reviews and modest airplay, was not the hit Karn and Virgin had expected, and stalled at number 98 in the UK chart. The apparent subject of the song's lyrics was diplomatic. Sylvian: 'I think I feel the same way that Mick feels about it. I don't think Mick particularly liked the single very much, but it was something he had to do. It's the first thing he's written and it was done at a time when he was very confused. It wasn't exactly a truthful statement.' Perversely there was no promo video made for the single yet there *was* one made for its B-side, 'The Sound Of Waves', which featured Karn and Hazel O'Connor made up like extras from *The Man Who Fell To Earth*. The relative failure of this and the Sylvian and Sakamoto single proved that it was Japan – the group – that was the saleable commodity; the group was more than the sum of its parts. Almost immediately after leaving AIR, Karn relocated to Nomis where Japan had reassembled to begin rehearsing for their final world tour.

It was by now becoming common knowledge amongst those in the industry that Japan had a limited life span, but still no official statement had been made confirming the split. Yet both Sylvian and Karn were open about the prospect in interviews and when the band had appeared on *The Old Grey Whistle Test* the previous March, they had been introduced as a group who had in fact already disbanded. Karn: 'I think if the band did split, Dave would be the one who would suffer most because I think he's incapable of carrying on by himself. The three of us worked much harder than Dave ever has and without us, he would find it very difficult. He is an excellent producer and if he could find a band that didn't know which direction to go in, if the songs were a bit flabby here and there, then he could take over and produce them and it would be great. That's what it's been like with Japan, it's the three of us working, but Dave steering. I think he'd find it very difficult unless he had people around him.' Jansen had no interest in going solo: 'My main focus was being a musician. I was utterly motivated to making a statement through playing an instrument and finding a voice, but I had nothing to say as a lyricist or songwriter – that was of no interest to me. The subject matter of Japan's songs was of little consequence and to this day I still have limited understanding of what many of the songs are meant to be about.' Sylvian himself was sanguine that summer. 'Since I finished the single with Ryuichi, I haven't felt the need to do anything,' he told journalist Betty Page. 'I had a few ideas but they were all half-hearted, so I didn't follow them up. I really lost interest in music and it's only just coming back.' He also appeared laissez-faire about Japan's commercial breakthrough. 'I'm so far removed from it,' he told Page, 'It's odd, because we haven't really done anything this year. Other than a few TV appearances, we haven't been together for months.' He was hardly enthusiastic about the forthcoming tour: 'If that tour wasn't there, it might not have happened. It's to get those four people back in one room in a working situation to see if we can carry on. It really is make-or-break time.' Page's conclusion was that 'Japan were dead and buried, but the corpse was contractually obliged to rise from its grave'.

At this point another ghost materialised. Japan's version of 'I Second That Emotion', re-released and remixed, was a huge UK hit that summer, peaking at number nine. The group didn't deign to promote it at all, letting the cartoony video, made back in 1979 do the legwork for them. At Nomis, Ippu Do guitarist Masami Tsuchiya (who had worked with Jansen on the Takahashi tour) joined them to, in Sylvian's words, 'breathe some life into the group'. Tsuchiya's guitar playing was noisy, masterful and almost irreverent and he looked great. He reckoned that to play with Japan was his 'destiny'. 'I think they wanted Masami, because he was a showman and, by comparison with me, quite wild,' observed David Rhodes. Johan Kinde happened to be in London for a week late that summer and was invited to pop into Nomis to watch Japan rehearse. 'The studio was really luxurious,' he recalls, 'and David was my idol. So just to see him sitting there! He was friendly and said, "Hello, how do you do?" and of course I was so nervous I started babbling, "Oh, I have a cold," and this and that – you know, actually telling him how I was, which is not what you're supposed to do, but I was so nervous! They sounded great of course and looked so cool, even rehearsing. They obviously lived the life they presented – it wasn't just a look.'

By late September a set list had been agreed on, after some discussion, naturally. 'All Tomorrow's Parties', 'Sensitive', Tsuchiya's 'Rice Music' and 'Bamboo Music' were all dropped after being initially pencilled in and Japan were once more ready to hit the road. Karn: 'This tour is a kind of test to see if it makes sense to go on as a collective unit. At the moment the group is split into two camps. On one side you have David and Steve, who are especially busy with the 'introverted' technical side, while Richard and I have developed in another direction. We want to make everything sound as 'natural' as possible, not just electronic. Rich and I have grown closer to one another while we working on my solo album; that record brought us together. In January [1983], we'll decide if it makes more sense to let everybody work on their own solo projects, but it doesn't mean the group will fall apart.' Jansen: 'Touring was the easy part. All the hard work is in rehearsals. Eight hours a day of repeatedly playing the songs until you'd developed a degree of autopilot as a fail-safe for live performance. Touring then becomes all about the quality of the hotels and the organisation of the transportation, the sound on stage and the state of mind before going on. If that's all good then it becomes a bit of a team holiday. Working only three hours a day – not every day – and exploring any number of sky bars. There is a sense of teamwork, and as the tour gathers pace and audiences are seen to be enjoying themselves, a confidence grows, with all the players in the team pulling their weight. That's a nice feeling.' Nick Huckle would not accompany the band on their swansong. In his place as tour manager was Jake Duncan, and John Punter was back at the mixing desk: 'My feeling was that it should be fun. We were doing it for the kids, really.'

The 'world tour' began in Sweden's Stockholm on 1 October. 'It was at a hall that was more suited to classical music,' says Kinde, who was in attendance at the group's invitation. 'And of course they were fantastic even though I preferred seeing them in rehearsal because I was the only audience member then!' A review of the show in *Schlager* magazine was however dismissive, citing the lack of melody and interaction with the 'elegant' audience, with the reviewer chastising Sylvian for singing in a way that was 'reserved and shallow like a bleached Bryan Ferry after a visit to a modern-day beauty parlour'. Once again, the bad review was based upon what Japan were not, rather than the ultra-chic, acquired taste that they were. Incredibly, even at this late hour, some reviews of the shows failed to see past the influence of the Bowie/Ferry axis. Such concerns barely mattered to Sylvian at this stage. 'Even now, we still hear these names, especially from people who don't like us,' he reasoned, 'then you're easily inclined to compare it. When you do like it, these things become irrelevant, because you concentrate on the true character of the music. For everything can be compared with

Itinery for the final tour, 1982

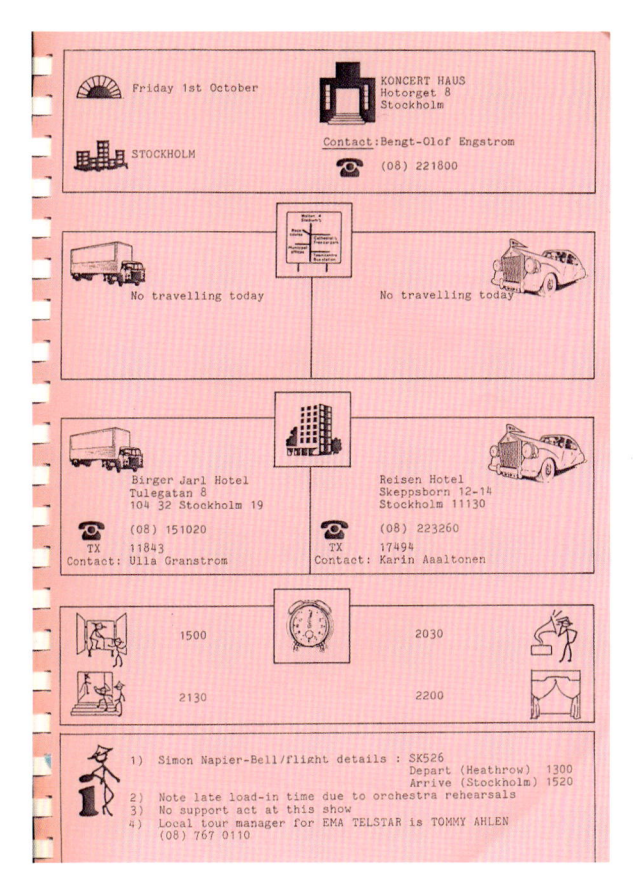

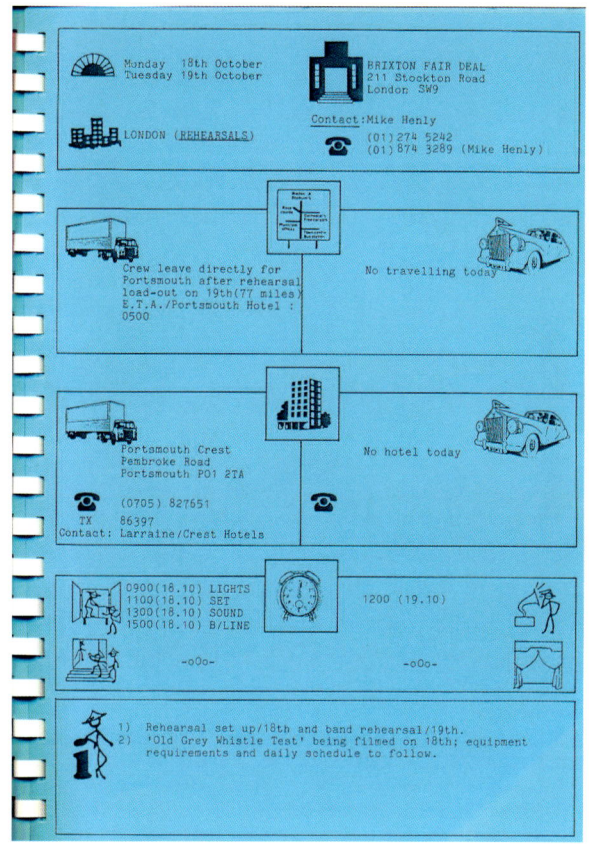

everything.' Kjell Paulsen, a schoolboy and aspiring journalist living in Oslo, recalls that, 'the synth/New Romantics thing was not as big in Scandinavia as it was in Britain. Sure, 'Tainted Love' and 'Don't You Want Me?' were hits, but it didn't change the music scene here. Japan were well known here, but not that popular. They were critically acclaimed, and the "in-crowd" liked them. Heavy metal was massive here in the 80s – bigger than the electro-pop bands. Japan were seen as quite arty. I also remember that many of my friends thought they looked feminine and gay, which in general was not a positive thing in their view.'

The tour then moved to Germany for two dates, where Japan's earlier trash-pop incarnation remained more beloved in some ways, but they still had a cool, cult appeal. Again, some songs from the Munich show were televised, illustrating that in a smaller club venue the band had become a singularly elegant and powerful force, with Sylvian surrendering to the music via subdued dance moves that less resembled actual dancing than a collage of frozen snapshots. The knowledge that this was the last time he would sing these songs no doubt fuelled his enthusiasm. Holland and Belgium followed, again with reviewers noting Japan's 'aloofness', although the audience were vocal and enthusiastic. In Brussels, Sylvian took time pre-sound check to speak to a journalist purporting to be from *Smash Hits*, although the interview never ran. In any case, it was the same old questions, e.g. 'What's next? What are your future plans? How's the tour?' etc., which Sylvian answered politely and efficiently, if wearily.

The audience at the Brussels show was bolstered by a UK contingent. Michael Giller was among the coachloads who had travelled especially to see the show. 'There were Sylvians everywhere,' he recalls, 'from the "almost Sylvian" to the "actually you look more like Margaret Thatcher" Sylvian. We

Sylvian, Le Palace,
Paris, October 1982
Sophie Delinanos

flounced into Brussels. The venue was a seated auditorium of modern design. All thoughts of architecture were soon forgotten when it became apparent that our party had been allocated the first three rows of the venue. What followed was as close to a stampede as we could muster. Safely settled in the second row, we were about 20 feet from the front of the stage. The security were either on strike or aware of our reputation. What seemed like a lifetime later, the lights dimmed and the haunting strains of 'Burning Bridges' filled the air. Despite a definite sense that the group were fine-tuning in preparation for the end-of-tour and end-of-band concerts in Britain and Japan, the first half of the show was as immaculate as ever. I remember 'Alien', 'Swing' and 'Canton' being mind-warpingly good. As always happens when you put a load of poseurs together, no one wants to be the first to drop the image and let go. Therefore the atmosphere was one of reverence and respect early on. By the time of 'Ghosts', it was almost meditative. The gig-changer came from a most unexpected source for me. Much as I love 'Still Life In Mobile Homes', I never regarded it as a track that could ignite a show, but on this night it was the song during which the band moved up a gear. Mick's gliding shuffles quickened in pace and the battered Stratocaster of Masami Tsuchiya began to howl and growl. At this point, most of us cast the image aside and let go. By the time of set closer 'The Art Of Parties', all it took was a warm smile and reserved beckoning gesture from Mr Sylvian, and a mass of fans lurched towards the stage and to our dream destination – within touching distance of our gods. It was like having Japan playing in your front room! As the band returned for the encore, Steve and Mick were shaking with laughter; oh, to have heard the joke. Taking his place behind his kit, Steve relayed the tale to David who broke up. Seeing David Sylvian really laugh is a rare and wonderful thing to see for those outside his inner circle; I say there should be more of it. There followed a spellbinding romp through a reworked 'Life In Tokyo'. I looked behind me and saw a sea of people – tourists and locals alike – dancing on their seats in a state of euphoria. No

Karn, Sylvian,
Le Palace, Paris,
October 1982
Sophie Delinanos

doubt aware that this would be the last time they would ever play 'Fall In Love With Me' in Belgium, the band launched into said song with all the androgynous angst and adolescent sex of old. By the end, David and Masami were throwing rock star guitar shapes, complete with jazz shoe on monitor – really! We jumped, we danced, we grinned like loons. It was pure, chemical-free ecstasy. And then they were gone and it was over.'

Japan then flew to Paris where they booked into the Hotel Napoleon. The group had a rare break in their tour schedule although even this was for the purpose of work. They were scheduled to shoot photos with Anton Corbijn for what would become the inner sleeve of their posthumous live album *Oil On Canvas*, some of which would also grace their last ever *NME* cover. Barbieri, who was there with girlfriend Gaye Jones, recalls: 'I think we must've been there for a couple of days as I remember doing a lot of sightseeing. We had a nice hotel just off the Champs-Élysées. We did a radio station interview and French TV filmed us before the show. Fin Costello, Anton, and Steve were taking shots of us around Paris.' Bourton: 'When we were in Paris on that tour, I had the *NME* there with Anton Corbijn. We'd finally got people to look beyond the make-up. It took the *NME* a long time and was a slow process, but we got there. I was at the photo shoot where Anton was taking test Polaroids of David and he showed David how to manipulate the image – scratch it and so forth – and David was instantly intrigued and started messing about with it. I still have that Polaroid.' Steve also took time to wander around the city and indulge his photography habit. For a week, posters of Sylvian, perhaps in a nod to the French surrealist movement, all in white and holding a trout, advertised the show citywide.

The gig itself was scheduled for 11 October at Le Palace, which until recently had been the infamous hangout of the Paris fashion elite. Bourton: 'At Le Palace I didn't notice Karl

Lagerfeld or Yves Saint Laurent there, but then that was the kind of crowd I was trying to steer Japan away from. They were the sort of people Connie would have encouraged and I was against. I didn't want them to be seen as mere clothes horses.' The gig itself was filmed for TV, with some tracks being broadcast on the popular *Megahertz* programme while the remainder gather dust in an archive. The band come across as both exuberant and relaxed, no doubt buoyed by the previous day's leisure time spent shopping, going for dinner and visiting galleries. In commercial terms, Japan were merely a passing chic fancy in France. Their albums appeared only in specialist charts and the press there was cursory although, to be fair, when presented with a list of possible magazine interviews, David had agreed only to *Vogue*. Renaud Haslan, then a young French fan, remembers that, 'journalists in France were narrow-minded and just couldn't get past the Roxy Music comparison, but from the end of 1981 onwards, the band started to make waves. 'Ghosts' and 'Bamboo Music' fell into that broad genre that started to define French music in the early 1980s, a kind of hybrid new wave that veered towards the exotic and bisexual with bands like Taxi Girl and Indochine, and singers like Alain Chamfort and Étienne Daho – the post-punk generation.' Sophie Delinanos was a Paris resident who ran possibly France's only Japan fanzine. 'Le Palace was full,' she confirms, 'but a lot of people were coming from England and Japan. I was lucky to be just close to the stage. David was always posing with his quiff and I remembered thinking that he was waiting for someone to catch his hair! I was very impressed by Mick's stage presence. Still, the one review I read of the show was unkind.' Despite Le Palace being a notorious nightspot in its own right, Japan did not hang around. Anxious to avoid any lingering fans, their exit was indecent and hasty. 'John Punter had a real go at me because we left him and his girlfriend behind at the venue after the show,' remembers Barbieri. 'I probably said we'd go back in the same car together and then couldn't or didn't keep the promise. There was always a bit of a "getaway" aspect after the shows though, because of the fans and security issues. Anyway, I took my telling off back at the hotel without protest.'

Before leaving Paris, (a city which Sylvian would briefly consider moving to for a while), an audience was granted with the *NME*'s Paul Morley. The resultant piece was typical of the *NME* when dealing with groups like Japan. The article, which came with its own 'further reading list' and a beautiful set of Corbijn photographs of Sylvian at Père Lachaise cemetery, was riddled with quotes from long dead poets and writers and nearly impregnable in its pseudo-intellectual density. The interview did at least offer in parts a clear insight into Sylvian's mindset at that particular moment – November 1982, when Japan could have had it all. Next to a photo of what appeared to be Sylvian praying to himself, the following quotes appeared like lines in some futurist manifesto: 'The live thing for me is rubbish,' Sylvian told Morley in his hotel room. 'It again amounts to nothing. Touring is not something I need to do and it's not something I intend to do.' When he was asked what 'people' meant to him, Sylvian replied 'useful', adding that Japan were 'the most useful people'. Asked to justify Japan, Sylvian answered simply: 'me'. On 'artificial intoxication' the singer was shockingly honest: 'The only thing I do is coke, but I only use it to speed up the process of the mind when I'm in such a low state that I feel I need to use it, when I feel trapped when my mind's too slow and lazy to work. I sometimes turn to that but it doesn't really help.' On music: 'I'm not even sure I want to continue with music. I've started painting recently.' Sylvian comes across as bored, overly intellectual, somewhat spoilt, and disaffected. He was a pop star removed from almost everything unnecessary to his art, and yet in this regard he had nothing to say. It had been a year since *Tin Drum* and he wouldn't write anything of worth again until the lyrics to 'Forbidden Colours' (which would be completed on 15 February 1983). Meanwhile, he was indulged by those around him in every respect. His stance may be almost utterly unsympathetic if it were not for the fact that the conversation took place halfway through a live tour. For Sylvian, touring was as tedious and exhausting, relatively speaking, as a nine-to-five job was for the average taxpayer. By Paris, Sylvian the 'pop performer' was flagging and he still had the stages of Britain and the Far East to endure.

After 10 days off, the next stop was the UK. Any technical issues had by now hopefully been ironed out and the band was in top form to tour a country that had finally and irrevocably fallen in love with them. Bourton: 'They had grown hugely in confidence by now. They were better than ever, live. We travelled in two Land Rovers for a lot of that tour; I was with David. We stopped to get fish and chips somewhere up in Northumberland and, as I was getting out of the vehicle, David said, "There's something rattling at the front of the car; can you have a look and see what it is?" So I said, "Sure." I went out and bent down and, as I was looking down and put my head against the grille, he tooted the horn, which is right at the front of the grille, and it frightened the shit out of me and I jumped about 30 feet in the air. When I came down I looked through the window and he was laughing his head off. He loved practical jokes.'

By now the tour almost had a family feel to it. Fin Costello was photographing the whole adventure, Punter travelled with his new North American girlfriend, and the band's onstage costumes (bar Karn's) had been designed by Tsuchiya's wife, Yuka. The other Yuka [Fujii] was a discreet presence, while Karn's girlfriend Orly was a regular visible fixture on the tour. She remembers the dynamic between Sylvian and Karn as being one of polite tolerance. 'There was no communication between them,' she says. 'The relationship had soured. They'd sit together if it was for a record company related dinner or whatever, but outside of that David rarely mixed with anyone. He stayed in his hotel room every night. Occasionally he'd go out with Jake the tour manager, but mostly he'd stay by himself. They even had different dressing rooms.' Angie Usher: 'It was my birthday and we were all quite drunk by the pool of the Holiday Inn in Birmingham [where Japan played three sold out nights], I think it was. They gave me a card signed by the whole band which I thought was sweet, but as presents they gave me a lot of tour merchandise, which I thought was funny. We were having a great time as usual and then David actually deigned to come down and say happy birthday to me, which I was amazed at. And when he arrived the whole atmosphere soured and went icy as if a headmaster had come into a party.'

Sandii with Banshees drummer Budgie, 1982

In Britain, a film crew appeared to document the tour for a long-form video to be released the following year and, at Sylvian's request, Sandii & The Sunsetz joined the group as support. 'David didn't treat us like a mere opening act,' recalls Sandii, 'he gave us a sacred place on that tour, and I'm still so very grateful. Maybe it's true that having us on that tour also helped give it some extra meaning for him, yes. He was so good to us. Mick was something else – quite mysterious and artistic; I wanted to get to know him. I think he and David balanced each other very well. They played their parts well, but I felt no sourness between them but a love. Whatever had happened, there was always a mutual respect.' The Sunsetz were well received by Japan's audiences and undoubtedly gave the tour some extra significance for Sylvian even if Jansen was by and large indifferent. 'I wasn't interested in the support groups. I don't mean as people, just didn't have the capacity to care about what other bands were trying to do, and the worst time to be distracted is before a show.' 'We were all on our best behaviour,' Karn would state. 'I only lost my temper once in the dressing room. David enjoyed having Sandii visit just before show time and she wouldn't stop going on about how wonderful we were, especially Dave. I blew my top and brusquely asked her to leave if she had nothing better to talk about.'

There was little else to complain about on this leg of the tour. Everyone could travel separately if they wanted to and each band member, finally, had his own hotel room. The venues, from Portsmouth to Edinburgh, were as big as Sylvian was comfortable playing and all sold out, sometimes several nights running. Wales and Ireland were not included for some reason. Bootleggers mooched out front at the venues, selling clumsy home-made posters and T-shirts; Sylvian and Karn (and Numan and Nick Rhodes) lookalikes thronged the entrances. In the weeklies there were reviews of course, but they no longer mattered. 'The overriding impression is one of a group who have achieved a stylish maturity,' said *Record Mirror*. 'It seems Japan have reached the zenith of their creativity with nowhere else to go,' said *ZigZag*, ' the sterility of perfection has left them out on a limb.' 'The ecstatic reaction they excite has little or nothing to do with any performance and more than a little with them just being there,' supposed the *NME*. Such reviews were akin to an attempt to hydrate the moon with a water pistol. Japan were autonomous, ubiquitous and above it all. Even themselves.

Betty Page, writing for *Noise* magazine, was one of the few journalists allowed all access on the tour. 'I had to prepare myself for my next big job, my final service to the army of Japan fans in Britain. I was off to report on the *Sons Of Pioneers*

191

Tour, the band's farewell, but I wasn't looking forward to it.' She'd give a detailed account of her meeting in her unpublished memoir *Beat Girl* (and in edited form in *Noise* magazine in late 1982) and it's worth quoting here at length:

'Rumours had been emerging that David Sylvian and Mick Karn weren't speaking; that they had demanded separate Range Rovers to travel in between gigs and separate dressing rooms. Then there were the preconditions to my doing an on-the-road feature – that I would under no circumstances travel with the band; that I must not attempt to interview David; that I made sure I spoke to Richard Barbieri and Steve Jansen. This supported the theory that David had lost control of the band (or indeed had lost interest in it) and a new democracy had established itself. I was fully anticipating a frosty atmosphere when I arrived at the Glasgow Apollo but consoled myself with the fact that I would be seeing Sandii & The Sunsetz again. Getting backstage was like trying to break into a secret government installation. The band's tour manager, Jake, chose to ignore my Access All Areas pass. He was too busy organising an SAS-style manoeuvre aimed at getting the fragile five out of the building and into their waiting cars. I retired hurt without so much as a glance at the group. He was only doing his job, but I was trying to do mine. This was the sort of nonsense music journalists had to put up with when a band was at the top of its game. I took the train to Edinburgh hoping for a better day. I wasn't getting past Jake and his clipboard, so enlisted the help of Virgin Records, who contacted the band directly to arrange a meeting. I discovered that David had a nasty rash due to malnutrition. He'd only eaten bread and water for three days. The theory was that he'd been denying himself sustenance in order to improve his performance, but this seemed far-fetched even for the enigmatic singer. Finally I got to have a meaningful conversation with the forbidding Jake, who apologised for the day before but said I'd not been on his list. He told me he'd spent many a month road managing the Bay City Rollers in their heyday, so he knew a thing or two about protecting a band from their fans (and journalists, I'd imagine). Now that Jake and I were mates, I got straight backstage and bumped into David in full make-up having his photo taken with Sandii. He smiled charmingly and seemed quite relaxed. I said hello to the rest of the group and there seemed to be no bad vibes at all. Steve sheepishly told me it wasn't their fault that I couldn't get to see them the night before. I forgave them. Frantic activity ensued in preparation for the "leap out". Jake shouted: "Okay, everybody, let's move!" Liggers such as myself were thrust out first, to be greeted by a wall of screaming girls being held back by the police. We got clear just as one girl made a run for it, but the band were already safely in their cars, zooming through the human wall. Back at the hotel, the automatic doors were firmly shut to anyone without a room key. It was a dramatic move, but necessary. The girls were animals. Steve, Richard and I set off for an Italian restaurant to do the interview and, to everyone's surprise, David decided to come too. He seemed remarkably chipper, but kept well out of range of my tape recorder. Richard and Steve "wanted to have their say" but when they finally did, it became even more obvious why the band were about to split. "The reaction on the tour has been so teeny," said Richard, between mouthfuls of pasta. "Little girls kept shouting out during pieces like 'Nightporter'. Once that happens, it ruins the whole gig."… I asked, as diplomatically as possible, if they thought the spokesmanship of Japan had resided for too long with one particular individual and if there were some aspects of the band that hadn't been properly represented. The answer surprised me: "I think in interviews that Dave hasn't come across as the person he is – ever. There seems to be more of an image built around him that differs from the actual person he is; there's a kind of alien feeling that comes across which is just not him." Later we arrived at the Holiday Inn in Newcastle. I spotted David in the hotel lobby and homed in for a quick chat. I told him I'd been forbidden from doing an interview with him but he agreed to answer a few questions as long as it didn't overshadow what the others had said. Feeling foolhardy, I proposed that he might actually be enjoying the tour (a very unlikely prospect). "Some nights it's good," he admitted, "but some nights I'm just parodying myself … in fact I almost see the whole show as a parody anyway, I know Steve and myself don't take it seriously at all. … It's like the end of a really good relationship between us all. We knew quite a long time ago that we weren't actually going to stay together, but we couldn't say so because of contractual things." When the tape recorder was switched off, David seemed relieved to have told me it was all over. It seemed such a waste – Japan had built up a huge fan base. After all those years of plugging away they were about to become one of the biggest bands of the 80s, but the cracks were too big to paper over. David fitted the image of a pop star even less comfortably than Marc Almond. He wanted to go back to spending his life in darkened rooms.'

Page does not exaggerate when she describes the mob scenes that were now following each Japan show. Japanese television footage of the group leaving the venue is on a par with the getaway scenes in the BBC 1973 Bowie documentary *Five Years*. 'It was strange,' says Huckle, 'to see David being mobbed like that, when only a few years previously we were mobbing Marc Bolan.' On arriving at the stage door, Japan would run through a makeshift corridor made of burly bouncers and roadies, beer guts straining beneath their *Sons Of Pioneers* T-shirts. A sea of Princess Diana hairdos and eyebrow-less teens screamed and threw themselves at the group as they ran heads down to the waiting van. The scenario was hilariously at odds with Japan's aesthetic. For Sylvian in particular such scenes were a final indulgence. The success of Japan had finally given him the time, space and money to begin working out who he was and what he really wanted to do, and he was now eager to move on and to leave everything Japan had become, and yet the very people who had provided the time and space – and money – wanted him to stay exactly as he was. Then again, not *everyone* liked Japan. Usher: 'Boy George would take the piss out of me when I went to see Japan, but then he was so bitchy that he would slag off anyone that wasn't him. I remember being in a cab on the way to see Japan at Hammersmith Odeon and seeing Roy Hay [of Culture Club] and his wife going in. I caught up with them and Roy's wife, Alison, said to me that George was slating them for going to see Japan. I think George hated any competition.'

'Nightporter' was released on seven-inch and 12-inch that October. With a video shot by the *Oil On Canvas* film crew, the single made a respectable number 29. A new version of 'Some Kind Of Fool' sung by Sylvian's friend, the French singer Pierre Barouh, had originally been pencilled in instead but was ultimately abandoned for reasons unknown. There was one last performance on *The Old Grey Whistle Test* on 18 October. Japan played 'Nightporter' and 'The Art Of Parties', their fastest and slowest songs, both now nearly two years old. As usual, John Punter had to help surreptitiously with the sound, merely suggesting tweaks to the BBC engineers as union rules disallowed him from operating the desk himself. For the same reason, a tape machine playing the brass parts to 'The Art Of Parties' even had to be hidden secretly among Barbieri's equipment, as this too was against the rules. Japan would never deign to be interviewed on the show and by now would no longer give interviews as a group anyway. 'There's no point,' said Sylvian that December, 'we differ in opinion so much the whole thing would turn into a discussion between ourselves and wouldn't lead anywhere.' There was no point now in agreeing on things as a band as, to all intents and purposes, there was no band.

Ticket prices for the regional shows were high for the time – it cost £6 to attend the Lancaster University shows. On the third night at the Manchester Apollo show, an Italian TV crew were in attendance. 'It would seem that in a bar after the show a rep got us to sign a usage contract,' remembers Jansen, 'but for whatever reason Simon tore it up right there and then – probably because we were making a live video of our own.' On 17 December, the Maxell Tapes sponsored *Sons Of Pioneers* tour finally made it to London. (Sylvian had apparently been first choice for Maxell's famous 'Break the sound barrier' TV ad that eventually featured Bauhaus's Peter Murphy). Hammersmith Odeon had been booked for six nights, evidently breaking all records at the time yet, 'We could have done much more,' says their agent Neil Warnock, 'but Sylvian had his limits.' Jansen: 'Playing Hammersmith was still a milestone as I'd been to see bands perform there only a few years earlier. These places are never as grand backstage as you would imagine.' There was a respectable number of celebrities in the audience for these shows, including Annie Lennox, Duran Duran, Billy Mackenzie, and ABC. Hank Marvin of the Shadows was even photographed with Japan backstage. Jansen: 'Seeing people like Hank Marvin backstage confused me a little.' One celebrity who didn't make it to the show was David Bowie. He had pulled up to the stage door in a limo and asked to be let in. 'Jake Duncan, the tour manager, apparently didn't believe it was him,' says Huckle, 'which is a bit strange. Anyway, the guys only found out about it after the show and they were absolutely furious! They gave Jake a right bollocking.' Sandii: 'I got to know Bowie a bit when I toured with him later on. He kind of admired Japan, but I got the feeling he was a bit competitive and was threatened by them at the time. I remember him saying to me, "Yes, they are very beautiful … so people say."'

As the performance on *The Old Grey Whistle Test* illustrated, Japan's performances by now were slick, well oiled and, apart from Tsuchiya's gorgeous guitar histrionics, held few surprises. Sylvian would later categorise this tour as merely 'posing for and with an audience'. For the first and last time in their existence, Japan were giving their audience what they wanted. After a lifetime of being the perennial glam pariahs, they were close to becoming public property. Surprisingly, the sound on the first night at Hammersmith was wanting, with some audience members being disgruntled at the prominence of Tsuchiya's solos, which at times appeared to be merely smeared across the surface. By the second night Punter had fixed this and by the final performance Japan delivered a moving, powerful show. 'Ghosts' was a true highlight by now, extended and stretched into a slowly exploding mushroom cloud of noise, with Karn contributing suitably Bowie-esque saxophone to great effect. (Karn would also sometimes take the opportunity during the song's extended instrumental intro to take a toke on a prepared spliff at the side of the stage). The atmosphere at the Odeon, already hysterical, was heightened by the knowledge that this was the final tour, although in reality few in the audience really believed they would never see Japan play in Britain again. There were already rumours of one big final show, pencilled in for either Wembley or the Covent Garden Opera House in the new year. Neither would transpire.

At the peak of Japan's popularity that November, Karn's debut album *Titles* was finally released. A beguiling mix of instrumentals and pop songs, the work was extremely likeable and completely out of sync with the then popular musical climate – and it barely charted. Karn was now a regular in both the pop and style magazines and the daily tabloids yet, despite his profile, lack of radio play seems to have stunted the sales of *Titles*. Reviews ranged from polite through bemused to cruel. 'He's still a hopeless Middle Eastern romantic,' wrote Betty Page, '99% uncommercial but very much state-of-the-art Karn – perhaps an acquired taste.' The usually besotted *Smash Hits* was much less taken, summing up the sound of the album as 'a hobbit jamming with a goblin at the bottom of Jaco Pastorius's garden'. Going against the image of him as being just a socialite, Karn himself 'preferred the more personal, instrumental side of the album, as for me it shows a progress of thoughts and ideas as they're going on.' The commercial fate of the album was doubly ironic because by now Sylvian was chastising Karn in print for wanting to pursue a 'pop path'. 'He likes the idea of being a pop star,' Sylvian said, making it sound like a put-down, 'and wants to go to every party.' Yet compared to Japan's most recent output, *Titles* was beautifully esoteric and much less fashionable than Sylvian's songs. Thus the Japan conundrum thrived, even during the group's dying days.

Following the final sold out Hammersmith show, Japan had six days' rest at home in London, peppered by the inevitable interviews, before leaving for the Far East leg of the tour, which was to begin with a show in Bangkok on 29 November. The change of scenery would have helped boost group morale, which was by now generally high if gig weary. Yet even at this late stage Sylvian was growing uncomfortable with the stage set, at one point wanting to ditch it. The *Sons Of Pioneers* set had in fact been designed by Arno and Innocenti, although Sylvian was unaware of this, having vowed never to work with the partners again after the 'Shit Tour'. 'We had to do it in secret,' recalls Innocenti, 'using someone else as a beard, although Simon was in on the whole thing. It amused him greatly.' The cost of redesigning the set at this late stage was deemed prohibitive and futile and so the tour wore on. Karn recalls the Bangkok show as being 'high in entertainment value; the audience were completely out of control, and it honestly became hard to hear ourselves above the din they made. Chaos ruled all around us, with people intermittently jumping onto the stage and throwing themselves off again.' The memories of this date are less clear for Jansen. 'The thing with touring is that the shows are the least eventful part of the whole business', he says, 'the performance you can do on autopilot and each venue looks the same from the stage and you don't particularly want to remember backstage, so there's very little that remains in my memory concerning the actual shows, but I do recall the Chinese fans being really enthusiastic. I think the only clear recollection I have of any concert was in Thailand where the security was non-existent. After getting off the kit to go play marimba in 'Ghosts', I got back to my chair and some kid was sitting in it. That's pretty memorable.'

By the first week of December, the group were settled in Hong Kong for two shows at the AC Halls. Sylvian 'disliked' Hong Kong and stayed in his hotel room whenever possible, writing letters, doodling, and playing with his Polaroid. Additional time was allowed for a press conference and to film on-location footage for the forthcoming live video. Jansen: 'I don't remember much about Hong Kong apart from the fact that we had a day or two off (except for taking a boat out with Fin Costello for some photos), and we were actually able to enjoy the hotel rooms for a change, and relax with some leisure time.'

It was now that certain financial matters came to a head. Napier-Bell had apparently hoped that the success of the tour would persuade Japan to carry on, but when it became evident that this wasn't to be, he decided to 'take his full commission', presumably a backdated one. What this meant was that at the end of a sold out tour, where the London dates alone had taken £100,000, Japan's individual members would receive nothing. When this became evident, Jansen and Barbieri threatened to go on strike. 'It would surprise

Japan at AC Hall,
Hong Kong
3 & 4 December 1982
Music Week Archive

LP inserts for Hong
Kong shows
Music Week Archive

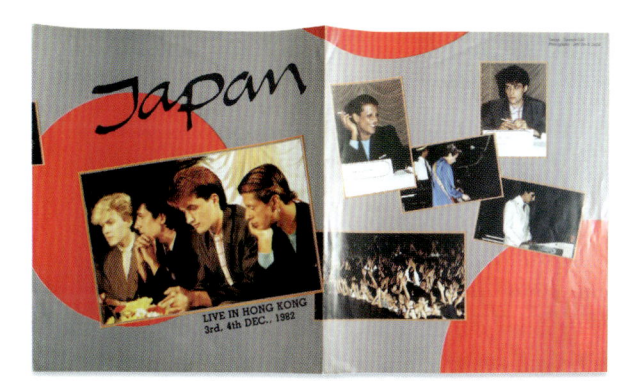

Audience at AC Hall,
Hong Kong
3 & 4 December 1982
Music Week Archive

Far right: Sylvian at
press conference,
Regal Meridian Hotel
Music Week Archive

Sylvian signing autographs on the final leg of the Japan tour
Keiko Kurata

a lot of people to know that the final world tour made us a total of £6,000 each,' explains Jansen, 'probably the most we'd seen, but even then we had to make a stand because at one point we were told there would be next to nothing.' Barbieri: 'With a few remaining shows to go, we were made aware that the band was not going to make any money. Steve and I decided to make a stand, went to Simon's hotel suite and said we weren't going to complete the tour unless we were paid something.' Jansen: 'After all, it's disappointing to think that the business end had taken their percentage from gross figures, creamed it off the top as it were, so their income was guaranteed from the outset. And when expenses started to eat away at profits it was all being sourced from the band's share. I reckon even the crew made more on that tour than we did.' In their manager's defence, Huckle says: 'For several years it was money going out and none in, much of which had to be paid back to someone – Hansa, Virgin, SNB or whoever. Plus, at that time the group were living in South Ken with all living expenses paid for.' Jansen: 'It wasn't so much of a showdown, as SNB didn't seem to be very bothered. He'd obviously pocketed his share and any cancellations would have been covered by insurance. He simply proposed a pathetic sum [£6,000]. If Richard and I didn't go on to finish the tour it would have meant the fans losing out, and there would have been some serious guilt trips imposed upon us by the rest of the crew.' For some reason, Karn was not included in this rebellion. If he had been, 'I would have called for a mutiny, a strike, unless our demands were met, and I wouldn't have budged an inch.' Sylvian apparently remained aloof. 'David would have been seeing a fair amount of income from publishing not to have to worry about it,' says Jansen, and so he remained absent from the discussion, counting down the days until the final show.

The first show of Japan's final Japanese tour was on 8 December at the Budokan, back where it all started in 1979. There was screaming from the off although this subsided to an eerie silence between some numbers. Sylvian: 'It was weird to be sat at the keyboard preparing for 'Nightporter' in total silence.' The set, which was broadcast live on radio, followed the Hammersmith shows, apart from 'Canton', which was saved until the encore when Sylvian finally ditched the silver spacesuit and reappeared on stage in a black suit, white shirt and black tie. For further encores, Akiko Yano and then husband Ryuichi Sakamoto joined in for a hesitant version of 'Bamboo Music'. Jansen then introduced Takahashi in Japanese as his 'wife', for a stilted attempt at 'Taking Islands In Africa'. Takahashi: 'This was the first song on which Japan collaborated directly with Sakamoto, and they may have attached a special significance to it as it was the song that essentially started their relationship with YMO. I remember David asking me during rehearsal if I wanted to sing it. On reflection, the key may have been a little low for me.' The final three pieces were 'Life In Tokyo', 'Canton' and finally the duet 'Goodnight', performed by Sylvian and Yano with Karn on sax. This show had a freer, more laid-back atmosphere than any other on the tour. Jansen: 'By that time we were into a routine which meant things ran smoothly, plus the Tokyo crew were always highly efficient, so I'd say that that show was more relaxed. Remember we'd just played in Thailand and Hong Kong where everything seemed to hang perpetually in the balance and was by contrast more stressful.'

Peter Barakan, Sakamoto's official translator and acquaintance of the band, was also in the audience. 'I did see them live, but only once, on what was the last tour. There definitely was a dichotomy between the musical direction they were heading in, and the idol-type reaction that their fans continued to have. I don't know whether to call it typical, as I can't think of another band of that kind who changed so dramatically.' The relaxed atmosphere continued in sound checks before the Tokyo shows at the Sun Plaza and Kosei Nenkin Hall with 'Nightporter' seguing into an ad hoc version of 'The Other Side Of Life'. After playing Tokyo for the final time, Japan moved through Osaka and Kyoto before reaching Nagoya where, on 16 December 1982, they played their last ever gig. This show, filmed by Yuka Fujii from the back of the hall, was up until the last few songs very much like any other Japan had played since the tour began the previous October. However, during the last few songs, the concert descended into a hybrid of onstage party and pantomime. 'The crew were planning some little surprises during the final show,' recalls Jansen, who by now had abandoned his check trousers and billowing white shirt for a more fetching black-on-black ensemble. 'The first clue was me being sprayed with water pistols during the marimba solo of 'Ghosts', and then I noticed someone wearing a Father Christmas suit at the side of the stage. But it wasn't until the encore that various people in costumes emerged. I didn't know who they were at first, then realised it was the crew, including Punter who was supposed to be front of house. The second encore saw the release of the ping-pong balls [during 'Fall In Love With Me']. We had no idea any of this was going to happen.' The encores saw various crew members dressed as pandas waving the Japanese flag, and Sandii and assorted Sunsetz dancing and joining in on backing vocals. Karn struggled with a champagne bottle, Sylvian and Jansen addressed the crowd and thanked the crew and then it was over. The screaming endured for some time with the audience unwilling to let Japan go, but eventually even the hoarse screams of, 'David', 'Rich', 'Mick', and 'Steve' passed into silence and the hall emptied. The cry for 'encore!', however, would reverberate soundlessly for decades to come.

Jansen: 'After the show, David and Masami took the train to Tokyo. Mick, Richard and I remained in Nagoya. We had a drink in the sky bar with the crew that evening which soon became jammed with fans, so we then did an impromptu signing whilst downing countless bottles of sake. I think this was the most memorable post-show gathering, due to the fact that many fans were taking photos.' The next day, back in Tokyo, Sylvian and Jansen appeared on the Sakamoto/Barakan radio show *Soundstreet*. The brothers, and indeed the hosts, sounded relaxed to the point of giggles. Sylvian admitted that he had felt slightly 'melancholy' immediately prior to the last show, but that the feeling had soon passed. 'It was more like getting a weight off of your shoulders than it being a big sad affair,' affirmed Jansen. There was one final party to attend. Jansen: 'That evening UDO threw a party for band and crew at their usual location for such events, The Cavern. It was a typically formal affair with the obligatory "sanbon-jime", a sort of formal clapping ceremony, similar to our "three cheers" I guess, applicable when the work is done and everything is wrapped up.' The now ex-members of Japan would then reassemble to work on the live album *Oil On Canvas* at AIR with John Punter. Japan had ended, but were not quite over yet.

The rumours had become reality – for the first time since 1974, Japan did not exist. The final tour had at least been thoroughly documented, because as well as being filmed for the forthcoming video release, Fin Costello had photographed it for a forthcoming book. 'My relationship with Japan was not unique but particularly interesting,' Costello would say. 'It was similar to several acts I had worked with over the years. I would work with a band for the time when we were complementary but a time always came when it was time to move on for both of us. I worked with Deep Purple for 35 years, but for most bands it generally lasted for three or four albums. My contribution came to an end amicably, just as the band broke up. I stayed on in Tokyo with my wife to supervise the production of the Japanese version of the book and have a holiday as we were all exhausted after such a long trip. Some people suggested that Duran Duran came to me because of Japan, but that's not so. Remember I did a lot more work with Rush, Aerosmith, and Ozzy at that time than I did with Japan. David and Mick used to tease me about the contrast.'

Napier-Bell was already committed to managing Sylvian but was also looking to other acts to bolster his roster, so as Japan were ending he signed up … Diana Dors. He also put the Nomis complex on the market. Delicia Burnell: 'They were a family and had grown up together and now they were growing apart. They were a band and things always go wrong with bands.' The members of the group had mixed feelings about the split. Sylvian and Karn seemed relieved at no longer having to be in the same room together. Jansen: 'I never had any qualms about splitting up and finding something else to do. We'd all pretty much had enough of working as a four-piece and there was enough recognition for the band to have made it feel worthwhile.' Barbieri: 'I certainly wasn't happy at the demise; it was so disappointing to have got to that stage of artistic and commercial achievement for it just to peter out. The relationship between Mick and David by that time was so negative and unstable that it really couldn't be rescued. There were many factors leading up to this, some I probably didn't even know about; Mick's girlfriend moving on to David, Mick wanting to make a solo album which David was against, refusals to do any extra tour dates or *The Old Grey Whistle Test* appearances – just too many negatives. Not unlike when someone dies, you dread the ending but when it comes, in a way it's a relief.' Jansen: 'It was often painful to be in the same room as David and Mick during this time, so once the band split it was a situation that no longer had to be tolerated by any of us. The band started from a very good and pure place with people I loved, but gave way to individual ambition. If things are going well as a team there are always going to be individuals that like to pick up the ball and run with it themselves. In my opinion, the split wasn't even remotely about a girlfriend, it was entirely driven by personal ambition, and I couldn't begrudge that. No one owed me a job in a band. We went into it together with no long-term promises, so the split was entirely diplomatic due to the fact that, as people, we were no longer in a stable enough position to make music together.' Orly: 'It was obvious Dave and Mick loved one another. They were brothers. But it's like in a family when the closest end up hating each other too. It was more competition than hate, brotherly competition.' Sylvian: 'With Japan there was, as you say, an aesthetic ideal: the whole band was put together around … well, mainly probably more my ideals than the others'. When it split up, I felt a kind of freedom. Those ideals were superficial anyway; a gloss on a package.' Huckle: 'To my mind it felt like a slow train crash that took place over several months.'

In splitting when they did, Japan froze themselves in the public eye at a point of unrealised and therefore eternal potential. To many they were on the verge of 'finally breaking through' and so when they did disband there remained the hope that Sylvian, Jansen, Karn, and Barbieri would one day realise their 'mistake' and reform. It had taken Japan a long time to win the hearts of their audience and as a consequence that audience would spend a long time letting the group go. The love for the group was bound up for many with youth itself and the endless possibilities that being young seemed to offer. But in the end there was no choice. The integrity that had made Japan who they were would also signify their end. Sylvian: 'It would have been harder to keep going than to stop. People said, "You've got a lot of courage to split up now when you're at the top," but for us it would have taken more courage to carry on. It would have been much, much harder to carry on than it was for us to split.'

Simon Napier-Bell
Harry Trezona

Soundmaker

THE COMPLETE MUSIC PAPER — 4th DECEMBER 1982

PRICE 35p

JAPAN SPLIT
INSIDE STORY
PAGE 23

ALEXEI SAYLE REVIEWS THE SINGLES

COMPREHENSIVE EQUIPMENT GUIDE WITH PRICES AND SPECS
STEVE STRANGE ★ CULTURE ★
EXCLUSIVE VIDEO CHART
AND McLAREN VIDEO
Plus — Jazz, Folk, Kits, D.I.Y.

Afterword
'Who would have dreamed of love never ending?'

Richard Barbieri, Hiroshima, Japan, 1983
Steve Jansen

Japan had grown apart. More specifically, Sylvian and Karn had grown apart. They no longer needed or wanted one another as they once did, either as friends or professionally. This was an inevitable consequence of growing up, and Japan would have split at some point as most groups do. The issues with Fujii, money, touring – these were symptoms that exacerbated the underlying tensions within the unit rather than being the cause of them. 'I would say the deterioration in the relationship between David and Mick brought the whole thing to a close,' explains Barbieri. 'Both were personally ambitious and there was evident friction between them as the band became successful and very high profile. David was very unhappy that Mick wanted to make a solo album, and also Mick's girlfriend taking up with David made things even worse. Steve and I were stuck in the middle of this and powerless to change its natural course. I fluctuated between the two sides, sometimes siding with one and then the other, depending on the issue, but never really falling out for long with either. I helped Mick with the keyboard programming for his solo album and I would feature on a couple of tracks on David's first album – so it wasn't as if we couldn't stand to work together anymore.'

Sylvian had begun to gather ideas for his debut solo album in the last few months of 1982, with 'Pulling Punches' being the first track he'd write for the forthcoming album. By early 1983 he had already decided on some of the personnel to accompany him on that album – and those who wouldn't. Jansen: 'It was a given that David would take the band's audience with him whatever he did, but surprisingly he asked me and Richard to work on his first album and tour, which clearly demonstrated that he didn't want to lose our creative input at all – so why split? Because he would effectively be working with Japan minus the element he wanted out of his life at the time – the one he felt most conflicted with. And, of course, being a solo artist enabled him to take on a more controlling role, which was always something of a need.' The success that Japan had strived for and attained had ended them. 'When a band becomes successful,' says Barbieri, 'you would think that it would strengthen the bond within the group, but in most cases that's when things start to unravel and when the group dynamic becomes something else. Ego, ambition, jealousy, ruthlessness, self-importance, etc., all this rises to the surface.'

With their last concert finally behind them, the ex-members settled into their new domestic lives. Everyone now had steady partners: Sylvian was with Fujii, Jansen with photographer Sheila Rock, Barbieri with make-up artist Gaye Jones, and Karn with Orly. As Jansen notes, Sylvian had the full support of Virgin and Nomis. Without similar resources, Jansen, Barbieri and Karn would struggle to find a corresponding focus. Orly: 'That last tour was great fun. Good memories. I then moved in with Mick. He was obviously unbelievably talented, but he was multi-talented and that was an issue for him. He struggled with which talent to focus on. Plus, the fact that he was a tortured soul. So, at one time he was writing for a ballet, also writing his own album, and he was sculpting. He needed a mentor. His management, record label, and publicist were all pulling him in different directions. If his heart was focused on a sculpture then his label would be trying to fix him up with a musician to collaborate with, so he'd have to do that; he was at cross-purposes a lot of the time. He needed the time to do what he needed to do at the right time.' Such dilemmas were not helped now by the fact that no one but Sylvian actually had a record deal. Meanwhile, the spectre of the group drifted on. In February, Hansa released a remix of the four-year-old 'All Tomorrow's Parties'. Enough of the heartbroken faithful bought it to take it to number 38 in the UK chart.

Perversely, the first thing the ex-members of Japan worked on after the split was a Japan album. In the first weeks of 1983, they reconvened with John Punter at AIR to work on the live album that would become *Oil On Canvas*. Virgin were keen as ever to capitalise on Japan's popularity and had initially suggested a greatest hits compilation. Sylvian, no doubt baulking at such a traditional rock and roll gesture, compromised by remixing and overdubbing the live tapes from the final tour. Although advertised as a live album, it was in fact almost completely reconstructed at AIR. 'If I remember correctly, as we'd just completed *Tin Drum* we asked Steve Nye to do our live sound on the final tour but he didn't want to do it,' says Jansen. 'So we then asked John Punter if he would be willing and he kindly obliged. It then made sense that he mix the live recording. The album was pretty much entirely re-recorded in the studio, except for the drums because there are too many microphones that capture other elements of the live sound for them not to be used. It's not really a live album at all; essentially it's a studio album. All the vocals and bass were re-recorded, some of Richard's and Masami's parts were too, wherever they weren't too exposed through the drum mics. Then there were parts on playback from a reel-to-reel tape deck which were used live and which made it onto the album. So the one thing people should consider when listening to that album is that the only parts they are hearing that they can truly be sure were being performed on the night, are the drums.'

Punter was happy to be working with the boys again and to have a chance to work with some of the *Tin Drum* material from which he had been excluded. 'Mixing a track is really where I put my signature on it,' he says, 'and I was happy to do that on the *Tin Drum* material. In fact, when I had been mixing the live show I had gone over the top now and then on those songs, especially the drums. The audience on the album sounds so muted because we didn't have audience mics. It was always intended to be a live album without an audience and of course Sylvian barely addressed them anyway; he was always quite minimalist in that respect – you don't hear him say anything between songs. But compared to the first show I did with them in Toronto, I think that by that final tour they had grown in confidence and ability a thousand-fold. And the reception and respect they were getting at the end certainly helped that.' It was Punter's job to go through the live tapes and assemble tracks he felt were the most worthy. He'd then compile a cassette of these for the band to review and an agreement about which ones to work on would be reached. The decision was mostly Punter's by this stage as the group trusted him implicitly and were also weary of the material itself. The sessions were civilised and low-key, with Karn in particular absenting the studio once his overdubs has been completed. Three new instrumentals punctuated the album with Sylvian's *Oil On Canvas* itself apparently summing up his feelings on the previous eight years. A simple, elegiac piano piece, one could almost hear Sylvian closing the piano lid on the group once the last chord faded. 'Once we finished mixing *Oil On Canvas*, that was it,' says Punter. 'We may have had dinner, but there was no big formal farewell as I recall. I saw Mick again years later when he played Toronto [in 1994] with Terry Bozzio. I just turned up and freaked him out by standing at the front of the stage, but I didn't really keep in touch with any of the others. I would sum up my time with them as wonderfully exciting, possibly one of the best times of my life. Just wonderful.'

The album's release was preceded by a live video of the same name filmed during the UK and Far East legs of the tour. The director, Anthony Lawson, had not found it a particularly enjoyable process. 'I got the job through the producer, Kevin Attew, who was a friend of mine,' he recalls. 'I'd never heard of Japan. I met them in Manchester on their tour and we had a brief meeting; they asked me what I'd done and so forth. It was pretty low-key and the room was very low-lit as I remember. They didn't make any particular impression upon me.' Japan had little interest in the medium of video and were merely going along with Virgin's and Napier-Bell's desires. 'Sylvian was very "cockney" I thought, very London,' says Lawson. 'They admitted that they weren't particularly dynamic on stage and as you can't really direct musicians in concert I had to come up with some sort of idea to get round this. So I decided to use very strong filters and Sylvian was very enthusiastic about that. So it was agreed and we began filming them shortly after. We shot two nights at the Hammersmith Odeon. I really took to Mick Karn; he had the most charisma I thought. I found the music a bit repetitive and I wasn't keen on Sylvian's singing. But that was okay, maybe it was for the best. I just treated it as a job.'

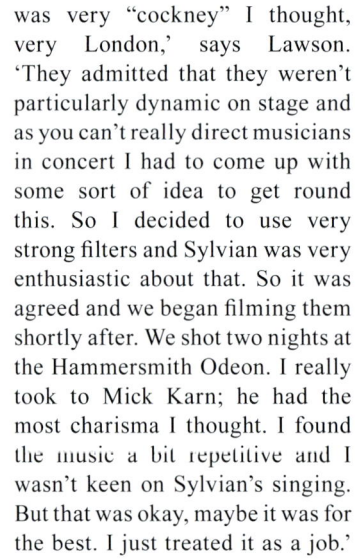

Sylvian was also treating the tour as a chore and by the time the touring party reached Bangkok his enthusiasm for all aspects of Japan was beyond waning. 'The idea of filming them in Bangkok and Hong Kong was to get some offstage action as it were,' says Lawson. 'So we shot a lot of footage of them at Aberdeen Harbour in Hong Kong, but then one of my assistants opened the film can in a car and it was exposed. We lost almost everything of that footage; we rescued a little bit of it. We were also running out of film. Add to this that I was supposed to meet them at some temples on the river in Bangkok to film more footage and they had gone to Pattaya! So we decided to film them going into the concert as they arrived – but we missed them. At this point, we actually hadn't seen the band at all in Bangkok! We couldn't catch up with them. Except for the little bit of footage in the harbour we had nothing. I had to lay it down with the producer, Kevin, at this point: "I *have* to have some face-to-face time with Sylvian! It's crazy to come all this way and not be able to shoot anything." We were all staying at the Holiday Inn on the harbour at this point, but they kept rushing off doing their own thing all the time. I told Kevin, "This is crazy! I can't be a director if I can't even get to them!" So eventually I was granted half an hour with Sylvian one evening beside the harbour where I managed to take some straightforward stills of him, which we slotted into the footage of 'Ghosts'.

It wasn't tense though. It was one of the easiest and most frustrating shoots I've ever done. I never got to know the guys at all – I never even went backstage. It was an odd shoot; they weren't very involved. At one point I asked if I was to shoot the audience and they kind of looked at one another and then back at me and said, "No. Why would we do that?" So that was strange. Sylvian didn't seem very bothered by any aspect of the film once we got started. I guess they'd already split up by then.'

The resulting film – the only official footage of Japan released live – was highly processed and filtered, resulting in an oddly anaesthetic feel that in fact suited the band's aesthetic. It appeared at times as if Japan were performing in front of a giant mirror. Some shots were by necessity filmed in isolation. 'I remember we didn't have enough footage of the keyboard player so had to set him up alone separately, poor fellow, and just shoot him miming.' Barbieri: 'The artist always pays for mistakes made by others.' Lawson: 'There was no master sync track so the music didn't always match, so the editor, Peter Shelton, had to do all the synching manually, relying on his ears and eyes. It turned out well I think but it was just a job, like shooting an advert for butter. The difference between shooting Japan and a butter advert was that the butter moved a bit more under hot lights. But I don't want to put Sylvian down, he had a niche and worked it well, but it just wasn't my kind of music. But you know who Mick Karn reminded me of? Maria Callas. I say that because I went to see Maria Callas in *Medea* in 1959 at Covent Garden, and although I wasn't all that keen on that particular opera and I could hardly see the stage from up in the gods, I just had to see her on stage at least once, and the extraordinary thing was that if she walked behind a pillar – and there were a lot of them for her to walk behind as I recall – I couldn't take my eyes off that pillar until she re-emerged. To me, that was charisma. Obviously Mick hadn't got it to that extent, but he seemed to be the one performer my eye was mostly drawn to during the Japan rehearsals, and I guess why I chose to operate the camera closest to him, in front of the stage, during the shows. I didn't think that David Sylvian had anything like Mick's visual draw, but I knew he'd be well taken care of by the other camera operators, because he was the bloke singing.'

The video was released in March and was heavily promoted, selling well enough to reach the top five of the national video chart. Virgin's marketing strategy of releasing the video before the more affordable album was no doubt designed to reap as many sales as possible for both. The fans, eager to hear and see Japan as live as possible, would buy the VHS or Betamax as soon as their pocket money would allow, but a video was no substitute for an album, and when that came out some months later they would purchase that too. Meanwhile, a preview from the forthcoming album was released. 'Canton (Live)/ Visions Of China (Live)' failed to pick up any airplay and stalled at 42. 'I fell asleep during this,' claimed Gary Kemp while reviewing the single for *Smash Hits*.

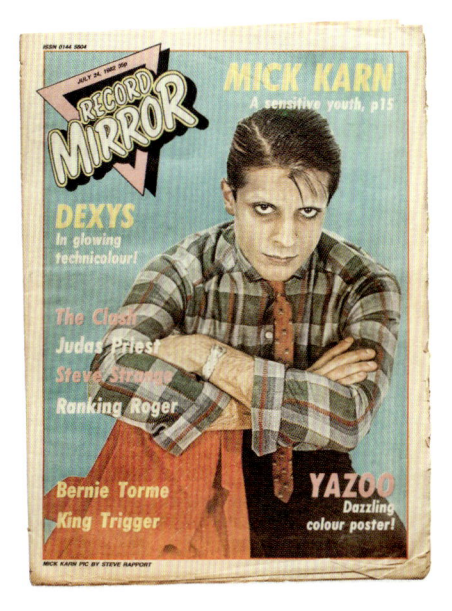

In June, the live album *Oil On Canvas* was released, with a double gatefold of beautiful photos of by Anton Corbijn portraying a seemingly anorexic group in Paris. It was Japan's highest charting album to date, peaking at number five. The actual cover itself was a striking departure in that it was the first time none of Japan featured on the cover. Instead, 'Head of JYM II', a painting by London-based expressionist Frank Auerbach featured. 'I had a problem looking at visual art up until I saw that painting of Auerbach's,' Sylvian would relate. 'I would walk around galleries, and I would appreciate the beauty of some of the work, the abstract nature, blah, blah, blah, but I was never moved, not like a piece of music would move me or a poem. So I was quite unprepared for the experience that I had with the Auerbach, and I can't tell you what I did or if I did anything to prepare me for that experience. I was just open to that moment. I must have been in a very open state of heart and mind, and was just blown away by one particular image. And the experience was as intense as any experience I'd had in music, and that was exciting because I just didn't think it possible.' Fujii had met Auerbach at an exhibition opening and mentioned the idea of using his work on the cover of the album. Auerbach responded that this was something he had always wanted and Huckle was duly put in touch with Auerbach's son who then licensed the image to Virgin.

At this point, Sylvian's relationship with his manager was souring. Huckle: 'He didn't want to go on with Simon and in fact asked me if I would manage him. I declined; I didn't think I was up to it.' At the same time, Sylvian's relationship with Virgin was flourishing. 'David and I got on very well,' recalls Simon Draper. 'I remember that it was a bit of a revelation when he realised I knew who Frank Auerbach was – in fact I owned an Auerbach. I have a big art collection; I'm very interested in art. But we also gave David a lot of freedom in what he wanted to do, which I thought he appreciated. I mean, we tried to do that with all our artists. We tried to "interfere positively" if you like. I never tried to second-guess the artists. We tried to give them a lot of freedom. We saw ourselves as facilitators.'

Karn meanwhile had grown estranged from his one-time manager, his label and Orly. Karn's romantic partner was now ex-Nomis staff member Delicia Burnell. She witnessed first hand his struggle to find himself creatively in the year following Japan's split. Deli: 'Mick was similar to David in many ways. He had a very strong work ethic, very centred on his creativity. But Mick had an amazing amount of ideas, and he could turn his hand to many things. But the nature of creativity is that you're also judged by it. It weighed heavily on him. It was the mainstay of his life. He needed to express so much in different ways it could be exhausting. And he was kind of the black sheep of his family in some ways despite his success. When we visited his family in Cyprus it was all food, food, food. I've never been so sick in my life. It was thought of as bad form if you didn't eat, and his father was a butcher of course. I think they always found it difficult that he chose that kind of work; they would have preferred him to be a farmer. It took a big shift in their attitude to be proud of him. He was also growing tired of being a "bass player for hire".' There was a sole single that summer: the Linn Drum-adorned 'After A Fashion' with Midge Ure. Even with the then requisite video shot in Egypt, it failed to pick up much airplay and charted only moderately. However, it did cement Karn's friendship with the ex-Ultravox singer. Orly: 'Him and Midge got on great and were friends to the end. There was no ego clash there. They thought each other was brilliant. Mick was so passionate about art, whether it was music or sculpture. I'll always remember his passion for his work above any particular work.'

Around this time, plans for Karn to open a London gallery finally imploded when the backers pulled out. A planned group project failed to materialise and a commission for the Ballet Rambert fizzled into the ether. At times it seemed like Karn was a man who could do anything, but was doing nothing. In fact he had demo'd an album's worth of material for Virgin as a follow-up to *Titles* during this period but, despite the songs being more straightforwardly pop than his debut, Virgin declined to fund a new album. He could still be seen at the occasional party and nightclub and remained an infrequent feature in the tabloids' gossip columns. He sometimes seemed like a pop star in lifestyle only. Deli: 'His taste in art was like his taste in music – very broad, from classical to modern – but I never heard him listen to anything "hard". His appearance was important to him; he took a lot longer to get ready to go out than I did.'

While his friends floundered somewhat, Sylvian's life came into bloom. His domestic life with Fujii seemed secure and fruitful, and he was making enough money to pay off his parents' mortgage and, most importantly, the sessions for his debut album, which he began in Berlin at the start of the summer, were going well, albeit plagued by technical issues with the studio itself. Free of the pressures of being in a group for the first time since he was a teenager, much of Sylvian's social life had shifted, but he was not quite the hermit that the press made him out to be. A friend since

1981, Mark Wardel grew closer to Sylvian once he left the rigorous confines of the group, and relates a typical night out that Sylvian undertook that year: '[My friend] David Bunny remembers being at my place in Dover Street in 83 when Sylvian phoned me from Legends to say he was at the club and would I like to come and hang out with him. So we walked around the corner to Legends. Bunny remembers me telling him on the way that he could come, but warning him to "behave" as he could be rather campily outrageous. Sylvian was sitting alone at a corner table (Yuka was away at the time), dressed entirely in black and wearing black shades which he never removed the entire time we were in the club. We had a few drinks and it became obvious that Sylvian was comfortable around Bunny and amused by his camp banter, and so he suggested that we went back to his place as he wasn't really comfortable in the club. Bunny also remembers Sylvian as being quite light-hearted and there being much laughter. We piled into David Bunny's little red Datsun and headed off to Sylvian's flat which was in Elm Park Mansions, Park Walk just off the King's Road. The flat was a small and basic rental-type place with hotel-type furniture. No luxuries or rock star trappings of any kind. He also remembers that they had a cat [Yuka's], which kept running up the curtains and got on our nerves.'

Much of this flat, including Sylvian's baby grand piano, which Huckle had had to hustle up the stairs with delivery men, and the cat – a Siamese called Oppi, would be documented by Sylvian in his book of Polaroids, *Perspectives*, which was released to coincide with an exhibition at Hamiltons Gallery the following summer. In addition, the book illustrated the trips he and Yuka took (with Nick Huckle driving) in 1983: Paris and the Alps that autumn, India in late winter. The photos were a portrait of a young man finally coming into his own, a golden period of growth and freedom. Jansen and Barbieri were also visitors to Elm Park Mansions as well as participants in Sylvian's solo album sessions. Barbieri: 'I think he simply didn't find his musical identity as a singer-songwriter until he left the band. I believe he wasn't happy with his work in the group. Unfortunately, when a frontman goes solo the impression given in the media is usually that the band were holding him back. 'Ghosts' was the spark, I believe, and that pointed the way.'

Sylvian's cachet as a 'serious' singer/songwriter was further illustrated that summer when his most recent collaboration with Sakamoto was an international hit. The title track of a new film, *Merry Christmas Mr Lawrence* (which starred David Bowie), the song was a glorious, orchestrated piece of mournful music that brought to mind the Walker Brothers. Sylvian had recorded the vocal earlier in the year in Tokyo. The video, directed by Godley and Creme, intercut footage of Sylvian miming in a sandpit with scenes from the film; conspicuously, Bowie was excluded. By the second day of filming Sylvian's fragile patience was exhausted. 'I got a call from him saying he wasn't coming in to finish it,' says Huckle. 'He didn't give a reason, just said he couldn't face it and they'd have to use the footage they already had. The directors weren't best pleased.' Following further recording sessions for *Brilliant Trees* in London, Sylvian saw in the New Year in Japan. Sylvian: 'There was a very memorable New Year's Eve spent in Kyoto with Yuka Fujii and the musician Stomu Yamashta. Stomu had something of the proselytiser about him, or maybe the temple master – knowledgeable on many a subject, a wonderful storyteller, passionate about Buddhism, Japanese culture and tradition, and of course music. I came away from that brief acquaintance with a greater appreciation for the subtleties and the difficulties of the path and its teachings.'

With the success of the album B*rilliant Trees* the following summer, which charted in the UK at number four in June 1984 and was raved over critically, Sylvian and Virgin had a right to be very pleased. It seemed that the singer/songwriter was now fulfilling all the potential ever afforded him, personally, creatively and commercially. With his life in full flower, further mainstays of his previous existence fell away. Sylvian had outgrown Napier-Bell by the time Japan had split, but had been bound to him contractually. Before the end of the year, Sylvian instead shifted managerial responsibilities to Richard Chadwick, with whom he and Yuka also formed a company – Opium (Arts) Ltd. Huckle: 'Dave had asked me if I could get him out of his contract with Simon. Dave already had the concept for Opium Arts around the time of the Paris/Alps trip, and was speaking of his vision of life sans Simon. But I think he was expecting a difficult time legally, breaking away, as there were still a number of years left on his Nomis contract. Also, at that time I think we felt Richard Chadwick was too tied in with Simon and Nomis to assist in any contractual disputes or whatever. After all, SNB had just negotiated Dave's solo deal with Virgin. However, there were a couple of things I think may have eased the eventual separation from Simon.

Firstly, at that time Simon was getting involved with Wham!, whom he would have seen as a ready-made cash cow, which came without many of the difficulties (artistic, financial and otherwise) that Dave might have given him in the future. Secondly, he clearly got on well with a chap called Jazz Summers, then a relatively new business partner of his, who seemed to think about management in the same way as him. These may have led Simon and Richard Chadwick to think that their best partnership years were behind them, and so some kind of more amicable split was agreed, with Chadwick taking on Dave, leaving SNB with Wham! and the other acts in the Jazz Summers stable.'

According to Napier-Bell, he had apparently decided to end his relationship with Sylvian during a visit to Berlin when he dropped in on the recording sessions of *Brilliant Trees*. 'Sylvian's new album was too uncommercial; I would give up managing him,' he'd recall. 'It was a hard decision, because over the previous seven years we'd been through a lot together.' Napier-Bell shifted his attentions from then on to globetrotting, fine dining, and Wham!. Shortly before this parting, Huckle himself simply disappeared. 'I can only express it as I had a kind of personal breakdown, probably brought on by taking on more than I could chew in respect of business dealings with Simon. All I remember is one evening walking up Gosfield Street [where Opium Arts was now based] in a daze and posting whatever float I was carrying for Dave through the office letterbox, then walking the streets of London and sleeping in various shop doorways for several days until I eventually pulled myself together.' A friend of Sylvian and Co since their school days, Huckle would never see Richard, Mick, Steve, or David again.

Freed from much of his past, Sylvian was finally being treated with the critical and commercial respect he hoped his work deserved. Yet he still maintained the pop star image – the make-up, the dyed bouffant hair, and the designer clothes. The look was as immaculate as ever, despite the occasional wispy beard. The dichotomy between his serious intentions and his appearance was either thrilling or uncomfortable depending on which magazines you bought. To see Sylvian's lyrics reprinted in *Number One* and *Smash Hits*, quoting Raymond Radiguet, Jean-Paul Sartre and Jean Cocteau was endearingly conspicuous. Yet side by side with Morrissey and U2 in the *NME*, his peroxide earnestness was beginning to look like something from a bygone era. Sylvian was now struggling with a self-confessed coke habit and various health issues, one of which finally forced him away from his beloved diet of junk food and into a dairy-free and meat-free regime. Although refusing to appear on *Top Of The Pops* and cancelling an appearance on *Wogan* for the single 'Red Guitar' at the last minute, Sylvian still gave interviews to everyone from *19* magazine to the Sunday supplements and appeared on radio seemingly weekly. It was a confusing state of affairs that wouldn't last. 1984 was to be Sylvian's final 'public' year. From then on he would transmute into the pop equivalent of the Left Bank poet to which he aspired to be.

Without a proper deal, Jansen and Barbieri had gone to work in Tokyo. 'Steve and I were commissioned to make a soundtrack for a space shuttle film by JVC in Japan,' recalls Barbieri. 'This recording became the *Worlds In A Small Room* ambient album.' This album would leak into the UK on import, but true to its instrumental nature it reaped little press or sales. Jansen and Barbieri had officially decided to work as a duo and shifted to the same management team that looked after Simple Minds, but it would be another three years before they surfaced as pop contenders in the guise of The Dolphin Brothers.

In 1983, as far as most Japan fans were aware, Jansen appeared to be pursuing photography in lieu of music, in the UK at least, when he was granted an exhibition at the Photographers' Gallery on 10 October. 'I've always considered photography to be an extension of recording, capturing a moment. It only takes a modicum of talent to learn the workings of a camera; I feel most of us have a potential for it, particularly when our surroundings are perpetually stimulated by change. Being on tour, all I had to do essentially was wait for scenes to present themselves. Recording was very much the focus from the age of about 16, and I think I began to feel compelled to record/document things. This led on to photography as well as keeping a journal for a while. There is also a correlation between the role of photographer and my role in music at that time. I've never been the type of person who is comfortable in the limelight, much preferring to be behind an instrument, behind the frontman who welcomes that kind of attention, working in the comparative darkness doing what I do without the desire to be seen doing it. I feel this gave rise to being a bit of an observer, behind the scenes, behind the camera.'

Jansen and Barbieri had in fact toured Japan that summer with Ippu-Do and Percy Jones, but their musical profile in the UK at this point was non-existent. Various offers of session work came to the duo, with Barbieri turning down Midge Ure, and Jansen accepting a live gig with Propaganda in 1985, but such a life was not something that ultimately appealed to either. Jansen: 'You need plenty of technique to be a session player and it's not something I focused on. I worked with people because they liked what I did, but I not necessarily did what they liked. It was quite boring work and at the same time stressful playing on other people's music. I never felt accomplished enough as a player to suit every type of music, which is what a session player needs to be.' Barbieri: 'After the split, the natural order of things took hold. There were no transitional problems for David to continue with the same record label, management and agent with the full support of the fan base that had been built up over the preceding years. Mick had some credit in the bank as the side man and would be supported by the label for a short while until sales dropped off, and Steve and I struggled.' Jansen: 'I'd virtually come out from school into being a professional musician and spent the next however many years sharing the workload with the same team. It felt good that there was a change coming and that I could look at things from my own perspective. It was a difficult adjustment though, simply because it was akin to stepping out from a bright light that's been hitting you in the face for the longest time ... looking around a bit dazed, trying to make some sense of your world. I actually spent a number of years simply trying to fit in with society in general, but I never really managed to pull it off.'

Karn eventually surfaced in November 1984 with a new collaborative project, Dali's Car. Featuring Karn himself handling all musical aspects of the venture, save occasional percussion by a more or less invisible drummer, the lyrics, melodies and vocals were left to ex-Bauhaus crooner Peter Murphy. Despite the enormous potential interest by the dormant Japan/Bauhaus audience, the album *The Waking Hour* – occasionally brilliant as it was – sounded like neither group and failed to sell. The duo split shortly before the album was released. '[Dali's Car] was only a name,' Karn would sigh, 'but the problem with any car is that there can only be one driver.'

In December 1984, Japan were but a beloved memory and Sylvian's commercial appeal was fading fast, as the poor chart placing of the final single from *Brilliant Trees*, 'Pulling Punches', proved. Still, Virgin finally got the greatest hits compilation they had been yearning for since 1982. Stalling at number 42, *Exorcising Ghosts* was nevertheless presented as an exquisite tableau with a sleeve by artist Russell Mills and a track listing compiled by Sylvian himself. The packaging was finally bereft of any images of the men who had helped make it; after all the peroxide and pancaked hype, only the music remained. 'The most evocative deep soul music ever made by white boys,' summed up Chris Roberts in *Sounds*, 'what we have here is something that some people will never understand.' The album's title was perfect – something you'd write on a school exercise book or in the foggy winter condensation of your teenage bedroom window. *Exorcising Ghosts* was the first Japan album this author was old enough to request as a Christmas present. But even at that tender age I knew the title was a misnomer; ghosts could be banished, cast out, ignored, and forgotten, but they could never truly die.

Special thanks to the following Pledgers

Penelope Hughes
Stephen Fiddes
Darren James
Alessandro Scotti
Keith Phillips
Veronica Merryfield
Natasha Charles
Shum, Tsz Kong
John McSherry
David Whiting
Paul Harris
Ian Brookings
Thomas Hastie
Danielle Hoareau
Logan Sky
Penny McLaughlin
Joe O
David John Nibloe
Donna Higuchi
Craig Hamlin

Mark Williams
Gareth Williams
Paul Jeff
Kevin Milburn
Clive Maidment
Ingo Kruschewski
Mark Deacon
Rene Yedema
Tony Johns
Thomas XXX
Julie Reed
Jan Skakle
Paul Haskell
Emma Brining
Dermot James
Karen Patrice Innes
Stefan C. Attrill
Philip Lowry
Simon Cross
Rebecca Olenchak

Simon Diabolic
Sven Jacobs
Gordon Bettes
Andy Bettess
Kevan McKeown
Alunia Skibinski
Matthew Love
Lee Mills
Shane McElligott
John Hagaar
Andrew Weston
John Ord
Alan Greenhalgh
Rob Phillips
Renaud C Haslan
Victoria Carter Clowes
Mark Redler
Stephen Evans
Erwin Barendregt

Sources and acknowledgements

Interviews with the author were conducted in person, via email, skype and by telephone.

David Sylvian did not contribute directly to this book, but I have quoted from an interview I conducted with him in 2005.

Portions of the '1980' chapter originally appeared in my piece for *Classic Pop* magazine.

Credits

Tim Bowness, Pete Morgan, and Lisa Quattromini at Burning Shed would like to thank:
Everyone who contributed to this book
Carl Glover
Sarah Gooderson
Rachel Hore
Rosie Morgan

Original interviews with the author:
Steve Jansen, Richard Barbieri, Rob Dean, John Punter, Steve Nye, Nick Huckle, William Newman-Norton, Sylvie Simmonds, Simon Napier-Bell, Rick Wernham, Neil Warnock, Chris Tsangarides, Peter Silver, Chris Carr, Par Can, Brian Cogan, Fin Costello, Margot, Marina Muhlfriedel, John Taylor, Keiko Kurata, Kumiko Amino, Pamela Turbov, Ann O'Dell, Pip Robinson, Simon Draper, Keith Bourton, Delicia Burnell, Barry Guy, Nicola Tyson, Allan Soh, Yukihiro Takahashi, Jeremy Lascelles, Phil Bodger, John Russell Taylor, Nick Robson, Nigel Walker, Angie Usher, Mark Wardel, David Rhodes, Steve Walker, Markus Innocenti, Edward Arno, Andy Rourke, Susan Blond, Peter Barakan, Sandii, Johan Kinde, Ricky Wilde, Kjell Paulsen,. Michael Giller, Renaud Haslan, Sophie Delinanos.

Magazines:
Sounds, NME, Melody Maker, Smash Hits, 19, Zigzag, Blitz, The Face, Bamboo, Music Life, Japan Fan Club, Onagu Senka, The Sunday Times magazine, Mojo, The Observer magazine, Vogue. Hot Press, Japan Fan Club Library, Noise, Trouser Press, Flexipop

Books:
You Don't Have To Say You Love Me
Black Vinyl White Powder
I'm Coming To Take You To Lunch
Simon Napier-Bell (Ebury Press)

Japan And Self Existence
Mick Karn (Lulu Books)

Praying To The Aliens
Gary Numan (Andre Deutsch Ltd.)

Hit Girl
Beverly Glick (unpublished)

Websites:
dangerousminds.com
skruff.com
simonnapierbell.com
nightporter.co.uk
musicradar.net
davidsylvian.com
davidsylvian.net

Thank you to Richard Barbieri, Rob Dean, Steve Jansen, Nick Huckle, Paul Rymer, Tim Bowness and Carl Glover for their seemingly endless patience and humour.

Thanks also to Mark Reynolds for giving me that tape and to Burning Shed (Tim Bowness and Pete Morgan) for taking this on.

Special thanks to Paul Lambden

Special thanks to Stephen Hemingway for his patience and understanding.

Burning Shed,
Unit B,
Yarefield Park,
Old Hall Road,
Norwich,
NR4 6FF,
United Kingdom

Cries And Whispers 1983-1991 is the long-awaited follow-up to *A Foreign Place*, Anthony Reynolds' hugely successful biography of the band Japan.

Following the musical adventures of Richard Barbieri, Rob Dean, Steve Jansen, Mick Karn and David Sylvian, the book takes in solo work, The Dolphin Brothers, Dali's Car, the brilliant but ill-feted reunion release *Rain Tree Crow*, and more.

First edition limited deluxe hardback with postcard signed by the author

Available now, exclusively from burningshed.com

ANTHONY REYNOLDS
Selected works

MUSIC
Albums

Pioneer Soundtracks (Jack) 1996
The Jazz Age (Jack) 1998
To Stars (Jacques) 2000
The end of the way it's always been (Jack) 2002
British Ballads (Anthony Reynolds) 2007
Life's too long - songs 1995 -2011 (Anthony Reynolds) 2012
A world of Colin Wilson. (Anthony Reynolds/Colin Wilson) 2012
Dr Freud's Casebook (with Charlotte Greig) 2014
Underwater wildlife (Anthony Reynolds) 2014

SOUNDTRACK
Adrift in Soho (2015)
Open my Eyes (2016)

Books
These Roses taste like ashes (collected lyrics, poetry and prose) 2001
The impossible dream: The Story of Scott Walker with the Walker brothers (Biography) 2009
Calling all demons (poetry) 2010

www.anthonyreynolds.net

Delicia Burnell,
Mask of confidence,
Mick Karn,
Turin 1987